Cultural Psychology of Coping with Disasters

Manfred Zaumseil • Silke Schwarz
Mechthild von Vacano • Gavin Brent Sullivan
Johana E. Prawitasari-Hadiyono
Editors

Cultural Psychology of Coping with Disasters

The Case of an Earthquake in Java, Indonesia

Springer

Editors
Manfred Zaumseil
International Academy for
Innovative Pedagogy Psychology
and Economics gGmbH at
Freie Universität Berlin
Berlin, Germany

Silke Schwarz
International Academy for
Innovative Pedagogy Psychology
and Economics gGmbH at
Freie Universität Berlin
Berlin, Germany

Mechthild von Vacano
Freie Universität Berlin
Berlin, Germany

Gavin Brent Sullivan
Leeds Metropolitan University
Leeds, United Kingdom

Johana E. Prawitasari-Hadiyono
Christian University of
Krida Wacana
Jakarta, Indonesia
Universitas Gadjah Mada
Yogyakarta, Indonesia

ISBN 978-1-4614-9353-2
ISBN 978-1-4614-9354-9 (eBook)
DOI 10.1007/978-1-4614-9354-9
Springer NewYork Heidelberg Dordrecht London

Library of Congress Control Number: 2013952455

Printed on acid-free paper

Springer is part of Springer Science+Business Media (www.springer.com)

Foreword

Interweaving Culture and Context in Our Understanding of a Society Facing Disaster

In this powerful book, the editors and authors provide an exemplar for an understanding of addressing disaster within a rich cultural context. As they state so well, stress and coping research, addressing trauma, and disaster responding have been presented in the literature as universal principles. They are also presented as apolitical. In fact, the vast majority of the literature is individualistic, White, and Western, control centered, and ignores power differentials and the role of oppression. It is further embedded within an elitist set of assumptions that people have the resources to come to treatment, that there are ample providers to administer such treatment, and that if successfully treated their core problems will be diminished (de Jong 2002). The central conceptual assumptions of both cognitive behavioral therapy and psychodynamic models is that stress is in the eye of the perceiver and so if we change the receiver's approach, viewpoint, or behavior, that remedy will follow. For resource-depleted or resource-lacking economic contexts or where the fundamental view of self is instead that the self is indivisible from the collective, these fundamental principles of Western psychology and psychiatry simply do not hold.

We might also on first blush think that a book on an earthquake in Indonesia would be too limited or specific to have wide universal value. However, because the authors consider this disaster in this specific place through a carefully considered cultural lens and through an open dialogue about how people are affected in culture, they make the case for a dialectic that is at the same time quite specific and quite universal. Further, by such careful and richly described comparison to Western, individualistic approaches, they provide a multilevel discussion that allows the reader to compare and contrast. They describe this using Conservation of Resources (COR) theory as an individual-nested in family-nested in tribe approach (Hobfoll 1988, 1998). Moreover, since a majority of the world's inhabitants and cultures are more collectivist than individualistic in their worldview and view of self, their study opportunes a deeper understanding of disaster reaction and intervention that is relevant to a majority of the world (Tol et al. 2012).

COR theory is one of several key frameworks that the authors call upon to frame their work. A lesser known aspect of COR theory is the FALL model—Fitting, Adaptation, Limitations, and Leniency. As readers digest this rich book, they might keep the FALL model in mind.

Fitting is key because resources do not necessarily fit demands, but rather people and social structures mold and alter resources to make them fit. It is an active, not a passive process. Moreover, in economically resource-lacking environments, the need to alter and mold resources to make them fit is a more necessary and dynamic process (Hobfoll 1998). It is also a process that can have dire consequences, because often resources are fit to meet needs in ways that deprive their future use and have limited capability. The use of child labor is one such example, because it helps both feed a family and harm the child's life.

Adaptation describes how people are looking to adapt to the overarching demands on their lives, even while they may be centrally attending to the immediate and critical demands of a disaster. Stress has evoked a learned helplessness model (Seligman 1975), whereas COR theory leads more directly to describe an adaptive model. In adaptation this book brings many examples and descriptions of how people shape themselves and their environments to adapt to challenges and meet demands. Further, throughout the book, but especially in the second half, the process of adaptation is illuminated within cultural context and a look to the preservation of life, family, and social bonds. The integration of concepts of spirituality—including a social-self view that includes the past, present, future, and spiritual afterlife—is both fascinating and illuminating, as this approach to self stands in such contrast to the mainly nonspiritual empirical literature from the West.

Limitations in the FALL model speak to the reality that economically challenging environments place multiple and oftentimes fundamental limitations on people's actions. Western psychology of coping envisions individuals that will be empowered if only they choose to be. Their shackles are seen as mental. Rather, collectivist societies are more constraining, at the same time that they may be more socially supportive. Economic realities place further limitations on access to services, availability of treatment, and even basic human rights. Indonesia has been plagued by religious and ethnic violence, as well as domestic abuse of women. Further, the Western expectation for a government that acts to protect the population cannot be assumed for much of the world, where police and government officials are often viewed as part of the corrosive and dangerous strain of violence, intolerance, and corruption, as they are in Indonesia (Human Rights Watch 2013). Further, the rights of women and minorities are not only not protected, but often undermined by officials for economic or political purposes.

Finally, an understanding of culture must unfortunately include an emphasis on the role of *Leniency*. What leniency means in cultural context is that for much of the world the rules do not apply to the privileged. Scholars of Indonesia explain the violence as a consequence of the "loss of the monopoly in the means of violence by the state," beginning with the political reforms of 1998 (Colombijn and Lindblad 2002). Other pockets of power exist in remnants of former politically leading Suharto clan or the army itself, as was recently seen in the military takeover of the government in Egypt. Leniency is fluid for much of the world, as it is sometimes the privilege of government, sometimes the result of powerful violent groups, or the power of the purse. This is not to say that Leniency and Limitations are not present in all parts of the world, but they are greater factors where government is nondemocratic and the greater the gradient between rich and poor.

Overall, we have much to learn from this volume. It is theoretically rich, deep in its analyses of context, difficulties and solutions, and hopeful in its emphasis on resiliency. The second half of the volume does an excellent job of interweaving treatment in the context of the fabric of society and how it is altered by disaster, as well as how we might best respond. It melds the psychological, sociological and anthropological in a way that contributes markedly to our understanding of trauma and recovery.

12 July 2013
Chicago

Stevan E. Hobfoll

References

Colombin, F. & Linblad, J. T. (2002). *Roots of violence in Indonesia: Contemporary violence in historical perspective*. Leiden: KITLV Press.

de Jong, J. T. V. M. (2002). Public mental health, traumatic stress, and human rights violations in low-income countries. In de Jong, J. T. V. M. (Ed.), *Trauma, war, and violence: Public mental health in socio-cultural context* (pp. 1–91). New York: Plennum-Kluwer.

Hobfoll, S. E. (1998). *Stress, culture, and community: The psychology and philosophy of stress*. New York: Plenum.

Human Rights Watch (2013). World Report 2013: Indonesia. http://www.hrw.org/world-report/2013/country-chapters/indonesia. Accessed 12 July 2013.

Seligman, M. E. P. (1975). *Helplessness: On depression, development, and death*. San Francisco: W. H. Freeman.

Tol, W. A., Patel, V., Tomlinson, M., Baingana, F., Galappatti, A., Silove, D., Sondorp, E., et al. (2012). Relevance or excellence? Setting research priorities for mental health and psychosocial support in humanitarian settings. *Harvard Review of Psychiatry, 20,* 25–36.

Foreword

Culture's Contagious Idea: From Perception to Inter-Being Coping

I have seldom read a book that has surprised me so, challenged, and enriched me so that I felt like crying out, "Al-hamdu lillahi," an expression of profound gratitude appropriate to both Tanzania, where I work, and Indonesia, where the authors of *Cultural Psychology of Coping with Disasters* are engaged. I have had a deep suspicion of psychologism in hazard and disaster research since my arrival in 1968 at Clark University as a beginning PhD student in geography. This was also the beginning of the infatuation with the psychological testing of "perception" by my geography professor, Robert Kates, his contemporary, Ian Burton, and their professor, Gilbert White. This trio is justly credited with creating and consolidating an American school of hazard research in the tradition of Harlan Barrows, White's teacher, who wrote in 1920 of "geography as human ecology" (Burton et al. 1978). The trouble was that none of my mentors had a deep understanding of psychology and the plurality of psychological approaches and theories, and their dabbling and eclecticism simply imported into geography of a handful of behavioral psychology's tests—thematic apperception, sentence completion, etc. What is worse, these tests were uncritically applied in cross cultural contexts (White 1974). Imagine my surprise to find a book that shows how rich an alternative existed in the 1960s and 1970s, when some of us rebelled against the reductionism and ethnocentricism of the environmental-behavioral turn in hazard research (Torry 1979; Waddell 1977; Hewitt 1983).

Cultural Psychology of Coping with Disasters provides a comprehensive, transdisciplinary review of coping theories and a framework for integrating cultural psychology into the study of coping with structural questions about the larger societal, political and economic systems in which individual and household coping takes place. Figure 2.1, "Dimensions and units of analysis for psychological and sociological approaches to coping" is destined to become as influential as the "pressure and release" framework (Blaikie et al. 1994), especially if the authors think of a snappier name for the framework (e.g., "pressure and release" became known as PAR or, more memorably, "the crunch diagram"). I will call it DUPS for short.

The other surprise I had in store was to see how broad a specialist seeming study of a particular earthquake in Indonesia turned out to be. There is a deeply intelligent discussion of field methods, the ethics of disaster research and timely reflections on participatory research. The latter has become de rigueur among PhD students working within the framework of political ecology (which has superseded human ecology) shared by anthropology and geography, and also among many international nongovernmental organizations (INGOs) working with communities in what is known as "community-based disaster risk reduction" (Delica-Willison and Gaillard 2012; ECB 2013). The four chapters in Part III, "Multidimentional Coping" will surely become as much discussed and used as the narrative and philosophically grounded expansion of the DUPS diagram. The chapter titles give a sense of the wide ranging and thoughtful content: "The Material Dimension of Coping: Socioculturally Mediated Biophysical Process," "The Social Dimension of Coping: Communal Negotiations of Social Benefits and Burdens," "The Life Conduct Dimension of Coping: Local Wisdom Discourses and Related Life Orientations," and "The Religious Dimension of Coping: The Roles of Cosmologies and Religious Practices."

There is so much that is timely and also timeless in its phenomenological wealth and multidimensional breadth. Well if not timeless, then it is likely to have a very long "shelf life". Recently, the story of war-injured people in Sierra Leone has been told (Berghs 2012; Wisner and Cole 2013), and the amputees themselves are said to reject the discourse of trauma (cf. Chap. 13 here). Books such as *Dead Aid* (Moyo 2009) and the specific evaluations of the Active Learning Network for Accountability and Performance in Humanitarian Action (ALNAP: http://www.alnap.org) show the relevance of the chapter on "Disaster Aid Distribution and Social Conflict". Gender mainstreaming and villager visions of their futures are also very timely as more and more women are coming to be seen as proactive leaders in the whole of disaster risk reduction and not only during the so-called "recovery" phase (see Gender and Disaster Network: www.gdnonline.org; and Grassroots Organisations Working Together in Sisterhood, GROOTS: http://www.groots.org).

I wish my introduction to psychology—as a grad student beginning to work academically on natural hazards in 1968—had not been so narrow. My only consolation is that the multiverse contains an alternative "me" in another "then" and "there" where my starting place is cultural psychology with all of its multidimensional and transdisciplinary power.

26 July 2013 Ben Wisner
Oberlin, Ohio

References

Berghs, M. (2012). *War and embodied memory: Becoming disabled in Sierra Leone.* Farnham: Ashgate.

Blaikie, P., Davis, I., Cannon, T., & Wisner, B. (1994). *At risk.* London: Routledge.

Burton, I., Kates, R., & White, G. (1978). *Environment as hazard.* New York: Oxford University Press.

Delica-Willison, Z., & Gaillard, J. C. (2012). Community action and disaster. In: B. Wisner, J. C. Gaillard, & I. Kelman (Eds.), *The Routledge handbook of hazards and disaster risk reduction* (pp. 711–22). London: Routledge.

Emergency Capability Building Project (ECB) (2013). *Towards resilience.* Baltimore: Catholic Relief Services.

Hewitt, K. (1983). The idea of calamity in a technocratic age. In K. Hewitt (Ed.), *Interpretation of calamities* (pp. 3–32). Boston: Allen & Unwin.

Moyo, D. (2009). *Dead aid.* New York: Farrar, Straus and Giroux.

Torry, W. (1979). Hazards, hazes and holes: A critique of the *Environment as Hazard* and general reflections on disaster research. *Canadian Geographer, 23*(4), 368–383.

Waddell, E. (1977). The hazards of scientism. *Human Ecology, 5*(1), 69–76.

White, G. (Ed.) (1974) *Natural hazards: Local, national and global.* New York: Oxford University Press.

Wisner, B., & Cole, E. (2013). Ask us how we survive. Review of war and embodied memory. *African Geographical Review* (in press).

Preface

Global media coverage of devastating disasters like the 2004 tsunami in the Indian Ocean, the 2010 earthquake in Haiti, and the recent disasters in Japan in 2011 lead us to recognize the continuing challenge faced by humanity when coping with disasters. Even beyond these colossal events, disasters are ubiquitous and historically persistent phenomena that have gained even greater relevance in the context of climate change. Of macroeconomic concern also is the fact that in recent years the world experienced the highest disaster losses ever recorded, which has resulted in continuously rising economic costs over the past 30 years (World Bank 2012).[1] In response to this heightened awareness about the collective impact of disasters, disaster research has grown into a transdisciplinary field, with discipline-based contributions ranging from engineering and geography to sociology, anthropology, history, and psychology. However, as we argue in this book, disaster studies lack a distinct cultural psychological approach, which conceptually connects research on subjective disaster coping to sociocultural approaches to disaster. Disasters are experienced and coped with subjectively, while embedded in sociocultural, historical, and environmental contexts.

The field of disaster research is still dominated by technocratic and universalist approaches (see Hewitt 2012), most often developed in high-income countries from the Global North and intended to be applied anywhere else, including middle- or low-income countries in the Global South. However, over the last decade, awareness about the value of local cultural resources has emerged and evolved in disaster research and international disaster management policies (see UNISDR 2005). The need for translation and transfer of expertise between the globalized field of disaster intervention and specific forms of local knowledge has gained increasing recognition (e.g., Mercer et al. 2010); however, the realization of such transcultural exchanges continues to be challenging in practice. For example, it is often the case that local knowledge is superficially acknowledged as isolated elements of culture which are

[1] Between 1980 and 2011, disasters have caused more than 3.3 million deaths and US$ 3.5 trillion in economic damages and losses across the world. Extreme weather events account for over 78 % of the events recorded over the same period and are responsible for two-thirds of the losses (US$ 2.6 trillion).

then integrated into strategies of disaster-risk reduction. Fundamental and implicit cultural assumptions about individuals, their social contexts and basic worldviews remain untouched in the application of globalized intervention strategies. However, in order for disaster aid and risk reduction to be sustainable and effective, planners and practitioners need to be sensitized to local practices, values, beliefs, social structures, and dynamics.

The main psychological contributions to disaster research have focused on psychopathological outcomes of disaster: the mechanisms and conditions by which disasters affect mental health and the effectiveness of associated psychological interventions (see MacFarlane et al. 2009). Other psychological approaches assimilate disaster into the broader theme of coping with stress, for example in cases of job loss, illness, or bereavement (see Chap. 2). The disaster psychopathology and coping approaches both identify universal psychological mechanisms that determine human behavior and experiences under challenging or threatening circumstances. Although these approaches turn our attention from a macro-level of analysis to a micro-level of subjective disaster experience, they operate with universalist assumptions which are built upon the individual as a separate entity. Social and cultural aspects are conceptualized as external moderating factors and a presumption is evident of clear boundaries between inner or private and outer or public realms. Thus, these theories fail to address how the sociocultural is intermingled with the individual inner, private, or cognitive aspects. Little research has examined the actual subjective experiences of people living and coping with disasters as individuals embedded in sociocultural settings. For this endeavor, the theoretical tools for disaster or coping research in psychology need to be expanded, which is the main goal of our book.

To bridge this research gap between sociocultural and psychological disaster approaches, we turn to cultural psychology and argue for a cultural psychology of coping with disasters. We develop our argument and approach by reviewing a broad range of theories, conceptual analyses, and policy-based arguments from anthropological disaster research to psychological coping theory and complement this discussion with findings from our research project in Indonesia. Our book provides a critical reevaluation of the complex phenomena of coping with disasters on a general level by applying an integrative theory of disaster coping to a specific context. The conceptual basis of our approach can be sketched by the three key terms of disaster, culture and coping.

Disasters are characterized by their large-scale impacts, causing loss and destruction in entire communities or regions that exceed available coping capacities and thus require outside assistance. Disaster coping always implies collective affectedness and the presence of or at least a need for external aid. Natural hazard agents such as earthquakes demonstrate how human existence (and social life) is embedded in physical environments. Disasters are framed as a long-term process of human–environment interaction, and, accordingly, coping with them needs to be understood within this relationship and framework.

In this book, culture is defined as the way people relate to the world and to themselves through meanings and practices. Culture is shared, (re)produced, and negotiated in multiple social contexts. For example, even though there are representations of Javanese culture as a monolithic corpus of knowledge, artistic, and social practices, there is not actually one single Javanese culture. The way people behave and view the world around them is shaped by their social stratification, political affiliation, transcultural interaction, or general life experience. We therefore follow the cultural psychological approach which situates the psychological subject in multiple contexts, while person and context mutually constitute each other.

Coping is a complex material–symbolic, cognitive–embodied, and individual–social process. It is embedded in structural and sociocultural contexts that not only produce or inhibit (forms of) agency, but also interpretatively frame the very "stressor" that is to be coped with and structure the embodied experience of suffering. Coping can neither be reduced to an "objective" material sphere nor be considered solely in symbolic terms. Subjective experiences, perceptions, emotions, and interpretations are socioculturally mediated or constructed *and* also bound to a biophysical materiality. The way people cope is significantly shaped by their actual access to resources. We further argue that coping processes are contingent upon micro- and macrodynamics of the individual life-course, community processes, and global histories. Research needs to consider the multiple (potentially contradicting) interests that actors bring to coping processes and practices, which do not necessarily relate to "coping" itself but to other dynamics that are not necessarily disaster-related.

Our theoretical argument is based on a review of the theoretical literature *and* grounded on an in-depth case study. Complexity cannot be captured by even the most elaborate theoretical model, and needs to be made clear and explicit through detailed explorative, qualitative case studies. Our strategy in this interpretative research was to turn the causal models of conventional coping theories into heuristic devices which are used to draw out the symbolical and practical meanings of concepts and their referential relations as used by people in a specific sociocultural setting (see Sect. 3.3); that is, instead of correlating strictly defined and categorized quantifiable variables, we chose an interpretative approach, asking our respondents for relevant concepts and explanations while posing questions about conventional coping themes. Our discursive and dialogical approach to theory and the empirical study resulted in the formulation of a multidimensional coping framework (see Part III), encompassing the material, social, religious, and life-conduct dimensions. In our case study, these dimensions serve as a productive analytical tool in which each dimension provides a particular lens to look at the complex phenomenon of coping. Instead of thinking about these dimensions as separate spheres or in terms of a hierarchical importance, we understand the dimensions as analytical perspectives that complement each other in gaining a deeper understanding of coping processes. We present our multidimensional coping framework as a research strategy to untangle *and* represent the complexity of coping processes.

The villages examined in our case study are located in Central Java, Indonesia, a geographical region with a long history of natural disasters. The study focused on the 2006 earthquake in the Yogyakarta province, which resulted in the destruction of 300,000 homes, 20,000 injuries, and almost 6,000 deaths (OCHA 2007). We examined the process of coping with disaster and related relief efforts in three affected villages, 2–5 years after the incident.[2] Our book reports the results of an international research collaboration, inspired by collaborative interdisciplinary and transcultural dialogue and reflection in the fields of psychology and anthropology between German and Indonesian authors and an author from Australia/New Zealand.

Our research was guided by the question of how people subjectively experienced, interpreted, and dealt with the disaster and the subsequent dynamics revolving around external aid resources. We also integrated a long-term perspective on coping and the local ways of dealing with persistent threats. Our analysis captures material, social, psychoreligious and emotional–habitual aspects of these coping processes in a four-dimensional framework and we demonstrate how contextual conditions influence these processes. We draw attention to the sociopolitical structures and relationships individuals have with different stakeholders, for example, the extent of trust that exists in a context of corruption. Within disaster studies, the 2006 Java earthquake is of particular interest because the large-scale governmental reconstruction program had a community-based approach. Financial resources were provided by the government and the program was administered and organized locally, drawing on the Javanese cultural resource of community self-help (*gotong royong*). The disaster gained global media attention and many local and international relief agencies were involved in a wide variety of interventions. Governmental and nongovernmental institutions combined social change agendas such as gender mainstreaming with their delivery of aid. The region, as is increasingly common in the current state of international disaster aid, became a laboratory of varying cultural influences and normative concerns, which generated new mixtures of "glocality".

This book illustrates the perspectives of disaster survivors and their life contexts. It is intended for many audiences because it contributes a theoretical argument to coping research, but it may also prove to be particularly useful for disaster researchers and practitioners. It provides a cultural psychological approach to understanding the psychosocial responses of people living in disaster-prone areas and to informing disaster management practices by including perspectives from disaster-affected communities.

Structure of the Book

This edited book is a result of a collaborative research process, with the full theoretical argument unfolding throughout the book. The first part introduces the theoretical foundation of our approach. Chapter 1 offers a critical and transdisciplinary

[2] The research with the title "Individual and collective ways of coping long-term with extreme suffering and external help after natural disasters: meanings and emotions" was funded by the Fritz Thyssen Stiftung from November 2008 to October 2011. The research project was carried out between the International Academy for Innovative Pedagogy, Psychology and Economics gGmbH (INA) at Freie Universität Berlin, Germany, while the responsibility for the implementation of the research project was in the hands of Prof. Johana Prawitasari-Hadiyono, Universitas Gadjah Mada, Faculty of Psychology, in Yogyakarta, Indonesia.

introduction to key paradigms, approaches, and controversies of disaster research and management. The authors examine a range of exemplary disaster research literature, pursuing core questions relevant to the overall goal of the book. Issues of human agency are addressed in relation to socioeconomic structures and exosemiotic or extradiscursive forces of "nature". The authors further examine how these approaches conceptualize the processes of human interaction with and adaptation to environments and identify the roles of cultural frames and forms of knowledge. Chapter 2 addresses the behavior, thoughts, experiences and feelings of individuals and communities exposed to strain and stress, introducing the various approaches associated with both psychological and broader social science-based understandings of coping. These models are similar to goal-based models of human nature, which understand human beings' basic motivation as moving toward goals while avoiding threats. This developing theoretical discussion is then used to analyze the extent to which these approaches can be applied in a disaster-related context. Our framework for a cultural psychology of coping with disaster is formulated in Chap. 3, beginning with the basic premise of how a cultural psychology approach highlights our understanding of the mutual constitution of person and context. We clarify understandings of subjectivity and agency and their relation to contexts before transferring these concepts to disaster contexts. A framework for coping that accounts for cultural specificities is developed by expanding upon appraisal-based and other coping models. We transcend the focus on cognitive and biologically founded processes, account for collective and locally specific modes of coping, and complement clinical and medicalizing approaches to disaster-related suffering with a focus on resilience and local forms of coping.

Part II of the book connects the theoretical considerations with the case study. Chapter 4 contextualizes our research in the ethnographic setting of Java, while Chap. 5 elaborates on the methodological basis of a culture-specific coping approach. Following Charmaz (2006) and Clarke (2005), we understand the research process, including data collection and theorizing, as a process of social action in which researchers construct the results in dialogue with others in particular places and times. We conceptualize the 3-year research process as a mutual process involving changes in views, conceptions, and methods. This transformation included the researchers as people, the organization of responsibilities and distribution of tasks, the management of financial resources, and the representation of the project at local and international forums. Our research in Java which exemplified this framework with its reflection process involving different research parties including participants, serves as a background for a general discussion of knowledge production, ethics, and empowerment in disaster contexts (see Chaps. 6–8).

In parts III and IV, we turn to our empirical case study of the 2006 Java earthquake. Part III uses the multidimensional coping framework to present the data. The Material Dimension (Chap. 9) refers to the biophysical side of disaster coping, which includes perceptions of physical destruction, rescue, relief, and reconstruction efforts, and subjective experiences of all of these features of the disaster. In the Social Dimension (Chap. 10), coping is understood as a social phenomenon that extends the understanding of traditional social support dynamics found in mainstream psychology. Communal coping efforts, power dynamics, and the re-negotiations of sociocultural-specific values and practices are all examined to explore the dynamics of a village struck by disaster. The Dimension of Life Conduct (Chap. 11) emphasizes the intertwining of sociocultural features with personalized, enacted codes of conduct. Differing local concepts of self and related control patterns are investigated here. The last chapter covers the Religious Dimension (Chap. 12). In disaster contexts, religion is an important resource for meaning-making, which helps people to find metaphysical explanations of events in addition to understanding their personal significance. Part IV then focuses on specific aspects of coping, which are analyzed across the (previously introduced) four coping dimensions. Chapter 13 contrasts the theme of "suffering" with the more common theme in international and Western contexts of "disaster mental health". Chapter 14 highlights the cultural-specific aspects of coping with the social conflicts resulting from aid distribution processes, a topic long neglected in individualistic and apolitical psychological approaches. Chapter 15 deals with risk management, before Part IV closes with a critical evaluation of gender mainstreaming issues in disaster contexts (Chap. 16). We conclude by weaving together our empirical findings with the theoretical considerations and addressing the general contributions a cultural psychological approach to coping with disaster may offer to the fields of psychology and disaster research and practice.

Manfred Zaumseil
Mechthild von Vacano
Silke Schwarz
Gavin B. Sullivan
Johana E. Prawitasari-Hadiyono

Acknowledgements The editors would like to thank Elise Serbaroli for her assistance in editing this preface.

References

Charmaz, K. (2006). *Constructing grounded theory. A practical guide through qualitative analysis*. London: Sage.

Clarke, A. (2005). *Situational analysis. Grounded theory after the postmodern turn*. Thousand Oaks: Sage Publications.

Hewitt, K. (2012). Culture, hazard and disaster. In B. Wisner, J. C. Gaillard, & I. Kelman (Eds.), *Handbook of hazards and disaster risk reduction* (pp. 85–108). New York: Routledge.

McFarlane, A. C., van Hooff, M., & Goodhew, F. (2009). Anxiety disorders and PTSD. In Y. Neria, S. Galea, & F. H. Norris (Eds.), *Mental health and disasters* (pp. 47–66). New York: Cambridge University Press.

Mercer, J., Kelman, I., Suchet-Pearson, S., & Lloyd, K. (2010). Framework for integrating indigenous and scientific knowledge for disaster risk reduction. *Disasters, 34*(1), 214–239.

Office for the Coordination of Humanitarian Affairs (OCHA). (2007). Cluster approach: Lessons learned: Yogyakarta and Central Java earthquake, Indonesia. http://star-tides.net/node/2081. Accessed 8 May 2013.

United Nations International Strategy for Disaster Reduction (UNISDR). (2005). Hyogo Framework for Action 2005–2015: Building the resilience of nations and communities to disasters. Geneva: UNISDR. http://www.unisdr.org/2005/wcdr/intergover/official-doc/L-docs/Hyogo-framework-for-action-english.pdf. Accessed 07 July 2013.

World Bank (2012). Disaster risk management http://web.worldbank.org/WBSITE/EXTERNAL/TOPICS/EXTURBANDEVELOPMENT/EXTDISMGMT/0,,menuPK:341021~pagePK:149018~piPK:149093~theSitePK:341015,00.html. Accessed 4 March 2013.

Contents

Contributors

Jeane A. Indradjaja Berlin, Germany

Lucia Peppy Novianti Institute for Community Behavioral Change, Yogyakarta, Indonesia

Johana E. Prawitasari-Hadiyono Center for Research and Community Service, Christian University of Krida Wacana, Jakarta, Indonesia

Universitas Gadjah Mada, Yogyakarta, Indonesia

Nindyah Rengganis Institute for Community Behavioral Change, Yogyakarta, Indonesia

Silke Schwarz International Academy for Innovative Pedagogy, Psychology and Economics gGmbH at Freie Universität Berlin, Berlin, Germany

Gavin B. Sullivan School of Social, Psychological and Communication Sciences, Leeds Metropolitan University, Leeds, UK

Tri Hayuning Tyas Department of Clinical Psychology, Faculty of Psychology, Universitas Gadjah Mada, Yogyakarta, Indonesia

Mechthild von Vacano Institute for Social and Cultural Anthropology, Freie Universität Berlin, Berlin, Germany

Tiara R. Widiastuti Institute for Community Behavioral Change, Yogyakarta, Indonesia

Manfred Zaumseil International Academy for Innovative Pedagogy, Psychology and Economics gGmbH at Freie Universität Berlin, Berlin, Germany

Part I
Theoretical Overview and Synthesis

Chapter 1
Understanding Disasters: An Analysis and Overview of the Field of Disaster Research and Management

Mechthild von Vacano and Manfred Zaumseil

Since the 1950s, disaster research has developed into a vast field of study, involving disciplines such as engineering, geology, meteorology, geography, sociology, psychology, and anthropology—just to name a few. A transdisciplinary field of emergency studies has emerged which even is claimed to have an independent status as a discipline of its own (Jensen 2010). In developing a cultural psychology of disaster, we position ourselves within this transdisciplinary field, initially by providing an overview of key issues. The following chapter will introduce current disaster research and discuss the potential advantages and pitfalls of each approach. Any analysis of such a complex, multifaceted, dynamic field is necessarily selective; we place special emphasis on concepts and tendencies that are relevant to formulating a cultural psychology of disaster. Important questions throughout this process include: How is the category "disaster" demarcated and construed, and what implications follow? How do the various approaches understand human–nature relations? How are "nature" and "human agency" perceived? How are historical and sociocultural contexts accounted for?

To offer an overview and orienting framework, the chapter begins with a brief introduction to disaster definitions and prevalent paradigms. We then discuss the key concepts of vulnerability, resilience, and risk with regard to their various meanings in distinct fields as well as their analytical potentials and pitfalls. An outline is provided of how disasters can be understood as occurring at the nexus of humans and nature. This covers such issues as society–environment interactions, human adaptation to hazardous environments, and implications of social, cultural, and political frames

M. von Vacano (✉)
Institute for Social and Cultural Anthropology,
Freie Universität Berlin, Landoltweg 9-11, 14195 Berlin, Germany
e-mail: m.vacano@fu-berlin.de

M. Zaumseil
International Academy for Innovative Pedagogy, Psychology and Economics gGmbH
at Freie Universität Berlin, Malteserstr. 74-100, 12249 Berlin, Germany
e-mail: zaumseil@zedat.fu-berlin.de

M. Zaumseil et al. (eds.), *Cultural Psychology of Coping with Disasters*,
DOI 10.1007/978-1-4614-9354-9_1, © Springer Science+Business Media, LLC 2014

of the category "disaster" itself. In the final section, we approach the issue of coping more closely, examining professional and nonprofessional ways of "managing" disaster and the interrelation between expert cultures and "local knowledge."

1.1 Introductory Review of Predominant Discourses

Any definition of a problem predetermines possible strategies for its solution. Therefore, examining different definitions of disaster can provide a useful framework to map the variety of approaches and should also reveal common patterns of hegemonic understandings. As the following examples illustrate, definitions of disaster vary over time between theorists, researchers, practitioners, and policymakers as well as within discipline-based approaches and across disciplines.

FEMA	"[A] disaster is commonly defined as a nonroutine event in time and space, producing human, property, or environmental damage, whose remediation requires the use of resources from outside the directly affected community." (Lindell et al. 2006, p. 7)
UNISDR	"[A disaster is] a serious disruption of the functioning of a community or a society involving widespread human, material, economic or environmental losses and impacts, which exceeds the ability of the affected community or society to cope using its own resources. Comment: Disasters are often described as a result of the combination of: the exposure to a hazard; the conditions of vulnerability that are present; and insufficient capacity or measures to reduce or cope with the potential negative consequences. Disaster impacts may include loss of life, injury, disease and other negative effects on human physical, mental and social well-being, together with damage to property, destruction of assets, loss of services, social and economic disruption and environmental degradation." (UNISDR 2009, p. 9)
Sociology	"[A disaster is] an event, concentrated in time and space, in which a society, or a relatively self-sufficient subdivision of a society, undergoes severe danger and incurs such losses to its members and physical appurtenances that the social structure is disrupted and the fulfillment of all or some of the essential functions of the society is prevented." (Fritz 1961, p. 655)
Sociology	"A disaster is a social situation characterized by nonroutine, life-threatening physical destruction attributed to the forces of nature, regardless of what other factors may seem to be involved." (Stallings 2005, p. 263, italics removed)
Geography	"A disaster occurs when a significant number of vulnerable people experience a hazard and suffer severe damage and/or disruption of their livelihood system in such a way that recovery is unlikely without external aid. By "recovery" we mean the psychological and physical recovery of the victims, and the replacement of physical resources and the social relations required to use them." (Wisner et al. 2004, p. 50)

Anthropology "[A disaster is] a process/event combining a potential destructive agent/force from the natural, modified, or built environment and a population in a socially and economically produced condition of vulnerability, resulting in a perceived disruption of the customary relative satisfactions of individual and social needs for physical survival, social order, and meaning." (Oliver-Smith and Hoffman 2002, p. 4)

Psychology "[A disaster is] a potentially traumatic event that is collectively experienced, has an acute onset, and is time-delimited; disasters may be attributed to natural, technological, or human causes." (McFarlane and Norris 2006, p. 4)

Disaster management agencies such as the US Federal Emergency Management Agency (FEMA) or the United Nations International Strategy for Disaster Reduction (UNISDR) offer rather practical definitions, demarcating a disaster as a nonroutine or disruptive event characterized by damage and losses that exceed the coping capacities of the affected communities and thus require external assistance or outside intervention. Similarly, a long tradition of disaster sociology has centered on disasters as interruptions of community functioning, an approach that is exemplified by Fritz's (1961) influential definition. Decades later, another constructionist strain of sociological disaster research emerged. As represented by Stallings (2005), authors in this tradition highlight the profoundly social nature of disaster. Framing something as disaster, they argue, always involves the demarcation of certain occurrences as disruptive or nonroutine events and the social processes of interpreting causalities.

Yet another influential understanding was formulated in the seminal publication *At Risk* by the geographers Blaikie et al. (1994, 1st ed.) and Wisner et al. (2004, 2nd ed.). Their differentiation of hazard from human vulnerability and their definition of disaster as the conjunction of both elements resonated far beyond the disciplinary borders of geography. For example, their approach strongly influenced the anthropologists Oliver-Smith and Hoffman (2002), who based their definition of disaster on Blaikie et al. (1994) while also adding a constructionist or relativist twist: that is, similar to constructionist approaches in sociology, Oliver-Smith and Hoffman's conception of disaster involves a cultural framing of the occurrence, in this case linked to *perceived* disruption. As a last example, we have selected a deeply psychological definition of disaster: Sociologists such as Fritz (1961) are concerned with community functioning, whereas psychologists such as McFarlane and Norris (2006) focus on individual functioning and thus the potential for mental health to be damaged by a disaster.

The discipline-based character of these definitions is apparent, but despite their differences they share a common understanding of at least four aspects: (1) The destructive character of an occurrence serves as a constitutive element, (2) the occurrence is categorized as a disruption to normality, (3) disaster is defined in relation to time, commonly as an event but sometimes as a process, and (4) the destructive and disruptive character of the occurrence is often linked causally to an element of dysfunction or overstrain, necessitating external assistance.

Table 1.1 Development of Disaster Paradigms (Based on Hilhorst 2007)

	Hazard (1950s–present)	Vulnerability (1980s–present)	Environment (1990s–present)
Casuality	Nature	Human	Human–nature
	Biophysical casuality	Social and structural casuality	Complex casuality
Temporality	Singular event	Process and structure	Process
	Emergency	Contingency	Long-term interaction
Policies	Technocratic disaster mitigation	Risk management	Risk reduction
	Emergency management	Vulnerability reduction	

Definitions not only specify disaster as a category of occurrence (or process) but also distinguish certain types of disaster according to their agent phenotypes; generally, a triple distinction is made between natural, technological, and social or human-induced hazards. Within the category of "natural hazard," Wisner et al. (2004) suggest six subcategories: famine, biological hazards (epidemics), floods, coastal storms, earthquakes, and volcanoes. Technological hazards include threats such as the release of toxic substances or explosions. Social hazards, by contrast, entail "willful attacks," civil conflict, or war. Reflecting increased attention to human–environment interaction, a fourth category of "socio-natural hazards" is emerging. It refers to seemingly natural hazards such as floods, landslides, or drought, which are now being recognized as anthropogenic, because the probability of these hazards increases due to human use of natural resources (UNISDR 2009).

This hazard-centered typology has been supplemented with or replaced by other distinctions, such as scope of disaster impact, speed of onset, duration, the size of the affected area, and social preparedness of the affected community (see, for example, Barton 1969; UNISDR 2009). According to these criteria, earthquakes are, for example, classified as sudden onset events of short duration, usually affecting a relatively small geographic area (UNISDR 2009).

Shifting Perspectives on "Natural" Disaster Across these different perspectives on disaster, scholarly and applied disaster discourses have followed broader disciplinary, practical, and policy developments. A rough sketch of shifting paradigms therefore provides another helpful orientation framework with which to navigate through the various approaches to disaster research. Following Hilhorst (2007), we identify three major paradigms in Western—and globalized—disaster research and management: the technocratic, hazard-centered approach; the vulnerability approach; and the mutual constitution approach (Table 1.1). Although these paradigms can be associated with specific periods of scholarship, they have not replaced each other sequentially but rather coexist and interact.

The field of disaster research came into being after World War II. Rooted in the scientific context of that time, these early approaches were technocratic in character and based on positivist assumptions (Jigyasu 2002). The understanding of disasters centered on geophysical hazards as external forces that attack communities and cause "natural" disasters. "Natural" hazards were typologically classified as geographical, geological, or meteorological and rendered predictable with measuring and monitoring techniques developed by the corresponding sciences of geology, meteorology, or engineering. According to this paradigm, appropriate disaster management and engineering structures could enable societies to prevent or ameliorate disaster (Jigyasu 2002). Scholars perceived failed attempts in terms of motivation to improve these efforts, striving for an ideal of control (Hewitt 1983).

However, the idea of technocratic control was soon supplemented by a behavioral approach. In his 1942 dissertation on flood management in the USA, Gilbert White warned against an overreliance on "structural," technocratic efforts and advocated adaptive or accommodative, "nonstructural" adjustments. He argued for behavioral changes rather than attempts to control flooding; people should receive training in proper disaster response behaviors and be able to anticipate and control the onset of a disaster situation. White (1986 [1942]) famously declared: "Floods are 'acts of god,' but flood losses are largely acts of man" (p. 12). By drawing attention to the element of human agency in disaster prevention, White's behavioral approach introduced a social element into science- and technology-based disaster management—an element that became a central focus of the vulnerability paradigm that followed.

The vulnerability paradigm criticized previous research for being technocratic and hazard centered and attempted to amend these shortcomings by highlighting the political–economic nature of disaster (e.g., Hewitt 1983; or later Blaikie et al. 1994; Wisner et al. 2004). The cause of disaster was no longer attributed to external forces of nature but rather to socioeconomic conditions and the distribution of access to resources (Hewitt 1983). Scholars have criticized the hazard perspective for failing to explain why some hazard agents develop into disasters, while others do not, or why disaster affects some people more severely than others. These new approaches indicate that biophysical processes may unfold as harmful events, but that their destructive impact actually results from people's vulnerabilities, such as unsafe settlement locations, inadequate housing, or fragile livelihoods. Through the concept of vulnerability, researchers turned their focus to the social factors that lead to disaster and which are (re)produced by social, economic, and political processes (Wisner et al. 2004). This shift in emphasis has meant that "natural" disasters are no longer understood as a singular, sudden-onset event caused by external forces but rather as something deeply embedded in "normal," everyday life and its socioeconomic structures (e.g., Hewitt 1983; Wisner et al. 2004, 2012).

The applied field of disaster management adopted the vulnerability paradigm in its own way: Under the banner of risk management, programs began to integrate preventive aspects of vulnerability assessment and reduction. Participatory approaches became a trend and post-disaster communities were encouraged to conduct their own hazard and vulnerability analysis (HVA) in order to develop and implement reduction measures for the future. These programmatic attempts necessarily reduced vulnerability to the microlevel of communities rather than tackling its root causes at a macrostructural level.

However, in the 1990s there was an increasing demand for the integration of a development perspective in disaster research and management. Critics, such as Lewis (1999), argued that vulnerability reduction should not only be part of post-disaster interventions but also be integrated into any development effort. Furthermore, these critics highlighted the fact that development policies did not necessarily lead to a reduction in vulnerability because conventional development was equated with economic growth or the rationalization of bureaucratic institutions (McEntire et al. 2002). An alternative understanding of "development" or "invulnerable development" (McEntire et al. 2002) was therefore proposed to integrate vulnerability reduction on a structural level, for example, by considering environmental aspects or settlement patterns.

Increasingly, these approaches addressed questions such as what development should look like if it incorporates sustainable risk reduction and what implications does this have for people's relationships to natural resources. These were precursory developments to the third disaster paradigm, which treats disasters as complex interactions between nature and society (Hilhorst 2007; this is often discussed in the context of human-induced climate change; for example Brown and Westaway 2011; Pelling 2010). In the discourse of disaster management, this shift has been reflected in the emergence of the claimed new category of "socio-natural hazard" (UNISDR 2009). Fundamental to this third paradigm is a refusal to see humans and nature as two distinct categories. A focus on nature as the decisive agent has given way to the concept of an environment shaped by human action or, one step further, to the idea of a socioecological system (SES) which is a biophysical–social combination of society and environment. Susceptibility to disaster is then understood as societal (mal)adaptation to hazardous environments or as a question of the resilience of SESs (Pelling and Manuel-Navarrete 2011). In addition, Hilhorst (2007) identifies complexity itself as a further characteristic of this third paradigm. In contrast to the relatively simple causalities within the vulnerability paradigm, society–environment relations are not only understood as interactive but also increasingly deemed to be chaotic and unpredictable.

In summary, recent hegemonic understandings have increasingly questioned the naturalness of "natural" disaster. The term "natural disaster" has thus been criticized for neglecting the role of human agency in disasters (Hewitt 1997; Bolin and Stanford 1998). Alternatively, Bolin and Stanford (1998) suggest understanding disaster as a conjunction of processes that "emerge or develop out of the interactions of environmental forces with the particularities of human settlements and the capacities of people in those settlements to deal with the consequences of those forces". While the vulnerability paradigm emphasizes the human side of disaster and focuses on the question of social and political inequalities, the environmental paradigm makes the human–nature relationship central and eliminates the binary of humans and their environment. The environmental paradigm also changes the analytical time frame of disaster; earlier notions of disasters as singular events have been replaced by a process-oriented understanding that highlights historical context. Accordingly, the processes of coping with disasters cannot be confined to the post-disaster situation but are rather embedded in a broader backdrop: "It is the pre-disaster conditions that mainly affect a society's ability to cope with hazard; it is its reconstruction operations that largely determine the effects of subsequent events" (Bankoff 2003, p. 157).

With the concept of vulnerability, the causes of disasters are rooted in social factors; from the environmental perspective, disasters are embedded in a constant process of human–environment interaction.

1.2 Key Concepts in Disaster Research and Management

No scientific or management-based discussion of disaster today could avoid the key concepts of vulnerability, resilience, and risk, which we will discuss in the following section. A focus on vulnerability reflects the change of paradigm in the 1980s, while resilience and risk did not achieve widespread resonance in disaster discourse until the following decade. As with many important concepts in widespread academic use, these three terms are subject to contrasting conceptual and definitional interpretations throughout the various disciplines and institutions of practice. However, a thorough, interdisciplinary review of these terms would exceed the scope of this section; accordingly, we have chosen to focus on prominent definitions from the fields of disaster management and research. To cover the disaster management perspective, we refer to definitions developed by experts under the umbrella of UNISDR (UNISDR 2009). To address the research literature, we draw on the work of at least one prominent advocate for each key concept. As all three key concepts also appear in psychology, we conclude this section with a short examination of their use in the psychological literature.

1.2.1 Vulnerability as Susceptibility to Harm

The rise of the vulnerability concept in disaster studies began in the 1980s and it now occupies a key role in many research and management approaches.[1] The vulnerability paradigm symbolized the shift from a hazard-centered understanding of disaster to a more sociopolitical view—a change from disaster reduction as a matter of technological potency to one of human responsibility. By emphasizing social, political, and economic conditions, the vulnerability paradigm led to a politicization of disaster. To fight the causes of disaster, the vulnerability approach stresses the necessity of deep-rooted (global) social change (more or less tied to a shift in the human–environment relationship). However, in the everyday practice of disaster management, actors tend to address vulnerability reduction on a small scale and most often adopt technical approaches to finding solutions.

[1] For an exhaustive account of vulnerability in disaster research and management, see Cutter (1996), Weichselgartner (2001) or Villagrán de León (2006).

UNISDR (2009) experts define vulnerability as "characteristics and circumstances of a community, system or asset that make it susceptible to the damaging effects of a hazard" (p. 30). By this definition, vulnerability is a precondition to disaster, with its relation to hazard defined as susceptibility. Accordingly, vulnerability exists independently of actual exposure and can vary within communities and over time. The United Nations experts elaborate:

> There are many aspects of vulnerability, arising from various physical, social, economic, and environmental factors. Examples may include poor design and construction of buildings, inadequate protection of assets, lack of public information and awareness, limited official recognition of risks and preparedness measures, and disregard for wise environmental management. (UNISDR 2009)

Technocratic and planning-related concerns prevail in this explanation, while social aspects are reduced to matters of cognitive and rational preparedness. Issues of socioeconomic distribution, for example, those that Hewitt (1983) highlights in his fundamental critique, could theoretically be read into this definition, but they are far from central. Instead, an inclination toward the paradigm of environmental management and environmental responsibility is conspicuous.

Similar to the UNISDR, FEMA authors Lindell et al. (2006) define vulnerability within the traditional framework of emergency management. They differentiate between hazard exposure, physical vulnerability, and social vulnerability as pre-impact conditions. Physical vulnerability refers to the potential of "adverse physiological changes or damage" and can refer to people (human vulnerability), other living beings and plants (agricultural vulnerability), or buildings (structural vulnerability). Social vulnerability, in contrast, is defined as the "potential for these extreme events to cause changes in people's behavior" (Lindell et al. 2006, p. 175) and can be further categorized as psychological,[2] demographic, economic, or political. Social vulnerability is determined by more or less structural deficits in "psychological resilience, social network integration, economic assets, and political power" and is distributed unequally among populations and geographic regions (Lindell et al. 2006, p. 77). The authors thus offer a rather simplistic distinction between physical vulnerability creating physical impact and social vulnerability causing social impact. They ignore any interrelation between social and physical processes—such as the social causes of physical destruction or casualties—and thereby do not match the insights provided by other understandings of vulnerability.

As representatives of the political vulnerability approach, Wisner et al. (2004)[3] conceptualize vulnerability as a complex and intertwined web of conditions and

[2] With respect to our goal of developing a cultural psychology of coping with disasters, it is worthwhile to mention that Lindell et al. (2006) define psychological vulnerability with reference to psychological coping theory following Lazarus and Folkman (1984; see Sect. 2.2.1). Psychological vulnerability is defined as a deficit in emotion-focused coping skills ("personal fragility") and problem-focused coping skills ("rigidity"). Furthermore, when combined with hazard exposure, psychological vulnerability is also considered a predicator of posttraumatic stress disorder (PTSD).

[3] In the following discussion, we refer to the second edition of *At Risk* by Wisner et al. (2004), even though the core concepts were already elaborated in the first edition by Blaikie et al. (1994).

deliberately emphasize the socioeconomic and political causes of disaster in their Pressure and Release (PAR) model. With PAR, the authors offer a three-stage causal model: Underlying any vulnerability are root causes of an economic, demographic, and political nature, including power distribution, gender relations, and ideological structures; but only the dynamic pressures of macro-forces and inadequate informational resources translate these root causes into the unsafe conditions that reflect the actual vulnerability of a particular population. These conditions are considered unsafe with regard to the physical environment, local economy, social relations, or public institutions. How this structural situation progresses into an actual disaster is explained using PAR's complementary Access model. The authors are particularly concerned with the unfolding of vulnerability at the microlevel of individuals and households, including dynamics of disaster impact, coping strategies, and the interactions among different actors involved. The model centers on livelihood as the foundation of ordinary existence and thus emphasizes people's access to material, social, and political resources. A lack or the uneven distribution of resources is a critical factor that determines the scope of vulnerability:

> [V]ulnerability located at the centre of the triangle [of political, social, and economic structures], ultimately reflects people's position in society (not only poverty) as a consequence of their ability or inability to secure access to a large, resistant and sustainable set of resources. (Wisner et al. 2012, p. 27)

The strength of the Access model lies in its socioeconomic emphasis at the microstructural level. However, this strength also turns out to be the model's weakness because it inclines toward economic reductionism, for example, when "social relations" are predominantly qualified in terms of economic or barter relationships. Similarly, it does not sufficiently account for the element of human agency, even while integrating it conceptually. By focusing mainly on economic and technological structures and by offering a causal and deterministic framework, both models fail to integrate the complex interactions between people and their changing environments. Human agency and interactions cannot be reduced to simple and predictable causal relations. Any deterministic framework will thus fall short of capturing and explaining the actual dynamics of disasters and disaster coping. The collapse and reconstruction of a house, for example, can be calculated and projected in economic and physical terms, but such a framework elides important sociocultural and psychological elements that mediate the disaster experience and recovery. Wisner et al. (2004) acknowledge their own shortcomings in integrating subjective experience, agency, and meaning and call for complementary approaches that necessarily rely on qualitative rather than quantitative research.

In general, the pitfalls of the political vulnerability approach lie in its understanding of vulnerability as encompassing elements of both victimhood and responsibility. The notion of victimhood particularly is apparent in vulnerability approaches that study certain "vulnerable groups" or even entire "vulnerable regions." The idea of "vulnerable groups," in particular, has been criticized for neglecting the fact that structural categories such as gender, race, immigration status, ethnicity, religion, and health status depend on specific societal and situational contexts (Wisner et al.

2012, p. 22). Vulnerability should always be seen in relation to a particular hazard and situation rather than attributed to static, essentialist factors; it is constantly (re)produced rather than structurally determined by physical and social conditions. A second point of criticism is derived from the way in which these approaches risk reproducing marginality by reducing "the vulnerable" to victims and downplaying people's capacities and agency. Bankoff (2003) argues that the vulnerability paradigm labels large swathes of the globe, for example, Southeast Asia, as underdeveloped, dangerous, and universally afflicted with disease, poverty, and disaster. The inhabitants of these regions are perceived as inferior, uneducated victims who need Western medicine, investment, preventative systems, and especially Western expertise to cope with these conditions. As Bankoff suggests, vulnerability often implies the responsibility of outside, expert knowledge to intervene and "help" as a counter to victimhood. However, a new understanding of responsibility has emerged in the discourses of climate change and development policy: Emphasizing the anthropogenic character of many disasters, vulnerability is understood as calculated self-destruction embedded in the human–environment relationship. Pessimism also prevails with a predicted global average increase in vulnerability that will lead to not only more disasters but also disasters with a greater impact (see McEntire et al. 2002; Lewis et al. 2011).

Thus, the concept of vulnerability refers to both a technocratically understood potential to be harmed and a socioeconomic susceptibility to the impact of hazards. Alexander (1997) suggests a more nuanced understanding of forms of vulnerability in order to distinguish between different ways in which people are potentially affected. He offers a typology of six distinct expressions of vulnerability, for example, the "total vulnerability" of the poor, who live in generally precarious conditions where disaster poses only one challenge among many others, in contrast to the "technocratic vulnerability" of the rich, who experience disaster as material loss but not as a matter of survival (and even their material losses are often covered by insurance).

1.2.2 Resilience as Adaptive Capacity

Some approaches to vulnerability already integrate adaptive capacity even if this is simply to recognize when it is absent. For Wisner et al. (2004), vulnerability exists when people in certain situations do not have the adequate capacity "to anticipate, cope with, resist and recover from the impacts of a natural hazard" (p. 11). Capacities are thus introduced as a positive counterpart to vulnerability, which has been criticized for its inherently deficit-oriented perspective, especially in the victimhood construction of vulnerable groups. In order to incorporate the coping capacities of various groups and individuals, scholars have established "resilience" as a new key concept to shift the conversation to more positive terms. However, like vulnerability, resilience is a word that has been imbued with many different meanings.

Resilience actually originates from physics to describe the capacity of a material or system to return to a state of equilibrium after being deformed or perturbed. The term was adopted more recently in the social sciences as a metaphor to describe the adaptive capacities of individuals, communities, and larger societies (Norris et al. 2008). For example, disaster experts under the umbrella of UNISDR define resilience as:

> [t]he ability of a system, community or society exposed to hazards to resist, absorb, accommodate to and recover from the effects of a hazard in a timely and efficient manner, including through the preservation and restoration of its essential basic structures and functions. (UNISDR 2009, p. 24)

The psychologists Norris et al. (2008) describe resilience "as a process linking a set of adaptive capacities to a positive trajectory of functioning and adaptation after a disturbance" (p. 130). Resilience becomes a factor in cases where a stressful event causes change: "Pre-event functioning" undergoes a crisis and experiences transient dysfunction. With resilience, however, the situation can be overcome through adaptive capacity and a mobilization of resources to achieve "post-event functioning" adjusted to the new environment. In contrast, vulnerability leads to persistent dysfunction. Building on this understanding of resilience, the authors develop a model of community resilience to describe the process of successful collective adaptability based on access to economic resources, relevant information, and relationships (in the sense of social capital; for further information, see Sect. 2.4.4).

Comparing the two definitions, it is clear that resilience always refers to something positive: either the ability or capacity to achieve the positive outcome (UNISDR) or the process by which these capacities are successfully exercised. Furthermore, both definitions relate resilience to successful adaptation. According to UNISDR experts, resilience can potentially involve resistance toward, absorption of, accommodation to, and recovery from adverse effects; therefore, it includes mitigation, containment, and/or coping. However, Norris et al. add a further distinction: If the people affected are successful in blocking a disturbance entirely, altogether preventing a crisis or a decrease in functioning, then the authors use the term resistance. Resilience, in contrast, describes a relatively successful navigation of a crisis. The concept of resilience draws its strength from expanding the analytical perspective and, therefore, disaster management strategies as well to include the possibility of a more or less successful encounter with a disaster (rather than implying that risk reduction means the nonoccurrence of a disaster; McEntire et al. 2002). A third commonality is that both approaches share an understanding of resilience as the self-organizing capacities and crisis management potential of communities or whole societies, which can develop and expand by learning from previous disaster experiences or improving risk reduction measures (UNISDR 2009; UNISDR 2004). The idea of resilience thus accounts for capacities endogenous to the community itself which the community can control better than macrostructural elements or the root causes of vulnerability (see Wisner et al. 2012).

However, the two definitions presented here differ in their relations to resilience: While the UNISDR definition frames resilience in terms of disaster hazards, Norris et al. formulate a much less specific understanding of resilience (and community resilience) as a process of adaptation to disturbance. This is similar to the interpretation of resilience in SES approaches such as climate change or more generally environmental change research (see Cote and Nightingale 2011; Pelling 2010; Brown and Westaway 2011). According to these approaches, "[r]esilience refers to the ability of a system to absorb disturbance without flipping into another state or phase" (Cote and Nightingale 2011). Resilience thus signifies the absorption of comprehensive systemic change.

Especially in comparison to vulnerability, the construct of resilience tends to lack specificity. Resilience usually represents a general improvement of adaptive capacities, whereas vulnerability relates to a particular event. In the model presented by Wisner et al. (2004), this point applies especially to the progression from vulnerability to "unsafe conditions" or "fragile livelihoods and unsafe locations" (Wisner et al. 2012), although even here the "root causes" remain relatively unspecific.

However, the processes set off by disasters are vast and include social changes beyond those related to hazard. The breadth of the changes can only be captured by a general concept such as resilience and adaptive capacity. If, for example, gender relations, power relations, forms of governance, or religious spirituality change, it is important to find out whether the community's resilience improves. Resilience would then serve as a criterion for risk reduction-oriented development policy. However, resilience has developed into a general and rather fuzzy concept which is not able to carry the weight of its multiple associations and uses. To counter this, researchers should account for the actual capabilities of people (Sen 1992) in disaster-prone areas, specifically their opportunities and abilities to attain desired and valued outcomes in the specific context.

The notion of resilience relativizes the anomalous nature of catastrophe and its responses. On both, the individual and community levels, academic discussions of resilience and adaptive capacities focus on preconditions for and processes of coping with enormous suffering in extreme situations. In contrast to the Western discourse that separates disaster from the rest of daily life, the resilience approach does not distinguish these cases qualitatively from other human and social experiences.

1.2.3 Risk as a Motivator for Prevention

Although the key concept of risk includes a general shift toward prevention, the paradigm of risk places much more responsibility on the individual and community levels than the structural paradigm of vulnerability. Across the disciplines and especially among applied and non-applied research approaches, the fundamental understanding of risk varies dramatically. Even though most risk researchers would agree that "risks are objective, subjective as well as socially constructed" (Zinn 2010, paragraph 13), the relative importance of the elements in this triad remains a matter of debate.

In disaster management, risk is defined as a "combination of the probability of an event and its negative consequences" (UNISDR 2009, p. 25). It is important to note that contrary to common usage, this definition does not equate risk with the possibility of an occurrence but rather with the consequences, the "potential losses" that are also described in technical contexts. Risk models and the scientific discourse on disaster risk reduction concentrate on "objectively measurable risk," which is normally assessed using a hazard and vulnerability/capacity analysis captured by the formula "risk = hazard × vulnerability" (Wisner et al. 2004). Risk assessment then provides a basis to raise risk awareness. Based on the principle of "bounded rationality," these authors assume that individuals take risks because they lack either understanding or knowledge (Burton et al. 1993). Disaster risk reduction is then concerned with the question of how, in the face of seemingly obvious threats, people can become better informed and change their behavior in such a way that their communities will engage in effective, independent, participatory, and sustainable prevention, or else adapt to changing environmental conditions. The adequate development of knowledge will ideally lead to disaster risk management in the communities affected (UNISDR 2004), which should also include other goals of development policy, such as sustainability, good governance, gender mainstreaming, or social justice.

The literature on risk reduction has a prescriptive character and aims to contribute to a better—that is, science-based—societal and communal approach to dealing with risk. Insofar as risk management aims to include action by the affected individuals themselves, the subjective approach to increasing risk awareness is relevant because it seeks to determine which factors influence (individual) risk awareness and how risk awareness can either be increased or adapted to an objective risk. These questions are usually examined in cognitive psychological research based on individual responses to risk situations collected with quantitative survey methods.

The corresponding field of applied research in mainstream psychology is equally concerned with risk perception and a "realist" approach to disaster management. Researchers in this area assume that there is an "objective" core of risk and try to investigate the biased, subjective perceptions of reality. Studies analyze how people's risk perceptions and interpretations deviate from a correct understanding of "objective" risks and how this relates to their values and belief systems (Zinn 2010). Critics of this approach fundamentally object to the cognitivist and individualist core of psychological risk-perception studies and highlight its insufficient consideration or simplistic reduction of human lives. Most studies are based on a normative ideal of the human subject as one who makes cognitive and rational decisions. If subjects of empirical studies then—necessarily—fail to measure up to this ideal, they are found to be acting upon biased perceptions and distorted mental processing. The goal then becomes challenging these biases, for example, through methodology or science, so that the ideal of rational calculation can lead to the "right" undistorted decisions. This rationalism, however, has been unmasked as biased itself and is in need of improvement; recently, the cognitive, rational subject has been replaced by a subject with a softer rationality that works quite successfully with heuristics (see Gigerenzer 2008; Kahneman 2011), intuition, and emotion (see Slovic and Västfjall 2010). Slovic and Västfjall distinguish between risk as feelings and risk as logic, whereby the former is based on instinct and intuition and the latter refers to a reasonable, scientific assessment of risk. Although intuitive reactions to danger might be reliable and effective in small-scale situations, intuition is insensitive to large losses of life and, accordingly, is thought likely to fail in the face of natural disasters (Slovic and Västfjall 2010).

As the following example illustrates, the distinction between subjective and objective risks is closely related to a binary opposition between laypersons with only biased and inadequate risk awareness and experts with objective "knowledge." In a recent study, Tekeli-Yeşil et al. (2011) examined factors that improve knowledge and increase risk awareness among Istanbul residents living in areas at high risk of earthquakes. Standardized questionnaires measured two dependent variables: risk awareness, measured as knowledge about earthquakes and earthquake mitigation and preparedness, and risk perception, assessed as respondents' judgments of the seismic risk at the location of their homes and the potential damage to their houses. In the analysis, residents' responses were compared to scientific or expert knowledge. For example, respondents were asked to spontaneously recite mitigation and preparedness measures. Their answers were then compared to a checklist of "correct" responses extracted from disaster management manuals. In the same study, the authors also deemed risk perceptions to be generally realistic because they matched or at least did not significantly differ from "actual" or "objective" risk levels, as assessed by the Department of Earthquake Engineering at the Boğaziçi University, Istanbul. However, the researchers found that the level of risk concern, compared to other threats and concerns, was too low among less educated participants and participants of a lower socioeconomic level. They also determined that these subjects had too little knowledge of the measures they should take in terms of risk reduction. One of the authors' main conclusions was to call for improved risk communication by the media and other stakeholders, especially with respect to mitigation and preparedness measures, and they placed their hope in the development of a general "safety culture."

In this type of study, the biased subject or the biased community must be enlightened by "knowing" experts about the probability of impending natural hazards in order to be prepared and gain control; at the same time, scientific and expert knowledge tends to have an elevated status (Flint and Luloff 2005). Furthermore, the focus on risk perception implies that risk reduction practices are a quasi-automatic outgrowth of cognitive enlightenment. However, risk perception by no means equals risk concern: any risk that is perceived still has to be seen as relevant, for example, in relation to other perceived risks (Solberg et al. 2010). In addition, risk concern still does not imply risk avoidance or reduction practices, because hazard adjustment is related to norms and dynamics in a sociocultural context (Solberg et al. 2010).

Moreover, "[r]isk is not an objective condition waiting to be perceived by individuals or calculated by analysts" (Bankoff and Hilhorst 2009, p. 686). Risk perception itself is shaped by sociocultural processes through which certain dangers are framed as "risk" (Flint and Luloff 2005). Obversely, the cultural anthropologist Michael Bollig (2012) offers a constructionist definition of disaster risk as "the culturally and socially embedded perceptions of future possible damage resulting from a variety of hazards" (p. 36). Similar perspectives have influenced sociological risk research with a stress on the necessity of studying the construction of risk and risk estimates more closely: What becomes an object of risk, and why or why not? Which social actors undertake which demarcations of risk and non-risk, and which assessments of risk are regarded as valid or invalid? In order to address these questions in a well-founded way, risk research must consider the political, institutional, and economic context of each situation (Tierney 1999).

The association of risk with particular assumptions of safety and control has been characterized as a distinctive feature of "modern" industrial societies, where notions of security emerge from an almost dialectical relation between science, technology, and social order (Macamo and Neubert 2008). According to Bankoff (2003), it is a Western myth to assume secure and ordinary life as a state of normality, and this myth can only be maintained by framing disasters as singular, disruptive events which are, by definition, excluded from normality. However, there are alternative ways of living with risk; instead of calculation and control, these include facing the future with a general attitude of uncertainty (Macamo and Neubert 2008). Accordingly, people have developed psychosocial mechanisms to live with uncertainty (Bankoff 2003) rather than building their worldview on the fantasy of human potency and control. If, for example, hazards are seen as frequent experiences and facts of life, then people have learned to live with these risks. Without necessarily articulating a conscious risk awareness, people have integrated practices of "risk reduction" and "disaster preparedness" into their common practices, stances, values, and "local knowledge" over centuries (Bankoff 2003). In the Philippines, for example, century-old practices buffer risks through local networks of mutual assistance (Bankoff and Hilhorst 2009). Thus, the critique of cognitive bias in risk perception studies should actually go much further: Risk perception does not by necessity correlate with risk reduction practices. Despite a failure to articulate risk awareness explicitly, people still incorporate strategies into their everyday practices that outsiders would identify as "risk reduction." As part of an expanded approach to risk perception research, nonnormative, conceptually open approaches to risk adjustment are needed; researchers could, for example, examine how people maintain psychological, social, and economic balance despite the evident presence of a threat—or of several threats—or determine what amount of certainty people deem necessary for everyday living.

At the same time, the "objective" risks identified by experts are often reflected only minimally in political action at the macrolevel. Daily politics involve many competing issues, and disaster risk reduction rarely has a good chance of being realized. Especially in cases where risk adjustment is weighed against short- or longer-term economic benefits, policy and investment decisions are based in large part on the society's willingness to take on risk and the perceived urgency of risk reduction. One example of this is Germany's nuclear phaseout following the Fukushima catastrophe in Japan (see Winter 2013). A society's relation to risk is therefore based on negotiations between various interests and positions, making risk a highly political category. What qualifies as risk and which risks demand risk reduction policies and practices should thus be investigated as a historically situated arena of social negotiation.

1.2.4 Vulnerability, Resilience, and Prevention in Psychology

The three terms introduced here not only are key concepts in the field of disaster research but also can be seen as key concepts in psychological discourse. Here, too, the concepts have undergone shifts in meaning and interpretation, as shown in the following section.

Theory and concept building on the topic of disaster and hazard often focuses on collectives, but very similar concepts have developed in parallel in psychology to focus on the individual level. Accordingly, many similarities are evident between concepts related to disaster and theories of psychological disturbance or disease.[4] For example, both are explained in an equilibrium model and seen as examples of decompensation that require outside help. In clinical psychology, "vulnerability" is seen as a disposition. Originally developed to describe the emergence of schizophrenia (see Zubin and Spring 1977), the concept was expanded to explain many other psychological diseases. According to the Diathesis–Stress model, any person can cope with stress and burden until the individual threshold of vulnerability is exceeded and illness results. For the individual, pathological breakdown then interrupts normal life. An exposure to inordinate stress has a similar function to hazard in cases of disaster and in both contexts vulnerability serves as a mediating concept.

In everyday understanding and within the fields of medicine and psychology, responsibility for decompensation has shifted from nature or fate to the afflicted person himself or herself (Herzlich and Pierret 1987). Increasingly, the individual is held responsible for becoming ill by leading a lifestyle inappropriate to his or her own vulnerability. With existing illnesses, the affected person is expected to practice adequate disease management. This is disease specific and conveyed to the patient through psychoeducational techniques within the framework of behavioral medicine (see, for example, Steptoe 2012), specifically as techniques of self-control in relation to the disorder. The "preventive self" (Lengwiler and Madarász 2010) is responsible for compensating for the individual's own vulnerability, similar to the community in community-based disaster risk management.

Vulnerability is compensated for in two different ways: Similar to the "vulnerable groups" approach, some authors presume that certain aspects of vulnerability cannot be changed—aspects that are either genetically predetermined or acquired through the individual's interactions with his or her environment. As a static, individual trait, vulnerability is measured by an array of indicators, such as sensory, motor, and regulatory irregularities (see Levit-Binnun and Golland 2012). Interventions are then initiated as compensatory measures; people practicing disease management must learn as to how to deal with their own vulnerability. Other theorists emphasize a dynamic interplay among a variety of protection and vulnerability factors that contribute to psychological health or illness (see Muris et al. 2011), a position which is conceptually closer to a process-based, contextual understanding of vulnerability (e.g., Wisner et al. 2004). In developmental psychopathology, researchers assume that challenging situations can lead to either increased psychopathology or resilience and that the development paths of both are influenced by a complex web of individual biological and psychological factors, experiences, choices, timing, and personal developmental history (Cicchetti 2010).

[4] Interestingly, Hewitt (1983) critiqued the predominant technocratic, hazard-centered paradigm of his time by comparing its conceptions of hazards with Foucault's analysis of the social emergence and management of madness.

Similar to developments in the disaster literature, a general conception of resilience has emerged in developmental psychology. Greve and Staudinger (2006), for example, describe resilience as a constellation of fit between individual resources, social conditions, and developmental challenges or problems. Through this constellation one successfully overcomes adverse developmental conditions with the help of regulatory (assimilative and accommodative) processes.

It is considered advantageous to improve one's resilience as part of a general competence in crisis management. While risk and vulnerability are projected onto a specific threat, and prevention is oriented toward avoiding specific diseases, resilience often refers to the achievement of positively connoted states of being, such as health, well-being, or fitness. This capacity-focused concept of resilience represents a major rethinking in favor of the positive strengths and virtues within the field of psychology, embodied by the development of a "Positive Psychology" (see Lopez and Snyder 2009). This shift eschews the victimizing, passive construction of the psychological subject in favor of expanding psychology beyond the scope of illness, overstrain, and processes that end in psychopathology. The new approach emphasizes ways in which psychological health, well-being, fitness, and happiness (Diener et al. 2010) are encouraged, created, and sustained in everyday life.

At the individual level, this shift in focus leads to problems similar to those identified in disaster discourse: one "realist" conception from the culture of expertise offers self-technologies to process risks and optimize resilience. Responsibility lies in the individual to exercise prevention, actively engage in problem solving, and achieve well-being and fitness. Rooted specifically in a North American worldview (Young 2006; McHugh and Treisman 2007; Watters 2010), this approach is supported by the growing prescription of psychoactive drugs (Frances 2013). As with the international framework of disaster management, this conceptual orientation and practice has increasingly been exported throughout the world (Watters 2010).

1.3 Conceptualizing Disasters as a Human–Nature Nexus

A situation only qualifies as a disaster if a natural hazard causes destruction and loss in human societies; hence, natural disasters are by definition located at the nexus of humans and nature. However, as the shifting disaster paradigms indicate, understandings of the human–nature relationship and its relevance for disaster studies have changed dramatically over time. The hazard paradigm depicted disaster as a consequence of natural forces and disaster mitigation as an effort to control these forces. Its historical counterpart, the vulnerability paradigm, highlighted human agency and shifted focus from the presumed naturalness of disaster to a sociopolitical and human responsibility to maintain living conditions that reduce harmful hazard impacts and increase people's capacity to face them. The environmental paradigm, in contrast, places human–nature interaction at the causal core of disaster, refusing to attribute this complex and dynamic interrelation solely to the agency of either nature or humans. It is therefore worthwhile examining the human–nature nexus more closely.

1.3.1 Disasters in Environments Shaped by Humans

Recently after an earthquake and subsequent tsunami destroyed the nuclear power plants at Fukushima, people worldwide witnessed how disasters emerge from a mutual interaction between the environment and human societies. As Luig (2012) suggests, this destructive example should put an end to debates on whether "humans" or "nature" are responsible for disasters and proved the obsolescence of the traditional Western nature/culture dichotomy. An alternative in current scientific discussion of disaster is to replace "nature" with "environment" because, unlike nature, environment is always a relational category, "a system representing a certain section of the external world to which actions and perceptions of a subject give significance" (Haltermann 2012, p. 61). Humans inhabit their environments physically and are mediated by symbols, and the manner in which they do it is embedded in specific historical and sociocultural contexts. According to this understanding, the category of environment is inherently cultural. Environment represents the external world as it is perceived and acted upon by humans from the perspective of utility (Haltermann 2012), for example, as natural resources. A strict differentiation between "human-made" or "built" versus "natural" environments is therefore misleading and should instead be viewed as a gradual distinction. Moreover, an environment is always a product and expression of political–economic processes (Bolin and Stanford 1998).

Within the fields of disaster research and management, the interaction between humans and the environment is invoked in many different ways. Some approaches contextualize the causes of disaster in the human–environment interaction in a fundamental way, in accordance with the principle that an earthquake on an uninhabited stretch of land is still an earthquake but is far from being a disaster (Tierney 2007). This understanding is based on the structural vulnerability approach, according to which a given hazard impact only becomes a disaster in the presence of vulnerability. In this view, a society as a whole can be more or less vulnerable, and this is understood as successful or unsuccessful mutuality: on the one hand, societies are better or worse in their adaptation to their respective environments; on the other hand, environments are better or worse in their responses to human activity (Hoffman and Oliver-Smith 1999). Through this evaluation of (mal)adaptation, every disaster is understood as being anthropogenic.

The UNISDR expert committee distinguishes "natural hazards" from "socio-natural hazards," implying that only some "natural" disasters have an anthropogenic origin; in other words, "human activity is increasing the occurrence of certain hazards beyond their natural probabilities" (UNISDR 2009, p. 28). The category of disaster (or hazard) here is one which would customarily be considered "natural" (e.g., drought or flooding) but is triggered or worsened by human interaction with the environment. The human use of resources increases the risk of disaster; for example, deforestation can cause landslides or draining wetlands can lead to flooding (Tobin and Montz 1997). The entire debate on climate change and the effects of global warming falls into this category. In these cases of "socio-natural hazards," the hazard itself already qualifies as being caused or amplified by human activity—in contrast to the previous understanding, where human responsibility is emphasized through the concept of vulnerability. Accordingly, disaster mitigation efforts take on different forms because socio-natural hazards can be reduced "through wise management of land and environmental resources" (UNISDR 2009, p. 28).

The socioecological system (SES) approach offers yet another analytical framework. The mutuality of the human–nature relationship is conceptualized so broadly that society–environment units are its starting point for analysis. Adaptation does not refer to human change that accommodates the environment but rather to a process in which whole dynamic, systemic units adapt themselves to changes that occur over a long period of time. Changes are understood as inherently produced through the complex interrelation of subsystems and attributed neither to singular environmental elements such as hazards nor to human agency alone.

All of these approaches contextualize disaster in a broadly conceived adaptation process of humans and the social and material structures they create. However, by emphasizing different aspects, these approaches have different strengths and weaknesses. For our investigation into coping with disasters, it is especially interesting to examine how these approaches envision the relationship between human agency and the environment.

Even if the environmental paradigm offers the potential to overcome the nature–culture dichotomy, many interpretations of the approach tend toward an environmentalist line of argumentation that runs the risk of entangling itself in this hegemonic, Western thought tradition. The hazard-centered paradigm focuses in particular on technocratic control of the environment, taking the position that humans can compensate for dangerous events through the deployment of appropriate technology; catastrophes result from a failure to use adequate technologies and preventative measures (Hewitt 1983; Bankoff 2003). By contrast, current discussions on climate change and related disaster risk reduction efforts draw heavily on an environmentalist discourse, which emphasizes human moral responsibility toward "nature" and warns against the destructive potential of human action. Arguments in favor of control and nature conservation both tend to place humans in opposition to nature by stressing human agency—the difference between them is that the former equates agency to potency, while the latter is tied more to responsibility. Murphy (1994) characterized this representation of the human–environment relationship as the "plasticity myth," because "nature" is construed as a pliable object subject to human rationality and use—an object to be manipulated, shaped, or harvested.

In contrast to these approaches, the SES approach within environmental change research conceives of society and environment together, as systems. Although it offers interesting impulses with regard to the complexity and mutuality of society–environment interactions, the conceptual framework of "systems" leans toward a mechanical view of the world. The idea of a system implies a constellation of functional and predictable relations and fails to account for the creative and unpredictable element of human agency (Hilhorst 2007). Only in recent years have environmental studies begun to expand their analyses beyond resources or infrastructure and started to address questions of perception and subjectivity (Brown and Westaway 2011).

However, entirely discarding the idea of mutual interaction in favor of human agency, as Hilhorst ultimately suggests, also misses the mark. If we take the mutuality of society–environment interaction as a starting point, then it is impossible not to recognize the dynamic interrelatedness of social structures, human agency, and biophysical environments. Not only is human agency embedded in social environments but social actors are also always embedded in biophysical environments. At the same time, forces of nature not merely are discursive constructs but also have their own agency.[5] The occurrence of a natural effect can impact sociocultural constructs such as when the Lisbon earthquake of 1755 caused a paradigm shift in the worldview at that time (Luig 2012). Because of this, the construction of the world or worlds needs to be conceptualized as being interrelated with extra-discursive forces. The exosemiotic agency of nature becomes apparent in hazard and disaster, but even then, it is a nature experienced through societal practices and constructs (Oliver-Smith 2002).

1.3.2 Cultural Adaptation to Hazardous Environments

Many natural hazards are systemic elements of a particular environment; the habitual presence of hazards normally leads to a situation in which societies have grown accustomed to them over time (Oliver-Smith and Hoffman 2002). This adaptation takes place on the material level, from the construction of houses to livelihood or settlement practices. For example, economic activities that generate mixed incomes, such as farming and home industries, buffer potential losses. However, social institutions can provide important flexibility in crisis response as well (Zaman 1999; Schmuck-Widmann 1996). Take, for example, the inhabitants of island chars in Bangladesh, where hazard constitutes a regular component of their livelihood strategies: floods irrigate, fertilize, and kill off pests; they make transportation routes easier to navigate; and they are a necessary prerequisite for fish to proliferate (Schmuck-Widmann 1996). It is only erosion, as a long-term effect of flooding or even a lack of flooding altogether, that becomes a problem. The example illustrates a way of life that faces not only a potential threat of hazard but also the impact of a hazard itself. Such instances of "living with disaster"—living with flood, drought, or volcanoes, as the case may be—demonstrate that a realized hazard does not necessarily lead to disaster. To what extent the impact causes damage or interrupts the "normality" of community life depends on the vulnerability of the people affected. The "living with disaster" approach (which should really be called "living with hazard") emphasizes the relevance of vulnerability, which can be reduced through adaptation to the environment or (implicitly) increased through certain development processes (Villagrán de León 2006). In this sense, disaster is also described as a society's inability to adapt to its environment: in "graphic ways, disasters signal the failure of a society to adapt successfully to certain features of its natural and socially constructed environment in

[5] Especially within debates on the social construction of nature, constructionists have been criticized for overemphasizing the discursive while neglecting the agency of nature.

a sustainable fashion" (Oliver-Smith 1996, p. 303). Here, adaptation can take place on several different levels: economic, ecological, social, or ideological.

By referring to "cultures of disaster," Bankoff (2003) introduces a further idea of cultural adaptation to environment. With the example of the Philippines, he shows how the long-term experience of living in hazardous environments leads to a historical–cultural adaptation process by which strategies for coping and risk reduction are developed. These strategies encompass land utilization, crop husbandry and diversification practices, mutual support systems, strategies to eliminate psychological distress, and the development of patronage relationships. Compared to the "living with disaster" approach introduced earlier, Bankoff places more emphasis on coping capacities for crisis behavior, addressing psychological aspects as well. Here, he draws on a remarkable article by the anthropologist Jon W. Anderson (1968), who already discussed "disaster-cultures" more than three decades earlier.[6] Bankoff agrees with Anderson's thesis that the more chronic a threat, the more culturally normal it becomes. Experience with the manifested hazard is integrated into the conceptual system or collective cultural knowledge and transmitted from one generation to the next, for example, through myths (Frömming 2006). Through cultural transmission individuals may have knowledge about hazardous situations even prior to a personal experience of exposure (Anderson 1968). In an acute emergency situation, they can resort to these cultural tools to assess and cope with the situation. Cultural adaptation to the environment thus provides not only pragmatic strategies but also interpretative schemes and psychological tools. One could also say that disaster in all of its facets is integrated into the cultural worldview so that the emergency situation does not actually overstep the boundaries of expected normality, even if it poses a disruption to everyday routines. Within this framework, cultural strategies can be specific to one particular hazard or can also respond to a general living with uncertainty (see Sect. 1.2.3).

In the interdisciplinary field of disaster research, the outcome of this adaptive process is commonly framed as indigenous or local knowledge. It is composed of technical, ecological, and historical knowledge of practices, beliefs, values, and worldviews (Dekens 2007) and characterized by its specific familiarity with local environments and by practices developed in long-term interaction with nature and its forces. With respect to natural disasters, local knowledge can include cultural techniques on three forms: prediction knowledge, direct and sustainable protection strategies, and techniques of coping with disaster and trauma (Frömming 2006). These categories are not limited to strategies specifically aimed at risk or hazard reduction as generally applicable social norms and taboos can also play a role in local disaster risk reduction. For example, in Flores, Indonesia, there is a religious taboo

[6] Anderson (1968) describes "disaster-culture" as "formulas generated by past accommodation of the culture's conceptual schema to yet another aspect of the environment. As a basic pattern of trying to understand perceived phenomena, they are elaborations that fit both the perceptions of the phenomena and the conceptual system of the culture which once established need not be continuously generated anew in each individual but can be transmitted as accomplished facts" (p. 304).

against panic reactions. In chaotic situations, people are to follow the unconditional imperative of running away as fast as possible without stopping to look around—a cultural rule that may save lives in the case of a volcanic eruption (Frömming 2006).

The concepts of "living with disaster" and "cultures of disaster" both emphasize local knowledge as a set of available capacities and offer an opportunity to think beyond the victimization inherent to the vulnerability paradigm. However, these approaches harbor their own reductionist limitations, which Spittler (1999) analyzes and illustrates using research debates about the drought in the Sahel: In this research context, scholars went so far as to advocate a "theory of survival strategies" as a counter-paradigm to that of local vulnerability, pointing to the high degree of environmental adaptation among the nomadic populations. They presumed a well-adapted, precolonial life in which people could confront hazard agents actively and with cultural preparation (see, for example, McCabe 2002). This, however, produces a new victim construct, that is, although affected groups are active in dealing with drought, they are painted as victims of (post)colonial power relations that prevent them from drawing on their "actual" survival strategies. Spittler rejects this argument and argues that not all locally adopted coping strategies have been eliminated; some endure just as before. Moreover, he questions whether ideal models of crisis behavior could ever be applied in practice and suggests that other precolonial, macropolitical influences such as war and slave raiding also had an impact on coping with crisis. In general, one should always ask whether the construction of precolonial, well-adapted cultures reflects a romanticizing tendency by the colonial others, especially because attributes such as "closeness to nature versus cultural alienation" have a long racist tradition.

As a second major criticism, Spittler disagrees with the reduction of culture to survival. Indeed, other values play a decisive role in human responses to disaster: During the Sahel drought 1984–1985, for example, the author experienced how Tuareg families still invested their scarce resources in buying proper clothes and celebrating prophet Muhammad's birthday in a festive way. As he put it, "living and dying with dignity counts more than survival at any price" (Spittler 1999, p. 166). In relation to coping with disaster, Wisner et al. (2004, p. 119) make a similar point that life is not only a question of survival but also a question of living well, or at least living in a way that seems worthwhile to the actors involved, such as with dignity or social cohesion.

However, beyond survival, a general question emerges concerning the relationship between adaptation to the environment and cultural practice ("doing culture"). The adaptive approach risks sliding into environmental determinism and identifying cultural practices as the direct results of ecological conditions[7] rather than seeing

[7] The socioecological approach in crosscultural psychology operates in a similarly deterministic way. This view assumes that culture represents a group's response to its physical environment, with certain requirements and limitations. This process produces certain technologies, social orders, and parenting styles, which then influence the development of personality. All of this has been examined through comparative correlation studies across different cultures, whereby cultural factors served as the independent variables (Whiting and Whiting 1975; Berry 1976).

those conditions as *one* influential and somewhat limiting factor. At the same time, the figure of cultural adaptation always contains a functional presumption: cultural practices are presumed to be efficient in their own terms and related to their own immediate goals—with survival as the ultimate goal. Coping is reduced to a mechanical response as if people operated with "no doubts and fears," always knew how to react, and behaved accordingly (Spittler 1999).

Yet another argument speaks against such narrow functionality: life does not stop at disaster impact nor do other social dynamics. For this reason, people not only adapt to a trigger situation and cope with a disaster but also continue living their lives—under changed circumstances. Thus disaster coping must always also be interpreted in relation to these non-disaster-related dynamics. For example, disasters can provide an opportunity to renegotiate social power relations. The occasion of disaster thus leads to societal dynamics that, in the absence of disaster, might have played out in exactly the same way, in a different way, or not at all (Stallings 1988). Like any major societal event, interpretations of disaster offer an arena in which to contest perspectives on society (Oliver-Smith 1996). Accordingly, interpretations of disaster function not only in terms of coping with the event itself but also in terms of sociopolitical interests: Discursive negotiations of causes may manifest controversial views on society and life in general. Schlehe (2010) demonstrates how religious interpretations of the 2006 Java earthquake actually point to competing views on the present state of Javanese society; some blame the prevalence of islamization and negligence of older "Javanese" traditions, while other statements position a lack of Islamic devotion as the root cause of the disaster. In order to examine processes of coping with disaster, Hilhorst (2007) advocates using a social version of the systemic complexity approach: Multiple social actors participate in the course of the event through their actions, assessments, decisions, and feelings. In an interactive manner, new dynamics emerge, spontaneity and creativity take effect, and conflicting interests undergo negotiation.

1.3.3 The Social Nature of Disasters

Although the vulnerability paradigm successfully drew attention to the social factors of disaster, some social scientists still argue that the inherently social nature of disaster remains insufficiently recognized in disaster theory (Quarantelli 2005; Tierney 2007). In order to comprehend what these authors mean, it is helpful to return to Stallings's (2005) definition of disaster as a *social situation* involving the *attribution* of destructive effects to natural forces. Stallings takes a constructionist standpoint by introducing socially defined causality instead of "real" causality and referring to the discursive framings of disaster. He considers the realist claim of scientific "objective" knowledge to be part of the social discourse itself.

The recent establishment of a "socio-natural hazard" category demonstrates the discursive nature of any typology, independent of its descriptive or analytical claim. That earthquakes, oilspills, and willful attacks—but not other adverse events—are all negotiated under the category of "disaster" points to the fact that disaster discourse in research and management is guided by both political and economic interests. US disaster management, for example, emerged from the Cold War context under a perceived urgency to prepare for nuclear attacks. This led to the inclusion of wilful attacks in the framework of emergency management. Similarly, the professional field of earthquake sciences emerged in the 1970s after a series of large earthquakes in California caused national concerns about macroeconomic and security consequences (Stallings 1995). Accordingly, constructionist sociological approaches highlight the political nature of disaster definitions and disaster management. Definitions of disaster determine which crisis situations set institutionalized mechanisms of disaster or emergency management in motion and, above all, which crises mobilize relief efforts and to what extent.

In a similar vein, it is important to examine what qualifies as a disaster and under which conditions. For example, earthquakes count as hazards with the potential to cause disaster, whereas heat waves are never framed as disasters even though they can be deadly. The decisive criterion is that disaster must specifically cause damage to property (Tierney 2007). Drabek (2006) poses the related question of why tornados tend to mobilize massive relief efforts, while acquiring funds for victims of famine or the human immunodeficiency virus (HIV) normally proves much harder. What qualifies as disaster has little to do with the disaster itself but rather with its discursive treatment. Subjectively experienced suffering or physical destruction is not random, purely constructed phenomena; rather, their framing and, therefore, their effects heavily depend on the discourses surrounding them. Accordingly, the social components of these phenomena represent a powerful discursive field where actors negotiate which kinds of suffering should be recognized as supraindividual "disaster suffering," and which should not.

Presenting an alternative to the macroeconomic bias of conventional disaster approaches, Barton (1969) introduced the psychosocial framework of "collective stress situations," which spans a broad range of adverse situations. If "many members of a social system fail to receive expected conditions of life from the system," Barton (1969, p. 38) suggests analyzing these situations from a perspective of collective stress. In this understanding, collective stress is conceptually linked to a collective experience of deprivation—that is, the insufficient satisfaction of human needs. Human needs and their deprivation encompass physical, physiological, and psychological aspects; collective stress situations therefore cannot be reduced to physical survival or functioning (Barton 2005). Furthermore, deprivation cannot be measured by universal standards; it depends on contextually specific definitions of normal life. People do not necessarily agree on which conditions are normal, so the author alerts the reader to potential disagreement over the recognition and demarcation of "social stress situations." Instead of "objective" criteria and macroeconomic concerns, Barton places the collective concurrence of subjective losses at the core of his theory with full awareness of the potentially inherent contradictions in this social-subjective understanding.

The criterion of disruption to normality must be examined just as critically as the criterion of damage. Starting with the vulnerability paradigm, disaster was envisioned as a manifestation of unequal, structurally rooted living conditions, contextualizing the seemingly singular "extreme event" in more broadly conceived socioeconomic processes. Especially in its political implications, the concept of vulnerability accounts for precarious living conditions as one form of everyday "normality," a recognition that the hazard-centered disaster approach neglects (or, as some would say, obscures for ideological reasons). The myth of a secure and ordinary life may derive from Western hegemonic assumptions (see Bankoff and Hilhorst 2009); however, such an outlook on life requires privileged living conditions even within Western societies, because this (such a state) is only ever achieved by a small percentage of the population. Vulnerability is thus distributed unevenly.

Moreover, myths of security and control may also increase vulnerability. This can occur when societies rely too heavily on human efforts to control environmental forces; in other words, when human agency is overestimated in the society–environment interaction. As early as the 1950s, for example, Gilbert White warned against continuing to settle areas susceptible to floods and relying too heavily on hazard control with dams. This myth is also tied to a culturally specific expectation of normality (Macamo and Neubert 2008). As evidenced by the increasing importance of the risk paradigm, disaster research and management in the hegemonic discourse still strives for calculable control of the event itself or of the complex dynamics of interaction. Omnipresent disaster management or disaster risk reduction in the form of measures prior to, in tandem with, and after the hazard event intend to reduce the fear of imminent threat as much as possible. This brings us back to the question of cultural approaches to danger, whether these are negotiated through security discourses or a presumption of uncertainty—and their close ties to culturally formed perceptions of the environment. A discourse of security goes hand in hand with the fantasy of a nature tamed by humans, whose externalized Other is the unpredictable natural danger. This natural danger is a disruptive force, an exception to the fundamental norm of equilibrium. However, the same natural hazards can also be seen as regular components of nature and human life. Especially in geographic regions where certain hazards occur frequently, Anderson (1968) has suggested referring to a cultural "normalization" of threat: "Threats are omnipresent potentialities of the environment to be taken into routine account as part of the background of life" (p. 298). Approaches to disaster always reflect cultural expectations: How normal is everyday life and how predictable or uncertain are future events? How disruptive are adverse occurrences? To capture these factors, Macamo and Neubert (2008) formulated a phenomenological, cultural-relativist definition of disaster that takes as its starting point the contextual perception of "disruption and normality." Especially for a psychological perspective on processes of coping with disaster, the issue of culturally shared expectations of the world plays a key role.

1.4 Professional and Nonprofessional Disaster "Management"

Turning from the conceptual issues discussed earlier, we can now focus on the applied field of dealing with disasters—or disaster "management." We begin with a brief outline of key topics related to psychological and social reaction patterns; the "nonprofessional" ways of responding that are discussed in disaster research. The following section introduces the highly professionalized field of disaster management, focusing specifically on its subfield of disaster mental health intervention. We end this section by elaborating on the relationship between the globalized expert culture of disaster management and the local capacities of people affected by disasters, particularly on context-specific forms of knowledge.

1.4.1 Psychological and Social Reaction Patterns

Psychological disaster research has mostly been concerned with the question of mental health outcome after disaster impact (see Sect. 2.2.5). In cases where individuals demonstrated a certain level of (psychological) vulnerability, psychologists saw exposure to disaster as a trigger for trauma and other pathological stress reactions (Paton et al. 2000). They felt that they should be responsible for addressing the mental health side of these supposedly singular occurrences. Psychological studies were mostly limited to investigating traumatization after disasters (see McFarlane et al. 2009). However, researchers have increasingly explored the assumed automatic link between disaster exposure and pathological outcomes. In the context of building a "positive psychology," the possibility of positive reactions to and growth outcomes from disaster has gained recognition (e.g., Paton et al. 2000); simultaneously, the research and intervention agenda has started to accommodate "resilience" and posttraumatic growth as new concepts.

Psychological reaction patterns that aggregate in mass behavior were a central focus of early disaster research in sociology. However, sociologists soon began debunking common assumptions about mass hysteria, personal breakdown, and antisocial behavior as "disaster myths." All of these myths shared a negative image of humanity by which humans respond irrationally and egoistically in disaster emergencies, disregarding the law and social norms as well as potentially spinning out of control, at least from a government perspective. All of these assumptions conceptualize a disaster as an extreme event that disrupts normality and attributes victimhood and (dangerous levels of) ineptitude to the persons affected. However, as early as the 1960s, the disaster sociologist Fritz (1961) suggested a much more positive framework to understand psychosocial disaster response patterns. According to this approach, negative psychological impact on disaster survivors is reduced by their social experience of "therapeutic adjustment":

> The widespread sharing of danger, loss, and deprivation produces an intimate, primary group solidarity among the survivors, which overcomes social isolation and provides a channel for intimate communication and expression and a major source of physical and emotional support and reassurance. (Fritz 1961, p. 689)

Instead of treating social groups as potentially ungovernable masses, Fritz stresses the resourcefulness of collectivity and shared experience. Refuting the assumption of quasi-natural egoism or the disintegrating effects of disasters, other researchers in this tradition have found solidarity to be an universally shared response to crisis, characterized by a reduction in status differences and increased generosity and helpfulness. Quarantelli and Dynes (1976), for example, found universal, cross-cultural community cooperation during the early stages of emergency, marked by a general willingness of those affected to help each other. However, this "brotherhood of pain" (Oliver-Smith 1999b) usually lasts only for a limited period of time and can tip over into conflict at a later stage.

Approaches such as the "therapeutic community" or the "brotherhood of pain" present a significant corrective to the disaster myth, but it is important to question whether they engage in myth building of their own: Both the emergency situation itself and the longer-term recovery process show evidence of both the myth and the counter-myth.[8] Solidarity might be followed by conflict; altruism can accompany egoistic behavior; and social disparity does not contradict heightened community experiences. It is interesting to note that although he is most often associated with his "brotherhood of pain" theory, Oliver-Smith has also offered a more nuanced perspective, for example, in his early study of a Peruvian earthquake (1979). Here, he developed a time-dependent relationship between solidarity and conflict, while also acknowledging the shifting forms of social identification within post-disaster processes. In the rescue situation immediately after the earthquake, when flight was a question of death or survival, the primary social focus was on rescuing oneself and one's family. Only in the subsequent early post-impact period did community solidarity and cooperation prevail and status differences among survivors appear to be suspended. However, this "brotherhood of pain" did not last long—it tipped over into conflict, at the latest with the advent of external aid (Oliver-Smith 1979). Today we assume that disaster can intensify solidarity as well as conflict (Tierney 2007), and both social dynamics have become central themes in sociological (and to some degree in anthropological) disaster research. In these fields, conflict is often coupled with external aid and the sudden availability of material resources that need to be distributed. The question of fair aid distribution can become a burden on the community and lead to feelings of envy or jealousy. However, in other respects, for example, with regard to political power relations, disasters may open "windows of opportunity" for competing actors to expedite their respective agendas (Oliver-Smith 1979), potentially leading to conflict as well.

1.4.2 Disaster Management Interventions

From early on, scientific research on disaster took place in close relation to national and later with international disaster management agencies. By now, there is a global network of state and non-state agencies whose intervention strategies adhere to policies prescribed by national legal structures or, at the international level, United Nations (UN) documents.

---

[8] The therapeutic community is most often described as a response to natural risk. Technological disasters tend to trigger more corrosive community processes "that break down the social fabric due to the ambiguity of risk" (Flint and Luloff 2005, p. 403). However, both of these assumptions lack empirical evidence (Flint and Luloff 2005).

It is a standard practice to picture disaster management as a cyclical progression of various phases or stages, also called the disaster management cycle. Most commonly, this cycle is divided into the four periods of hazard mitigation, disaster preparedness, emergency response, and disaster recovery. Mitigation seeks to prevent disaster occurrence or minimize its likelihood and impact; the construction of dams against floods is one example of such measures. According to FEMA, mitigation attempts to either "control the hazard source" and prevent damage in developed areas or else decrease potential hazard exposure through adapted settlement or construction measures (Lindell et al. 2006). If mitigation aims to avert or limit disaster impact, preparedness refers to protective measures that ensure an effective response at impact; it encompasses emergency drills or public awareness campaigns. These two categories of pre-disaster activities are complemented by two post-disaster activities: Emergency response refers to the immediate aftermath and includes rescue efforts, evacuation and first aid, the provision of emergency supplies, and the restoration of basic public services. Once the situation has been stabilized, the phase of disaster recovery is reached, sometimes referred to as rehabilitation or reconstruction. This fourth period lasts until community activities have returned to normal or to a state "as normal as possible" (Lindell et al. 2006, p. 21).

It is important to note that technocratic political strategies of disaster management are changing in response to the shifts in disaster research described in Sect. 1.1. The understanding that disaster emerges only if a hazard and vulnerability coincide has been integrated into evaluation models such as the hazard vulnerability analysis (HVA). As indicated by its name, the HVA offers communities a tool to identify potential hazards, estimate the probability of harmful events, and foresee their potential consequences for different social groups and institutions (Lindell et al. 2006). The second shift in thinking from vulnerability toward resilience finds its expression in a broader understanding of risk reduction today. Rather than responding reactively to singular disaster events and their consequences through emergency services, disaster management has developed into a continuous "total disaster risk management," according to which appropriate measures should be integrated into each phase of the disaster management cycle in order to reduce the overall disaster risk.

As a general trend, preventative measures have gained importance in disaster management (see UNISDR 2005; Wisner et al. 2012). At the international level, the Hyogo Framework for Action 2005–2015 outlines necessary disaster loss reduction measures on the part of different sectors and actors, such as national and local governments (Lavell et al. 2012), international agencies (see Arnold 2012), disaster experts, local actors and communities (Delica Willison and Gaillard 2012), and civil society (see Thompson 2012). The framework formulates five priorities for action:

(1) Ensure that disaster risk reduction is a national and a local priority with a strong institutional basis for implementation.
(2) Identify, assess and monitor disaster risks and enhance early warning.
(3) Use knowledge, innovation and education to build a culture of safety and resilience at all levels.
(4) Reduce the underlying risk factors.
(5) Strengthen disaster preparedness for effective response at all levels. (UNISDR 2005)

A normative character prevails throughout both older and more recent models of (total) disaster management, prescribing how societies should handle hazards (O'Brien et al. 2012). Disaster experts define what needs to be known and what needs to be done. A broad range of manuals and guidelines have been developed to foster sustainable reduction to disaster losses by building the resilience of nations and communities. In addition to disaster-specific risk reduction, the actors involved also strive to boost social and economic resilience[9] in order to mitigate in a more comprehensive manner the underlying risk factors (i.e., as proposed in the fourth priority of the Hyogo Framework for Action). Community-based risk management approaches that draw on "participatory" techniques enjoy special popularity. Using a variety of moderation techniques, the affected populations are integrated into the risk management process by presenting their own evaluation of the risk situation and undertaking adequate preventative and reactive measures. However, the fundamentally prescriptive impetus endures simply through the institutional framework of participatory risk management: the assertion that a risk exists which needs to be managed never comes into question. The experts' claim to possess "objective" risk knowledge remains unquestioned and necessarily leads to asymmetrical relations between the external disaster professionals and the communities involved. As a result, the prescriptive, universally conceived, rational and expert-based approach to disaster stands in opposition to culturally sensitive, locally specific approaches to daily life and dealing with risk.

On an international level, the technical–economic, organizational, and political side of disaster management still dominates. It shapes the complex coordination of direct emergency aid in disaster responses: the long-term (re)construction of material, administrative, and economic structures as well as future-oriented risk management. This macrolevel largely draws on technical rationality. Central goals include effective planning, logistics, and coordination, often alongside political objectives such as good governance, social justice, gender justice, and poverty reduction. This practical level follows normative considerations, describing how things should be if the actors are to work successfully and effectively. By representing processes of dealing with disaster sequentially, in phases, models such as the disaster management cycle present an ideological image of orderly disaster management and successful coping through controlled actions (Dombrowsky 2005). In reality, however, there are always discrepancies between the model and the actual conditions on the ground. These can include alternate interpretations of the disaster based on local knowledge and local experience in coping with hazards, as well as local, sociocultural structures that stand in opposition to the rationality and interests of those providing aid.

[9] Disaster-specific risk reduction includes approaches that demand a broad and sustainable environmental policy in the long term, as well as approaches that encompass specific policies tailored to the individual disaster. Social resilience is strengthened by human rights approaches (see Dale and Carmalt 2012), including policies for gender mainstreaming (see Acar and Ege 2001; UNISDR 2005). Economic resilience should result from sustainable livelihood approaches and poverty reduction programs, as well as social protection approaches through social insurance, assistance efforts, and social funds, provided, for example, by the World Bank (Peacock and Prater 2012).

The aid business itself has increasingly been questioned as a means of political manipulation to pursue specific, mostly Western agenda in the name of humanitarian efforts (see Arnold 2012). In response to criticisms such as these, several guidelines and frameworks have been formulated to establish standards for disaster aid (see Sphere Project 2011; ALNAP 2008), including minimum standards for the quality of humanitarian response and demands for conflict-sensitive program management. Following the basic principle of "do no harm" (Anderson 1999), these documents call for the avoidance or reduction of aid-related social conflict. However, considering the expansive distribution of material resources over the course of reconstruction efforts and the likelihood that the corresponding mechanisms of advantage and disadvantage will emerge in crisis situations, this maxim represents an enormous challenge and, in most cases, can only be followed to a certain extent. Moreover, conflict potential often increases when actors follow additional hidden or overt agenda while providing aid, an observation that has been noted with regard to some gender mainstreaming and civil rights approaches. Successful relief efforts must instead consider their own long-term effects and aim to strengthen the local economy or local structures of community self-help rather than weaken them through new dependencies (see ALNAP 2008). Another development is that donor organizations and aid agencies themselves have increased their coordination efforts through policies, such as the cluster approach which was, for example, applied in the 2006 earthquake on Java (MacRae and Hodgkin 2011; Arnold 2012).

1.4.3 Interventions in Disaster Mental Health

A significant component of humanitarian responses to disaster is the area of mental health. The various practical approaches and recommendations are closely tied to the interdisciplinary field of disaster mental health (see, for example, Neria et al. 2009). In addition, a trend toward professionalization in the field of psychology has produced a new subdiscipline of disaster psychology (see Reyes and Jacobs 2006).

The *Sphere Handbook* (Sphere Project 2011) on minimum standards in humanitarian responses to disaster outlines mental health and psychosocial support organized as a pyramid of intervention. At the top of this pyramid are specialized services provided by psychiatrists, psychiatric nurses, or psychologists. One section lower, we find basic support by nonmental health professionals such as general doctors or community workers. The broad foundation of the intervention pyramid comprises unspecific measures that lead to the activation of social networks, for example, or measures targeting general social protection. According to this model, experts from the fields of psychiatry and psychology are primarily responsible for specialized mental health-care initiatives, even though the broader scope of mental health-care intervention goes far beyond the field of the experts. The Sphere standards further suggest that psychosocial approaches should be integrated into all sectors of humanitarian aid (even in technical fields).

For a long time, the expert fields of psychiatry and clinical psychology have predominantly focused on the identification and treatment of posttraumatic stress disorder (PTSD) as an individual response to disaster (see McFarlane et al. 2009). However, along with a general criticism of the PTSD concept (see Sect. 2.2.5), researchers disagree on the significance of PTSD for public health (Van Ommeren et al. 2005). Bonanno et al. (2010) reviewed psychosocial disaster consequences and intervention programs from the individual to the community level and found a relatively low rate (below 30 %) of mental health problems such as PTSD, grief, depression, anxiety, stress-related health problems, increased substance abuse, and suicidal thought among disaster survivors. Instead, the authors emphasize resilience and criticize the growing tendency toward extensive prophylactic psychological interventions in the immediate aftermath of disaster. Interventions such as critical incident stress debriefing (CISD), for example, have proven ineffective or even harmful (Bonanno et al. 2010). Debates continue over appropriate working approaches and strategies in the area of disaster response, and a fundamental consensus is still lacking (Hobfoll et al. 2007). Ager (2006) identifies four core issues for debate: How culturally appropriate are existing intervention models? Which understanding of "psychopathology" or "suffering" are they based on? What priority should be given to mental health concerns in the context of complex emergencies? How can larger populations benefit from psychosocial interventions?

An important milestone in attempts by professionals to reach a consensus occurred with the reporting of the findings of an international panel of 20 experts on the study and treatment of people exposed to disaster and mass violence (Hobfoll et al. 2007). The panel formulated five rather general essential elements of immediate and midterm mass trauma intervention: (1) promotion of a sense of safety, (2) promotion of calm, (3) promotion of a sense of self- and collective efficacy, (4) promotion of connectedness, and (5) promotion of hope. Considering the heterogeneity of disaster situations, the authors rejected the idea of drawing up specific guidelines or courses of action. The experts supported and elaborated their findings both on the individual level of coping with stress and trauma and on the level of communities and social systems. Their report offers pragmatic suggestions that avoid taking a pathologizing perspective on trauma and has since become a central reference point for many subsequent approaches.

One such approach is psychological first aid (PFA), an intervention tool for trained professionals helping children, adolescents, adults, and families in the immediate aftermath of disaster and terrorism (Brymer et al. 2006; Ruzek et al. 2007; Vernberg et al. 2008). It is considered *first* aid insofar as it can be complemented by secondary psychological assistance or other more specialized therapeutic interventions, adapted to survivors' needs and the time frame (Ruzek et al. 2007). Based conceptually on the principles formulated by Hobfoll et al. (2007), PFA is organized into eight core actions (Brymer et al. 2006): Initial actions include establishment of contact and engagement, provision of physical safety, and efforts to produce emotional comfort and stabilization. Later actions focus on calming and reducing high arousal, numbing, or emotionality. Furthermore, the authors call on aid providers to gather information in order to identify immediate problems and current needs. Other core actions include providing practical assistance, connecting with available social supports, disseminating information on coping, and building links to collaborative services. Finally, aid providers should educate survivors about stress reactions, adaptive coping strategies, and other opportunities to seek help. PFA offers a range of specific recommendations intended to suit individualized needs and be sensitive to situational contexts (Vernberg et al. 2008). The authors consider their approach to be "culturally informed" as well as sensitive and acceptant to different forms of communication, expression of emotions, religious orientations, and values (Brymer et al. 2006). In general, the orientation toward broad principles should encourage flexibility.[10]

Another practice-oriented initiative by the Society for Community Research and Action (SCRA) draws on the American field of community psychology and aims to transcend the individual perspective and focus on expert knowledge so prevalent in other approaches. The *Manual for Planning and Action to Help a Community Recover from Disaster* (SCRA 2010) reads as a "how to" manual for stakeholders willing to engage in their communities. Like PFA, the manual refers to the principles formulated by Hobfoll et al. (2007), but it is guided by basic community psychology values. It focuses on positive community action—strength, social justice, community resources, participatory action, and flexibility in multiple contexts—but neglects issues of power and social inequality. Furthermore, it fails to account for the cultural specificity of social contexts.

Thus, current approaches encourage broad, low-threshold interventions that can then provide a basis for specialized services (if necessary). The *Disaster Mental Health Handbook* of the American Red Cross (2012) recommends that psychological triage prioritize clients with risk markers, such as loss of a family member or a history of mental health issues. However, all clients and responders can benefit from PFA. If individuals are not calmed or reassured by the secondary assessment, further forms of crisis intervention or referral to a mental health provider in the community may be appropriate. A diagnosis of trauma in terms of PTSD occurs only when symptoms persist over a longer period of time—at least 1 month, according to the current Diagnostic and Statistical Manual of Mental Disorders (DSM-5) by the American Psychiatric Association.

1.4.4 Expert Cultures and Local Knowledge

As indicated in most definitions of disaster quoted previously, outside intervention is constitutive of disaster management. The entire field is based on a distinction between affected people, victims, or survivors and external professionals. Many elements

[10] Bonanno et al. (2010) regret the dearth of empirical evidence to support the effectiveness of PFA and its accompanying psychoeducational materials, citing the difficulty of conducting controlled intervention research in the aftermath of disasters as one barrier to improved knowledge. In our view, however, this critique overlooks the fact that context-sensitive flexibility is an essential component of PFA which, by necessity, stands in opposition to rigid mental health evaluation techniques that require a very high degree of standardization.

of disaster management have been globalized, for example, through UN agencies and international policies, offering a universal framework of outsider knowledge to "manage" the way people cope in their specific local contexts. While skepticism toward survivors' response patterns prevailed in early disaster research and the vulnerability paradigm saw affected populations as (potential) victims, the key concept of resilience changed the previous paradigms because it allowed researchers to acknowledge people's capacities and called for the integration of these resources into daily practice. In order to increase the efficiency of preventative disaster risk reduction strategies, aid practitioners began to deploy participatory methods in order to take advantage of locally available capacities. In conjunction with this process, previously neglected local knowledge (Dekens 2007; Bankoff 2003) was increasingly recognized as a valuable resource. Researchers and practitioners developed frameworks to collect systematically and analyze local knowledge (Dekens 2007), while other initiatives attempted to synthesize local and outsider knowledge in participatory disaster risk reduction programs (for example, Mercer et al. 2007, 2010).

However, even with such new developments, old assumptions persist and the relation between outside intervention and local community capacities remains challenging. Realist theoretical positions based on an understanding of risk as an objective given, assume risk reduction to be of equally objective interest to local people. Following this logic, local populations should be ready to jump on board participatory strategies that involve sharing their local knowledge in order to integrate local and scientific knowledge into a cooperative effort. However, it is important to ask whether these programs actually succeed in overcoming the traditional top-down approach to disaster risk reduction in which solutions are developed outside of the specific context to which they are applied (Mercer 2012; Riley 2009; Stirrat and Henkel 1997). Sillitoe (2010), once a pioneer of promoting indigenous knowledge in development initiatives, has become rather skeptical about the chances of harmoniously combining indigenous (or local) knowledge and scientific knowledge. The failure of such approaches may trace back to the logic behind the shift toward participation: this reorientation was derived not only from a recognition of local capacities but also from the experience that outside interventions failed by ignoring the local context and its specific needs and conditions. Sometimes these interventions even caused harm by inadvertently altering social structures in a permanent way. The shift toward participatory approaches therefore emerged from the shortcomings of top-down logic, but not from an intention to abandon this logic altogether. As a result, the participatory approach has had little effect on the deeper level of power relations and knowledge claims. In addition, over centuries of contact colonized and marginalized groups have developed a deep mistrust toward Western promises of a better life through technology and development (Sillitoe 2010).

Paralleling these implementation challenges, the category of local knowledge itself is a matter of debate at a conceptual level—and some failures in practice might be associated with these problems. Local knowledge is always rooted in local people's way of life, in "their culture." The debate over understandings of local knowledge thus recapitulates larger conversations about the concept of culture. Local knowledge is not monolithic, static, or self-contained but rather heterogeneous, dynamic, and hybrid (see Schlehe 2006): Within any given "local culture," different knowledge, practices, and strategies exist, and not necessarily everyone agrees on their uniform expression. Specifically, like any form of knowledge, local knowledge is plural and contested. Just as nobody would claim that people's knowledge in European or North American societies has stopped evolving, local knowledge is always dynamic in nature and subject to historical processes. These processes encompass the integration of and interaction with new elements; local knowledge is thus mutable and globally intertwined (Frömming 2006). In the context of this debate, authors such as Dekens (2007) have formulated an understanding of local knowledge that is sensitive to these points of criticism and also counteracts the danger of ecological determinism and survival reductionism as discussed in Sect. 1.3.2:

> A local knowledge system is composed of different knowledge types, practices and beliefs, values, and worldviews. Such systems change constantly under the influence of power relations and cross-scale linkages both within and outside the community. As such, local knowledge and practices need to be understood as adaptive responses to internal and external changes which result (or not) in disaster preparedness at local level. (Dekens 2007: VIII)

More radical critiques reject the notion of local knowledge itself, so long as it is framed in opposition to "knowledge" or "global knowledge." By burying the specific historical and sociocultural roots of "knowledge," this dichotomy reifies the same power hierarchy that local knowledge discourses intend to overcome (Agrawal 1995). However, the fact that Western, technically oriented solutions so often fail due to the specific challenges of sociocultural contexts provides evidence that these solutions are much less universal than people claim; indeed, ultimately they "are just as firmly anchored in a specific milieu as any other system of knowledge" (Agrawal 1995, p. 425). Questions of knowledge and power thus play a central role both for those promoting local knowledge and for those rejecting the notion entirely. Explicit articulations of local knowledge often convey indigenousness and ethnic identities and assert or seek recognition for these. In this regard, self images and ascribed characteristics (e.g., from government agencies) combine in ways that can be ambivalent, as local knowledge in terms of indigenous capacities always fuses elements of both empowerment and glorified romanticism, as we discussed in Sect. 1.3.2 with respect to a "closeness to nature."

In order to move beyond a monolithic understanding of "locals" and "outsiders," each with their own knowledge, and to analyze questions of power without reproducing them conceptually, it is helpful to draw on Hilhorst's (2007) actor-centered approach. This view envisions the entire field of social responses to disaster as interactions between different social domains. In doing so, she considers scholars to be actors as well, grouping them together with disaster management practitioners in one domain. Politicians and bureaucrats constitute another domain in which they propagate patterns of risk governance. Finally, Hilhorst delimits the domain of local response. Each social domain represents an area of social life in which discourses, values, commitments, and practices are shared, but inner transformation, differentiation, conflict, and negotiation also take place (Hilhorst 2007). Throughout the interactions among these various social domains, individual and institutional actors hold a range of different power positions, which occur and are reproduced in relation to material and social resources. Hence, disaster management itself represents an interesting, complex, "cultural" field of study composed of social actors pursuing their respective agenda in a web of constant interaction (Hilhorst 2007; Hilhorst and Jansen 2010). These dynamics are subject to a wide variety of influences that we can analyze in terms of macroeconomics, politics, culture, or organizational structure, to name just a few. Examples include the competitive dynamics among aid agencies; the coordination process between large organizations or umbrella organizations and case-specific national politics; and the element of personal interaction in disaster aid.

1.5 Concluding Remarks

No well-grounded discussion of disaster can escape the challenge of addressing the topic's complexity. Disasters are multidimensional processes in which physical and social elements intertwine to potentially affect all aspects of human life (Oliver-Smith 1999a). Disasters involve a certain degree of collective impact but are experienced subjectively, shaped but not determined by biophysical and sociocultural contexts. A characteristic of disasters is their destructive nature, but distinctions between "crisis" and "disaster" are purely definitional, serving to advance a (political) categorization of suffering that implies different approaches and different claims to external aid. For a long time, scholars emphasized the sudden and disruptive character of disaster, locating this category of destructive events beyond normal life and, in the case of "natural" disaster, beyond human responsibility. In contrast, structural approaches have argued that disaster represents a manifestation of preexisting vulnerabilities, which express themselves as damage or loss as a result of the impact of hazards. "Natural" disasters are also considered man-made and seen as long-term processes rather than sudden, disruptive events. In the environmental paradigm, both of these elements are tied to nature once again with disaster understood as a web of complex interactions between humans and the environment (Hilhorst 2007). Vulnerability then becomes a question of whether societies are able to adapt to their environments. This last perspective places stronger emphasis on biophysical agents, but in contrast to the hazard paradigm, it frames these agents as environment rather than as independent forces of nature. In contrast to nature, the environment always represents a category tied to human beings—lived, used, shaped, and interpreted through cultural practice. Like disaster itself, coping with disaster always occurs at the nexus of society and environment, incorporating both the exosemiotic agency of the biophysical world and its human interpretations and related practices. Over a long period of time, experience with the environment contributes to a collection of specific knowledge—"local knowledge"—that people draw on as a coping mechanism in cases of concrete disaster occurrences.

Researchers representing the environmental approach may not only integrate analytical elements of structural vulnerability but also emphasize the complex and dynamic interplay of many different factors which are not limited to the role of societal structures. On the theoretical level, this implies that agency can be attributed to any number of affected or participating actors—in contrast to the vulnerability paradigm, which risks construing vulnerable groups and persons as purely passive victims. With the shift toward resilience, a complementary perspective has emerged to focus on the capacity of affected communities and individuals to cope with crises, mitigating the potential for further disasters. Thus, societies, communities, households, or individuals are no longer seen as simply more or less vulnerable but also as more or less capable of adapting to adverse conditions. In contrast to resistance, which would entail preventing disasters altogether, resilience points to the relative physical and temporal extent of damage, and its processual character. Local knowledge has a positive connotation in the context of disaster, often equated with mitigation strategies or other forms of resilience. However, critical approaches often run the danger of interpreting local knowledge as automatically "better" for supposedly being more primordial and closer to nature. But, like any other expression of culture, local knowledge is plural, contested, historically situated in a globalized world, and articulated by specific individuals. This is precisely where we see the main value of the local knowledge discourse: it points to a plurality of knowledge resources that far exceeds the hegemonic scientific base of globalized disaster management.

A technocratic perspective has remained prevalent in recent attempts to integrate local knowledge into disaster management. Local knowledge is mostly reduced to a neat package of practical, local strategies for everyone involved to apply or dismiss in disaster risk reduction efforts. More general cosmologies such as culturally expected normality or human–nature relations are rarely addressed or even seen as obstacles to disaster risk reduction (Hewitt 2012). However, subjective experiences are shaped by the way people perceive and inhabit their worlds; cosmologies and sociocultural practices therefore represent an integral element of any coping process. A cultural psychology of coping with disaster thus requires scholars to account for the emic point of view, or rather the plurality of emic perspectives.

Furthermore, it is important to localize hegemonic disaster research. The hegemonic perspective originated under specific historical conditions and in specific regions of the world. In mainstream research, institutions in the USA have established themselves most strongly (Tierney 2007, Lindell et al. 2006). From the very beginning, mainstream disaster research developed in close connection with the demand for applicable knowledge and corresponding strategies for state, non-state, and later international institutions tasked with helping people overcome and prevent disasters. In many regards, it is therefore an applied science (Tierney 2007), showing conceptual proximity to disaster management as a form of intervention and governmentality. Approaches seen as less applicable, such as constructionist analyses, are criticized for producing irrelevant knowledge that cannot feed directly into disaster management or improve the lives of people affected by disaster (Wisner et al. 2004). However, Tierney (2007) sees disaster research as increasingly open to constructionist insights; we, too, consider that such non-applied meta-perspectives are absolutely necessary to overcome the all-too-pragmatic logics of intervention because on the one hand, they point out that disasters and dealing with disasters need to be contextualized in broad, historical fields of power and societal relationships, while, on the other hand, they enable researchers to broaden their perspectives by helping to challenge the framework of "disaster" and the effects of that framework. Social constructionist insights are useful in questioning power structures, identifying cultural and hegemonic biases, and increasing sensitivity toward cultural specifics by localizing supposedly "universal" knowledge.

Acknowledgments The editors would like to thank Sophia Perl for assistance with editing and translating parts of this chapter from German into English.

References

Acar, F., & Ege, G. (2001)."Women's human rights in disaster contexts: How can CEDAW help?" Paper prepared for the Expert Working Group meeting, Ankara, Turkey. UN Division for the Advancement of Women. http://www.un.org/womenwatch/daw/csw/env_manage/documents/EP4–2001 Oct 25.pdf. Accessed 10 May 2013.

Active Learning Network for Humanitarian Practice (ALNAP). (2008). *Responding to earthquakes 2008: Learning from earthquake relief and recovery operations*. London: ALNAP. http://www.alnap.org/publications/pdfs/ALNAPLessonsEarthquakes.pdf. Accessed 10 May 2013.

Ager, A. (2006). Towards a consensus protocol for psychosocial response in complex emergencies. In G. Reyes, & G. A. Jacobs (Eds.), *Handbook of international disaster psychology. Volume 1: Fundamentals and overview* (pp. 51–64). Westport: Praeger.

Agrawal, A. (1995). Dismantling the divide between indigenous and scientific knowledge. *Development and Change, 26*(3), 413–439.

Alexander, D. (1997). The study of natural disasters, 1977–1997: Some reflections on a changing field of knowledge. *Disasters, 21*(4), 284–304.

American Red Cross. (2012). Disaster mental health handbook. Disaster services. http://www.cdms.uci.edu/PDF/Disaster-Mental-Health-Handbook-Oct-2012.pdf. Accessed 10 May 2013.

Anderson, J. W. (1968). Cultural adaptation to threatened disaster. *Human Organization, 27*(4), 298–307.

Anderson, M. B. (1999). *Do no harm: How aid can support peace or war*. London: Lynne Rienner.

Arnold, M. (2012). International planning systems for disaster. In B. Wisner, J. C. Gaillard, & I. Kelman (Eds.), *Handbook of hazards and disaster risk reduction* (pp. 603–616). New York: Routledge.

Bankoff, G. (2003). *Cultures of disaster: society and natural hazard in the Philippines*. London; New York: RoutledgeCurzon.

Bankoff, G., & Hilhorst, D. (2009). The politics of risk in the Philippines. *Disasters, 33*(4), 686–704.

Barton, A. H. (1969). *Communities in disaster: A sociological analysis of collective stress situations*. Garden City: Doubleday.

Barton, A. H. (2005). Disaster and collective stress. In R. W. Perry & E. L. Quarantelli (Eds.), *What is a disaster: New answers to old questions* (pp. 125–152). Philadelphia, PA: XLibris.

Berry, J. W. (1976). *Human ecology and cognitive style*. New York: John Wiley.

Blaikie, P., Cannon, T., Davis, I., & Wisner, B. (1994). *At risk: Natural hazards, people's vulnerability and disasters*. New York: Routledge.

Bolin, R. C., & Stanford, L. (1998). *The Northridge earthquake: vulnerability and disaster*. London; New York: Routledge.

Bollig, M. (2012). Social-ecological change and the changing structure of risk, risk management and resilience in a pastoral community in northwestern Namibia. In U. Luig (Ed.), *Negotiating disasters: politics, representation, meanings* (pp. 31–58). Frankfurt a. M.: Lang.

Bonanno, G. A., Brewin, C. R., Kaniasty, K., & La Greca, A. M. (2010). Weighing the costs of disaster: consequences, risks, and resilience in individuals, families and communities. *Psychological Science in the Public Interest, 11*(1), 1–49.

Brown, K., & Westaway, E. (2011). Agency, capacity, and resilience to environmental change: Lessons from human development, well-being, and disasters. *Annual Review of Environment and Resources, 36*(1), 321–342.

Brymer, M., Layne, C., Jacobs, A., Pynoos, R., Ruzek, J., Steinberg, A., et al. (2006). *Psychological first aid field operations guide* (2nd ed.). Los Angeles: National Child Traumatic Stress Network and National Center for PTSD. http://www.ptsd.va.gov/professional/manuals/manual-pdf/pfa/PFA_V2.pdf. Accessed 26 May 2013.

Burton, I., Kates, R. W., & White, G. F. (1993). *The environment as hazard*. (2nd ed.). New York: Guilford.

Cicchetti, D. (2010). Resilience under conditions of extreme stress: A multi-level perspective. *World Psychiatry, 9*(3), 145–154.

Cote, M., & Nightingale, A. (2011). Resilience thinking meets social theory: Situating social change in socio-ecological systems (SES) research. *Progress in Human Geography, 36*(4), 475–489.

Cutter, S. L. (1996). Vulnerability to environmental hazards. *Progress in Human Geography, 20*(4), 529–539.

Dale, C. H., & Carmalt, J. C. (2012). Human rights, disasters and state obligations. In B. Wisner, J. C. Gaillard, & I. Kelman (Eds.), *Handbook of hazards and disaster risk reduction* (pp. 61–70). New York: Routledge.

Dekens, J. (2007). *Local knowledge for disaster preparedness*. Kathmandu: International Centre for Integrated Mountain Development (ICIMOD). Online: http://preventionweb.net/go/2693. Accessed 10 May 2013.

Delica Willison, Z., & Gaillard, J. C. (2012). Community action and disaster. In B. Wisner, J.C. Gaillard, & I. Kelman (Eds.), *Handbook of hazards and disaster risk reduction* (pp. 711–722). New York: Routledge.

Diener, E., Ng, W., Harter, J., & Arora, R. (2010). Wealth and happiness across the world: Material prosperity predicts life evaluation, whereas psychosocial prosperity predicts positive feeling. *Journal of Personality and Social Psychology, 99*(1), 52–61.

Dombrowsky, W. R. (2005). Not every move is a step forward. In R. W. Perry & E. L. Quarantelli (Eds.), *What is a disaster: New answers to old questions* (pp. 79–96). Philadelphia, PA: XLibris.

Drabek, T. E. (2006). Sociology, disasters, and emergency management: History, contributions, and future agenda. In D.A. Mc Entire (Ed.), *Disciplines, disasters and emergency management: The convergence and divergence of concepts, issues and trends in the research literature*. Emmitsburg, MD: Emergency Management Institute, FEMA.

Flint, C. G., & Luloff, A. E. (2005). Natural resource-based communities, risk, and disaster: An intersection of theories. *Society & Natural Resources, 18*(5), 399–412.

Frances, A. (2013). *Saving normal: An insider's revolt against out-of-control psychiatric diagnosis, DSM-5, Big pharma, and the medicalization of ordinary life*. New York: HarperCollins.

Fritz, C. E. (1961). Disasters. In R. K. Merton & R. A. Nisbet (Eds.), *Contemporary social problems* (pp. 651–694). New York: Harcourt, Brace and World.

Frömming, U. U. (2006). *Naturkatastrophen: Kulturelle Deutung und Verarbeitung*. Frankfurt a. M.: Campus.

Gigerenzer, G. (2008). *Rationality for mortals. How people cope with uncertainty*. New York: Oxford University Press.

Greve, W., & Staudinger, U. M. (2006). Resilience in later adulthood and old age: Resources and potentials for successful aging. In D. Cicchetti & D.J. Cohen (Eds.), *Developmental psychopathology, Vol. 3: Risk, disorder and adaptaion* (2nd ed., pp. 796–840). Hoboken, NJ: Wiley.

Haltermann, I. (2012). The perception of natural hazards in the context of human (in-)security. In U. Luig (Ed.), *Negotiating disasters: Politics, representation, meanings* (pp. 59–78). Frankfurt a. M.: Lang.

Herzlich, C., & Pierret, J. (1987). *Illness and self in society*. Baltimore: Johns Hopkins University Press.

Hewitt, K. (1983). The idea of calamity in a technocratic age. In K., Hewitt (Ed.), *Interpretations of calamity from the viewpoint of human ecology* (pp. 3–32). London; Boston; Sydney: Allen & Unwin.

Hewitt, K. (1997). *Regions of risk: A geographical introduction to disasters*. Eastbourne: Longman.

Hewitt, K. (2012). Culture, hazard and disaster. In B. Wisner, J. C. Gaillard, & I. Kelman (Eds.), *Handbook of hazards and disaster risk reduction* (pp. 85–108). New York: Routledge.

Hilhorst, D. (2007). Complexity and diversity: unlocking social domains of disaster response. In G. Bankoff, G. Frerks, & D. Hilhorst (Eds.), *Mapping vulnerability* (pp. 52–66). London; Sterling, VA: Earthscan.

Hilhorst, D., & Jansen, B. J. (2010). Humanitarian space as arena: A perspective on the everyday politics of aid. *Development and Change, 41*(6), 1117–1139.

Hobfoll, S. E., Watson, P., Bell, C. C., Bryant, R. A., Brymer, M. J., Friedman, M. J. et al. (2007). Five essential elements of immediate and mid-term mass trauma intervention: Empirical evidence. *Psychiatry, 70*(4), 283–315.

Hoffman, S. M., & Oliver-Smith, A. (1999). Anthropology and the angry earth. An overview. In: S. Hoffman, & A. Oliver-Smith (Eds.) (1999), *The angry earth. Disaster in anthropological perspective* (pp. 1–15). New York; London: Routledge.

Jensen, J. (2010). The argument for a disciplinary approach to Emergency Management Higher Education. FEMA. http://training.fema.gov/EMIWeb/edu/highpapers.asp. Accessed 10 May 2013.

Jigyasu, R. (2002). Reducing disaster vulnerability through local knowledge and capacity. http://ntnu.diva-portal.org/smash/get/diva2:123824/FULLTEXT01. Accessed 6 June 2013.

Kahneman, D. (2011). *Thinking, fast and slow*. New York: Farrar, Strauss and Giroux.

Lavell, A., Gaillard, J. C., Wisner, B., Saunders, W., & van Niekerk, D. (2012). National planning and disaster. In B. Wisner, J. C. Gaillard, & I. Kelman (Eds.), *Handbook of hazards and disaster risk reduction* (pp. 617–628). New York: Routledge.

Lazarus, R. S., & Folkman, S. (1984). *Stress, appraisal, and coping*. New York: Springer.

Lengwiler, M., & Madarász, J. (2010). Präventionsgeschichte als Kulturgeschichte der Gesundheitspolitik. In M. Lengwiler, & J. Madarász (Eds.), *Das präventive Selbst. Eine Kulturgeschichte moderner Gesundheitspolitik* (pp. 11–28). Bielefeld: Transskript.

Levit-Binnun, N., & Golland, Y. (2012). Finding behavioral and network indicators of brain vulnerability. *Frontiers in Human Neuroscience, 6,* Art. 10. doi: 10.3389/fnhum.2012.00010.

Lewis, J. (1999). *Development in disaster-prone places*. London: IT Publications.

Lewis, J., Kelman, I., & Lewis, S. A. V. (2011). Is "fear itself" the only thing we have to fear? Explorations of psychology in perceptions of the vulnerability of others. *Australasian Journal of Disaster and Trauma Studies, 3,* 89–103. http://preventionweb.net/go/24421. Accessed 13 June 2013.

Lindell, M. K., Prater, C. S., & Perry, R. W. (2006). *Fundamentals of emergency management*. Emmitsburg, MD: FEMA Emergency Management Institute. http://training.fema.gov/EMIWeb/edu/fem.asp. Accessed 10 May 2013.

Lopez, S. J., & Snyder, C. R. (Eds.) (2009). *Oxford handbook of positive psychology* (2nd ed.). New York, NY: Oxford University Press.

Luig, U. (2012). Negotiating disasters: An overview. In U. Luig (Ed.), *Negotiating disasters: Politics, representation, meanings* (pp. 3–26). Frankfurt a. M.: Lang.

Macamo, E., & Neubert, D. (2008). Erwartung an Sicherheit. Subjektive Katastrophenwahrnehmungen und Bedingungen der Bewältigung am Beispiel Mosambiks und Deutschlands. In K. Rehberg (Ed.), *Die Natur der Gesellschaft. Verhandlungen des 31. Kongresses der Deutschen Gesellschaft für Soziologie* (pp. 858–874). Frankfurt a. M.: Campus.

MacRae, G., & Hodgkin, D. (2011). Half full or half empty? Shelter after the Jogjakarta earthquake. *Disasters, 35*(1), 243–267.

McCabe, J. T. (2002). Impact and response to drought among Turkana pastoralists: Implications for anthropological theory and hazard research. In S. M. Hoffman & A. Oliver-Smith (Eds.), *Catastrophe & culture: The anthropology of disaster* (pp. 213–236). Santa Fe: School of American Research Press.

McEntire, D. A., Fuller, C., Johnston, C. W., & Weber, R. (2002). A comparison of disaster paradigms: The search for a holistic policy guide. *Public Administration Review, 62*(3), 267–281.
McFarlane, A. C., & Norris, F. H. (2006). Definitions and concepts in disaster research. In F. H. Norris, S. Galea, M. J. Friedman, & P. J. Watson (Eds.), *Methods for disaster mental health research* (pp. 3–19). New York: Guilford Press.
McFarlane, A. C., van Hooff, M., & Goodhew, F. (2009). Anxiety disorders and PTSD. In Y. Neria, S. Galea & F. H. Norris (Eds.), *Mental health and disasters* (pp. 47–66). New York: Cambridge University Press.
McHugh, P. R., & Treisman, G. (2007). PTSD: A problematic diagnostic category. *Journal of Anxiety Disorders, 21*(2), 211–222.
Mercer, J. (2012). Knowledge and disaster risk reduction. In B. Wisner, J. C. Gaillard, & I. Kelman (Eds.), *Handbook of hazards and disaster risk reduction* (pp. 97–108). New York: Routledge.
Mercer, J., Dominey-Howes, D., Kelman, I., & Lloyd, K. (2007). The potential for combining indigenous and western knowledge in reducing vulnerability of environmental hazards in small island developing states. *Environmental Hazards, 7*(4), 245–256.
Mercer, J., Kelman, I., Suchet-Pearson, S., & Lloyd, K. (2010). Framework for integrating indigenous and scientific knowledge for disaster risk reduction. *Disasters, 34*(1), 214–239.
Muris, P., Mayer, B., Reinders, E., & Wesenhagen, C. (2011). Person-related protective and vulnerability factors of psychopathology symptoms in non-clinical adolescents. *Community Mental Health Journal, 47*(1), 47–60.
Murphy, R. (1994). *Rationality and nature*. Boulder: Westview Press.
Neria, Y., Galea, S., & Norris, F. H. (Eds.) (2009). *Mental health and disasters*. New York, NY: Cambridge University Press.
Norris, F. H., Stevens, S. P., Pfefferbaum, B., Wyche, K. F., & Pfefferbaum, R. L. (2008). Community resilience as a metaphor, theory, set of capacities, and strategy for disaster readiness. *American Journal of Community Psychology, 41*(1/2), 127–150.
O'Brien, G., Bhatt, M., Saunders, W., Gaillard, J. C., & Wisner, B. (2012). Local government and disaster. In B. Wisner, J. C. Gaillard, & I. Kelman (Eds.), *Handbook of hazards and disaster risk reduction* (pp. 629–640). New York: Routledge.
Oliver-Smith, A. (1979). Post disaster consensus and conflict in a traditional society: The 1970 avalanche of Yungay, Peru. *Mass Emergencies, 4,* 39–52.
Oliver-Smith, A. (1996). Anthropological research on hazards and disasters. *Annual Review of Anthropology, 25,* 303–328.
Oliver-Smith, A. (1999a). What is a disaster? Anthropological perspectives on a persistent question. In A. Oliver-Smith, & S. M. Hoffman (Eds.), *The angry earth: Disaster in anthropological perspectives* (pp. 18–34). New York: Routledge.
Oliver-Smith, A. (1999b). The brotherhood of pain: Theoretical and applied perspectives on post-disaster solidarity. In A. Oliver-Smith, & S.M. Hoffman (Eds.), *The angry earth: Disaster in anthropological perspectives* (pp. 156–172). New York: Routledge.
Oliver-Smith, A. (2002). Theorizing disasters: Nature, power, and culture. In S. M. Hoffman, & A. Oliver-Smith (Eds.), *Catastrophe & culture: The anthropology of disaster* (pp. 23–48). Santa Fe, NM: School of American Research Press.
Oliver-Smith, A., & Hoffman, S. M. (2002). Introduction: Why anthropologists should study disaster. In S. M. Hoffman & A. Oliver-Smith (Eds.), *Catastrophe & culture: The anthropology of disaster* (pp. 3–22). Santa Fe, NM: School of American Research Press.
Paton, D., Smith, L., & Violanti, J. (2000). Disaster response: Risk, vulnerability and resilience. *Disaster Prevention and Management, 9*(3), 173–179.
Peacock, W., & Prater, C. (2012). Social Protection and Disaster. In B. Wisner, J. C. Gaillard & I. Kelman (Eds.), *Handbook of hazards and disaster risk reduction* (pp. 687–696). New York: Routledge.
Pelling, M. (2010). *Adaptation to climate change: From resilience to transformation.* London: Routledge.

Pelling, M., & Manuel-Navarrete, D. (2011). From resilience to transformation: The adaptive cycle in two Mexican urban centers. *Ecology and Society, 16*(2), 11. http://www.ecologyandsociety.org. Accessed 22 December 2011.

Quarantelli, E. L., & Dynes, R. (1976). Community conflict: Its absence and its presence in natural disasters. *Mass Emergencies, 1,* 139–152.

Quarantelli, E. L. (2005). A social science research agenda for the disasters of the 21st century. In R. W. Perry & E. L. Quarantelli (Eds.), What *is a disaster: New answers to old questions* (pp. 325–396). Philadelphia, PA: XLibris.

Reyes, G., & Jacobs, G. A. (Eds.) (2006). *Handbook of international disaster psychology*. Westport, CT: Praeger.

Riley, K. (2009). Participation and the state: Towards an anthropological view of the 'new participatory paradigms'. *New Proposals: Journal of Marxism and Interdisciplinary Inquiry, 2*(2), 24–30.

Ruzek, J. I., Brymer, M. J., Jacobs, A. K., Layne, C. M., Vernberg, E. M., & Watson, P. J. (2007). Psychological first aid. *Journal of Mental Health Counseling, 29*(1), 17–49.

Schlehe, J. (2006). Kultur, Universalität und Diversität. In E. Wohlfart & M. Zaumseil (Eds.), *Transkulturelle Psychiatrie. Interkulturelle Psychotherapie. Interdisziplinäre Theorie und Praxis* (pp. 51–57). Heidelberg: Springer.

Schlehe, J. (2010). Anthropology of religion: Disasters and the representations of tradition and modernity. *Religion, 40*(2), 112–120.

Schmuck-Widmann, H. (1996). *Leben mit der Flut. Überlebensstrategien von Char-Bewohnern in Bangladesh. ASA-Texte*. Berlin: Hilbert & Pösger.

Sen, A. (1992). *Inequality reexamined.* Oxford: LinkClarendon Press.

Sillitoe, P. (2010). Trust in development: Some implications of knowing in indigenous knowledge. *Journal of the Royal Anthropological Institute, 16*(1), 12–30.

Slovic, P., & Västfjäll, D. (2010). Affect, moral intuition, and risk. *Psychological Inquiry, 21*(4), 387–398.

Society for Community Research and Action (SCRA). (2010). Task force for disaster, community readiness, and recovery. http://www.scra27.org/disaster_recovery_manual. Accessed 23 Nov 2012.

Solberg, C., Rossetto, T., & Joffe, H. (2010). The social psychology of seismic hazard adjustment: re-evaluating the international literature. *Natural Hazards and Earth Systems Science, 10*(8), 1663–1677.

Sphere, Project. (2011) Sphere handbook: Humanitarian charter and minimum standards in disaster response (3rd Rev. ed.). http://www.sphereproject.org/handbook. Accessesd 22.06. Jun 2013.

Spittler, G. (1999). Stress, crisis and catastrophe. Communication and survival strategies of Tuareg nomads during a famine. In U. Kracht & M. Schulz (Eds.), *Food security and nutrition. The global challenge* (pp. 157–168). New York: St. Martin's Press.

Stallings, R. A. (1988). Conflict in natural disasters: a codification of consensus and conflict theories. *Social Science Quarterly, 69*(3), 569–586.

Stallings, R. A. (1995). *Promoting risk: constructing the earthquake threat.* Hawthorne, NY: Aldine de Gruyter.

Stallings, R. A. (2005). Disaster, crisis, collective stress, and mass deprivation. In R. W. Perry & E. L. Quarantelli (Eds.), *What is a disaster: New answers to old questions* (pp. 237–274). Philadelphia, PA: XLibris.

Steptoe, A. (Ed.). (2012). *Handbook of behavioral medicine: Methods and applications*. New York: Springer.

Stirrat, R. L., & Henkel, H. (1997). The development gift: The problem of reciprocity in the NGO world. *Annals of the American Academy of Political and Social Science, 554,* 66–80.

Tekeli-Yeşil, S., Dedeoğlu, N., Braun-Fahrlaender, C., & Tanner, M. (2011). Earthquake awareness and perception of risk among the residents of Istanbul. *Natural Hazards, 59*(1), 427–446.

Thompson, M. (2012). Civil society and disaster. In B. Wisner, J. C. Gaillard, & I. Kelman (Eds.), *Handbook of hazards and disaster risk reduction* (pp. 723–735). New York: Routledge.

Tierney, K. J. (1999). Toward a critical sociology of risk. *Sociological Forum, 14*(2), 215–242.

Tierney, K. J. (2007). From the margins to the mainstream? Disaster research at the crossroads. *Annual Review of Sociology, 33*(1), 503–525.

Tobin, G. A., & Montz, B. E. (1997). *Natural hazards: Explanation and integration*. New York: Guilford Press.

United Nations International Strategy for Disaster Reduction (UNISDR). (2004). Living with risk. A global review of disaster reduction initiatives. http://www.unisdr.org/we/inform/publications/657. Accessed 4 June 2012.

United Nations International Strategy for Disaster Reduction (UNISDR). (2005). Hyogo Framework for Action 2005–2015: Building the resilience of nations and communities to disasters. Geneva: UNISDR. http://www.unisdr.org/2005/wcdr/intergover/official-doc/L-docs/Hyogo-framework-for-action-english.pdf. Accessed 7 July 2013.

United Nations International Strategy for Disaster Reduction (UNISDR). (2009). UNISDR Terminology on Disaster Risk Reduction. Geneva: UNISDR. http://www.unisdr.org/files/7817_UNISDRTerminologyEnglish.pdf. Accessed 22 June 2013.

Van Ommeren, M., Saxena, S., & Saraceno, B. (2005). Mental and social health during and after acute emergencies: emerging consensus? *Bulletin of the World Health Organization, 83*(1), 71–74.

Vernberg, E. M., Steinberg, A. M., Jacobs, A. K., Brymer, M. J., Watson, P. J., Osofsky, J. D., et al. (2008). Innovations in disaster mental health: Psychological first aid. *Professional Psychology: Research and Practice, 39*(4), 381–388.

Villagrán, D.e León, J. Carlos. (2006) Vulnerability: A conceptual and methodological review. UNU Institute for Environment and Human Security (UNU-EHS), No. 4. http://www.ehs.unu.edu/file/get/3904. Accessed 3 June 2012.

Watters, E. (2010). *Crazy like us: The globalization of the American psyche*. New York: Free Press.

Weichselgartner, J. (2001). Disaster mitigation: the concept of vulnerability revisited. *Disaster Prevention and Management, 10*(2), 85–94.

White, G. F. (1986). Human adjustment to floods. In R. W. Kates & I. Burton (Eds.), *Selected Writings of Gilbert F. White* (pp. 10–25). Chicago: University of Chicago Press.

Whiting, J., & Whiting, B. (1975). *Children of six cultures: A psychocultural analysis*. Cambridge: Harvard University Press.

Winter, G. (2013). The rise and fall of nuclear energy use in Germany: Processes, explanations and the role of law. *Journal of Environmental Law, 25*(1), 95–124.

Wisner, B., Blaikie, P., Cannon, T., & Davis, I. (2004). *At risk: Natural hazards, people's vulnerability and disasters* (2nd ed.). London: Routledge.

Wisner, B., Gaillard, J. C., & Kelman, I. (2012). Framing disaster: Theories and stories seeking to understand hazards, vulnerability and risk. In B. Wisner, J. C. Gaillard, & I. Kelman (Eds.), *Handbook of hazards and disaster risk reduction* (pp. 18–33). New York: Routledge.

Young, A. (2006). Trauma und Verarbeitung in den USA nach dem 11. September. Ein anthropologischer Blick auf virtuelle Traumata und Resilienz. In E. Wohlfart & M. Zaumseil (Eds.), *Transkulturelle Psychiatrie. Interkulturelle Psychotherapie. Interdisziplinäre Theorie und Praxis* (pp. 391–410). Heidelberg: Springer Medizin.

Zaman, M. Q. (1999). Vulnerability, disaster, and survival in Bangladesh: Three case studies. In A. Oliver-Smith, & S. M. Hoffman (Eds.), *The angry earth: Disaster in anthropological perspective* (pp. 192–212). New York: Routledge.

Zinn, J. O. (2010). Biography, risk and uncertainty: Is there common ground for biographical research and risk research? [59 paragraphs]. *Forum Qualitative Sozialforschung/ Forum: Qualitative Social Research, 11*(1), Art. 15., http://nbn-resolving.de/urn:nbn:de:0114-fqs1001153. Accessed 13 May 2013.

Zubin, J., & Spring, B. (1977). Vulnerability: A new view of schizophrenia. *Journal of Abnormal Psychology, 86*(2), 103–126.

Chapter 2
Understandings of Coping: A Critical Review of Coping Theories for Disaster Contexts

Manfred Zaumseil and Silke Schwarz

2.1 Introductory Review of Dominant Approaches

This chapter addresses the behavior, thoughts, experiences, and feelings of individuals who have been exposed to strain or stress. While Chap. 1 covered approaches to understanding and handling "natural" disasters, this chapter addresses the psychological and broader social science-based approaches to handling stress and strain. We then analyze these approaches to determine the extent to which they can be applied in a disaster-related context.

Historically, the subject of coping took root in the mainstream psychologies in the 1960s as a means to mitigate the negative consequences of stress (Folkman 2011). For a long time, the primary psychosocial consequences of disasters were viewed to be the harm and damage suffered by the individual. Generally speaking, an individual's stressful life circumstances were considered only in terms of their potential to negatively affect that individual's ability to function mentally, physically, and socially. It was only later that the positive aspects were recognized as well. Bonanno et al. (2010) and Masten and Narayan (2012) demonstrate the many different ways in which adaptive functioning can occur following a disaster. Under normal circumstances, disasters do not result in psychological and social collapse. In fact, they tend to yield a wide variety of trajectories, most of which are positive in nature. As a result, concepts such as resilience and competence became increasingly important, not only in the macrosocial field of disaster management (see Chap. 1) but also in the area of psychological functioning.

The mainstream psychological coping models can be seen as one specific way of looking at the process of handling strain. These models are similar to the goal-based models of human nature (Carver and Connor-Smith 2010), in which the basic

M. Zaumseil (✉) · S. Schwarz
International Academy for Innovative Pedagogy, Psychology and Economics gGmbH
at Freie Universität Berlin, Malteserstr. 74-100, 12249 Berlin, Germany
e-mail: zaumseil@zedat.fu-berlin.de

S. Schwarz
e-mail: silke.schwarz@fu-berlin.de; silgnschwarz@yahoo.de

M. Zaumseil et al. (eds.), *Cultural Psychology of Coping with Disasters*,
DOI 10.1007/978-1-4614-9354-9_2, © Springer Science+Business Media, LLC 2014

motivation of human beings is to move toward (that is, approach) goals while avoiding threats.

From the very beginning, one of the strengths of the psychological coping models was the fact that they were conceived to yield both positive and negative results. These models address both successful and unsuccessful attempts to manage challenges or threats. Another strength of these models is that they attempt to draw a connection between internal and external elements: with coping models, challenges and threats (internal and external, for example, sickness or an earthquake) and personal resources (internal and external, for example, a high perceived self-efficacy and a resource-rich social environment) are viewed as interrelated factors.

In the first part of this chapter, we examine psychological person-centered coping models (PCCMs; Sect. 2.2). We then explore models that emphasize a broader context (Sects. 2.3 and 2.4) which focus on social and material resources. The former represent the dominant models for stress research in the mainstream psychologies (Folkman 2011). Depending on the model in question, the main focus lies either in the cognitive processes of appraisal and emotion regulation (Sect. 2.2.1), attribution of meaning (Sect. 2.2.2), religious forms of coping (Sect. 2.2.3), future-oriented forms of coping (Sect. 2.2.4.), or on the conceptualization as a mental health problem (Sect. 2.2.5).

In contrast, the resource-oriented coping theory addressed in Sect. 2.3 places more emphasis on the social and material contextual features of stress processes. In these theories, stress is generally viewed as a loss of resources (Hobfoll 1998). In the field of community psychology and in research on social support, the social context and social interactions are more central components in considering an individual's ability to combat strain. Social support is examined both as a part of the PCCM approaches (as an individual mobilizable resource) (Sect. 2.2) as well as in approaches that adopt a more context-specific understanding of coping (Sect. 2.3).

Sociology and related social science specializations also feature models in which coping and the resilience of the community in question are studied as social or collective processes. This approach shows strong similarities with the perceptions of disaster management discussed in Chap. 1. When considering community resilience or the application of social capital, the coping capabilities of large social units (for example, villages and neighborhoods) are of primary importance (Sect. 2.4).

The diagram in Fig. 2.1 provides an overview of the numerous perspectives and dimensions covered by the approaches to coping developed in both psychological and social science contexts. The units of analysis vary in size and their interaction with stressful events can be examined over longer or shorter periods of time, as needed. The diagram displays the past or prior history of stressful and overwhelming experiences. A coping episode can also be selected as a unit of analysis for a particular individual. This episodic approach forms the basis for the most influential psychological model, the appraisal-oriented psychological approach (Lazarus and Folkman 1984). In newer approaches in developmental psychology, coping is viewed as an adaptive process associated with a potentially long-term series of interactions with a potentially challenging environment. These approaches take into account the fact that a series of stressful episodes can lead to changes both in the individual and in the

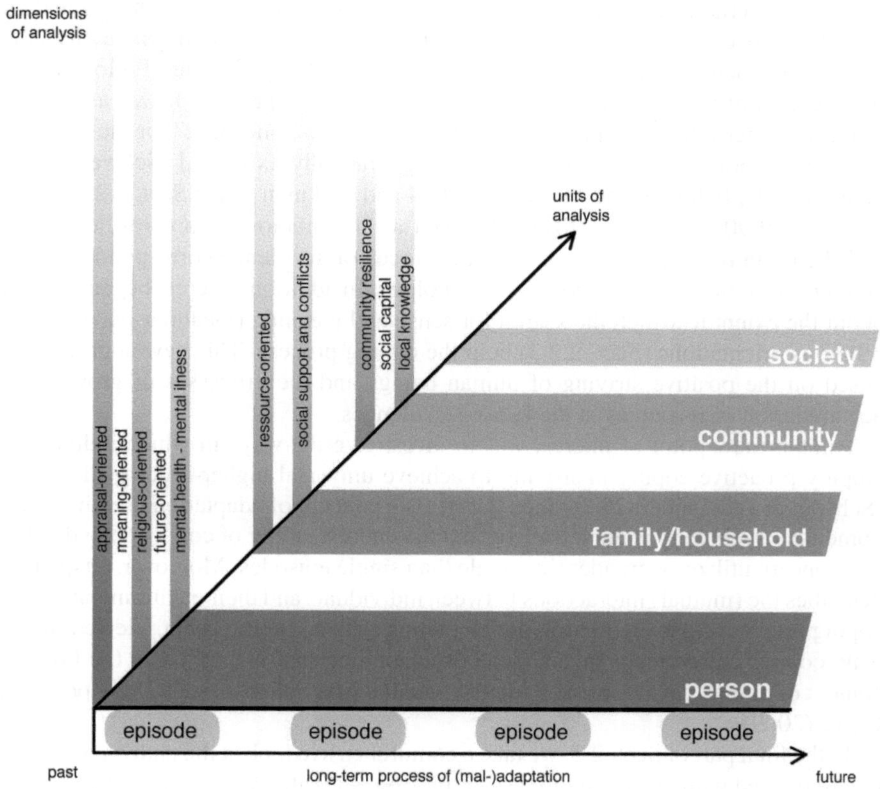

Fig. 2.1 Dimensions and Units of Analysis for Psychological and Sociological Approaches to Coping (DUPS)

environment itself (Skinner and Zimmer-Gembeck 2007; Leipold and Greve 2009). In addition, future-oriented coping is beginning to play an important role (Aspinwall and Taylor 1997; Schwarzer and Taubert 2002). Coping models that take the larger context into account include conceptualizations based on dyadic relationships as well as coping at the level of the household (as shown in the access model proposed by Wisner et al. 2004). Models of adaptation for larger social units in hazardous environments were introduced in Chap. 1. We draw upon these models at the end of this chapter.

2.2 Coping as an Individual Process

One of the most prominent individual approaches to understanding stress is the basic psychological model of coping (Lazarus 1966; Lazarus and Folkman 1984; Sect. 2.2.1). The development of this model led to a major boom in coping research as well as to extensive additions to the model. These revisions are briefly noted in

Fig. 2.1. In certain subfields of psychology (particularly those that concentrated on cognitive processes, health and illness, emotions, development, and personality), the coping approach continued to develop as it was applied to new issues. Following our introduction of the basic model, we address these developments. It was as a result of these changes, for example, that the understanding of "meaning" for the different cognitive appraisals in the context of coping gradually expanded (Schwarzer and Taubert 2002; Folkman and Moskowitz 2004 and Folkman 2011; Sect. 2.2.2).

In the 1990s, Folkman (2011) observed a reorientation toward resilience and well-being in research on stress. This new focus on resilience corresponded to the emergence of the branch of positive psychology. In addition, interest began to grow about the extent to which the search for sense and meaning (meaning-making) and religious orientations (Sect. 2.2.3) help the coping process. This new approach focused on the positive striving of human beings and the processes of growth and accumulation of resources in the face of challenges.

Another new point of interest was to investigate the ways in which individuals employ proactive coping in striving to achieve universal higher-order goals in life (Schwarzer and Taubert 2002; Sect. 2.2.4). The concept of adaptation used in developmental psychology is universalistic and the understanding of coping embedded in this concept utilizes a broader time scale than single episodes. Moreover, adaptation describes the (mutual) interactions between individuals and their environment, while coping refers exclusively to a single interaction with a specific event. Viewed in this way, coping represents a special type of adaptation that is applied to the broader context of human development by developmental psychologists such as Leipold and Greve (2009).

In the final part of Sect. 2.2, we take a comprehensive look at the pathways of coping associated with health and illness or, more specifically, with psychopathological categories and the need for therapeutic support. The process of coping with extreme suffering takes on a special status. Normally, this process is not addressed within the framework of general psychological coping literature and is instead treated as "trauma" in the branch of clinical psychology (Sect. 2.2.5).

2.2.1 Appraisal-Oriented Approaches

This aspect of the coping literature was developed in the 1960s in response to findings on the harmful effects of stress on health and well-being. The primary goal was to identify the factors that could potentially reduce these harmful effects. At first, these factors were purely person-centered; they were viewed as psychoanalytically inspired defense mechanisms and as stable properties of the personality like optimism or extraversion (see Carver and Connor-Smith 2010). This remained the dominant view until Lazarus (1966) proposed a model of coping based on the interactions between the individual and the situation, an approach that ultimately developed into the transactional cognitivist appraisal-oriented model of coping (Lazarus and Folkman 1984).

Person-centered approaches in this tradition claim universal generalizability and explain behavior from the perspective of the individual person. These approaches establish a connection between the external situation and the resources of the person in question. The coping process begins when the internal resources (for example, specific skills or abilities) and external mobilizable resources (for example, social support) no longer correspond to a demanding situation. This is then defined as a stress-inducing situation. One important turning point in what was previously an objective, behaviorist psychology was the assertion that this lack of correspondence was not determined *objectively*, but *subjectively*, by means of the cognitive appraisal of the individual exposed to the situation. This appraisal comprises the individual's subjective evaluation of both the demanding situation as well as the personal (internal) and external (social and material) resources (Schwarzer and Taubert 2002).

> Coping is defined as the person's constantly changing cognitive and behavioral efforts to manage specific external and/or internal demands that are appraised as taxing or exceeding the person's resources. (Folkman et al. 1986, p. 993)

According to Lazarus and Folkman (1984), in primary (or demand) appraisal, a person evaluates whether or not there is any challenge, threat, harm, or loss with respect to commitments, values, or goals in his or her interaction with the environment. In secondary (or resource) appraisal, the person evaluates what can be done to overcome or prevent harm or to improve his or her prospects for a beneficial outcome. With regard to personal resources, the individual's subjectively perceived competence (perceived self-efficacy) is considered to be crucial (Schwarzer and Taubert 2002).

A cognitive appraisal is an individual's evaluation of the significance of what is happening in the world for his or her personal well-being (Lazarus 1991). Coping comprises two distinct functions: the internal emotion-focused coping, which serves to regulate emotions, and the problem-focused (or instrumental) coping, which serves to change the problematic person–environment situation. Problem-focused coping changes the relationship between the person and his or her environment, while emotion-focused coping induces internal changes in a person's attention or personal meanings (Folkman and Lazarus 1988). Beginning with the appraisals, emotions accompany the entire coping process. Emotions are analyzed as cognitive systems with an orientation function and tied psychobiologically to an appraisal pattern (for example, sadness to the relational theme of irrevocable loss). Lazarus (1999) emphasizes that emotions are relatively quick reactions in that they flow from the way in which we appraise events as they occur and as more information becomes available:

> These appraisals are characterized by negative emotions that are often intense. [. . .] Emotions continue to be integral to the coping process throughout a stressful encounter as an outcome of coping, as a response to new information, and as a result of reappraisals of the status of the encounter. (Folkman and Moskowitz 2004, p. 747)

Subsequently, Lazarus (1991) incorporated coping into a complex cognitive–emotional system. According to Lazarus, the process of evaluating environmental situations triggers certain specific emotions that have evolved to benefit adaptation processes. In a debate with Shweder (1993) regarding the universality of emotions, Lazarus (1993) argued that while certain core themes remain constant in any culture, different cultures define specific criteria for identifying these themes (for example, the necessary criteria for defining a personal insult).

Since the introduction of the coping model, a multitude of types of coping strategies were studied which appeared to be similar in empirical studies despite being derived from very different theoretical frameworks. For example, Folkman and Lazarus (1980) distinguished problem-focused coping (active change of the situation) from emotion-focused coping (control of the negative feelings if the situation cannot be changed), but in practice the coping strategies that people use are often mixtures of these strategies that cannot be separated. Skinner et al. (2003) suggested viewing different forms of coping as action types and proposed that these coping forms are adaptive in relation to the environment, the social resources, and the individual's own preferences and orientations. Within this typology, they defined five core categories: "problem solving, support seeking, avoidance, distraction, and positive cognitive restructuring" (p. 239).

The deciding factor in the expansion of coping research was the fact that the newly developed measuring techniques opened up the coping construct to quantification and empirical testing. However, the elaborate coping theory proposed by Lazarus (1991) was difficult to operationalize and presented problems with regard to the stability, generality, and dimensionality of coping (Schwarzer and Schwarzer 1996). In addition, a quantitative, measurement-based approach is limited in its ability to investigate special properties, for example, cultural distinctiveness, and places far more emphasis on universally applicable systems of coping. Subjectivity and subjective meanings are reduced to highly simplified elements (see Shweder 1993). Constructions are understood as part of a private, idiosyncratic process which has its universal roots in the core relational themes of the accompanying emotions. Both are anchored in a biological evolutionary adaptation model. According to Lazarus (1991, 1999), while meaning does not emerge from the sociocultural sphere, it is certainly modified by variables within this area.

2.2.2 Meaning-Oriented Approaches

Lazarus (1991, 1999) abandoned the behavioral model in which mind and behavior were seen solely as a response to environmental stimuli. He suggested examining the relationship between person and environment and introduced a relational perspective. Threat is viewed as a relational meaning that "a person constructs from the confluence of personality and environmental variables" (Lazarus 1999, p. 12) and "appraisal refers to the evaluative process by which the relational meaning is constructed" (p. 13).

Park (2010) further expounded upon the conception of meaning defined in the appraisal-based coping approach: *meaning-making* refers to the processes people utilize in order to reduce the discrepancy between their appraised situational meaning and global beliefs and goals. It also refers to the development of explanations for varied reactions to adversity and a key distinction is between global and situational meanings. Another construct, *benefit-finding*, relates to the process of identifying benefits in adversity. It refers to perceptions of change as measured by self-report instruments (Pakenham 2011).

Global meaning refers to the individual's general system of orientation. Global meanings form the core schemas through which people interpret their experience of the world. They comprise beliefs, global goals, and a subjective sense of meaning and purpose. *Situational meaning* is appraised in the context of a particular environmental encounter. Situational meanings focus on the question of whether a particular event is threatening or controllable as well as on the causes of the event, and any implications it might have for the future (Park 2010). According to Park (2010), a discrepancy between appraised situational meaning and global meaning will create distress and result in an intense motivation to reduce this discrepancy through meaning-making. This process makes it possible for an individual to recover from a stressful event. Meaning-making is therefore both an automatic, unconscious process as well as an active coping activity. Automatic processes include, for example, intrusive thoughts about the stressful event and avoidance of reminders, among other things. Active coping may include identity-related appraisals. In some cases, these appraisals may lead to feelings of shame, guilt, or pride (Tracy and Robins 2004).[1]

If the situational appraised meaning is changed as a result, this phenomenon is referred to as assimilation; if global beliefs and goals are changed, this is known as accommodation. The process of meaning-making implies a cognitive component (integrating experience with preexisting schemas) as well as an emotional processing component (experiencing and exploring emotions). The foundation for viewing changes in the external situation versus internal changes to the individual was already established in the distinction between problem-focused versus emotion-focused coping (Lazarus and Folkman 1984). However, in the recent conceptualization, meaning—along with emotion—assumes a more important role. Brandtstädter (2006), Leipold and Greve (2009), and Brandtstädter (2011), for example, expanded the relationship between accommodation and assimilation into a dual-process model of developmental regulation. Given the dramatic changes to the environment, accommodative processes are critical, meaning that individuals' life goals are modified to correspond with the actual situation.

Park (2010) points out that the mere search for meaning in the face of a catastrophic experience may not necessarily be beneficial to the health of the individual. Rumination may involve repetitive thoughts that introduce negative emotions without identifying a solution. The deciding factors are the products of the meaning-making process (*meanings made*). These meanings result in the subjective sense of having *made sense*. This may include a feeling of acceptance, a perception of growth and

[1] For example, a man may be proud that he has coped successfully by fulfilling the social expectations of a man or as the head of a household. Another man may feel a sense of shame with respect to his male identity because of ongoing fear or difficulty managing extreme emotions (Tracy and Robins 2004).

positive life changes, as well as the integration of the event into the identity of the individual. Park (2010) states that while there are complex constructs of meaning in theory, the operationalization of meaning-making efforts and *meanings made* tend to be rather simplistic. Although one of the central assumptions is that highly stressful events cause a *shattering* (Janoff-Bulman 1992) of the general orienting system and global meaning, there is little evidence to indicate that this shattering actually takes place. However, "it is clear that meaning-making attempts and meanings made are reported by most individuals facing highly stressful events" (Park 2010, p. 290).

Examples of Meaning-Making in the Context of Disasters Garrison and Sasser (2009) conducted a qualitative investigation of benefit-finding and meaning-making in families who recovered from the impact of Hurricane Katrina and were able to return to their houses. In their study, a number of different factors were included under the heading of benefit-finding: improved relationships within the family, insight into the importance of building relationships with people rather than objects, and pride about successful coping. The study found that sense-making resulted in the insights that "everything has a reason" (p. 118) and that the "storm taught us to see the important things" (p. 118). Attribution to a higher power could mean that "God had his reason" (p. 118; reference to God by 37 % of respondents) or that respondents "interfered with mother Nature" (p. 118). Less than half of the interviewees expressed a "general acceptance" (p. 118) of the storms. Additionally, most of the respondents expressed optimism with regard to their futures and the authors found that humor played an important role in meaning-making.

One interesting question inquires as to whether such challenges can be accepted as mixed experiences. The Western model is one in which the aim is to reduce negative emotions and increase positive emotions. In contrast, Eastern or Asian approaches to emotions often allow for mixed emotional experiences, which combine both positive and negative aspects, to be accepted without attempting to unify these aspects or reduce negative emotions. This acceptance may make it easier to cope with the range of personal and social experiences inherent to the most difficult of circumstances. It is still unclear whether research on stress and disasters supports this view on mixed emotions (what Miyamoto et al. 2010 and Miyamoto and Ryff 2011 call *dialectical emotions*).

In a similar study on the subject of faith, crisis, coping, and meaning-making conducted by Marks et al. (2009), four different age groups were compared in order to draw conclusions about the relationship between disaster and psychological development. Respondents in the younger age groups (average age 37–54) viewed the storm Katrina that occurred 3–6 months and 6–14 months prior to the study primarily as a crisis (in the sense of a developmental challenge or turning point), while respondents from the older age groups (average age 74–91) tended to view the storm as an additional life experience. Respondents attributed the storm to God and "Mother Nature." One prevalent idea was that hurricanes served as a lesson in humility from which people had to learn to accept a lack of control. However, it is striking that both religious and nonreligious respondents shared the view that it is important to do their best in the face of their struggles and, ultimately, to make the best of the situation.

2.2.3 Religious-Oriented Approaches

Religious coping has two contrasting dimensions: It not only can be seen as a specialized type of meaning-oriented approach to coping, but also represents far more than a search for meaning in situations of stress. Religious coping is often associated with special types of social integration; it is also related to the idea of social support. Orientations, beliefs, and practices associated with spiritual or religious life exert a significant influence upon the appraisal processes and coping strategies.

Spirituality is generally defined as an introspective, individual experience while *religiosity* describes a community experience. These two ideas are related, rather than being independent constructs. Through a combination of both constructs, individuals are able to seek support from a divine being as well as from other members of a religious community, make meaning in the face of distressing events, and ultimately promote resilience, healing, and well-being (Bryant-Davis et al. 2012).

According to Pargament (2011), religion adds a distinctive dimension to the coping process. In his view, religion is the search for significance in the sacred (Pargament 2011) and "religious coping is a search for significance in times of stress" (Pargament 1997, p. 90). The sacred is the common denominator in both religious and spiritual life. It represents the most important objective sought by religious-spiritual individuals, and, as such, is tightly interwoven in the course of their lives (Hill and Pargament 2008). *Sacred* refers not only to God and higher powers, but indeed to any element that is tied to God and therefore "imbued with spiritual qualities like transcendence, boundlessness and ultimacy" (Pargament 2011, p. 272).

The idea of a universalist conception of religiosity, which is independent of contextual and cultural associations and serves as a universal property of humanity, blossomed in the 1980s and 1990s in line with the development of a number of instruments for measuring religiosity (see Hill and Hood 1999). Pargament (1997, 2011) and Pargament et al. (2000) postulated that, during stressful life events, common religious beliefs can be translated into specific methods of coping. They not only showed how different religions opt for different systems of coping, they also demonstrated how the same religion, applied to different cultural contexts, might stimulate completely different methods of coping with painful and difficult life events. Pargament (1997), like Park (2010; see earlier discussion), states that people bring their own personal *orientation systems* to bear on stressful situations. This orientation system is the special way in which a particular individual perceives and interacts with the world: "It consists of habits, values, relationships, generalized beliefs and personality" (Pargament 1997, 99 f.). Religious orientation makes up a part of this comprehensive orientation system. The culture helps to shape the coping mechanism and is itself reshaped by these forms of coping. However, Pargament's universalist, person-centered approach makes only minor concessions toward relativizing the culture-specific differences between the world religions.

According to Pargament (2011), every religious coping effort has a common end, that is, to enhance significance. This can be done by conserving or transforming significance. With conservation, the emphasis is on protecting or maintaining that which is of significance. With transformation, significance is maximized by attempts to change the nature of significance itself (Pargament 1997). This concept is very similar to the ideas of assimilation and accommodation used in the meaning-making approach (see Park 2010) as well as to the developmental approaches to coping (see Leipold and Greve 2009). According to Pargament, transformations take place only on an individual basis within the religious belief systems. Believers first seek to interpret the events they encounter in ways that allow them to conserve and confirm their existing meanings. It is only in extreme situations that they then seek to modify or transform the beliefs that make sense to them (for example, in the case of conversion or disavowal of previous beliefs).

The search for meaning filters and influences the interpretation of the situation. The system of religious beliefs, which is in turn a part of the general person-specific belief system, mediates between the situation at hand and the solution to the problem. Pargament portrays this accepted religious belief system (insofar as it is related to coping) as an array of opinions that are shared to variable and measurable degrees by the adherents of that system.

Difficulties arise in the religious coping approaches when it comes to gaining mastery and control because one subcategory of religious coping is relinquishment of control. Cole and Pargament (1999) discuss the paradox of the phenomenon of *spiritual surrender* in which people do their best while still relinquishing control to the higher being. They see this phenomenon as a universal response offered by many religions as an answer to human limitations. As part of this practice, person-centered control itself is surrendered in order to attain emotional and spiritual objectives (Cole and Pargament 1999). We believe that the authors transcend the cognitivist coping model (see Sect. 2.2.1) when they write, "spiritual surrender is much more than a cognitive shift. It is an experiential shift as well, one that involves changes in motivation, affect, values, perception, thought, and behavior" (p. 185).

According to Pargament (1997), the most helpful varieties of religious coping are those associated with a perception of God as supportive and feelings that God is loving and should be trusted to care for one's burdens. Perceptions of God as benevolent are particularly beneficial for coping. For some people, perceptions of a partnership with God are advantageous, and many derive strength from their religious communities. The social support they receive can ease the burden of coping. Overall, those aspects of religious coping were the only ones Pargament considered to be generally advantageous. Other forms of religious coping such as pleading—that is seeking control indirectly by pleading to God for a miracle or a divine intervention—appear to have either mixed or predominantly negative effects (similar to the view of God as punisher).

2.2.4 *Future-Oriented Coping*

Future-oriented coping is founded on the basic theoretical assumptions of the appraisal-oriented model introduced in this chapter and refers to an individual's strategies for handling future threats and challenges. In this respect, this type of coping represents one psychological approach to risk management. We addressed the collective dimensions of the topic of disaster risk in Chap. 1. We determined that it is difficult to assess the sociocultural-specific ways in which individuals handle risk using existing universalist models.

In the psychological coping research, future-oriented behavior was primarily analyzed in the context of individual health threats. Psychological models were developed with the aim of achieving universal validity. In the field of health promotion, there are both collective and individual strategies for handling risk. In a Western context, there is a heavy focus on the latter approach as well as on the rational control paradigm. It is with this in mind that Schwarzer et al. (2003) formulated the individual stages of the motivational and volitional process in their health action process model.

In the case of both disaster risk management and health-related action, there is still only a tentative relationship between the perception of a risk and the practical action taken to counter this risk. The assumption is that there are a series of universal psychological mechanisms that prevent precautionary behavior. Slovic and Västfjäll (2010) have shown that intuitive action in risk situations can lead to confusion and irrational behavior. Gigerenzer (2008) and Kahneman (2011) analyzed the weaknesses (and strengths) of risk heuristics and demonstrated that it is extremely difficult to weigh up multiple risks simultaneously. Because the perception of a potential threat causes unpleasant feelings, the individual turns to the process of wishful thinking (Lazarus and Folkman 1984). As a result of this process, the individual begins to assume that the threat is not serious or that he or she will not be affected. This corresponds to what is referred to as the optimism bias in risk perception (see Chap. 1). In some cases, a positive illusion in the form of unrealistic optimism was identified (that is, situations in which people believe they will be personally immune to a disaster, such as an impending earthquake; Burger and Palmer 1992). In another strategy, the individual associates any potential effects of the threat with external conditions rather than with his or her own behavior.

On a theoretical level, there are different conceptions of future-oriented coping known as *proactive coping*, that is, a "process of anticipating potential stressors and acting in advance either to prevent them or to mute their impact" (Aspinwall 2011, p. 334). In their conceptualization of proactive coping, Aspinwall and Taylor (1997) and Aspinwall (2011) propose a five-step model of future-oriented coping. This process starts with a general move toward resource accumulation. The process continues with the identification of potential stressors, the initial appraisal of their potential for threat, and the regulation of any accompanying negative emotions. Preliminary coping efforts are focused on relieving or diminishing the effect of the stressor as well as eliciting feedback and using it to regulate the initial appraisal and preliminary coping efforts. Proactive coping as an individual endeavor has mainly developed in the context of threats to health; however, it has also been extended to threats in the fields of work, aging, and social relations. Although Aspinwall (2011) suggests that proactive coping should be extended to stressors in dyadic relations or families as well as to large-scale collective proactive coping problems, this theoretical framework has yet to be developed.

Schwarzer and Taubert (2002) propose a different, more differentiated terminology. Their terminology takes into account not only the timeline of the threat but also the certainty (or uncertainty) of the risk. This is an important dimension in the context of disasters because some disasters such as earthquakes develop rapidly and the effects are unpredictable. In this model, along with *reactive coping*, which relates to an event in the past, there are three additional forms of coping: preventive coping, anticipatory coping, and proactive coping. With *preventive coping*, a critical event may or may not occur in the distant future. This type of coping is associated with uncertainty and requires the management of unknown risks. This model corresponds to Aspinwall's (2011) definition of proactive coping. *Anticipatory coping* refers to a certain, imminent threat. In contrast, the concept of proactive coping proposed by Schwarzer and Taubert (2002) is not directly associated with a threat; instead, it is an "effort to build up general resources that facilitate promotion toward challenging goals and personal growth. In proactive coping, people have a vision" (p. 28). In this reading of *proactive coping*, future-oriented behavior is not dependent upon a threat. Goal management, rather than risk management, is central to this understanding. The focus of self-regulatory goal management is an active engagement with challenges and "ambitious goal setting and tenacious goal pursuit" (p. 29). Schwarzer and Taubert (2002) therefore categorize lifestyle choices characterized by active, future-oriented planning and accumulation of resources as coping behaviors.

In positive psychology, future-oriented behavior has increasingly been conceived of as separate from risk and threat. In this field, eustress is conducive to development and perceived as a positive challenge. If we view the selection and accumulation of skills and resources as strategies for self-regulatory goal management in the process of individual striving, the individual's stock of resources will make the individual more resilient in the event of a disaster. However, to date there has been little research on the relationship between the cultural context, and environments with fewer resources, and an individual's perceptions of the future.

Future orientations can be viewed as a part of future-oriented coping and developmental psychology as well. In these fields, they are understood as multidimensional processes that combine motivational, cognitive, and behavioral components (Kotter-Grühn and Smith 2011; Seginer 2008). Future orientations tend to be associated with hope, even under stressful circumstances, and, according to Seginer (2008), these attitudes comprise both culturally specific as well as universal components. Seginer shows that individuals who are part of collective societies (see Sect. 2.4) are able to draw upon the goals of their community as a reservoir of communal or religious ideologies that have been practiced since childhood. In contrast, individuals from individualistic societies have less community-based support and must find and pursue their own personal goals.

Resilience has come to serve as a bridge concept between episodic periods of coping and the lifelong objective of human development. Leipold and Greve (2009) understand development as "the maintenance and implementation of the individual's abilities to use regulation processes to adapt to a challenging situation" (p. 42) and resilience as "successfully overcoming adverse developmental conditions" (p. 40). Following Brandtstädter (2011), there are two equivalent transformation processes working in tandem as part of episodic coping and lifelong development: the first is an intentional, personal assimilative mode in which the individual's life situation is brought into alignment with his or her expectations and goals. The second is a sub-personal accommodative mode which involves revising standards and goals to suit the given possibilities for action. According to Brandtstädter (2011), neither mode has primacy. He criticizes prior coping research, which, in his view, focuses mainly on the persistent pursuit of goals while neglecting the accommodative processes. Leipold and Greve (2009) limit intentional, planned agency by viewing the entire accommodative mode as sub-personal, that is, as a regulation process that takes place partially outside of the individual's personal control, and which, to some extent, is not accessible to the individual on a conscious level. Accommodative processes are necessary when a threat is unavoidable or when a challenge cannot be faced; they play an important role in the individual's ability, for example, to successfully handle the aging process. Developmental psychologists have shown that older individuals modify their life goals and meanings in such a way as to create a kind of well-being paradox: in spite of their limited opportunities (and potential illness), they are relatively content with their lives (Baltes 1997; Kotter-Grühn and Smith 2011).

2.2.5 *Impacts of Extreme Stress on Mental Health*

Following the changes in general coping theory and research, there also has been a considerable shift in the perspective on the impacts of extreme stress on mental health. In the beginning, the field of *disaster psychology* (see Reyes and Jacobs 2006) was identical to the fields of mental health disorders after a disaster and trauma psychology. Since the 1990s, there has been a gradual expansion in the perspective which focuses on the diversity of human responses to extreme stress. Prior to that development, this diversity was buried in trauma discourse, which, with the introduction of the posttraumatic stress disorder (PTSD) diagnosis to the Diagnostic and Statistical Manual of Mental Disorders (DSM III 1980) by the American Psychiatric Association, dominated the psychological research and practice of the time (see Bonanno et al. 2010). The reemergence of this diversity focused on the following aspects:

- Typically, there is a considerable amount of diversity in the longitudinal trajectories of responses to stress including resistance, resilience, recovery, and delayed and persistent dysfunction (Norris et al. 2009).
- Severe manifestations of problems are observed only in a small percentage of exposed individuals (Bonanno et al. 2010).
- Aside from PTSD, disasters may result in other psychological problems such as depression, anxiety, grief, stress-related health problems, substance abuse, and suicidal behavior (Bonanno et al. 2010)

- There is a cultural specificity in responses to extreme stress. These were studied as *idioms of distress* or *cultural syndromes*, triggering a discussion about the cross-cultural validity of PTSD (Hinton and Lewis-Fernandez 2011).

The concept of trauma originated in the context of the two world wars. Extreme suffering was then designated as PTSD in the American diagnostic system (DSM III, then IV and V), thereby laying claim to universal validity. One prerequisite for a PTSD diagnosis is a clearly defined traumatic event. A traumatic event in this sense implies an exposure to a threat of death or grievous bodily injury directed toward an individual or another person. Symptoms of this syndrome include intrusive distressing memories, dreams and flashbacks of the traumatic event(s), and distress at exposure to trauma-related triggers. Additional criteria include negative changes to cognition, mood, arousal, and reactivity. Disturbances cause significant distress and impairment of function which persists for longer than 1 month.

The categorial illness or disorder systems utilized by international classification bodies require universally applicable divisions between sick and healthy individuals. With PTSD, however, the assumption tends to be that there is no qualitative difference with respect to normal processes. According to Bonanno et al. (2011), PTSD is best understood as a continuous dimension and the "specification of a diagnostic cut-point will always be arbitrary to some extent" (p. 513).

The universally constructed psychological explanations take different disruptions in memory (Brewin 2011) as well as emotional and cognitive processing into account (Foa and Rothbaum 1998; Ehlers and Clark 2000; Steil et al. 2003). However, according to Pitman et al. (2012) and Schmahl (2009), the field has yet to identify the definitive disorder model. On a phenomenological level, in the psychiatric literature (for example, Friedman et al. 2011) it has been proven that exposure to a wide variety of different traumatic events (disasters, violent experiences resulting from war, accidents, and rape) results in the same consistently identifiable pattern of disturbances (ensuring coherence and reliability of PTSD identification).

In their broad overview of the costs of disaster for individuals, families, and communities, Bonanno et al. (2010) showed that the psychological cost for survivors (especially the number of PTSD cases) had been overestimated in the literature, whereas the broader impact in other areas had been underestimated. Norris et al. (2002a, b) and Norris (2005) published a comprehensive review and meta-analysis of the empirical literature and concluded:

> Samples were more likely to be impaired if they were composed of youth rather than adults, were from developing rather than developed countries, or experienced mass violence (for example, terrorism, shooting sprees) rather than natural or technological disasters. [...] Within adult samples, more severe exposure, female gender, middle age, ethnic minority status, secondary stressors, prior psychiatric problems, and weak or deteriorating psychosocial resources most consistently increased the likelihood of adverse outcomes. (Norris et al. 2002a, p. 207)

Bonanno et al. (2011) estimate that 5–10 % of individuals exposed to these conditions developed a PTSD. If the exposure is particularly intense and persists over an extended period of time, the rate may increase, although it seldom rises above 30 %. Hobfoll (2011), on the other hand, disputes these figures and criticizes the "initial optimism about how many people are resilient in the face of major stress" (p. 128) with references to the high numbers of mental health problems found in his study of distress during the ongoing terrorism in Israel (Hobfoll et al. 2012). Bonanno et al. (2011) argue that most studies that demonstrate higher numbers of PTSD involve the faulty application of diagnostic methods by emphasizing average differences in a number of symptoms between exposed and nonexposed groups, for instance. Other mental disorders, problems, or impairments may accompany PTSD or become dominant disorders. These phenomena may include grief, depression, anxiety, stress-related health problems, increased substance abuse, and suicidal ideation. The more serious occurrences of these problems tend be under 30 % of a population directly affected by a potentially traumatic event (Bonanno et al. 2010).

The decisive turning point in the study of the psychological repercussions of disasters was proposed by Norris et al. (2009) and Bonanno et al. (2010). Their approaches no longer rely on the frequency of identified cases of illness following a disaster; instead, they focus on the analysis of longitudinal and other trajectories of successful or unsuccessful adaptation in the wake of a disaster. In this approach, resistance is equated with no dysfunction, resilience with a transient perturbation for several weeks, and recovery with dysfunction followed by a return to pre-event functioning (Bonanno 2004). Symptoms may display a cyclical course or emerge after a considerable amount of time (Norris et al. 2009). In chronic dysfunction, the initial stress reaction persists.

This thinking along the lines of trajectories resulted in a theoretical and methodological shift in research on the psychological consequences of disasters (Bonanno and Mancini 2012). Specifically, Hobfoll (2011) demonstrated that PTSD is not necessarily accompanied by dysfunction:

> People may experience distress and disease and yet remain committed and absorbed in their life tasks as parents, partners, workers, citizens, and friends. (Hobfoll 2011, p. 128)

The concept of posttraumatic growth (PTG) focuses on the ostensibly counterintuitive and paradoxical finding of apparent gain as a result of the negative experience, that is, that people may experience a significant positive change in life and new meaning (Tedeschi and Calhoun 2004). In the field of positive psychology (Snyder and Lopez 2011), this phenomenon is viewed in terms of its positive effects:

> Posttraumatic growth is the experience of positive change that occurs as a result of the struggle with highly challenging life crises. It is manifested in a variety of ways, including an increased appreciation for life in general, more meaningful interpersonal relationships, an increased sense of personal strength, changed priorities, and a richer existential and spiritual life. (Tedeschi and Calhoun 2004, p. 1)

The processes that occur after an experience of extreme stress are now viewed as diverse phenomena and are no longer focused on disease and dysfunction. Research on resistance, resilience, and adaptability has enabled stronger connections to be established between coping concepts and the topics of development and future orientations. However, many studies equate a decreasing severe-to-moderate symptom trajectory with resilience (by Norris et al. 2009 or by Hobfoll et al. 2008), meaning that it is defined from a negative, rather than a positive, standpoint. In addition, studies also often refer to *partial* or *subliminal* PTSD, thereby increasing pathologization as well as the need for individual therapy (Young 2006). We address different cultural understandings of human suffering and other responses to disasters in Chap. 3.

2.3 Individual Coping Within Social Contexts

When researching human responses to disasters, the disciplinary context influences the formulation of the research question and determines the form of investigation: The mainstream psychological approaches referenced in Sect. 2.2 focus on identifying generalizable rules which are rooted in human mental structures and reflected in social behavior. The individual is the focal point. From a social science perspective, the approach is reversed. The goal is to determine the extent to which individual experiences and actions are affected and produced by sociocultural conditions and topics. Models that rely on a complex interplay—or a reciprocal structure—between the individual and the social represent a synthesis between mainstream psychological models and social science-based models. These models are examined in Sect. 2.4.

Only a few of the psychological approaches focus more on context and emphasize the social embedding of individual behavior, although constructs such as social support and social conflict are becoming influential. In the theoretical approaches by Hobfoll (2001, 2011) and Hobfoll and Buchwald (2004), the conservation of resources theory, coping is explained primarily from the viewpoint of human nature. However, in his integration of real sociocultural and material conditions, Hobfoll demonstrates that the stress process must be understood as a complex set of interactions between these elements.

2.3.1 A Resource-Oriented Approach

The stress coping theory proposed by Hobfoll (2001, 2011), Hobfoll and Buchwald (2004), and Hobfoll et al. (2011) focuses on the objective elements of threat, loss, and common appraisals rather than subjective, idiographic appraisals. In this way, they ensure that exclusive focus is not placed on the individual and prevent the theoretic–analytical dissociation of the individual from his or her sociocultural and material contexts. The theory is based on the premise that human beings will strive for resource gains, that is, for things they value most highly. Value is attributed to resources based on the specific cultural context. These resources may be considered worthy in and of themselves or because they promote the retention or acquisition of other resources:

> Resources include object resources (for example car, house), condition resources (for example employment, marriage), personal resources (for example key skills and personal traits such as self-efficacy and self esteem) and energy resources (for example credit, knowledge, money). (Hobfoll 2011, p. 128)

The list of particular resources mirrors the diversity of cultural settings with their individualistic and collective ideals. Hobfoll (2001) uses a cultural term with a hierarchical structure of *individual-nested and family-nested in tribe*. Here, he is referring to Boas (1940).

Resource loss is an important component in the stress process, and it receives a disproportionate amount of emphasis in comparison with resource gain. This principle is known as *loss primacy*. The second principle—termed *resource investment*—is future oriented. This principle posits that individuals invest resources in order to protect themselves from loss, recover from loss, or acquire new resources. This process results in a pool of resources which Hobfoll terms *resource caravans*. Families and individuals are dependent upon resource-enriching environments; otherwise "they fail to develop their resource caravans mainly out of circumstances that are beyond their and their families' control" (Hobfoll 2011, p. 129). Those who possess resources are more capable of gain, and this leads to further gain. However, loss cycles will be more influential than gain cycles. If the loss of resources continues, individuals become increasingly vulnerable to the effects of stress and fall into a spiral of loss, a process that can have serious consequences. In situations of loss, a paradoxical, opposite process comes into play; here, the salience of gain increases in situations of resource loss. This process, which Hobfoll (2011) refers to as third principle, is reported to play a role in traumatic situations and resiliency efforts.

The Conservation of Resources (COR) theory is less an input–output model of coping with stress than a model for the commerce of stress and resources within social contexts. In this model, both successful and unsuccessful adaptation may occur. In this broader context, the episodes of coping are viewed as adaptation processes. In Hobfoll's model, social support is a valuable resource which is closely related to resiliency. The theory offers an understanding of coping that sees individualistic and communal coping as a continuum:

> We need to widen the social aspects of coping efforts and move from self-regulation to self-in social settings regulation. (Hobfoll 1998, p. 130)

According to Hobfoll (1998), there is a *stress crossover* between individuals within the community; that is, the stress experienced by one person influences the stress experienced by another person, a partly involuntary sharing of resource loss. He also analyzes the dynamics of intragroup stress and the different demands within the community (between those who are stronger and those who are weaker in the group or community). In addition to stress crossover, there is also a transfer or crossover of resources. Hobfoll and Buchwald (2004) explain the common sharing of resources by describing the barriers between different individuals within a community to be more or less permeable.

He does not use a typology to represent the different ways of coping. Instead, he relies on a multiaxial model in which individuals are characterized by their position along the axes. On the first axis, we find the degree of coping activity; this axis spans from very active, through cautious action, to passive avoidance. The second axis represents the dimension of prosocial versus antisocial coping. In prosocial coping, the individual seeks social support and mutual cooperation. In antisocial coping, the individual strives to obtain advantages at the cost of others. On the third axis, which incorporates findings from Japan, a country representing rather inter-connected selves, besides American findings representing predominantly autonomous and independent selves, Hobfoll introduces a distinction between direct and indirect coping strategies. Indirect action is often found in communities that strive to maintain harmony. It is a diplomatic–strategic form of action. An individual acts in such a way as to disguise the intentions of this action from his or her interaction partner. This way, the individual will not lose face if he or she makes a mistake (Hobfoll 1998).

According to Hobfoll (1998), the COR theory can incorporate the idea that coping actions represent not only individual but also collective actions: In this model, actions are embedded in a historical and cultural context, and assessments are not made independently by single individuals, but in fact represent large-scale perceptual and interpretive structures that are shared within the community. This applies to the perceived meaning, relevance, and threats associated with a particular situation as well as to the perception of the individual coping efforts and, in particular, the collective coping efforts, surrounding the situation.

2.3.2 Social Support and Social Conflict

The concept of social support has also begun to draw more attention in mainstream psychology; however, it is important to note that the different approaches to stress each incorporate different conceptualizations of social support:

> [Social support] may be regarded as resources provided by others, as coping assistance, as an exchange of resources, or even as a personality trait. Several types of social support have been investigated, such as instrumental or tangible (assist with a problem, donate goods), informational (give advice), and emotional (offer reassurance, listen empathetically). (Schwarzer and Knoll 2007, p. 244)

Social support was integrated into the appraisal-oriented stress approaches and assumed a functional role as one resource factor. Evidence from studies in the field of individual health and illness shows that support has an indirect enabling effect on coping. It increases perceived self-efficacy, which in turn improves an individual's potential to obtain support from social networks. In dyadic relationships, Schwarzer and Knoll (2007) observed a resource transfer from the individual providing the support to the individual receiving it. In the approach proposed by Schwarzer and Knoll, when considering coping in couples in which one partner suffers from severe illness, the focus lies not on the shared process of coping with a severe illness, but rather on the ways in which the sufferer perceives the support provided and the effectiveness of this support. In this respect, an individual's subjective appraisal remains as the dominant function in appraisal-oriented coping.

However, divergent interests and social conflicts are difficult to model from a social support perspective. Hobfoll (1998) states that the availability of social support is dependent upon power and status. According to him, certain people are nested in settings which offer them rank and privilege. Those lacking in status and power suffer social discrimination almost independently of their own behavior. However, those with power, status, and privilege are faced with developmental conditions—Hobfoll refers to these as "caravan passageways" (Hobfoll 2011, p. 129)— which lead to social exclusion. The concept of passageways can be extended to neighborhoods, work environments, and other contexts. These passageways are responsible for an individual's access to cultural capital, material goods (for example, inheritance), and social support. The mastery and self-efficacy attributed to individuals is therefore viewed as a function of their positions in a privileged passageway for their resource caravans (Hobfoll 2011). The individual's ability to seek social support is dependent upon the availability of this support in a real context, a factor which tends to be neglected in the various appraisal-oriented coping approaches.

The concept of social support has influenced the practice of disaster psychology, that is, interventions to prevent PTSD by education about what to expect rather than reliving the experience such as was the case in critical incident stress debriefing. Kaniasty and Norris (1993), Norris et al. (2005), and Kaniasty (2012) developed a model to illustrate how different subgroups of disaster survivors experience social support or a lack thereof. This model is connected to Hobfoll's COR theory. The authors differentiate between the constructs of *social embeddedness* (quantity and types of relationships with others), *received support* (actual receipt of help), and *perceived support* (the belief that help would be available if needed).[2] Specific properties of the disaster, such as severity of exposure and displacement as a result of the disaster are relevant to the social support dynamics in coping efforts. The authors proposed a social support deterioration model (Kaniasty and Norris 1993) that they continued to develop over a series of studies on different disaster types (for latest results, see Kaniasty 2012). The model aims to generate general predictions about the dynamic social processes at work after disasters. It links both social support and social conflict with factors such as distress, trauma, and well-being. The model starts with the often-reported finding that "natural" disasters elicit the provision of widespread mutual aid and support. The social support deterioration deterrence model predicts that the experience of having received social support in the initial period of solidarity will distort the perception of reality in which social support is actually deteriorating. According to the model, this exaggeration of perceived available support is the reason behind feelings of well-being or reduced distress and pathology. Postdisaster social bitterness may emerge due to dissatisfaction with aid, social support, interpersonal constraints, and conflicts, leading to increased distress and pathology (Kaniasty 2012).

The sociological approaches to social conflicts and the resolution of these conflicts are more generalized:

> Social conflict [is] a struggle over values or claims to status, power, and scarce resources, in which the aims of the conflict groups are not only to gain the desired values, but also to neutralize, injure, or eliminate rivals. (Coser 1967, p. 232)

[2] It is important to note that the actual amount of support received as determined by the investigation is a value provided by the respondent, not an objectively determined quantity.

In conflict resolution theory and practice, there is an ongoing discussion about the universality or cultural specificity of ideas of fairness and justice (Deutsch 2000). The crucial factor in postdisaster settings is distributive justice:

> [It] is concerned with the fair allocation of resources among diverse members of a community. Fair allocation typically takes into account the total amount of goods to be distributed, the distributing procedure, and the pattern of distribution that results. (Maiese 2003)

Wagner-Pacifici and Hall (2012) see the issue of power as a crucial aspect in conflict resolution. Preconflict power relations also factor into postdisaster dynamics. The authors point to the difference between the resolution of a conflict and mere end of the conflict. Both concepts may play an important role in postdisaster conflicts (especially in dealing with possible conflicts along the helping process) as part of the long-term communal process of coping with disaster. The authors question whether reaching a resolution is always desirable. In their introduction to the approach of conflict transformation utilized by Mahatma Gandhi, Kurtz and Ritter (2011) write:

> Resolution carried with it a danger of cooptation (Gleichschaltung), an attempt to get rid of conflict when people were raising important and legitimate issues.

Reconciliation processes may also mean that people are no longer given a position to air their grievances. People may be expected not to raise issues of injustice anymore which helps to maintain the status quo instead of allowing for renegotiation for a more just social system. While, for some, participating in reconciliation practices may generate solidarity and even community pride which, in turn, affords healing, others may feel excluded or more isolated.

2.4 Coping as a Social Process

The individual-subjective perspective in psychology has been transgressed primarily as a result of Hobfoll's COR theory (see Sect. 2.3.1). Feelings of stress as well as access to and control over resources all have a collective dimension. The goal is to understand the reasons why as well as how communal coping strategies and prevention measures develop. Hobfoll continues to emphasize the importance of social and gender-related inequalities rooted in the power dynamics within a given society and their effect on an individual's access to and control over resources and opportunities to develop a resource pool. With this notion, he sketches out the sociocultural and material boundaries of human agency. However, to what extent is the current international scientific discourse on coping and related methods itself a cultural product with a Western cultural bias? And to what extent do culture- and gender-specific biases exist in the psychological concept of coping (see Sect. 2.4.1)? In the section that follows, we address a possible synthesis between mainstream psychological models and social science-based models. This synthesis takes the form of complex interactions or reciprocal structures between the individual and the social. These models are addressed in the Sects. 2.4.2 and 2.4.3.

2.4.1 *Biases in Psychological Coping Approaches*

Certain types of action and experience are ignored in the mainstream psychological coping theories (see Sect. 2.2). The value—or lack of value—attributed to certain elements based on cultural or perspective-based biases tends to remain hidden, rendering these judgments difficult to address or criticize.

2.4.1.1 Androcentric Biases

Based on the models illustrated in the previous sections and the corresponding quantitative measurement instruments, there are significant gender differences that may hint at an androcentric bias. For example, women report more somatic and posttraumatic stress symptoms than men (Zeidner 2006). The lifetime prevalence of PTSD among women is also twice that among men (Breslau 2001; Kimerling et al. 2002).[3] This higher prevalence among women is reported to be independent of the type of traumatic event (Norris et al. 2002b) as well as the cultural background (Norris et al. 2002a) and age of the subject (Kessler et al. 1995). Norris et al. (2002a) also found that women are twice as likely to develop PTSD after a disaster-related experience. On a similar note, Rubonis and Bickman's (1991) meta-analysis demonstrates that women show higher levels of PTSD symptoms and more pronounced affective responses to disaster-related experiences.

Research has shown that women tend to have larger social networks; in addition, they are more willing to offer social support (Schwarzer and Leppin 1989; Kessler et al. 1995) and more likely to implement social strategies when coping with a problem (Thoits 1991; Ptacek et al. 1994). Women rely less on direct strategies and more on prosocial coping (Hobfoll and Buchwald 2004). According to the transactional model, emotional coping is less effective and offers fewer health benefits in comparison with problem-focused methods (Billings and Moos 1981). A number of different studies show that women tend to focus on the emotional aspects of a problem and engage in avoidance behaviors as part of the coping strategy (Billings and Moos 1981; Araya et al. 2007). These empirical findings have been used, for example, as an explanation for the fact that women are more likely to suffer from depression (Aneshensel and Pearlin 1987). Men's emotion-focused coping strategies, on the other hand, frequently take the form of aggression against third parties or drug and alcohol consumption (Carver et al. 1989).

Hobfoll et al. (1994) demonstrate the impact of perceived control over one's own life on the coping process: If the individual has a higher level of perceived control, he or she tends to be more problem-focused. Men report a higher level of

[3] The work of Kimerling et al. (2002) provides a solid overview of the existing empirical studies in the area of gender and PTSD. However, it falls short of producing an integrated conceptual framework and there are no explanatory models or clinical recommendations. In general, PTSD and trauma research is limited with regard to gender-related topics, both on a conceptual level as well as on an empirical level (see Simmons 2007).

perceived control in comparison to women. This style of coping is associated with less psychological stress—unless the situation is completely uncontrollable (Zeidner and Hammer 1992).[4] There is also empirical evidence for gender differences with regard to the critical events that men and women experience over the course of their lives. Here it is assumed that women have been exposed to more situations in which they have had limited authority and control (Billings and Moos 1981; Geller and Hobfoll 1993; Hobfoll et al. 1994; Hobfoll and Buchwald 2004). In contrast, Porter et al. (2000) assume that empirical differences between the genders do not actually reflect gender-specific behavior, but instead can be traced back to different memory processes based on gender role stereotypes (see also Simmons 2007; Hatch and Dohrenwend 2007).

Although different theories emerged to explain the existence of these gender specifities, the empirical research contained assumptions and references that are not immediately apparent. For example, some of these theoretical approaches are based on sociocultural factors while others are based on evolutionary biology. The latter approach is always associated with deterministic assumptions, which can pose problems from a feminist perspective. As implied by the title of the article by Tamres et al. (2002) *Sex differences in coping behavior*, the text focuses on the supposed biologically determined sex differences rather than on socioculturally constructed gender differences. Differences in coping are automatically accounted for based on differences in the biological sex of the individual. Generally speaking, mainstream psychological coping research usually lacks a theoretical and practical definition of gender. There are only a few authors who work to incorporate newer, feminist theoretical discussions (for example Range and Jenkins 2010; Tang and Lau 1995; Hobfoll et al. 1994; Nezu and Nezu 1987; Eisler et al. 1988).

A further problem lies in the fact that the underlying cultural understanding is not expressly stated. Western theorists proposed most of the gender theory applied in international contexts and much of the empirical research has been conducted in Western countries. It is not clear whether these theories adequately represent other sociocultural conditions.

From a feminist psychological perspective, it is crucial for theoretical models to take sociocultural and structural contexts into account instead of relying solely on individual factors. The transactional stress theory does not meet these requirements. Feminist approaches address individual problems in conjunction with institutional frameworks and societal routines (for example Mejia 2005). Without these, there is a risk of adopting an essentialist view with regard to male or female identity, and thereby reinforcing this sexual binary instead of exploring diversity. Hobfoll's COR theory leans in this direction, as it includes the element of social embeddedness. However, only sociological approaches are able to adequately accommodate this idea.

---

[4] Empirical studies in the area of problem-focused coping have yielded contradictory findings. In some studies, men show a higher level of problem-focused coping (Folkman and Lazarus 1980), while, in other studies, this form of coping is more common in women (Vitaliano et al. 1985). Further studies showed no differences between the genders (Rosario et al. 1988; Tamres et al. 2002; Zeidner 2006).

2.4.1.2 Ethnocentric Biases

Markus and Kitayama (2010) suggest that psychological concepts display a Eurocentric or North American bias. Most studies have centered on individuals socialized in either a North American or Western European context. In an effort to pursue a universalist model, findings have been generalized without explicit mention of their cultural bias. Generally speaking, we can see the different Western sociocultural contexts as rather distinctive cultural contexts in which the individual person is viewed as the source of all thought, feeling, and action. These assumptions about human nature as focused on individual striving imply specific ideas about the self and human agency, ideas that are reflected in appraisal-oriented coping models.

Cultural psychologists such as Markus and Kitayama (2010), on the contrary hand, differentiate between two types of sociality in which different modes of being or senses of self are represented. The first sense of self is seen as connected, related, or interdependent with others. In this cultural context, prescribed tasks require and encourage individuals to fit in with others, take on the perspective of others, read the expectations of others, and use others as referents for action. These interdependent relationships may be harmonious or prone to conflict. In the second model, an independent self, interaction with others produces a sense of self as separate, distinct, or independent from others. These differences between a primarily independent and a primarily interdependent self are considered to be universalist orientations that appear more or less everywhere around the world. These orientations are heavily dependent upon the social context, and, based on the given context, one or the other tends to emerge as dominant.

> When the schema for self is interdependent with others and this schema organizes agency, people will have a sense of themselves as part of encompassing social relationships. People are likely to reference others, and to understand their individual actions as contingent on or organized by the actions of others and their relations with these other. (Markus and Kitayama 2010, p. 425)

In the appraisal-based coping models, which rely upon an independent self, the focus is different: In these models, individuals with a high level of self-efficacy engage in active, problem-solving control over their environment. This type of individual actively pursues social support, seeks out information, etc. The individual always remains the center of action. Even the secondary control process (in the system proposed by Skinner et al., 2003, this is referred to as accommodation) does not imply joint or less conscious action. While primary control involves influencing objective circumstances, secondary control "refers to the process by which people adjust some aspect of the self and accept circumstances as they are" (Morling and Evered 2006, p. 269). The authors stress this twofold property of secondary control and suggest that it is adaptive for coping in interdependent cultural contexts. However, developmental psychologists criticize the Western privilege of active control strategies and emphasize the importance of accommodative processes, particularly for older subjects (Brandtstädter 2006, 2011; Leipold and Greve 2009).

In their meta-analysis, Fischer et al. (2010) draw a connection between the independent and interdependent conceptions of self and religious affiliation. They analyze the relative importance of interpersonal and intrapersonal coping in Muslim and Christian faiths and connect appraisal-oriented coping with the social psychological conceptions of intergroup behavior and social identity.

> The Christian core self is relatively individualistic, whereas the Muslim core self is oriented more toward the collective. As a consequence, it is hypothesized that when confronted with a stressful life event, Muslims are more likely to adopt interpersonal (collective) coping strategies (such as seeking social support or turning to family members), while Christians are more likely to engage intrapersonal (individualistic) coping mechanisms, such as cognitive restructuring or reframing the event. (p. 365)

We, however, believe that religion and cultural context are inherently interdependent and, therefore, that the construction of a global Muslim or Christian identity is impracticable.

In the mainstream psychological approaches reviewed in this chapter, when behavior is explained, the individual—complete with all related structures and functions—is the primary concern. The active, goal-striving, and appraising human being pursues his or her goals, even under adverse circumstances, or is willing to modify these circumstances if necessary.

The opposing model, in this case, would be the conception of subjectivity in the sociological theory proposed by Bourdieu. He views the social aspect as the driving force and subjectivity as a component of an individual's habitus (Bourdieu 2002):

> When we speak of habitus, we maintain that the individual, and even the personal and the subjective, are social, collective properties. The habitus is socialized subjectivity. (Bourdieu and Wacquant 2006, p. 159)[5]

On the one hand, the habitus means that the individual is not able to move independently and intentionally within a social context. He or she is confined to certain predefined principles of the social order. The social context itself is shaped by property and power relationships. On the other hand, the habitus remains an open disposition system which is subject to continuous change through new experiences. An individual's actions are not determined solely through the internalization and embodiment of social structures; while these factors may limit the scope of the individual's opportunities for independent action, they do not determine his or her behavior. However, the habitus represents the limits of the individual's conscious knowledge of his or her possible agency.

Normally, the habitus corresponds with the individual's environment. This relationship is based on the fact that the habitus is created by the environment. This approach explains the stability of orientations and opinions. On this basis, it is possible to understand the idea of local knowledge—knowledge which has influenced coping practices in "natural" disasters for generations—embedded in practical behavior as described by Bankoff (see further). However, a dramatic event such as a disaster can also modify the habitus to the point at which it no longer corresponds with reality. The individual loses his or her orientation and must engage in a conscious effort to renew and reconstruct this orientation, a process which subjects it to

---

[5] Translation from German by Devin Martini.

possible changes. Structural ritualization theory refers to these effects of disruptions and deritualization. Disasters may result in a breakdown of social and personal ritualized practices, their impacts on the societal order, and the ways people may cope with or adapt to such experiences by reconstituting old or new ritualized practices (Knottnerus 2012).

Even if this conception only partially applies, it could dramatically affect the understanding of coping by limiting the scope of conscious, planned agency. If individuals view their ideas and practical orientations for action as foregone conclusions resulting from their social environment and inherent resource differences with domination and subordination, then coping with a threat must be viewed in this context as well. With this in mind, it is necessary to focus on the types of action that express these foregone orientations. These include performative, ritual, and intuitive actions that pervade everyday social activities and help to reinforce and reproduce these principles or order. It is crucial to possess information about the orientations of the social subgroup and its position in the social power structure in order to investigate the group's habitus (as this strongly influences opportunities for action and potential coping strategies) and gain insight into potential avenues of transformation. This may make it easier to understand the reasons why, after a disaster, it is difficult to establish a risk management strategy by means of persuasion with rational arguments (see Chap. 1 on the subject of handling risk).

A disaster brings about dramatic changes that are perceived as a broadly shared experience of being disaster survivors. Afterward, life is never the same for many people. This makes it necessary to process and manage any changes that may occur. We discussed this on the level of meaning (as the difference between situational and global meaning) as well as in the context of religious coping (as a means of conserving or transforming significance). The transformation models tend to focus primarily on individual, cognitive-based processes.

However, it is also possible to investigate the dynamics between conservation and transformation after a serious disaster and the related relief processes with respect to social negotiation processes (see Schwarz 2012; see Chap. 16). At present, there are few models available to describe collective difference management after major shocks. These types of models might be described as collective constructions and reflexive processes which take the form of collective discourses and forms of cooperative living, for example, in a family or community. In addition to these discursive and practical forms of management, there are also performative types of action that take the form of ritualistic behavior, for example processions, collective commemoration, performances, etc. According to Bhandari et al. (2011), the ritualized social activities enhance the capacity of individuals and groups to adapt or cope with various uncertainties and challenges created by disasters before, during, and after their occurrences as ritualized behavior fosters access to skills and local knowledge:

> Rituals also generate and reinforce emotional intensity and collective beliefs, thereby strengthening group ties, social support, and social networks. Furthermore, the reconstitution of RSPs [ritualized social practices] subsequent to disasters, enables people to adapt or cope with disruptive consequences of such events by providing coherence, direction, and a sense of stability (and therefore security) in their lives. (p. 27)

2.4.2 Coping as Collective Agency

If we separate the process of coping with disasters from the individual and view it instead as a broad social process, we must return to the understandings of disaster management covered in Chap. 1. These understandings place less emphasis on psychological concepts and focus instead on the areas of knowledge surrounding wide-ranging social processes, techniques, methods of organization, and physical processes. In disaster literature, the term *coping* is used to designate human agency within the process of dealing with disasters:

> Coping is the manner in which people act within the limits of existing resources and range of expectations to achieve various ends. (Wisner et al. 2004, p. 113)

The reasonable course of action follows from a scientifically based prescriptive model which, under ideal circumstances, is adapted to suit the actual life circumstances of the individuals involved. Wisner et al. (2004) understand politically motivated recommendations for action as a type of coping at the level of political action.

There is a long-standing debate in philosophy and social science about the question of whether or not collective agents can be considered legitimate constructs in social ontology, and concerning the nature of their agency (Dubreuil and Hardy-Vallée 2012). It is the question of whether an organization or a community can be viewed as a collective actor. According to Roth (2011), one central problem for the theory of shared or collective agency is how to establish an interpersonal structure of participatory intention. He cites Gilbert (2009), who sees it as essential that each participant has an obligation to do his or her part. According to her, groups form a plural subject whose intentions cannot be reduced to the sum of individual intentions (Gilbert 1989). Dubreuil and Hardy-Vallée (2012) summarize:

> An agency collectivist believes that collectives, under certain conditions, can be construed as a single agent. An agency individualist believes that no group or organization, under any condition, can be construed as a single agent; only individuals are agents. (p. 9)

According to Kashima et al. (2005), the tendency to ascribe as much agency to groups as to individuals is more prominent in East Asian cultures than in Western cultures. Although we consider this to be a rather essentialist view of culture, we nevertheless agree with the idea that for the purposes of an everyday understanding of the subject—as well as in social science—collective actors are constructions, and that it can be both productive and beneficial to interpret their actions within a social field or arena as intentional.

We disagree with Dubreuil and Hardy-Vallée (2012) in their objective, mechanistic explanation of agency. If we acknowledge collective actors (such as NGOs and local or national authorities), it is still difficult to estimate the extent of their influence within a social arena filled with competing powers and interests (for example, within a community), and to determine the rationality and values behind the behavior of these actors. In addition, by examining the group as a whole, we fail to acknowledge the diverse interests and power relationships within the group. Another conceptual difficulty lies in the fact that a community is sometimes recognized as a single actor (for example, in the concept of community resilience), while other times it is seen as a social arena composed of collective actors. Therefore, we understand collective agency as being very limited in its coherence due to diverging interests and power differences within a group. Furthermore, it may apply only at limited times where there are genuinely shared goals and attention; differences might quickly reemerge, for example, after communal rebuilding or rescue activities.

The conceptualization of collective agency is crucial to understanding the ways in which disasters—and responses to these disasters—unfold. Wisner et al. (2004) claim to adopt a realist approach so that they can regard risk as an objective hazard that exists and can be measured independently of social and cultural processes. The corresponding theories and methods associated with this epistemology are techno-scientific, statistical, and actuarial. Wisner et al. (2004) add a weak constructionist perspective and make the assumption that objective hazards are mediated by social and cultural processes. The realists aim to promote reasonable strategies that align with the interests of the people living under unsafe conditions. During international meetings, they fight to reach statements of intent to change these situations.

Realists such as Wisner et al. (2004) tend to interpret discursive or system analysis approaches as destructive, negative criticism against humanitarian organizations and, ultimately, the potential of human agency. They express disillusionment toward the approach advanced by Hilhorst and Jansen (2010) called *humanitarian space*. It is a way to analyze the role of social actors in shaping the everyday realities of humanitarian action, and investigate the ways in which these actors interact with disaster survivors and recipients of aid. This perspective is less a means of structuring what needs to be done and more a way of understanding postdisaster social conflicts. Hilhorst and Jansen (2010) question how the reasons for which some people become eligible to receive aid and others do not are conditioned by institutional interests, the local sociocultural fabric, and power differences among aid recipients. Discursive and system analysis approaches view the actors in postdisaster contexts as pawns of social interests and power relationships. These approaches illustrate the limits of individual agency, that is, a person's capacity to influence his or her surrounding and the social structures in which he or she lives.

2.4.3 Social Capital, Community Resilience, and Local Knowledge

The following three key concepts expand the psychological coping theory to include a collective dimension, an experience-based dimension, and a local dimension:

2.4.3.1 Social Capital

Definitions of social capital are diverse; so, too, are the associated understandings of the potential and limits of collective agency. Many authors (Portes and Landolt 1996; Woolcock 2010; Poder 2011) agree that social capital is a very wide-ranging, controversial concept that is not yet founded on solid science. However, even though the strong, theoretical scientific basis behind the approach has yet to be provided, the concept has practical benefits in that it draws together experts on a variety of different subjects.

One of the most popular approaches is Putnam's (1995) conception based on the understanding proposed by Coleman (1988). According to these authors, social capital resides in social relationships, as well as in networks, groups, and voluntary associations formed by members of the community. For Putnam (1995), social capital is characterized by the features of the networks, norms, and social trust that facilitate coordination and cooperation for mutual benefit.

The approach spans the different types of groups and networks that people can call upon (*structural* social capital) and the respondents' subjective perceptions of the trustworthiness of other people and key institutions (often referred to as *cognitive* social capital). There is a distinction between a *bonding* social capital (that relates to people who are demographically similar, like family members, neighbors, close friends, and work colleagues), *bridging* social capital (that relates to people who do not share many of the same characteristics), and *linking* social capital (that relates to people in positions of authority). Bridging and bonding social capital are "essentially horizontal (that is, connecting people with more or less equal social standing), linking social capital is more vertical [. . .] across power differentials" (Grootaert et al. 2004, p. 4).

According to Poder (2011), there are two fundamentally different approaches to and understandings of social capital. As described above, for Coleman (1988) and Putnam (1995), social capital refers to the nature and scale of a wide variety of informal networks and formal civic organizations. This means that social capital can decline for a given social unit (see Putnam 1995). It resides with the social unit and not with the individual. For Bourdieu (1980) and Portes and Landolt (1996), on the other hand, social capital refers to the resources (like information, ideas, assistances, etc.) available to individuals through their relationships. The main focus lies on individual resources instead of on group characteristics. These resources vary between different individuals, based on their strategic positions within the group. The resources are social in the sense that they are only accessible through the individual's relationships. Social capital is related to power and influence, that is, to features that produce differences between individuals.

In summary, the first version of social capital (as a characteristic of groups) can be described as an integral element in the agency or coping of an entity, for example, a community. Subjective observations of community members are used to estimate the extent to which the community in question deviates from the ideal model of a community that is capable of action. Models such as these often neglect the importance of conflicts, power relationships, and unequal distribution of resources within the community. These are the critical aspects of the resource-oriented model of social capital (Bourdieu 1980; Portes and Landolt 1996).

2.4.3.2 Community Resilience

Social capital can be understood as one element in the broad concept of community resilience. Securing and increasing social capital is the goal of the community-based approaches to disaster risk management (see Chap. 1). Norris et al. (2008) developed a special ideal type model for disasters. They understand community resilience as a "set of networked adaptive capacities" (p. 135). The community capacities are made up of different elements that need to be strengthened in order to increase communal resilience. To promote *economic development*, it is necessary to foster a diversity of economic resources and equitable distribution of income and resources against a backdrop of interdependencies at the macroeconomic level. Under the heading of *social capital*, the authors include network structures and linkages as well as social support, which mainly refers to helping behaviors within family and friendship networks. In the relationships between individuals and their larger neighborhoods and communities, social capital implies a sense of community, a concept which includes a major investment in community issues, place attachment, and citizen participation. This requires *information* about the danger and behavioral options. Here, *communication* refers "to the creation of common meanings and understandings and the provision of opportunities for members to articulate needs, views, and attitudes" (p. 140). *Community competence* is viewed as networked collective agency based on critical reflection, and implies participation, collective efficacy, and empowerment. The model combines many approaches and identifies a number of barriers that stand in the way of achieving the *desired level* of community resilience. This target outcome of community resilience can be measured in the form of community wellness (Norris et al. 2008). Like any understanding of community resilience, the ideal type model reflects certain value-based ideas about good community functioning. Subjective wellness or well-being represents a controversial method of evaluation, particularly in community psychology.

Critical community psychologists such as Nelson and Prilleltensky (2010) shed light on these core values and differentiate between the personal and collective domains of well-being. The values of self-determination, caring, compassion, and health fall under the domain of personal well-being, whereas respect for diversity, participation, and collaboration are defined as relational well-being, and support for community structure, social justice, and accountability are considered to be aspects of collective well-being. The authors address the way in which value conflicts are handled within this domain. The values formulated by Nelson and Prilleltensky reflect a Western, secular orientation and claim universal validity. However, it is possible that there are many differences between this idea and other sociocultural orientations.

In the social process of coping after a disaster, which includes major interventions by external sources of aid informed by value-based goals and motives, it is important to carry out an intensive discussion of the different understandings of value and justice. We do not approach the local orientations as homogenous, closed, or static. Indeed, we expect to discover diversity, contradiction, and dynamic relationships between local understandings (see Beatty 1999; Ricklefs 2008; Berninghausen et al. 2009; Schlehe 2010).

2.4.3.3 Local Knowledge

Local knowledge represents another means of accessing shared coping resources, one that places these resources in their historical and local contexts. Societies share an interdependent relationship with the world that they inhabit (Chap. 1). This interdependent relationship produces cultural interpretations and practical behaviors that allow societies that inhabit hazardous environments to develop corresponding cultural adaptations and manage these hazards using historically derived methods. These methods consist of technical, ecological, and historical knowledge as well as practices, beliefs, values, and worldviews (Dekens 2007) that affect different aspects of society: all the way from economic structures and characteristics of social relationships to mental structures (Bankoff 2004).

These context-specific manners are generally referred to in the literature as local knowledge (Sillitoe 2010; Dekens 2007; Bankoff 2004; Jigyasu 2002). Local knowledge is knowledge that is shared and distributed through social channels. As such, this knowledge is produced and reproduced by individuals in historical processes. This does not imply explicit, conscious knowledge. Rather, based on Bourdieu's concept of habitus, local knowledge is integrated in the subjectivity of the individual as agency: individuals are able to react to their environment in a reasonable way without any reliance on conscious, rational planning. Unlike in the appraisal model, the individual does not arrive at the coping response through an individual, conscious engagement with a challenge or strain.

In Chap. 1, we established the fact that, in the process of relief management, control is regained in the situation following a disaster through a rapid mobilization of science-based expert knowledge. This type of mobilization often results in a mixing of local and science-based resources as well as different cultures of knowledge and skills. The experts enter with universal knowledge and aid and meet local people who are equipped with regionally specific, inherited information and abilities. Bankoff (2003, 2007) assumes that environments in which people are repeatedly confronted with hazards result in cultural adaptation. He formulates a local definition of coping which includes this historical dimension:

> The strategies adopted by communities to reduce the impact of hazards or avoid the occurrence of disaster are known as coping practices and are based on the assumption that what has happened in the past is likely to repeat itself following a familiar pattern. [. . .] Variously referred to in the literature more generally as informal security system or local capacities and more specifically as indigenous technical knowledge or appropriate technology such coping practices include the specialized knowledge of skilled individuals as well as the social knowledge held by the communities at large. (Bankoff 2004, p. 32)

The idea of local knowledge therefore contains an *indigenous rationality* that does not necessarily correspond to the Western idea of a goal-oriented individual. This idea is also present in the psychological coping models and approaches to international disaster management. They tend to overemphasize individual capacity for action and control, while local knowledge focuses on the collective capacity.

In addition, the idea of *local knowledge* includes inherently power-critical components. This is due to the fact that local knowledge always serves as an alternative or counterargument to hegemonic knowledge forms which claim universal validity of theories developed in Western countries to be applied worldwide. This applies, for example, to the way in which institutionalized disaster management is handled in the context of a disaster. The indigenous rationality of local knowledge, on the contrary is neglected, devalued, and marginalized (see Bankoff and Hilhorst 2009). For this reason, some emphasize the necessity of integrating local knowledge into disaster management.

Through its focus on local capacities, local knowledge discourses and practices add a level of cultural identity and cultural identity politics to coping. However, the juxtaposition of local versus global knowledge is somewhat artificial because global elements are long-standing components of local knowledge (even before the disaster).

2.5 Concluding Remarks

In psychological perspectives on coping, the development of important lines of theory and empirical investigation allows for the expansion of an approach to coping with disasters that can include cultural–psychological features. In this field, the general approach is to seek the psychological mechanisms that determine human behavior and experience under challenging or threatening circumstances.

Our first question was about the role of the relational conception of environment and person in coping with stress. Lazarus (1991, 1999) understood this process as a series of transactions in which the situations become a perceived event with a personal connotation. In his model, the goal-striving individual carries out continuous appraisals and reappraisals of situations in such a way that any resulting emotional reactions have an orientation function. This introduced a subjective dimension to stress in which the appraisals of the individual relative to motives are central. Coping behavior, or human agency, can be focused on the situation as an active means of solving a problem, or on the person (through a process in which individuals change meanings and process emotions). Coping was defined as showing effort under pressure, whether or not this process is successful. Change or adaptation in meanings and orientations were expanded into meaning-oriented approaches in subsequent theories and extended to include religious coping approaches because, in times of threat or difficulty, the search for significance becomes particularly salient. However, within the appraisal-based coping approach, the functional role of finding meaningfulness and religious coping was primary that both can have health benefits. Future-oriented coping can be understood as a private form of risk management, although previous research has primarily viewed this type of coping in relation to threats to the health of the individual. In the proactive coping model (according to Schwarzer and Taubert 2002), the focus shifted from specific threats to an accumulation of resources in the sense of a nonspecific increase in resilience. In developmental psychology, these approaches were expanded into adaptive development models with assimilative and accommodative processes (see Brandtstädter 2011).

Perspectives on the possible effects of extreme stress and disasters on mental health have changed in recent years. The clinical model, which held that extreme stress leads to illness, has become less dominant (in both theories and postdisaster practice). Instead, the conception that exposure to extreme stress can lead to a number of different trajectories—with primarily positive outcomes and infrequent negative outcomes—is now more influential. This new interest shifted attention in theorizing and research to the influences that govern these processes.

Hobfoll's (2001, 2011) COR theory expanded the appraisal-based understanding of coping to include the gain or loss of resources which are considered to be critical to the stress process. Spirals of fatal loss result in extreme stress in traumatizing situations. This focus on resources draws a stronger link between person-centered processes and the context, which, for example, can reveal the orientations that determine the value of certain resources. Social processes such as the exchange of resources between community members or the distribution of stress in social networks are also taken into account. A culture-bound dimension of coping was also added to the model. In the appraisal-based model, social support is viewed primarily in terms of its functional role in the coping process; COR theory, in contrast, differentiates coping based on the conditions of the availability of this social support in the social arena. Kaniasty (2012) developed special postdisaster trajectories concerning the perception of this availability. The research of these dynamics also incorporates social conflicts and the observation of collective coping processes.

Our critical review shows that, in the field of psychology, social and cultural aspects always remain on the outside, as moderating factors, and cannot be addressed in terms that are intermingled with their inner, private, or cognitive aspects. On applying this understanding to gender, the androcentric bias of the common conception of coping becomes disguised and "sex" is mostly viewed as an essentialized, biological variable; a theoretically viable concept of gender is still missing which takes structural and contextual conditions into account. Similarly, cultural context is often reduced to ethnicity which is equated with one's sense of ethnic origin. Cultural and feminist psychology and concepts from the fields of anthropology and sociology, which are highlighted in the next chapter, suggest that these definitions must be expanded. For example, coping models that are considered to be universal contain constructs that are anchored in Western thought and research, particularly the monadic ideology of the subject as an independent self and an expression of active, cognitively directed problem solving or self-improvement.

Of course, it is an exciting prospect to be able to apply certain basic concepts of psychological coping in an expanded model of coping that includes social, cultural, and material resources. It is interesting to be able to both understand externally focused problem-solving activities, as well as work on the leading systems of orientation, as aspects of coping and consider a diverse range of coping methods. The notion that coping is to be viewed as an effort made under demanding situations—regardless of the success of this effort—is productive insofar as each judgment about the success or failure of coping efforts represents a normalizing and therefore questionable proposition. We think that coping must be viewed as a social process; the exclusive reliance on the individual perspective is ultimately an artificial, Western construction, which bears more resemblance to laboratory situations than real-life circumstances. We further address this issue in the next chapter.

In order to expand the understanding of nonindividualistic coping processes, we discussed notions of collective coping and collective agency which were initially introduced in Chap. 1 as potential criticisms of psychological models of risk reduction. We argued that these models fail to address issues in terms of structures of power, control, and unequal distribution of resources. Moreover, our analysis showed that the capacity of the agency planning and acting in the collective interest is highly limited by structural considerations. Additionally, the actions tend to reflect a habit or a performative means of reinforcing distinctions within social relationships. Social capital cannot be understood merely as part of the capacity of a community carefully attempting to build community resilience, but rather as a series of networks used to promote certain interests. The positive notion of collective agency and related constructions—such as feelings of solidarity, a sense of community, the conception of social capital in civil society, and ideas of participation and empowerment—are concepts that can be treated as options for collective coping within the social arena and which must assert themselves against the interests of other agencies. A discursive analytical approach offers points of access for investigating these types of multiple, probably contradicting processes. The options of local knowledge and practice can also be accommodated by these types of formulations and the question remains as to the conditions under which these factors have a chance to resonate in community and higher-level political arenas.

Acknowledgment The editors would like to thank Devin Martini for assistance with editing and translating parts of this chapter from German into English.

References

Aneshensel, C. S., & Pearlin, L. I. (1987). Structural contexts of sex differences in stress. In R. C. Barnett, L. Biener, & G. K. Baruch (Eds.), *Gender and stress*. New York: Free Press.

Araya, M., Chotai, J., Komproe, I. H., & de Jong, J. T. V. M. (2007). Gender differences in traumatic life events, coping strategies, perceived social support and sociodemographics among postconflict displaced persons in Ethiopia. *Social Psychiatry Psychiatric Epidemiology, 42,* 307–315.

Aspinwall, L. G. (2011). Future-oriented thinking, proactive coping, and the management of potential threats to health and well-being. In S. Folkman (Ed.), *The Oxford handbook of stress, health and coping* (pp. 334–365). New York: Oxford University Press.

Aspinwall, L. G., & Taylor, S. E. (1997). A stitch in time. *Psychological bulletin, 121*(3), 417–436.

Baltes, P. B. (1997). On the incomplete architecture of human ontogeny. *American Psychologist, 52*(4), 366–380.

Bankoff, G. (2003). *Cultures of disaster*. London: Routledge.

Bankoff, G. (2004). The historical geography of disaster: 'Vulnerability' and 'local knowledge'. In G. Bankoff, G. Frerks, & D. Hilhorst (Eds.), *Mapping vulnerability* (pp. 25–36). London: Earthscan.

Bankoff, G. (2007). Living with risk; coping with disasters. *Education about Asia, 12*(2), 26–29.

Bankoff, G., & Hilhorst, D. (2009). The politics of risk in the Philippines. *Disasters, 33*(4), 686–704.

Beatty, A. (1999). *Varieties of Javanese religion*. Cambridge: Cambridge Univ. Press.

Berninghausen, J., Kerstan, B., & Soeprapto-Jansen, N. (2009). *Schleier, Sarong, Minirock, Frauen im kulturellen Wandel Indonesiens*. Bremen: Kellner Verlag.

Bhandari, R. B., Knottnerus, J. D., & Okada, N. (2011). Urban ritual events and coping with disaster risk: A case study of Lalitpur. Nepal. *Journal of Applied Social Science, 5*(2), 13–32.

Billings, A. G., & Moos, R. H. (1981). The role of coping responses and social resources in attenuating the stress of life events. *Journal of Behavioral Medicine, 4,* 139–157.

Boas, F. (1940). *Race, language, and culture.* New York: Macmillan.

Bonanno, G. A. (2004). Loss, trauma, and human resilience: Have we underestimated the human capacity to thrive after extremely aversive events? *The American Psychologist, 59*(1), 20–28.

Bonanno, G. A., Mancini, A. D. (2012). Beyond resilience and PTSD: Mapping the heterogeneity of responses to potential trauma. *Psychological Trauma: Theory, Research, Practice, and Policy, 4*(1), 74–83.

Bonanno, G. A., Brewin, C. R., Kaniasty, K., & La Greca, A. M. (2010). Weighing the costs of disaster: Consequences, risks, and resilience in individuals, families and communities. *Psychological Science in the Public Interest, 11*(1), 1–49.

Bonanno, G. A., Westphal, M., & Mancini, A. D. (2011). Resilience to loss and potential trauma. *Annual Review Clinical Psychology, 7,* 511–535.

Bourdieu, P. (1980). Le capital social: Notes provisoires. *Actes de la Recherche en Sciences Sociales, 31,* 2–3.

Bourdieu, P. (2002). Habitus. In J. Hillier, & E. Rooksby (Eds.), *Habitus* (pp. 27–32). Aldershot: Ashgate.

Bourdieu, P., & Wacquant, L. J. D. (2006). *Reflexive Anthropologie.* Frankfurt am Main: Suhrkamp.

Brandtstädter, J. (2006). Adaptive resources in later life: Tenacious goal pursuit and flexible goal adjustment. In M. Csikszentmihalyi, & I. S. Csikszentmihalyi (Eds.), *A life worth living: Contributions to positive psychology* (pp. 143–164). New York: Oxford University Press.

Brandtstädter, J. (2011). *Positive Entwicklung. Zur Psychologie gelingenden Lebens.* Heidelberg: Springer/Spektrum Akademischer Verlag.

Breslau, N. (2001). The epidemiology of posttraumatic stress disorder: What is the extent of the problem? *Journal of Clinical Psychiatry, 62,* 16–22.

Brewin, C. R. (2011). The nature and significance of memory disturbance in posttraumatic stress disorder. *Annual Review of Clinical Psychology, 7,* 203–227.

Bryant-Davis, T., Ellis, M. U., Burke-Maynard, E., Moon, N., Counts, P. A., & Anderson, G. (2012). Religiosity, spirituality, and trauma recovery in the lives of children and adolescents. *Professional Psychology: Research and Practice, 43*(4), 306–314.

Burger, J. M., & Palmer, M. L. (1992). Changes in and generalization of unrealistic optimism following experiences with stressful events: Reactions to the 1989 California earthquake. *Personality and Social Psychological Bulletin, 18,* 39–43.

Carver, C. S., & Connor-Smith, J. (2010). Personality and coping. *Annual Review of Psychology, 61*(1), 679–704.

Carver, C. S., Scheier, M. F., & Weintraub, J. K. (1989). Assessing coping strategies: A theoretically based approach. *Journal of Personality and Social Psychology, 56,* 267–283.

Cole, B. S., & Pargament, K. I. (1999). Spiritual surrender: A paradoxical path to control. In W. R. Miller (Ed.), *Integrating spirituality into treatment* (pp. 179–198). Washington, DC: American Psychological Association.

Coleman, J. S. (1988). Social capital in the creation of human capital. *The American Journal of Sociology, 94,* 95–120.

Coser, L. (1967). *Continuities in the study of social conflict.* New York: Free Press.

Dekens, J. (2007). Local knowledge for disaster preparedness. Kathmandu: International Centre for Integrated Mountain Development (ICIMOD). Online: http://preventionweb.net/go/2693. Accessed 10 May 2013.

Deutsch, M. (2000). Justice and conflict. In M. Deutsch, & P. T. Coleman (Eds.), *The handbook of conflict resolution: Theory and practice* (pp. 43–68). San Francisco: Jossey-Bass Inc.

Dubreuil, B., & Hardy-Vallée, B. (2012) Collective agency: From intuitions to mechanisms http://citeseerx.ist.psu.edu/viewdoc/summary?doi=10.1.1.81.7868. Accessed 10 May 2013.

Ehlers, A., & Clark, D. M. (2000). A cognitive model of posttraumatic stress disorder. *Behaviour Research and Theory, 38*(4), 319–345.

Eisler, R. M., Skidmore, J. R., & Ward, C. H. (1988). Masculine gender-role stress: Predictor of anger, anxiety, and health-risk behaviors. *Journal of Personality Assessment, 52,* 133–141.

Fischer, P., Ai, A. L., Aydin, N., Frey, D., & Haslam, S. A. (2010). The relationship between religious identity and preferred coping strategies: An examination of the relative importance of interpersonal and intrapersonal coping in Muslim and Christian faiths. *Review of General Psychology, 14*(4), 365–381.

Foa, E. B., & Rothbaum, B. O. (1998). *Treating the trauma of rape*. New York: Guilford Press.

Folkman, S. (2011). Stress, health and coping: An overview. In S. Folkman, & P. E. Nathan (Eds.), *The Oxford handbook of stress, health, and coping* (pp. 3–14). New York: Oxford University Press.

Folkman, S., & Lazarus, R. S. (1980). An analysis of coping in a middle-aged community sample. *Journal of Health and Social Support, 21,* 219–239.

Folkman, S., & Lazarus, R. S. (1988). Coping as a mediator of emotion. *Journal of Personality and Social Psychology, 54*(1), 466–475.

Folkman, S., & Moskowitz, J. T. (2004). Coping: Pitfalls and promise. *Annual Review of Psychology, 55*(1), 745–774.

Folkman, S., Lazarus, R. S., Dunkel-Schetter, C., DeLongis, A., & Gruen, R. J. (1986). Dynamics of a stressful encounter: Cognitive appraisal, coping, and encounter outcomes. *Journal of Personality and Social Psychology, 50*(5), 992–1003.

Friedman, M. J., Resick, P. A., Bryant, R. A., & Brewin, C. R. (2011). Considering PTSD for DSM-5. *Depression and Anxiety, 28,* 750–769.

Garrison, M. E. B., & Sasser, D. D. (2009). Families and disaster. In K. E. Cherry (Ed.), *Lifespan perspectives on natural disasters* (pp. 113–130). Dordrecht: Springer.

Geller, P. A., & Hobfoll, S. E. (1993). Gender differences in preference to offer social support to assertive men and women. *Sex Roles, 28,* 419–432.

Gigerenzer, G. (2008). *Rationality for mortals. How people cope with uncertainty*. New York: Oxford University Press.

Gilbert, M. (1989). *On social facts*. New York: Routledge.

Gilbert, M. (2009). Shared intention and personal intention. *Philosophical Studies, 144,* 167–187.

Grootaert, C., Narayan, D., Nyhan, J. V., & Woolcock, M. (2004). *Measuring social capital: An integrated questionnaire*. Washington, D.C.: The World Bank.

Hatch, S. L., & Dohrenwend, B. P. (2007). Distribution of traumatic and other stressful life events by race/ethnicity, gender, SES and age: A review of the research. *American Journal of Community Psychology, 40,* 313–332.

Hilhorst, D., & Jansen, B. J. (2010). Humanitarian space as arena: A perspective on the everyday politics of aid. *Development and Change, 41*(6), 1117–1139.

Hill, P. C., & Hood, R. W. (1999). *Measures of religiosity*. Birmingham: Religious Education Press.

Hill, P. C., & Pargament, K. I. (2008). Advances in the conceptualization and measurement of religion and spirituality: Implications for physical and mental health research. *Psychology of Religion and Spirituality, 58*(1), 64–74.

Hinton, D. E., & Lewis-Fernandez, R. (2011). The cross-cultural validity of posttraumatic stress disorder: Implications for DSM-5. *Depression and Anxiety, 28,* 783–80.

Hobfoll, S. E. (1998). *Stress, culture and community*. New York: Plenum Press.

Hobfoll, S. E. (2001). The influence of culture, community, and the nested-self in the stress process: Advancing conservation of resources theory. *Applied Psychology, 50*(3), 337–421.

Hobfoll, S. E. (2011). Conservation of resources theory: Its implication for stress, health and resilience. In S. Folkman, & P. E. Nathan (Eds.), *The Oxford handbook of stress, health, and coping* (pp. 127–147). New York: Oxford University Press.

Hobfoll, S. E., & Buchwald, P. (2004). Die Theorie der Ressourcenerhaltung und das multiaxiale Copingmodell eine innovative Stresstheorie. In P. Buchwald, S. E. Hobfoll, & C. Schwarzer (Eds.), *Stress gemeinsam bewältigen* (pp. 11–26). Göttingen: Hogrefe.

Hobfoll, S. E., Dunahoo, C. L., Ben-Porath, Y., & Monnier, J. (1994). Gender and coping: The dual-axis model of coping. *American Journal of Community Psychology, 22*(1), 49–82.

Hobfoll, S. E., Canetti-Nisim, D., Johnson, R. J., Palmieri, P. A., Varley, J., & Galea, S. (2008). The association of exposure, risk and resiliency factors with PTSD among Jews and Arabs exposed to repeated acts of terrorism in Israel. *Journal of Traumatic Stress, 21,* 9–21.

Hobfoll, S. E., Hall, B., Horsey, K. J., & Lamoureux, B. E. (2011). Resilience in the face of terrorism: Linking resource investment with engagement. In S. M. Southwick, B. T. Litz, D. Charney, & M. J. Friedman (Eds.), *Resilience and mental health: Challenges across the lifespan* (pp. 253–263). Cambridge: Cambridge University Press.

Hobfoll, S. E., Hall, B. J., & Canetti, D. (2012). Political violence, psychological distress, and perceived health: A longitudinal investigation in the Palestinian authority. *Psychological Trauma: Theory, Research, Practice, and Policy, 4*(1), 9–21.

Janoff-Bulman, R. (1992). *Shattered assumptions: Towards a new psychology of trauma*. New York, NY: Free Press.

Jigyasu, R. (2002). Reducing disaster vulnerability through local knowledge and capacity. http://ntnu.diva-portal.org/smash/get/diva2:123824/FULLTEXT01. Accessed 06 June 2013.

Kahneman, D. (2011). *Thinking fast and slow*. New York: Farrar, Straus and Giroux.

Kaniasty, K. (2012). Predicting social psychological well-being following trauma: The role of postdisaster social support. *Psychological Trauma: Theory, Research, Practice, and Policy, 4*(1), 22–23.

Kaniasty, K., & Norris, F. H. (1993). A test of the support deterioration model in the context of natural disaster. *Journal of Personality and Social Psychology, 64*(3), 395–408.

Kashima, Y., Kashima, E., Chiu, C. Y., Farsides, T., Gelfand, M., Hong, Y.-Y., et al (2005). Culture, essentialism, and agency: Are individuals universally believed to be more real entities than groups? *European Journal of Social Psychology, 35*(2), 147–169.

Kessler, R. C., Sonnega, A., Bromet, E., Hughes, M., & Nelson, C. B. (1995). PTSD in the national comorbidity survey. *Archives of General Psychiatry, 52,* 1048–1060.

Kimerling, R., Ouimette, P., & Wolfe, J. (Eds.). (2002). *Gender and PTSD*. New York: Guilford.

Knottnerus, J. D. (2012). *Ritual as a missing link: Sociology, structural ritualization theory, and research*. Boulder: Paradigm Publishers.

Kotter-Grühn, D., & Smith, J. (2011). When time is running out: Changes in positive future perception and their relationships to changes in well-being in old age. *Psychology and Aging, 26*(2), 381–387.

Kurtz, L. R., & Ritter, D. (2011). Conflict resolution, provocation or transformation? Ask Gandhi. American Sociological Association. http://works.bepress.com/lester_kurtz/36. Accessed 14 Feb 2013.

Lazarus, R. S. (1966). *Psychological stress and the coping process*. New York: McGraw-Hill.

Lazarus, R. S. (1991). *Emotion and adaptation*. London: Oxford University Press.

Lazarus, R. S. (1993). From psychological stress to the emotions: A history of changing outlooks. *Annual Review of Psychology, 44,* 1–21.

Lazarus, R. S. (1999). *Stress and emotion. A new synthesis*. London: Free Association Books.

Lazarus, R. S., & Folkman, S. (1984). *Stress, appraisal, and coping*. New York: Springer.

Leipold, B., & Greve, W. (2009). Resilience: A conceptual bridge between coping and development, *European Psychologist, 14*(1), 40–50.

Maiese, M. (2003). Distributive justice. http://www.beyondintractability.org/essay/distributive_justice/. Accessed 31 March 2013.

Marks, L. D., Cherry, K. E., & Silva, J. L. (2009). Faith, crisis coping and meaning making after Katrina. In K. E. Cherry (Ed.), *Lifespan perspectives on natural disasters* (pp. 195–215). Dordrecht: Springer.

Markus, H. R., & Kitayama, S. (2010). Cultures and selves: A cycle of mutual constitution. *Perspectives on Psychological Science, 5*(4), 420–430.

Masten, A. S., & Narayan, A. J. (2012). Child development in the context of disaster, war, and terrorism: Pathways of risk and resilience. *Annual Review of Psychology, 63,* 227–57.

Mejia, X. E. (2005). Gender matters: Working with adult male survivors of trauma. *Journal of Counseling & Development, 83,* 29–40.

Miyamoto, Y., & Ryff, C. (2011). Cultural differences in the dialectical and non-dialectical emotional styles and their implications for health. *Cognition and Emotion, 25,* 22–30.
Miyamoto, Y., Uchida, Y., & Ellsworth, P. C. (2010). Culture and mixed emotions: Co-occurrence of positive and negative emotions in Japan and the U.S. *Emotion, 10,* 404–415.
Morling, B., & Evered, S. (2006). Secondary control reviewed and defined. *Psychological Bulletin, 132,* 269–296.
Nelson G., & Prilleltensky, I. (Eds.). (2010). *Community psychology: In pursuit of liberation and well-being*. Houndmills: Palgrave/Macmillan.
Nezu, A. M., & Nezu, C. M. (1987). Psychological distress, problem solving, and coping reactions: Sex role differences. *Sex Roles, 16,* 205–214.
Norris, F. H. (2005). *Range, magnitude, and duration of the effects of disasters on mental health: Review update 2005*. Dartmouth: Dartmouth Medical School and National Center for Posttraumatic Stress Disorder.
Norris, F. H., Friedman, M. J., Watson, P. J., Byrne, C. M., Diaz, E., & Kaniasty, K. (2002a). 60,000 disaster victims speak: Part I. An empirical review of the empirical literature, 1981–2001. *Psychiatry: Interpersonal & Biological Processes, 65*(3), 207–239.
Norris, F. H., Friedman, M. J., & Watson, P. J. (2002b). 60,000 disaster victims speak: Part II. Summary and implications of the disaster mental health research. *Psychiatry: Interpersonal & Biological Processes, 65*(3), 240–260.
Norris, F. H., Baker, C. K., Murphy, A. D., & Kaniasty, K. (2005). Social support mobilization and deterioration after Mexico's 1999 flood: Effects of context, gender, and time. *American Journal of Community Psychology, 36*(1–2), 15–28.
Norris, F. H., Stevens, S. P., Pfefferbaum, B., Wyche, K. F., & Pfefferbaum, R. L. (2008). Community resilience as a metaphor, theory, set of capacities, and strategy for disaster readiness. *American Journal of Community Psychology, 41*(1–2), 127–150.
Norris, F. H., Tracy, M., & Galea, S. (2009). Looking for resilience: Understanding the longitudinal trajectories of responses to stress. *Social Science & Medicine, 68*(12), 2190–2198.
Pakenham, K. I. (2011). Benefit finding and sense making in chronic illness. In S. Folkman, & P. E. Nathan (Eds.), *The Oxford handbook of stress, health, and coping* (pp. 242–268). New York: Oxford University Press.
Pargament, K. I. (1997). *The psychology of religion and coping*. New York: Guilford Press.
Pargament, K. I. (2011). Religion and coping: The current state of knowledge. In S. Folkman, & P. E. Nathan (Eds.), *The Oxford handbook of stress, health, and coping* (pp. 269–288). New York: Oxford University Press.
Pargament, K. I., Koenig, H. G., & Perez, L. M. (2000). The many methods of religious coping: Initial development and validation of the RCOPE. *Journal of Clinical Psychology, 56,* 519–543.
Park, C. L. (2010). Making sense of the meaning literature: An integrative review of meaning making and its effects on adjustment to stressful life events. *Psychological Bulletin, 136*(2), 257–301.
Pitman, R. K., Rasmusson, A. M., Koenen, K. C., Shin, L. M., Orr, S. P., Gilbertson, M. W., et al (2012). Biological studies of post-traumatic stress disorder nature reviews. *Neuroscience, 13*(11), 769–787.
Poder, T. G. (2011). What is really social capital? A critical review. *The American Sociologist, 42,* 341–367.
Porter, L. S., Marco, C. A., Schwartz, J. E., Neale, J. M., Shiffman, S., & Stone, A. A. (2000). Gender differences in coping: A comparison of trait and momentary assessments. *Journal of Social and Clinical Psychology, 19*(4), 480–498.
Portes, A., & Landolt, P. (1996). The downside of social capital. *The American Prospects, 26,* 18–21.
Ptacek, J. T., Smith, R. E., & Dodge, K. L. (1994). Gender differences in coping with stress: When stressor and appraisals do not differ. *Personality and Social Psychological Bulletin, 20,* 421–430.

Putnam, R. D. (1995). Bowling alone: America's declining social capital. *Journal of Democracy, 6*(1), 65–78.
Range, L. M., & Jenkins, S. R. (2010). Who benefits from Pennebaker's expressive writing paradigm? Research recommendations from three gender theories. *Sex Roles, 63,* 149–164.
Reyes, G., & Jacobs, G. A. (Eds.). (2006). *Handbook of international disaster psychology. Fundamentals and overview*. 4 Volumes. Westport: Praeger.
Ricklefs, M. C. (2008). Religion, politics and social dynamics in Java. In G. Fealy & S. White (Eds.), *Expressing Islam* (pp. 115–136). Singapore: Institute of Southeast Asian Studies.
Rosario, M., Shinn, M., Morch, H., & Huckabee, C. B. (1988). Gender differences in coping and social supports: Testing socialization and role constraint theories. *Journal of Community Psychology, 16,* 55–69.
Roth, A. S. (2011). Shared agency. In E. N. Zalta (Ed.), *The Stanford encyclopedia of philosophy*. http://plato.stanford.edu/archives/spr2011/entries/shared-agency/. Accessed 05 June 2013.
Rubonis, A. V., & Bickman, L. (1991). Psychological impairment in the wake of disaster: The disaster-psychopathology relationship. *Psychological Bulletin, 109*(3), 384–399.
Schlehe, J. (2010). Anthropology of religion: Disasters and the representations of tradition and modernity. *Religion, 40*(2), 112–120.
Schmahl, C. (2009). Neurobiologie. In A. Maercker (Ed.), *Posttraumatische Belastungsstörungen* (pp. 51–64). Heidelberg: Springer.
Schwarz, S. (2012). *Eine kritische und kultursensible Sicht auf das Mainstreaming von Gender in einem Katastrophenkontext: Umstrittene Gendergerechtigkeitsvorstellungen, ein heuristisches Modell sozialen Wandels und Strategieprozessvorstellungen. Betroffenen- und AktivistInnen-sichtweisen.* Doctoral dissertation, Fachbereich Erziehungswissenschaften und Psychologie, Freie Universität Berlin.
Schwarzer, R., & Leppin, A. (1989). Social support and health: A meta-analysis. *Psychology and Health, 3,* 1–15.
Schwarzer, R., & Knoll, N. (2007). Functional roles of social support within the stress and coping process: A theoretical and empirical overview. *International Journal of Psychology, 42*(4), 243–252.
Schwarzer, R., & Schwarzer, C. (1996). A critical survey of coping instruments. In M. Zeidner & N. S. Endler (Eds.), *Handbook of coping: Theory, research, applications* (pp. 107–132). Oxford: Wiley.
Schwarzer, R., & Taubert, S. (2002). Tenacious goal pursuits and striving toward personal growth: Proactive coping. In E. Frydenberg (Ed.), *Beyond coping* (pp. 19–35). Oxford: Oxford University Press.
Schwarzer, R., Sniehotta, F. F., Lippke, S., Luszczynska, A., Scholz, U., Schüz, B., et al. (2003). On the assessment and analysis of variables in the health action process approach. http://userpage.fu-berlin.de/~gesund/hapa_web.pdf. Accessed 05 June 2011.
Seginer, R. (2008). Future orientation in times of threat and challenge. *International Journal of Behavioral Development, 32*(4), 272–282.
Shweder, R. A. (1993). Everything you ever wanted to know about cognitive appraisal theory without being conscious of it. *Psychological Inquiry: An International Journal for the Advancement of Psychological Theory, 4*(4), 322–342.
Sillitoe, P. (2010). Trust in development: Some implications of knowing in indigenous knowledge. *Journal of the Royal Anthropological Institute, 16,* 12–30.
Simmons, C. A. (2007). Speculation as to why Women "get" PTSD more often than men. *Women & Therapy, 30*(1/2), 85–98.
Skinner, E. A., & Zimmer-Gembeck, M. J. (2007). The development of coping. *Annual Review of Psychology, 58,* 119–144.
Skinner, E. A., Edge, K., Altman, J., & Sherwood, H. (2003). Searching for the structure of coping. A review and critique of category systems for classifying ways of coping. *Psychological Bulletin, 129*(2), 216–269.

Slovic, P., & Västfjäll, D. (2010). Affect, moral intuition, and risk. *Psychological Inquiry, 21*(4), 387–398.

Snyder, C. R., & Lopez, S. J. (Eds.). (2011). *Oxford handbook of positive psychology*. Oxford: Oxford University Press.

Steil, R., Ehlers, A., & Clark, D. M. (2003). Kognitive Aspekte der Behandlung der posttraumatischen Belastungsstörung. In A. Maercker (Ed.), *Therapie der posttraumatischen Belastungsstörungen* (pp. 91–106). Berlin: Springer.

Tamres, L. K., Janicki, D., & Helgeson, V. S. (2002). Sex differences in coping behavior: A meta-analytic review and an examination of relative coping. *Personality and Social Psychology Review, 6*(1), 2–30.

Tang, C. S., & Lau, B. H. (1995). The assessment of gender role stress for Chinese. *Sex Roles, 33*(7/8), 587–595.

Tedeschi, R. G., & Calhoun, L. G. (2004). Posttraumatic growth: Conceptual foundations and empirical evidence. *Psychological Inquiry, 15*(1), 1–18.

Thoits, P. A. (1991). On merging identity: Theory and stress research. *Social Psychology Quarterly, 54*(2), 101–112.

Tracy, J. L., & Robins, R. W. (2004). Putting the self into self-conscious emotions: A theoretical model. *Psychological Inquiry, 15*(2), 103–125.

Vitaliano, P. P., Russo, J., Carr, J. E., Maiuro, R., & Becker, J. (1985). The ways of coping checklist: Revision and psychometric properties. *Multivariate Behavioral Research, 20*(1), 3–26.

Wagner-Pacifici, R., & Hall, M. (2012). Resolution of social conflict. *Annual Review of Sociology, 38*, 181–199.

Wisner, B., Blaikie, P., Cannon, T., & Davis, I. (2004). *At risk: Natural hazards, people's vulnerability and disasters*, 2nd ed. London: Routledge.

Woolcock, M. (2010). The rise and routinization of social capital, 1988–2008. *Annual Review of Political Science, 13*(1), 469–487.

Young, A. (2006). Trauma und Verarbeitung in den USA nach dem 11. September. In E. Wohlfart & M. Zaumseil (Eds.), *Transkulturelle Psychiatrie. Interkulturelle Psychotherapie* (pp. 391–410). Heidelberg: Springer.

Zeidner, M. (2006). Gender group differences in coping with chronic terror: The Israeli scene. *Sex Roles, 54*(3/4), 297–310.

Zeidner, M., & Hammer, A. (1992). Coping with missile attack: Resources, strategies, and outcomes. *Journal of Personality, 60*, 709.

Chapter 3
A Cultural Psychological Framework for Coping with Disasters

Manfred Zaumseil, Mechthild von Vacano, Silke Schwarz, Gavin B. Sullivan and Johana E. Prawitasari-Hadiyono

Incorporating the notion of complexity from recent approaches into disaster research, we argue for a theory of coping that transcends the universalist and individualist assumptions of coping theory. We locate this approach in cultural psychology and base our reconceptualization of coping processes on the core assumption of a permeating co-constitution of person and context. Context contains notions of material, symbolic, and social surroundings, whereas the person is always embedded in multiple contexts simultaneously. Agency, therefore, is engendered and inhibited in person–context relations. Instead of developing yet another coping model of universal psychological functioning, we opt to replace causal assumptions by referential relations and argue for an interpretative research approach to coping in context, one that integrates existing coping models as heuristic devices. Drawing from the insights of disaster research, we further broaden our understanding of coping and

M. Zaumseil (✉) · S. Schwarz
International Academy for Innovative Pedagogy, Psychology and Economics gGmbH at Freie Universität Berlin, Malteserstr. 74-100, 12249 Berlin, Germany
e-mail: zaumseil@zedat.fu-berlin.de

M. von Vacano
Institute for Social and Cultural Anthropology,
Freie Universität Berlin, Landoltweg 9-11, 14195 Berlin, Germany
e-mail: m.vacano@fu-berlin.de

S. Schwarz
e-mail: silke.schwarz@fu-berlin.de; silgnschwarz@yahoo.de

G. B. Sullivan
School of Social, Psychological and Communication Sciences,
Leeds Metropolitan University, City Campus, LS1 3HE Leeds, UK
e-mail: g.sullivan@leedsmet.ac.uk; gsullivan34@yahoo.com

J. E. Prawitasari-Hadiyono
Center for Research and Community Service,
Christian University of Krida Wacana,
Jl. Tanjung Duren Raya No. 4, 11470 Jakarta, Indonesia
e-mail: jeprawitasari@ukrida.ac.id

Universitas Gadjah Mada, 55281 Yogyakarta, Indonesia

M. Zaumseil et al. (eds.), *Cultural Psychology of Coping with Disasters*,
DOI 10.1007/978-1-4614-9354-9_3, © Springer Science+Business Media, LLC 2014

conclude by presenting coping as complex material-symbolic, cognitive-embodied, and individual-social processes that are contingent on the micro- and macrodynamics of the individual life course, community processes, and global histories.

3.1 Basic Assumptions of a Cultural Psychology Approach

From the outset, it is important to address the theoretical and methodological propositions of a cultural psychology (Cole 1996; Kitayama and Cohen 2007; Miller 2002; Greenfield 2000; Belzen 2010) and a sociocultural psychology (Markus and Hamedani 2007) that can be applied to disasters. From this perspective, psychological processes are seen as grounded in particular sociocultural historical contexts. Psychological phenomena are considered to be constituted by cultural meanings and practices rather than formed in a manner that is independent of sociocultural input (Miller 2002).

> Sociocultural psychology requires spanning the divides created by the many familiar and foundational psychological binaries that is, person-situation, individual-environment, culture-social structure, and self-society, that conceptualize people as separate from their "surrounding" contexts. (Markus and Hamedani 2007, p. 6)

Following Markus and Hamedani (2007), we do not assume that sociocultural contexts only determine the forms of behavior but rather emphasize that people actively interact with multiple contexts; in our view, sociocultural and psychological features create each other in a process of mutual constitution. For an understanding of context and psychological processes, several consequences can be derived from this perspective, as follows:

Moving Beyond Dualisms Any binary juxtaposition of context and psychological processes tears apart elements that belong together because they mutually constitute one another. Personal and sociocultural features thus cannot be separated.

Accounting for a Multiplicity Of Contexts The mutual constitution of psychological processes and contexts implies that psychological processes differ based on the context with which they share a co-constitutive relationship. In other words, there are fundamentally different ways of being a person in different contexts.

Broadening the Context Sociocultural models tend to highlight ideas, practices, systems of meanings, representations, and values as contextual characteristics. However, other aspects of contexts also require consideration. These aspects can include the material environment—experienced and perceived through practices and interpretations—or social constellations of difference and power.

Accounting for Agencies The idea of mutual constitution implies the agency of both the person and the context. Human agency can change contexts—or rather, it can be self-referential and aim for personal transformations—but sociostructural and material contexts not only represent arenas of human agency, they also determine the limitations of this agency.

Interpretive Approach The mutual constitution of psychological and contextual features evolves along a process of social construction and implies that there is no separate reality that is independent of the person acting within it. In order to investigate this constitution, we think it is appropriate to adopt a phenomenological interpretive approach (in the sense of Schütz and Luckmann 1973; Bruner 1990). The self–context relationship is no longer construed in terms of cause and effect or correlations; instead, psychological phenomena are embedded in collective systems of practice and knowledge. The meanings of these components can only be understood within their referential contexts (Straub and Thomas 2003; Straub and Chakkarath 2010; Cole 1996), and thus require interpretative research strategies.

Conceptualizing Change and Stability We understand both—context(s) and the self—as dynamic constructs that may transform in cycles of mutual constitution (Markus and Kitayama 2010). However, this type of dynamic relation does not necessarily imply change. Most sociostructural contexts appear to be stable rather than in flux, although this stability is also (re)produced in persistent person–context dynamics.

A brief comparison with assumptions of traditional cross-cultural psychological approaches might serve to clarify the strengths of a framework based on the cultural psychological assumptions outlined above. In cross-cultural psychology, researchers validate the universality of existing psychological theories in diverse cultural contexts in order to develop universal models that predict behavior on a worldwide scale. Cross-cultural psychology operationalizes culture as an antecedent or independent variable while trying to quantify cultural differences. Thus, sociocultural context is separated from psychological dynamics and considered to be an index rather than a process. In the *ecocultural approach* of cross-cultural psychology employed by Berry (1976, 2001) for instance, human psychological diversity is explained through ecological and sociopolitical influences and a set of variables that link these influences to psychological characteristics. Here again, cultural context is treated as an independent variable and the environment is related to psychological features in a deterministic way. As already indicated, we do not adopt this type of analytical separation between person and context; instead, we assume a pervasive co-constitution. Rather than investigating causal relations, we look for referential relationships between meanings in cultural practices and therefore allow for cultural or, more broadly, contextual specificity while avoiding universal presumptions.

Our understanding of subjectivity as permeated by sociocultural features draws on a social constructionist epistemology.[1] In accordance with the cultural historic approach (Vygotsky 1985) and symbolic interactionism (Mead 1934), we assume that developments in psychological processes originate in social processes, while mediation is achieved via language (see Gergen 1999) and performative acts (Gergen and Gergen 2010). Social constructionism is thus an important theoretical tool: The

[1] However, we expand social constructionism to include the notion of a materialist social constructionism (Clarke 2005) and embodiment in a broader sense, drawing from Bourdieu's (2002) concept of habitus.

self and knowledge about the world are constructed in social practices and there are many different possible variations, none of which can be verified by objective access to the world as it really is (Goodman 1978). This results in the creation of a multitude of person–context units. In the deconstruction of truth claims, we can enquire about the motives behind any particular version of constructed reality but different positions with regard to various power relations become apparent. However, social constructionist approaches often remain confined to the symbolic and rarely account for agency in an active sense, for example, humans shaping and changing the world they inhabit.

3.2 Rethinking the Person–Context Relationship

As we have highlighted above, the co-constitutive relationship of persons and contexts is central to our cultural psychological approach. We deliberately chose to develop our theoretical approach around the notion of context as a broad category. Culture—as the obvious concern of cultural psychology—is located conceptually in and in-between context(s) and person(s). In the following section, we further define our understanding of context.

3.2.1 Meaning and the Material

The contextual aspects of experience and action receive differing degrees of cultural psychological emphasis depending on whether the focus is placed on the intentional world of meanings, interactions, and the semiotic subject (Mead 1934; Bruner 1990; Shweder 1993) or on tool use, everyday practical action, artifacts, and material and institutional structures (Cole 1996). We combine these two main perspectives as both refer to the complex connections between humans and their man-made material or immaterial contexts and structures, which are continuously renewed and changed through human practice and shared experience. In a similar vein, Marcus and Hamedani (2007) developed a broad understanding of the sociocultural context, which entails meanings, interactions, and cultural products. Defining the "sociocultural," they wrote:

> Thus, it includes both *meanings*—ideas, images representations, attitudes, values, prototypes and stereotypes—and what is often termed the *sociostructural*—cultural products, interpersonal interactions, institutional practices and systems—and person–situation contingencies, all of which embody, as well as render material and operable normative patterns prevalent in a given context. (p. 5, italics in original)

Different metaphors are employed to describe the ways in which the personal and the material context relate to one another. In his ecological model, Bronfenbrenner

(1981) used the image of concentric circles[2]. These circles encompass personal development and represent a series of nested systems. This metaphor is useful to illustrate how the micro and macro contexts are permeated by one another. However, this reduces context to the mere surroundings, to environment and proximate causes. Cole (1996) offered another metaphoric understanding of "context as that which weaves together" (p. 135). Contexts are not immutable, and systems or threads of contexts can recombine in new patterns. Context is both inherent and constructed. It is—to employ Cole's perspective again—constructed by the actions of the subjects and held together through the use of tools, or mediating artifacts.

3.2.2 Communities as Social Context

Marcus and Hamedani's (2007) definition of context as including meanings and social structures recognizes the additional important social element of context. While meaning always refers to shared, though potentially contested, interpretations, a focus on *socio*structural features includes, among other things, interpersonal relations and institutions. On this view, there are multiple social contexts and these are connected to the practice of social interaction.

The community provides a perspective on social context, one which is frequently used and which has found its application in the field of community psychology. Building on Campbell (2001), who suggested an understanding of community based on the three dimensions of sentiment, space, and social structure, Kagan et al. (2011) specified a meaningful notion of community. In their account, sentiment "operates in a psychological, cultural and symbolic sense" (Kagan et al. 2011, p. 74) and resembles the construct of a *sense of community* (Sarason 1974) with a focus on shared symbols and understandings as well as a shared emotional attachment to a group and location or place.

On an analytical level, community can be understood as a social actor or a social field (in the sense of Bourdieu 1986). In the latter example, social actors and individual persons act in more or less conflicting ways based on their membership in social groups and their interests. In contrast, the understanding of community as an actor normally relies on an ideal type model in which the community functions as a social unit of agency (e.g., in the sense of community resilience): social support, sense of belonging, and social bonds of affection and cooperation are emphasized while coercion and the potential conflicting interests of community members tend to be neglected. However, both the harsh reality of exclusion and the concurrent processes of internal solidarity need to be accounted for.

---

[2] The microsystem (e.g., family and neighborhood), the mesosystem (the interaction of two microsystem environments), the exosystem, the macrosystem (the larger cultural context), and the chronosystem (the context of passing time). These events may have an impact on a particular birth cohort.

Furthermore, inequalities in power and resources permeate communities and social contexts in general. In order to establish a comprehensive view of the socio-cultural aspects, it is important also to adopt the approaches of critical (community) psychology, which draw attention to disadvantage, oppression, marginalization, racism, poverty, and colonization (Nelson and Prilleltensky 2010; Kagan et al. 2011; Markard 2010).

3.2.3 Subjectivity and Agency

In order to account for the *mutual* constitution of person and context, concepts of agency address the human capacity to shape social and material worlds. However, approaches differ with regard to the question where they locate the sources of agency. For cultural psychologists Markus and Kitayama (2010), the sense of agency is a central component of the self:

> A self is the "me" at the center of experience—a continually developing sense of awareness and agency that guides actions and takes shape as the individual, both brain and body, becomes attuned to various environments. Selves incorporate the patterning of their various environments and thus confer particular and culture-specific form and function to the psychological processes they organize (e.g., attention, perception, cognition, emotion, motivation, interpersonal relationship, group). In turn, as selves engage with their sociocultural contexts, they reinforce and sometimes change the ideas, practices, and institutions of these environments. (p. 420)

To view the "me" as the center of experience and the sense of agency as individualistic is one particular way of understanding the self. The way in which people associate and experience agency is context bound in and of itself (Markus and Hamedani 2007). The sense of agency is not a characteristic of the individual; it is created dynamically in the mutual constitution of person and context (Markus and Hamedani 2007). In Western psychology, however, this notion of self has been (re)produced as a universalistic fallacy of the independent self (Markus and Hamedani 2007). It leads to a normative understanding of the self as autonomous, intrinsically motivated, and engaged in control, influence, and self-expression, rather than as socially interdependent and adjusting to others' expectations. However, for many people, the binary of individual self and social context may seem strange. They may associate "experience" more closely with collectively shared realities and not assume that the "me" aspect is central, because experience can be simultaneously social and subjective, collective and individual (Kleinman and Fitz-Henry 2007). The psychological (emotions and actions) is inherently social and does not emerge from the inner, individual self. To develop an understanding of the relationship between the sociocultural and the psychological, bridging terms such as practice and (a non-cognitively-simplified understanding of) meaning can be particularly useful.

If we understand people as products of the social context which they in turn are able to shape, we see being social and "having" agency as basic to the human condition. Yet, the agency people have is also socially embedded, as Ortner (2006) pointed out:

> [I]ndividuals or persons or subjects are always embedded in webs of relations, whether of affection and solidarity, or of power and rivalry, or frequently of some mixture of the two. Whatever "agency" they seem to "have" as individuals is in reality something that is always in fact interactively negotiated. (p. 151)

In the following sections, we apply these insights to a reconceptualization of coping processes, where these are traditionally understood in cognitive terms.

3.3 Reconceptualizing Coping Processes in Person–Context Relations

The appraisal-based coping approach made it possible to relate the individual psychological responses in a stressful situation to the situational context. Deriving the term from pragmatism, Lazarus (1999) described the situation–person relationship as a "transaction" in order to emphasize the personal connotation of events perceived as stressful. It is on this subjective basis alone that people appraise the situation by evaluating the relationship between themselves and the environment. However, it remains problematic with this approach and more recent iterations that person and context are treated as distinct entities separated into cause and effect relationships. This separation stands in direct conflict with the cultural psychological understanding of person and context, described above, as permeating one another.

3.3.1 Replacing Causal Assumptions by Referential Relations

The appraisal-based model is based on functionalist assumptions of cause–effect relations and distinguishes between antecedents, which are usually located in the "context" (situational demands, constraints, values, and beliefs), mediating processes (idiosyncratic appraisals and applied coping strategies), and effects (emotional, social, and moral coping outcomes). This model relies on the basic distinction between problem-focused coping, which refers to coping efforts directed toward the external condition(s) causing stress, and emotion-focused coping, which describes inward-directed coping efforts, such as the management of an individual's own thoughts or emotions.

On the whole, we use the Lazarus model in a heuristic fashion and replace the focus on causal relations between variables with referential relations of meanings. This means that we do not attempt to correlate constructs such as social support, self-efficacy, or well-being, as emphasized by questionnaires. Instead, we view these assumed interrelations as a point of reference for a heuristic research strategy; the different forms of coping established in quantitative coping research serve us as an analytical inspiration in the sense of the sensitizing concepts of grounded theory (see Sect. 5.3). Instead of relying on universalist psychological mechanisms, our goal is to develop strategies for identifying relationships in specific contexts. We do not separate and correlate the variables of central characteristics of the various coping models (i.e., the antecedents, mediating processes, and effects of stressful and overwhelming experiences). We are far more interested in examining behavior in the given context from an emic perspective and determining what it means, for example, when research participants explain that their relationship to Allah allows them to accept the death of someone close to them, when they tell us about their methods and attitudes that were positive with regard to reconstruction work, or how they deal with the pain of the betrayal they experienced due to the way in which aid was distributed. This way we can deduce specific forms of coping imbedded in particular contexts.

3.3.2 Appraisal and Meaning-Making in Social Context

Within its individual, idiosyncratic framework, Lazarus' (1999) appraisal-oriented model can be called constructivist. The point of departure for this model from our social constructionist perspective is the subject's personal, subjective appraisal and reappraisal of the dynamic, mutually reciprocal, person–environment relationship. For our purposes, we need to contextualize and expand the individual in a constructivist manner because "individual" processes of evaluation and perception are not self-referential, but in fact are permeated by complex sociocultural processes. To a certain extent, Hobfoll's (1998, 2011) work has already developed in this direction with his attempt to proceed from self-regulation in stress contexts to self-in-social-setting regulation by placing the dynamics of resource loss and gain *in a social context* at the center of his model.

Another approach, which is more cognitivist than the appraisal in the Lazarus model, is the understanding of meaning-making processes proposed by Park (2005, 2010). In Park's model, subjective appraisals of the situation are related to subjective general orientations (global meanings). This understanding has an arbitrary, or random, component and subjective orientations are not linked to discourses and social meanings. In terms of its functional purpose in the process of coping, meaning is only relevant insofar as it is a by-product of the mind of the individual doing the coping. Instead of adopting such a reductionist view of mind (cf. Bruner 1990), we promote an interpretive approach which relates personal meanings to different local, global, and imported meanings of the intentional world. In order to construct meaning, people use (various) symbolic systems, which are deeply embedded in culture as well as in language and material artifacts.

The perspective we adopt is consistent with Markus and Kitayama's (2010) view that "meanings, beliefs and values are externalized and materialized in the world (D'Andrade 1995) and, thus, no longer need to be packed in the head of each individual member of the cultural group" (p. 287). Meanings are negotiated in the social fields in which the person is embedded and cannot therefore be reduced to their functional role in the coping process. Thus, meaning-making processes can only be analyzed using interpretative research strategies that situate meanings within multiple person–context constellations.

3.3.3 *Incorporating Practice Theory*

In appraisal-oriented coping models, the subject is an active, goal-striving individual with idiosyncratic values and beliefs that reflect her or his appraisal of the situation and her or his personal resources. Thus, these models emphasize the cognitions, motives, and goals of the person in question. Here, a double division is drawn between the individual and her or his social context as well as between the mind and the body. This double division is rooted in a particular conception of the subject, the self, and emotions which is prevalent in Western thinking; this conception separates inner experience and outside expression and implies a culture of individuality and interiority (Taylor 1989). The mind–body division results in cognition being valued more highly than emotion. Body and emotion are removed from the arena of socialization and placed within the sphere of universal physiology, biology, and evolution. Lazarus' (1991, 1993, 1999) view also derives emotions and their orienting functions (relational emotional themes) from biology and evolution. On this view, culture only directs the specific orientation of the emotions. However, the body is more than biology; it is a "mindful body" (Scheper-Hughes and Lock 1987) constituted in interaction with the social context. Thus, we choose to supplement the cognitive orientation with another understanding grounded in practice theory.

Here, the body, or emotions, are viewed as context-specific forms of socialization (Scheer 2012). Based on this understanding, emotions emerge from acquired bodily knowledge. As emotional practices, emotions are generated within their social contexts and power relations. Throughout history, emotions have been formed in a wide variety of social ways: by being mobilized, named, communicated, and regulated (Scheer 2012). Scheer provides a compelling account of the emotional socialization that led to the different forms of Protestant inwardness. Thus, in coping situations, emotions are not physically created and managed (controlled) by the mind; they are embedded in—and perpetuate—these histories of social shaping. However, in relation to other aspects also, practice theory helps to counteract the cognitivist bias, for example, with respect to religious coping. Although the predominant approaches to religious coping view religiosity as a cognitive process that can be examined by asking questions about an individual's conscious convictions, the cultural psychologist Belzen (2010) argues that religion should be understood as one of a number of different, practical, shared activities. Religion then regulates conduct, though this cannot be viewed as the conscious following of rules; it is more a habitus (in the sense of Bourdieu, see Chap. 2) than a goal-directed behavior. The "doing" of religion would thus need to be considered an inseparable aspect of religious coping; individual or collective forms of prayer, then, have to be analyzed as an embodied experience and not "just" in terms of expressive or communicative aspects.

3.3.4 *Accounting for Power Differentials*

Because Lazarus' individualist coping model neglects the social element of coping processes, it also ignores all questions of power. In his resource-oriented approach, Hobfoll situated the coping subject in social contexts and addressed the question of power. His metaphor of *resource caravan passageways* (see Sect. 2.3.1; Hobfoll 2011) therefore serves as a helpful reference point to grasp the conceptual implications of the possibilities and limits of agency. Social structures of discrimination and privilege have a significant influence on individual resource dynamics, and power differentials are potentially reproduced in coping processes: People who lack status and power experience continuous social discrimination almost independently of their own behavior, whereas privileged access to resources reproduces beneficial conditions for personal developments and leads to further status enhancements. The mastery and/or self-efficacy attributed to individuals in coping processes needs to be interpreted against this background: These aspects indicate the function of a privileged position, or a privileged passageway of resource caravans (Hobfoll 2011), rather than individual functioning itself.

Moreover, if we go one step further and think of coping as a social process (see Sect. 2.4), these processes need to be situated in productive constellations of power in an even more profound way. Critical community psychologists have pointed to the fact that histories of colonialism and the ongoing dynamics of oppression and liberation in different (post)colonial contexts shape adaptation processes (see Nelson and Prilleltensky 2010; Kagan et al. 2011). Because the "culture" of cultural psychology "is continually shaped by socio-historical and political processes intertwined within the globalized history of power" (Reyes and Sonn 2011, p. 203), coping is embedded in larger power structures and dynamics. Thus, different patterns of coping cannot be attributed to an essential characteristic of that social group (e.g., "women" as vulnerable or emotional) but have to be addressed in conjunction with institutional frameworks and societal routines. This line of argument has been pursued, for example, by feminist psychologists such as Mejia (2005). Such a power-critical perspective requires theorists to link macrostructures of coping to the microprocesses of coping: national or global politics influence the way people cope, as they structure available resources in a significant way—in material, infrastructure, and discursive terms. To stay with the two structural categories already mentioned above, colonial orders and gender norms are internalized and embodied experiences, again varying according to specific contextual constellations. As such, they are continuously (re)produced—and challenged—throughout coping processes.

3.3.5 Abandoning Universalism for the ("Cultural") Particular

All of the points mentioned above reflect the most basic implication associated with a cultural psychology of coping: a farewell to all forms of universalism. In Sect. 2.4.1.2 we elaborated on the universalist claims of coping models and their implicit Eurocentrism. Universalist theories of psychological coping mechanisms treat psychological functions as if they were independent of the context and function solely as characteristics of the individual. Some approaches address cultural diversity using an additive strategy in which they take the forms of coping that appear in a particular cultural context and add one or two forms that presumably appear in members of other cultures (e.g., harmony control, see Morling and Fiske 1999, or indirect control, see

Hobfoll 1998). It was using this type of strategy that psychiatric classifications were expanded to include culture-bound syndromes—a kind of exotic psychopathology of "folk illnesses"—which, regardless of the context, were ascribed to the individual as a cultural particularity within the framework of a universal model of psychological functioning (or dysfunctioning). In this way, cultural plurality is incorporated into psychological models only in a superficial way; their claims to universalism, on the other hand, remain unquestioned.

Religious coping is subject to equally superficial treatment within the framework of cross-cultural psychology. In these models, religion is viewed as monolithic Christianity or monolithic Islam (see Sect. 2.2.3); it is artificially separated from the local sociocultural context and broken down into abstract mathematicized relations between variables as part of the drive to quantification in psychology (see Machado and Silva 2007). A cultural psychological understanding of religion, on the contrary, assumes that religiosity cannot be defined in general terms and that researchers can only approach religion through its cultural, contextual, and historical components. This type of understanding requires us to take a hermeneutic-constructivist approach to religion and religious coping:

> [A]s there exists no religion in general, but only specific forms of life that fall under the label of "being religious," and as psychology should not strive to identify supposedly basic elements of psychic functioning valid for all subjects, regardless of time and place, a psychology of religion should aim to determine how a specific religious form of life generates, incorporates and regulates the psychic functioning of the persons involved. (Belzen 2010, 344f.)

In Java, for example, we find a variety of Islamic forms of life that integrate older Javanese cosmologies and practices to a greater or lesser degree (see Sect. 4.1). However, even those who claim to live according to "pure" Islamic principles articulate their identities in a global, national, but also very communal context in which religious plurality is negotiated against a privileged position of Islam, with Islam being a contested field of interpretation itself. Religious meanings and public expressions of religiousness are thus always embedded in religiopolitical discourses, which are deployed and negotiated by actors sometimes without explicit intentions. This applies to both religion in everyday life and to religious coping in a crisis. Religion is only one example and it is important to add that secular worldviews are just as grounded in their respective contexts and oriented toward a *particular* way of seeing the world.

Within his universalist frame of conservation of resources (COR) theory, Hobfoll offers several reference points for conceptualizing coping as situated in context(s). Not only does he account for status and power differences (see earlier discussion), he also allows for a cultural relativist perspective on coping resources: he considers these resources to be dependent upon their relative value in a specific cultural context. This type of understanding may help to develop a material social constructionist understanding of material resources: because while food supply and/or physical security are not purely discursive matters, nevertheless, they are still imbued with contextual meaning and social value.

Example 1: Alternative Perspectives on (Disaster) Mental Health Disaster mental health is largely separate from stress-coping research. It has developed as a specialized field with its own terminology and as a universal approach to extreme suffering. This approach is largely driven by a medical logic and posits that universally recognized psychological disorders appear in disaster survivors when a traumatic event occurs within a person's local environment (external), causing a vulnerable psyche (internal) to be "weakened". The diagnosed disorder is a function of the individual, meaning that it is separate from the context and must be treated in the individual and in the community using medical discourses and practices. This understanding is associated with a decontextualization, which is particularly prevalent in the international disaster aid scene. This renders it extremely difficult to attempt a sociocultural recontextualization of psychological suffering in the wake of disasters (Breslau 2004). In contrast to this understanding, we recommend viewing suffering as "inherently subjective, local and pluralistic in nature" (Priya 2012, p. 214). In the case of persistent and extreme psychological impairments in the aftermath of a disaster, the question presents itself: how have the affected parties arrived at this assessment and how should their assessment be handled in the local sociocultural context. Furthermore, expressions of embodied experiences and emotions (local) as idioms of distress[3] can also point to emic interpretations of fright as well as emic models for overcoming it. However, as with "local" knowledge, there may also be numerous interactions between local idioms or practices and imported Western concepts (see Abramowitz 2010 in particular). This can be seen in the use of the imported term "trauma," in numerous languages and its connection to local meanings.

3.4 Coping from a Disaster Theoretical Perspective

Although it is mostly formulated on a macrolevel, we suggest reading the disaster literature with regard to its possible contribution to an understanding of coping processes in disaster contexts. In recent disaster approaches, disasters are seen as processes rather than as singular events; they are broadly contextualized in time and situated in historically (re)produced social structures or human–environment relationships. Overall, this process has been characterized as multidimensional (Oliver-Smith 1999) insofar as it potentially affects all aspects of human life—environmental, economic, political, social, or ideological. In addition, the environmental paradigm has promoted an understanding of disasters as complex mutual interactions between human societies and nature (Hilhorst 2007). If we combine this perspective with our cultural psychological notion of mutual person–context constitution, context can refer to human society (in different scales), to the physical environment ("nature"), *and* to the complex mutual interaction between these arenas. The environment, as we argued in Sect. 1.3.1, is an inherently social category because the way individuals

[3] Local idioms of distress are considered to be dependent on local knowledge; they are viewed as "those particular ways in which members of sociocultural groups convey affliction. Idioms vary across cultures, depending on the salient metaphors and popular traditions that pattern the human biological capacity for experiencing distress" (Hinton and Lewis-Fernández 2010, p. 210).

experience the forces of nature is mediated through interpretations and practices that are socially shared, diverse, and potentially contradictory.

Constructionist authors in particular have pointed to the fact that a "disaster" is constituted by a social process of demarcating certain situations as extraordinary "events" and interpreted these categorization processes against the backdrop of political and economic structures and motivations (see Sect. 1.3.3). Most definitions of disaster converge when it comes to highlighting the collective large-scale impact of disasters in which their destructive effects lead to a disruption of "normal" life. Within the hazards paradigm, as well as implicitly in many recent approaches, disasters are conceived as external forces affecting a larger social unit or community, with an impact that exceeds the coping capacities of the community itself, thus necessitating external aid. Coping with disasters always contains a collective notion of suffering and the allocation of external resources is dependent upon whether or not the collective adverse situation is recognized as a disaster or not. Therefore, whether or not a given situation is included in or excluded from the category of disaster has an important influence on coping dynamics. By suggesting a much broader category of social stress situations, in which "many members of a social system fail to receive expected conditions of life from the system," Barton (1969, p. 38) portrays such definitional processes as contested fields in which the recognition of subjective suffering and need is negotiated. The very recognition of plight is at stake when people frame their situation of loss and destruction as part of a process of meaning-making.

Yet another interesting aspect lies in the cultural construction of the disaster event as a disruption of normality. This construction implies a relative high degree of stability, security, and predictability in "normal" life. All these are notions that can be tied to a particular privileged outlook on life; however, to many people in the world, life may be uncertain. The ways in which people cope with disasters should thus be interpreted against the backdrop of what people consider to be normal. Furthermore, these strategies need to be contextualized in their individual and collective experiences of potentially chronic adversity, in its multiple forms. In this way, the periodization of disaster, for example, understanding a disaster as a singular event, is a form of collective meaning-making in and of itself; the same idea is reflected in the idiosyncratic appraisal in which the individual interprets a certain situation as "stress" when compared to other life challenges.

Another important point of reference for our study is the discourse on local knowledge. In a broad sense, the discourse on local knowledge helps us to examine the extent to which any knowledge is situated within a particular context (see Sect. 1.4.4) and allows us to analyze privileged knowledge claims, such as universalist assumptions about human functioning. The assumption of local knowledge as something positive, derived from more sustainable ways of life, has a positive bias and needs to be questioned in analysis and, ultimately, abandoned. However, the empowering implications of local knowledge as a conscious, explicit discourse countering global—mainly Western—hegemony contribute an important view of coping processes as socially situated. We thus identify twofold coping resources with regard to the local knowledge discourse as a set of particular coping capacities and as a means of reinforcing "local" pride in these capacities. In this regard, local knowledge is yet another example of the complex embeddedness of coping processes in sociopolitical macrocontexts, a fact which lends support to our argument that coping is always more than a functional response to stress.

The notion of the "local" in local knowledge further allows us to situate coping in long-term processes of human–nature interaction in which experience with the local environment is culturally transmitted in explicit—or moreover, implicit—ways. However, this knowledge should by no means mistakenly be viewed as static, isolated, or monolithic. It is also important to note that this knowledge is not merely a matter of cognitive knowledge; it also includes habitualized bodily "knowledge" (see Sect. 3.3).

Example 2: Alternative Perspectives on Disaster Risk Reduction Within the last decade, disaster risk reduction has gained traction in disaster management and research. The international disaster literature presents risk reduction as a global strategy and uses generalized models to identify the conditions that contribute to or hinder risk reduction. The entire field of risk management is grounded in specific notions of risk, human agency, control, or security and a normative imperative of prevention (see Sect. 1.2.3), but the everyday integration of *disaster* risk needs to be contextualized in terms of people's diverse living conditions, which may be characterized by multiple uncertainties and threats. In this respect, it is important to examine the circumstances in which the global discourses and strategies for action and the local understandings and practices are created and carried out. We identify two problems here: first, that notions of risk can be extremely divergent and second, that the same difficulty may apply to the notions of risk "reduction" and the consequences for related action plans. In Chap. 1 we argued that risk is not an objective phenomenon, but rather a social construct created in a local context and that risk reduction measures are not automatically derived from risk perception. Here, in the active component of risk reduction, the cultural psychological conceptions take on central importance: How are the local understandings of action and/or local practices constituted? How are actors' perceptions of action influenced by global and adopted external risk reduction strategies and how do these different understandings interact with one another? In the context of disaster literature, understanding the possibilities and limits of human agency is key (not only in relation to social structure). For us, it is important to learn how local events are understood and associated with meanings in the context of a disaster, how they are linked to local and external influences, and which individuals, authorities, or organizations are ascribed with agency (and concomitantly with responsibility) for risk reduction.

3.5 Critical Characteristics of a Cultural Psychology of Coping with Disasters

By formulating a cultural psychology of coping with disasters, it is our goal to close the theoretical gap between sociocultural disaster research, which has been prominently developed in the disciplines of anthropology and sociology, and universalist psychological research approaches to disaster or stress. The cultural psychological perspective is reflected in the fact that our analysis begins at the nexus between local events and the subjective experiences and actions of the affected parties. We view individuals as embedded in multiple contexts and at the same time, we consider the person–context relationship to be mutually or co-constituting. Personhood, therefore, is contained within different forms of social interaction as well as in symbolic meanings, material manifestations, and performative behaviors while simultaneously helping to create these phenomena. Our analytic perspective thus aims to understand subjective coping processes with regard to disaster while positioning these processes within person–context relations.

If disasters are multidimensional processes (Oliver-Smith 1999), then it is reasonable to think that coping with disasters is also multidimensional: Coping processes are embedded in structural and sociocultural contexts that not only produce—or inhibit—agency, but also interpretatively frame the very "stressor" to be coped with and structure the embodied experience of suffering. Following the disaster research paradigm of *complex* interactions between nature and human described in Sect. 1.1, we argue for a complexity theory of coping.

Coping is a complex material-symbolic, cognitive-embodied, and individual-social process. Coping can neither be reduced to an "objective" material sphere nor to a symbolic arena in which the environment and resources are deemed to be solely a matter of perception. Subjective experiences, perceptions, emotions, and meaning are socially mediated, constructed, and simultaneously linked to a biophysical materiality. The way in which people cope is significantly shaped by their actual access to resources. However, the mediation between the material and symbolic takes place; an individual's actual losses or gains (e.g., reputation, property, power and capabilities) represent an important component of subjectivity. In addition, personal–subjective responses to disaster are products of an individual's (religious) orientation system or practiced habitus. In the sense of mindful bodies, the habitus comprises the physical and emotional side of experience, action, and performance; body and emotions are linked to the context through an individual's socialization history and can be understood on this basis. Coping processes cannot be reduced to what decontextualized individuals think, feel, and do; at the same time, the individual component, which is based on different interests, experiences, and positions in power relationships and personalities, must not be neglected for the sake of a broader collective context, be that the individual's community or "culture" (i.e., macro-reduction of individual differences). As interpretative (meaning) or behavioral (habitus) patterns imply, coping is never an idiosyncratic process. Nevertheless, it is analytically necessary to examine personal methods of coping and relate them to their complex social contexts. While a cultural psychological perspective on collective coping efforts focuses on the subjective involvement of multiple actors, these collectives may refer to different social units—from the family to the village, the congregation, or the nation.

Coping processes are contingent upon the micro- and macrodynamics of an individual's life course, community processes, and global histories. Accordingly, coping processes are driven by multiple potentially contradictory interests, which do not necessary relate to "coping" itself, but to other—not necessarily disaster-related—dynamics. A cultural psychology of coping therefore needs to include the broader picture and abandon functionalist assumptions. The challenge is to comprehend—or at least try to comprehend—what is subjectively at stake for the different actors involved when they rely on any given method of coping.

Throughout this chapter, we developed our argument for a person–context situated understanding of coping, elaborating on multiple aspects of context, which we view as a broad, and necessarily vague, category. Because any theoretical framework based on this type of person–context understanding would need to accommodate these hazy notions of context, we borrow the conceptual framework of complexity from disaster research and suggest framing coping (with disasters) as a complex process. At the same time, we do not want to imply that complexity is a sufficient means of describing the local and subjective dynamics of coping with disasters; such answers can only be found in qualitative, interpretative, in-depth studies localized in specific settings. In our research strategy, we turn the causal models of conventional coping theory into heuristic frameworks of relational references, while at the same time opening our analytical perspective by integrating a multidisciplinary body of disaster research and reviewing relevant ethnographic literature.

Acknowledgment We would like to thank Devin Martini for assistance with editing and translating parts of this chapter from German into English.

References

Abramowitz, S. A. (2010). Trauma and humanitarian translation in Liberia: The tale of open mole. *Culture, Medicine, and Psychiatry, 34*(2), 353–379.
Barton, A. H. (1969). *Communities in disaster: A sociological analysis of collective stress situations*. Garden City: Doubleday.
Belzen, J. (2010). Psychology of religion: Perspectives from cultural psychology. *Mental Health, Religion & Culture, 13*(4), 329–347.
Berry, J. W. (1976). *Human ecology and cognitive style*. New York: Wiley.
Berry, J. W. (2001). Contextual studies of cognitive adaptation. In J. M. Collis & S. Messick (Eds.), *Intelligence and personality: Bridging the gap in theory and measurement* (pp. 319–333). Mahwah: Lawrence Erlbaum.
Bourdieu, P. (1986). Der Kampf um die symbolische Ordnung. Pierre Bourdieu im Gespräch mit A. Honneth, H. Kocyba & B. Schwibs. *Ästhetik und Kommunikation, 16*(61/62), 142–164.
Bourdieu, P. (2002). Habitus. In J. Hillier & E. Rooksby (Eds.), *Habitus* (pp. 27–32). Aldershot: Ashgate.
Breslau, J. (2004). Cultures of trauma. *Culture, Medicine and Psychiatry, 28*(2), 113–126.
Bronfenbrenner, U. (1981). *Die Ökologie der menschlichen Entwicklung. Natürliche und geplante Experimente*. Stuttgart: Klett-Cotta.
Bruner, J. (1990). *Acts of meaning*. Cambridge: Harvard University Press.
Campbell, C. (2001). Social structure, space, and sentiment: Searching for common ground in sociological conceptions of community. *Research and Community Sociology, 10,* 21–57.
Clarke, A. (2005). *Situational analysis. Grounded theory after the postmodern turn*. Thousand Oaks: Sage.
Cole, M. (1996). *Cultural psychology: A once and future discipline*. Cambridge: Harvard University Press.
Gergen, K. J. (1999). *An invitation to social construction*. London: Sage.

Gergen, M. M., & Gergen, K. J. (2010). Performative social science and psychology [13 paragraphs]. *Forum Qualitative Social Research, 12*(1). http://nbn-resolving.de/urn:nbn:de:0114-fqs1101119. Accessed 04 July 2013.

Goodman, N. (1978). *Ways of worldmaking*. Indianapolis: Hackett.

Greenfield, P. M. (2000). Three approaches to the psychology of culture: Where do they come from? Where can they go? *Asian Journal of Social Psychology, 3,* 223–240.

Hilhorst, D. (2007). Complexity and diversity: Unlocking social domains of disaster response. In G. Bankoff, G. Frerks & D. Hilhorst (Eds.), *Mapping vulnerability* (pp. 52–66). London: Earthscan.

Hinton, D. E., & Lewis-Fernández, R. (2010). Idioms of distress among trauma survivors: Subtypes and clinical utility. *Culture, Medicine, and Psychiatry, 34*(2), 209–218.

Hobfoll, S. E. (1998). *Stress, culture and community*. New York: Plenum Press.

Hobfoll, S. E. (2011). Conservation of resources theory: Its implication for stress, health and resilience. In S. Folkman & P. E. Nathan (Eds.), *The Oxford handbook of stress, health, and coping* (pp. 127–147). New York: Oxford University Press.

Kagan, C., Burton, M., Duckett, P., Lawthom, R., & Siddiquee, A. (2011). *Critical community psychology*. West Sussex: Wiley-Blackwell.

Kitayama, S., & Cohen, D. (Eds.). (2007). *Handbook of cultural psychology*. New York: Guilford.

Kleinman, A., & Fitz-Henry, E. (2007). The experiential basis of subjectivity: How individuals change in the context of societal transformation. In J. Biehl, B. Good & A. Kleinman (Eds.), *Subjectivity. Ethnographic investigations* (pp. 52–65). Berkeley: University of California Press.

Lazarus, R. S. (1991). *Emotion and adaptation*. London: Oxford University Press.

Lazarus, R. S. (1993). From psychological stress to the emotions: A history of changing outlooks. *Annual Review of Psychology, 44,* 1–21.

Lazarus, R. S. (1999). *Stress and emotion. A new synthesis*. London: Free Association Books.

Machado, A., & Silva, F. (2007). Toward a richer view of the scientific method: The role of conceptual analysis. *American Psychologist, 62*(7), 671–681.

Markard, M. (2010). Kritische Psychologie: Forschung vom Standpunkt des Subjekts. In G. Mey & K. Mruck (Eds.), *Handbuch Qualitative Forschung in der Psychologie* (pp. 166–181). Wiesbaden: Verlag für Sozialwissenschaften.

Markus, H. R., & Hamedani, M. G. (2007). Sociocultural psychology: The dynamic interdependence among self systems and social systems. In S. Kitayama & D. Cohen (Eds.), *Handbook of cultural psychology* (pp. 3–39). New York: Guilford Press.

Markus, H. R., & Kitayama, S. (2010). Cultures and selves. A cycle of mutual constitution. *Perspectives on Psychological Science, 5*(4), 420–430.

Mead, G. H. (1934). *Mind, self, and society*. Chicago: University of Chicago Press.

Mejia, X. E. (2005). Gender matters: Working with adult male survivors of trauma. *Journal of Counseling & Development, 83*(1), 29–40.

Miller, J. G. (2002). Bringing culture to basic psychological theory: Beyond individualism and collectivism: Comment on Oyserman et al. *Psychological Bulletin, 128*(1), 97–109.

Morling, B., & Fiske, S. T. (1999). Defining and measuring harmony control. *Journal of Research in Personality, 33*(4), 379–414.

Nelson, G., & Prilleltensky, I. (2010). *Community psychology. In pursuit of liberation and well-being*. Houndmills: Palgrave Macmillan.

Oliver-Smith, A. (1999). What is a disaster? Anthropological perspectives on a persistent question. In A. Oliver-Smith & S. M. Hoffman (Eds.), *The angry earth: Disaster in anthropological perspectives* (pp. 18–34). New York: Routledge.

Ortner, S. A. (2006). *Anthropology and social theory: Culture, power, and the acting subject.* Durham: Duke University Press Books.

Park, C. L. (2005). Religion as a meaning-making framework in coping with life stress. *Journal of Social Issues, 61*(4), 707–729.

Park, C. L. (2010). Making sense of the meaning literature: An integrative review of meaning making and its effects on adjustment to stressful life events. *Psychological Bulletin, 136*(2), 257–301.

Priya, K. R. (2012). Social constructionist approach to suffering and healing: Juxtaposing Cassell, Gergen and Kleinman. *Psychological Studies, 57,* 211–223.

Reyes, C. M., & Sonn, C. C. (2011). (De)colonizing culture in community psychology: Reflections from critical social science. *American Journal of Community Psychology, 47*(1/2), 203–14.

Sarason, S. B. (1974). *The psychological sense of community: Prospects for a community psychology*. San Francisco: Jossey-Bass.

Scheer, M. (2012). Are emotions a kind of practice (and is that what makes them have a history)? A Bourdieuan approach to understanding emotion. *History and Theory, 51*(2), 193–220.

Schütz, A., & Luckmann, T. (1973). *The structures of the life-world*. Evanston: Northwestern University Press.

Scheper-Hughes, N., & Lock, M. M. (1987). The mindful body: A prolegomenon to future work in medical anthropology. *Medical Anthropology Quarterly, 1*(1), 6–41.

Shweder, R. A. (1993). Everything you ever wanted to know about cognitive appraisal theory without being conscious of it. *Psychological Inquiry: An International Journal for the Advancement of Psychological Theory, 4*(4), 322–342.

Straub, J., & Chakkarath, P. (2010). Kulturpsychologie. In G. Mey & K. Mruck (Eds.), *Handbuch Qualitative Forschung in der Psychologie* (pp. 195–209). Wiesbaden: Verlag für Sozialwissenschaften.

Straub, J., & Thomas, A. (2003). Positionen, Ziele und Entwicklungslinien der kulturvergleichenden Psychologie. In A. Thomas (Ed.), *Kulturvergleichende Psychologie. Cross-cultural psychology* (pp. 29–80). 2nd ed. Göttingen: Hogrefe.

Taylor, C. (1989). *Sources of the self: The making of the modern identity*. Cambridge: Cambridge University Press.

Vygotsky, L. S. (1985). *Thought and language*. Cambridge: MIT Press.

Part II
Context, Method and Reflexive Commentaries on the Case Study

Following the theoretical contributions concerning disasters and coping with their impacts, Part II focuses on contextualization and knowledge production. Chapter 4 presents our case study in Java, Indonesia as a contextual ethnographic introduction exemplifying key sociocultural aspects of the 2006 earthquake post-disaster management context and characteristics of our three research sites.

The discussion of adequate contextualization leads to questions of knowledge production in the context of disasters. Chapter 5 develops a methodological basis for a culture-specific coping approach, including specific propositions about the contextual particularity of human subjectivity and agency. Using grounded theory to reveal specific ways of coping in particular contexts, we demonstrate and recommend the potential of a qualitative research approach. The results of this research process have the potential to be transferable without claiming generalizability. The example of the research in Java and the reflection that took place with the participants leads to a more general discussion about knowledge production in the context of disasters. The research process, including data collection and theorizing, is understood as a process of social interaction in which researchers construct the results in dialogue with others in particular places and times. We consider our 3-year case study a mutual change process in views, concepts and methods. The transformation included the researchers as people, the organization of responsibilities and distribution of tasks, funds and the representation of the project on local and international forums.

Any research project further constitutes a form of contextually situated social practice. In our case, the research (as the empirical inspiration for the book) was an international collaboration and was characterized by transcultural dialogue (Chaps. 6-8). Chapter 6 problematizes tensions between formal norms in research ethics and practical requirements, revealing ethical dilemmas for researchers that touch upon the emotional and interpersonal relationship to the village residents as research participants. Chapter 7 reflects on the multiplicity of roles, power and epistemology from an Indonesian earthquake survivor–researcher collaborating in the international team. The last contribution (Chap. 8) addresses practical experiences, gratifications and challenges of implementing participatory research in a post-disaster community, reflecting on the process from the first steps of building rapport until the final participants' presentation of media products.

Part II
Context, Method and Reflexive Commentaries on the Case Study

[illegible]

Chapter 4
Contextualizing the Research: Introduction to the Case Study in Java, Indonesia

Manfred Zaumseil, Mechthild von Vacano and Silke Schwarz

Our book argues that research on coping with disaster should be grounded in a local setting, integrating a local sociocultural, political, and historical context and making use of any ethnographic literature available. In Part II–IV of our book, we base our theoretical argument for a cultural psychology of coping with disaster on a particular case study of the 2006 Java earthquake. This chapter introduces readers to the sociocultural research setting of Java and the specific earthquake event. It can also be read as an example of how to account for the local context in cultural psychological research on disaster coping.

Ethnographic literature of Java is rich and diverse, and reviewing this literature requires critical reading. Much has been written about Java, and academics have debated about representations of "culture" and the reproduction of power structures in research. A brief review of the available literature on Java would offer both a backdrop for getting acquainted with the research site and a meta-reflection on dealing with culture. At the same time, any endeavor to write a single chapter on the sociocultural context of Java is inevitably selective and cannot account for the complexity and historical depth of many dynamics.

Our empirical study is based on a case study of three villages in the Bantul District of the Special Province of Yogyakarta that, together with Klaten (in the neighboring Province of Central Java), was most severely affected by the 2006 earthquake. In the following sections, we contextualize the sociopolitical setting of our research and introduce the readers to the broader scenario of the 2006 earthquake in Java. We

M. Zaumseil (✉) · S. Schwarz
International Academy for Innovative Pedagogy, Psychology and Economics gGmbH
at Freie Universität Berlin, Malteserstr 74-100, 12249 Berlin, Germany
e-mail: zaumseil@zedat.fu-berlin.de

M. von Vacano
Institute for Social and Cultural Anthropology
Freie Universität Berlin, Landoltweg 9-11, 14195 Berlin, Germany
e-mail: m.vacano@fu-berlin.de

S. Schwarz
e-mail: silke.schwarz@fu-berlin.de; silgnschwarz@yahoo.de

M. Zaumseil et al. (eds.), *Cultural Psychology of Coping with Disasters*,
DOI 10.1007/978-1-4614-9354-9_4,

then reflect on the selection criteria of our research sites (Mulya Sari, Sendang, and Sido Kabul) and characterize these rural communities in regard to socioeconomic structures and the damage caused by the 2006 earthquake.

4.1 Introduction to the Ethnographic Setting

Cultural representations of "Java" and "Javaneseness" are a highly politicized field, which needs to be interpreted against a postcolonial backdrop of regional, national, and global (power) dynamics. Contemporary self-representations of the Javanese culture fall into a contested arena, where multiple actors compete to define their particular normative understanding of being Javanese. Ethnographic literature has tended toward orientalist representations of Java as a refined, mystical "other" in comparison to an (implicit) image of "rational" Europe. In classical ethnographic writings, the "Javanese" have been over-generalized and -typified, as in the interpretative approach of Clifford Geertz (1973) and many of his followers. This approach excludes cultural dynamics, inner diversity, and external influences from the scientific endeavor. Reflecting on postcolonial critiques on the concept of culture, authors such as Pemberton (1994), Boellstorff (2002), and Antlöv and Hellman (2005) have rejected the monolithic and seemingly timeless representations of the Javanese culture. They point out the risk such a research poses in reproducing the cultural images of state propaganda in favor of the ruling elites, for example, in regard to the notions of social harmony and acceptance. In a third wave of criticism, Bråten (2005) and Stange (1991) accused the discussion about the hidden purposes behind the construction of "Java" and the "Javanese" of being too academic and "Western." They call for a focus on the real experience of life and human engagement in Java, based on a dialog between those who live "Javanese" lives (including scholars and nonscholars) and outside researchers (Bråten 2005). Our research project follows the suggestion of conducting careful empirical work in a transcultural research dialog without the ambition of painting a clear-cut picture of Java or "the Javanese self." Nevertheless, for theoretical sensitization (in the framework of grounded theory), it is important to be familiar with the existing ideas and representations of "Java" and the "Javanese."

4.1.1 A Glimpse into Indonesia's National History

As is the case in many postcolonial states, the territory that is today referred to as "Indonesia" is a product of anticolonial struggle, in Indonesia's case against Dutch rule. Given the vast extent of the islands and the plurality of ethnic identities and languages they encompass, cultural plurality and national unity form a dynamic tension, as expressed in the national slogan of "Unity in Diversity." Since the early formation of Indonesian nationalism at the beginning of the twentieth century, Java and the Javanese culture have occupied a privileged position within the multicultural state and have been construed as a superior cultural resource (see Woodward 2011; Li 2000). Key concepts of national ideology and political rule drew heavily from Javanese cosmologies. For example, Indonesia's first president and national hero, Sukarno (1945–1967), was frequently referred to as a just king (*ratu adil*), a common cultural image of a promised ruler to bring prosperity and peace (see Antlöv 2005). Later, during president Suharto's authoritarian New Order regime (1967–1998), these Javanized concepts of a harmonious nationhood were spread systematically through political indoctrination in school education and obligatory training courses for university students and civil servants (see Antlöv 2005).

During this period, the political elites of the New Order defined Indonesia as a *pancasila* democracy[1] as opposed to a Western democracy. Their version of democracy emphasized the harmonious interaction between different societal groups, which was protectively guarded by the military and ruled by a wise and caring president as "father" of the nation (see Antlöv 2005). The cynicism of this idyllic vision of political life becomes obvious when considering the fact that the New Order regime was based on the massacre of between 200,000 and 1 million people in 1965–1966 (historians disagree on the exact numbers) (Cribb 2002). The outburst of violence was directed against everyone presumed to be a "communist," including members of the ethnic Chinese minority and "godless" *kejawen* Muslims (see later). During the New Order regime itself, the ideology of "harmony" was enforced through substantial limitations of political freedom and violent repressive measures against any opposition to the system. The regime restricted political life to three political parties, and village residents were forbidden to engage in any political activity, as they were construed as dangerous "floating masses." This systematic depolitization of "the masses" was legitimized by anticommunist propaganda and the stereotype of rural populations being especially vulnerable to (communist) political manipulation, thus not capable of being political subjects. Political Islam was perceived as another threat to national peace and the militarist political rule and therefore forced into a minor role during the New Order regime. Capitalist economic development was instilled as a key national value; however, the developmental benefits concentrated on Java, especially the capital Jakarta, while other regions were reduced to the role of suppliers, primarily of natural resources and export products. Thus, Java was privileged not only culturally, but also economically.

In 1998, after nationwide demonstrations, President Suharto resigned and the New Order regime came to an end, followed by a process of democratization and decentralization. Soon after, a myriad of social and political groups, embracing their newly gained political freedom, began publicly articulating their interests. These groups included secular human rights groups, indigenous people's movements, traditionalist revivalists, orthodox political Islamic groups, and seemingly everything in between. Public controversies on the core values of Indonesian society increased. At the same time, violent conflicts in various regions of Indonesia broke out (see Henley

---

[1] Having its etymological origins in an old Javanese language, *pancasila* stands for the national formula of five principles upon which the Indonesian Constitution is based: belief in the one and only God; just and civilized humanity; unity of the nation; democracy "guided by the inner wisdom in the unanimity arising out of deliberations amongst representatives"; and social justice (unofficial translation of the 1945 Constitution of the Republic of Indonesia, see http://www.embassyofindonesia.org/about/pdf/IndonesianConstitution.pdf. Accessed 30 June 2013).

and Davidson 2008). Despite the changes and formal democratization, the end of the New Order was only a partial regime change, because many personnel continued in various levels of the military and bureaucracy (Heryanto 2004). Decades of depoliti-zation and the recent disappointments with post-New Order democracy (corruption, persistent economic hardship, and violent conflicts) have left their marks on many Indonesian citizens in relation to "politics." Many still share a deep-rooted skepti-cism against any overt political activism. This, however, does not mean that they lack strong (political) opinions on the state of society. If researchers want to gain an understanding of current village dynamics, they must consider these historical effects and the multidirectional processes of the post-Suharto era.

4.1.2 Characteristics of Religious Life

Religion (*agama*) was a key component of the developmentalist New Order ide-ology. Every citizen needed to affiliate with one of the five recognized religions: Islam, Protestant Christianity, Roman Catholic Christianity, Hinduism, and Bud-dhism (Woodward 2011). Anyone one who did not at least nominally affiliate with one of these religions was officially marked as "not having a religion yet" (*belum beragama*). As this wording indicates, having a proper religion was construed as progressive and modern. In contrast, alternative religions were associated with back-wardness and atheism (or any suspicion thereof), with the enemy stereotype of "godless communism." Woodward (2011) argues that the official criteria against which religions were to be measured were implicitly Islamic. The criteria included "an all-encompassing way of life governed by fixed statutes, belief in the oneness or unity of God, a Holy Book, and a prophet to whom knowledge of the above was revealed" (p. 7). While Protestantism and Catholicism fulfill these normative criteria, creative interpretation was required in order to encompass Hinduism and Buddhism.[2] But the definition successfully discredited a myriad of regional religions, including the mystic Javanism or *kejawen* (Henley and Davidson 2008).[3]

According to the 2010 national census, 95 % of the population in Java adhere to Islam and a minority 3 % to Christianity (BPS 2011). Thus, official statistics suggest an almost mono-religious composition and fail to capture the various, and potentially conflicting, ways of interpreting and living Islam in Java. Anthropologi-cal scholarship has generated elaborate debates on classificatory schemes grasping these varieties of Islam in Java,[4] mainly agreeing with regard to one major distinc-tion, which is the relative importance of *kejawen* elements within Muslim practice.

[2] For an exemplarily account on how Balinese Hinduism was reshaped to come close to these criteria see Howe (2005).

[3] These narrow categories of *agama* persist; however, Confucianism has been included into the list as part of slow steps toward recognizing the ethnic Chinese minority in Indonesia in post-Suharto Indonesia (see Schlehe 2011).

[4] Clifford Geertz popularized the distinction between orthodox Muslims (*santri*) and nominal Mus-lims, who only formally acknowledge Islam while adhering to older Javanese religious and ancestral

The term *kejawen*, or Javanism, refers to cosmologies and practices that are articulated as "real" Javanese tradition. For a long time they have been characterized as pre-Islamic, Hindu, and Buddhist inspired, though Woodward (1989, 2011) challenged this notion by revealing Sufi Islamic elements in *kejawen*. While clear-cut classifications of religious varieties in Java (for example, Geertz 1960) have proven insupportable, it seems productive to understand orthodox Islam and *kejawen* Islam as two referential resources for Muslim life in Java, where some people rely more on the former and other people more on the latter. Ricklefs (1979) has argued for multiple shades of grey between the polar ends and Beatty (1999) suggested a great variety within "Javanism" and "practical Islam" in the countryside, with fluent transition in between. He further emphasized the dynamic interplay between these two poles as the particular characteristic of religion in Javanese rural life.

When orthodox Islam and *kejawen* are contrasted, the former is generally characterized by an emphasis on religious obligations, regular prayer and the submission of the believers to Allah as a higher, distant omnipotent God (see Beatty 1999). Another key element is the merit logic of potential reward for good believers in this life or afterlife. With regard to life conduct and guiding ethical principles, the orthodox Islamic scheme is characterized by religious rules classifying actions as "recommended, neutral, disapproved and forbidden" (Beatty 1999, p. 182, referring to Levy 1969). These rules and distinct guiding principles can be derived from religious sources of the Quran or its interpretations by religious leaders.

Kejawen, on the other hand, is portrayed as the complete opposite of orthodox Islam. *Kejawen* followers locate God in the heart of humans, as humans are "fundamentally part of the Divine essence" (Mulder 1983, p. 11). Accordingly, formal prayer, such as the five daily prayers, and mosque attendance play a subordinate role, because religious experience and practice is inherent in any aspect of life. The human existence itself is seen as a religious experience. *Kejawen* morality and codes of conduct are not guided by external authorities, such as God or religious leaders. Wisdom and guidance is found in self-reflection and insight into the ultimate (divine) oneness of life. There are no external criteria to judge human actions or for judging other people's behavior (Anderson 1990/1972). Beatty (1999) highlights that Javanists value "internally motivated acts" over obligations: "What comes from oneself and is freely given is superior to what is done to order" (p. 182). Within *kejawen*, Islam further integrates the belief in a world animated by spirits (Schlehe 2006) which are addressed in various rituals–a practice which orthodox Muslims would refuse as idolatry.

The difference between orthodox Islam and *kejawen*, as commonly portrayed in ethnographic literatures, can be summarized in the following way:

---

traditions (*abangan*). As a third category he identified the religious practices of the urban gentry elites (*priyayi*) as a noble version of *kejawen* (Islam). Koentjaraningrat (1985) differentiates between a "syncretistic variant of Javanese Islam, in which pre-Hinduistic, Hinduistic and Islamic elements are combined into one integrated system" (the *agami Jawi Islam*) and a "more puritan variant of Javanese Islam" (p. 316).

> Where Islam promises heaven through ritual compliance and devotion to the Koran, Javanism (*kejawen*) takes the everyday world as its key text and the body as its holy book. (Beatty 1999, p. 158)

This binary of orthodox Islam and *kejawen*, however, should be seen as a continuum rather than opposites. In his study on the village of Banyuwangi in Eastern Java, Beatty has shown that most people fall somewhere between the poles. Other authors have pointed to the need to further differentiate the two categories.[5]

According to official state policy, *kejawen* Islam is not recognized as an official religion (*agama*), but can formally be practiced as culture (*kebudayaan*) (Woodward 2011). From a research perspective, it is important not to reproduce such normative and exclusive definitions of religion. Therefore, we refer to a broad anthropological understanding of religion as "the ways in which people link up with, or even feel touched by, a meta-empirical sphere that may be glossed as supernatural, sacred, divine or transcendental" (Meyer 2006, p. 6). This definition allows an inclusive understanding of religion, crucial for an open qualitative approach.

4.1.3 "Javanese" Psychologies[6]

According to *kejawen* cosmology, macro- and micro-cosmos reflect each other. Individual, society, nature, and cosmos form an inseparable constellation, which ideally should be of harmonic balance (Magnis-Suseno 1981). Javanese cosmology translates into a particular Javanese self-psychology (e.g., Koentjaraningrat 1985; Geertz 1960; Mulder 1983, 1990; Magnis-Suseno 1981). A core concept is the notion of personhood consisting of an outer phenomenological realm (*lahir*) and an inner essential realm (*batin*).[7] *Lahir* ties humans to the biophysical world and *batin* relates humans to morality and the ultimate meaning and oneness of life (Mulder 1983). *Lahir* and *batin* constitute inseparable aspects of human existence that humans should strive to match as supplementing each other. According to *kejawen* ideals, such synchrony can be practiced through ascetic exercises. Any religious practice (such as Islam's five obligatory daily prayers) lacking inner devotion (*batin)* is disdainfully dismissed (see Beatty 1999). Through the intuitive feeling of *rasa*[8], the inner realm affords the possibility to connect oneself with the essence of all existing life and the divine spiritual dimension of earthly things. A quiet *batin* reveals the deeper meaning of life

---

[5] Geertz (1960) further dichotomized the orthodox *santri* Muslims as traditionalists and modernists, Koentjaraningrat (1985) offered a distinction of several currents within the "*kebatinan kejawen*" movements and Ricklefs (2008) emphasized the varieties of pro-Islamizing forces.

[6] We refer to "Javanese" psychologies, because many of the concepts we present in this section can be derived from *kejawen* cosmology, but are culturally shared far beyond *kejawen* Islam, including "Javanese" Christians.

[7] Woodward (2011) points out that these two key concepts of "Javanese" cosmology and mysticism are based on the Islamic concepts of outward (*zahir)* and inner (*batin*) modes of piety.

[8] As Stange (1984) explains, *rasa* relates to the physical and emotional aspects of feeling and implies "intuitive feeling" as a category of epistemic access to (mystical) truth.

and the rules of the cosmic course of events. With the practice of *kejawen* mysticism, or *kebatinan*, the inner resources (*batin* and *rasa*) are cultivated in order to attain a noble and refined (*halus*) inner nature, which reflects in a person's outer behavior and appearance (*lahir*). Ideally, a person should control her or his passions (*hawa nepsu*) and egotism (*pamrih*), both considered unrefined (*kasar*) feelings, in order to avoid disrupting harmonious social relations, provoking conflicts and tensions in the community, and endangering social peace (Magnis-Suseno 1981).

Since the inner and outer realms constitute interdependent aspects of personhood, ethical principles are expressed in codes of conduct that offer people practical orientation for regulating their motivations and emotions (see Chap. 11). Ethnographers in Java have worked out several codes of conduct, slightly diverging in their selection and emphasis. Common aspects include modesty as the inner freedom from self-interest (*sepi ing pamrih*). Modesty implies letting go of material values (Magnis-Suseno 1989). It leads to a calm self-ownership, patience, and an ability to humbly accept one's assigned role in society. Sincerity (*ikhlas*) refers to one's character, where a person's behavior and existence is closely tied to inner morality. It implies psychological resilience through detachment from the external world: "It is 'not caring,' on the premise that if one does not care about worldly things they cannot hurt or upset one" (Geertz 1960, p. 241).

Patience (*sabar*) is yet another core code of conduct, which is grounded in the awareness of a human's limited capacity to determine the course of life and the acceptance that everything has its own time, which cannot be forced or rushed (Magnis-Suseno 1989). Patience counts as a sign of inner calmness and strength, expressed in a practical way of facing challenges. All of the above-mentioned conduct codes are closely related to the code of cautious mindfulness (*waspada-éling*), which refers to the awareness of the human existence in its general cosmic but also specific social context (see Magnis-Suseno 1989). Awareness in this connection should not be understood as rational cognitive knowledge, but rather as containing insights through intuitive feeling (*rasa*).

The ideal that humans should accept (*nrimo*)[9] their fate derives from the awareness of a cosmic order and a human's moral obligation to respect this order of life. Ethnographers have offered various interpretations and valuations of this concept in regard to the notion of passivity that it entails. Authors such as Koentjaraningrat (1960) have highlighted the notion of predetermination and how "Javanese" see human life as unavoidably predetermined. Magnis-Suseno (1981) highlights that *nrimo* does not mean apathetically giving in to everything, rather reacting reasonably to disappointments and adversity without breaking down or struggling against them. From his point of view, *nrimo* enables people to seek freedom from external, material constraints, providing them with an inner independence (Mulder 1990). From this perspective, acceptance relates to the aspects of life that cannot be changed. Thus, it might be a helpful psychological mechanism to cope with disappointment and adversity in a "rational" way (Magnis-Suseno 1989). The ideal of knowing one's place in life and accepting and being grateful for it does not free humans from their

[9] Some authors use the alternative spelling of *nrima*.

obligation to strive for their best (Mulder 1990). Diverging interpretations of *nrimo* depend on diverging understandings of fate (*takdir*). In this regard, Geertz (1960), for example, identified differences even among orthodox Muslims. While his traditionalist orthodox Muslim interviewees perceived their fate as predetermined and prosperity deriving from piety and moral goodness, his modernist orthodox respondents emphasized the need to work and strive for self-improvement. The success of human efforts, however, is still believed to depend on God's will.

Political elites have further emphasized that accepting the order of life includes accepting existing social power structures. The *nrimo* code of conduct is thus transfered to a political context of those being ruled having to accept being ruled. Ethnographers of "Javanese" culture have reproduced such discourses, as was the case with Darmatputera, who euphemized political rule as joyful obedience of the subjects to their Lord (Antlöv 2005). With regard to political stability or change, Magnis-Suseno (1989) construed a similarly problematic "Javanese" subject, by emphasizing the high value of fulfilling each respective task in life (*ramé ing gawé*) as opposed to "changing the world."

Most of these codes of conduct, or "Javanese" ethics, are based on the interdependent relationship of inner and outer, and self and other (Beatty 1999). Therefore, psychological wellbeing expressed in concepts such as inner peace (*tentram*) merges psychological and social conditions (Mulder 1990).

4.1.4 Characteristics of Rural Community Life

The idealized Javanese village has served as a basis for national identity and state propaganda (Antlöv 2005) because of the ideal village community spirit. This ideologically romanticized village lives in social harmony (*rukun*) and shows collaborative effort. Its residents are ready to help each other, lend their workforce for the common good (*gotong royong*), and make their decisions in common deliberation (*musyawarah*), wisely led by the elite.

However, the very unit of "the village" is not as organic as it may seem. Rural communities were officially defined through historical administrative demarcations, which only roughly resonated with residents' subjective and collective processes of belonging (cf. Rigg 1994). The unit of the village (*desa*), for example, was introduced by colonial administration (Breman 1980), whereas the Japanese occupation during World War II left its mark in the subdivision of neighborhood units (*rukun tetangga*, abbreviated *RT*) (Koentjaraningrat 1961). Today, both of these units are part of a dense hierarchical system of administrative control, according to which each village is divided into smaller units of hamlets (*dusun*) divided into neighborhood units. Another administrative level used to exist between hamlet and neighborhood, the *rukun warga* abbreviated *RW*, which persists as the informal reference unit of *kampung*. The fact that *kampungs* still have informal leaders (*Mbah kaum*), who are perceived as institutions of experience and wisdom, points to the emotional relevance of the *kampung* unit.

With Mulya Sari, Sendang, and Sido Kabul,[10] we included three rural communities into our case study that are hamlets of 600–700 residents, belonging to three different villages (*desa*) of 9,000–3,000 residents. Each hamlet is broken down into four or five administrative neighborhood units (RT) or two or three informal *kampung* units. In respect to coping efforts on the community level, these various units became highly relevant (see Chap. 10): These differing sociopolitical reference units may cause friction between formal, informal, and emotional affiliation, because institutionalized recovery and reconstruction assistance was based on the formal administrative structures. State policies mostly address the village or hamlet level, but, in terms of everyday life, the neighborhood or *kampong* (communities) are much more relevant, both practically and emotionally.

The literal meaning of *rukun tetangga* (social harmony of neighbors) reflects an emphasis on social harmony (*rukun*) as a key value in cultural representations of Java. As the principle of acceptance, *rukun* needs to be interpreted against its ideological background and as a meaningful concept for people in Java (see Antlöv 2005). As an ideal for community relations, *rukun* needs to be achieved and maintained by the active effort of each community member (Mulder 1990, Schweizer 1989). This includes her or his engagement in social community life through participation in collective rituals, community work, and gatherings, as well as through a readiness to help neighbors, for example, hosting important ceremonies. Active participation in community life is regarded an important contribution to a prosperous and harmonious village, while withdrawal from such obligations is perceived as a potential disruption of community coherence. Village residents can and are mostly expected to engage in various group activities from farmers' groups to Quran recitation sessions to informal lottery circles (*arisan*). Further gender-specific night watch (men) and public health (women) groups exist. *Rukun* is closely associated with the principle of mutual assistance (*gotong royong*). As Bowen (1986) thoroughly elaborates, *gotong royong* is another ideologically loaded term, used for state interests but still emotionally and practically relevant to community residents:

> The term corresponds to genuinely indigenous notions of moral obligation and generalized reciprocity, but it has been reworked by the state to become a cultural–ideological instrument for the mobilization of villagers. (Bowen 1986, p. 546)

Village residents have historically been responsible for the construction and maintenance of village infrastructure. They are expected to take care of public village facilities such as graveyards, roads, assembly halls, sanitary facilities, and water canals. Especially since the New Order regime, this form of collective, unpaid labor for village development is framed as *gotong royong*. In this context, *gotong royong* is better translated as "community work" rather than "mutual assistance."

The *rukun* ideal reflects in the expectation how village politics are to work. Decision-making should take place in a process of mutual deliberation (*musyawarah*), where decisions are reached in consensus rather than majority. This ideal intersects with power structures and the high relevance of status in regard to who can speak his

---

[10] The names of the research sites have been changed to ensure anonymity.

(or her) mind. For instance, most decision-making forums are men-only gatherings. People have a clear idea on who in the village counts as a public figure (*tokoh*), is able to speak and take responsibility and who is "just a common villager" (*orang kecil, orang awam*), not expected to speak openly in a similar way. The cultural imperative of subordinating one's opinion and interest to the group (Mulder 1983) does not apply equally to everyone.

As a general rule, overt expressions and conflicts should be avoided by all (Mulder 1983), including the ruling elites. Successful political guidance is, among other factors, measured by a generally peaceful community (Magnis-Suseno 1989). But such inhibition of public conflicts should not be mistaken for an absence of conflict. People find other more indirect and subversive ways of expressing their disagreement or protest (Schweizer 1989). However, *rukun* does not just imply the repression of overt conflicts, but also the reduction of conflicts on a fundamental level. In the context of religious diversity in a Javanese village, Beatty (1999) described how plurality was integrated into community practice. Using the example of the collectively practiced ritual meal of *slametan*, he shows how much effort was devoted to finding a collective language and to maintaining a collective ritual practice across religious differences. Rather than interpreting *rukun* in terms of its potentially repressive effects, Beatty (1999) emphasized a shared "willingness to make concessions in order to maintain social harmony in the neighborhood" (p. 156).

4.1.5 Socioeconomic Context

Administratively speaking, the Bantul district belongs to the Special Province of Yogyakarta and is characterized by its proximity to the city of Yogyakarta. In comparison to other rural regions in Java, the Bantul district offers more employment opportunities and markets in nearby Yogyakarta. In our research sites, most households relied on a mixed-income livelihood, combining agriculture with sand mining, construction labor, or industries supplying larger businesses outside the village. A few maintained small home businesses, producing, for example, noodles, tofu, ceramics, and bricks. None of these livelihoods generate steady income nor do they provide access to a social security system including health insurance or pensions. Very few village residents were employed on a regular basis in factories or in the service industry of the city periphery. Even fewer worked in government institutions or for the military. In general, these regular employment opportunities are seen as particularly desirable, because they are prestigious and include social security services such as health insurance and pensions. Considered within the larger Indonesian context, national and international labor migration serves as an important source of income, often used to provide for other family members or to accumulate capital to start a business or build a house.

Access to and availability of social security institutions are very limited. While basic medical treatments are available free of cost at government-mandated community health clinics (*Pusat Kesehatan Masyarakat,* or *Puskesmas*), any hospitalization will cost the affected family a large sum, which is usually paid through informal networks but foremost by the family. With regard to pension, children are expected to provide for their elderly parents. For the younger generation, education is seen as a key to success. Schooling fees, however, limit access to education. Thus, it is common that, among siblings, only one child will continue schooling while the other(s) work to support her or his education.

4.2 Contextualizing the 2006 Java Earthquake

Being located where the Eurasian, Pacific, and Australian tectonic plates meet, Indonesia has a long history of seismic and volcanic hazards. Other frequent disasters include landslides, hurricanes, floods, or fires (Torrente et al. 2008; PDRSEA 2008). Comparing the frequency of the disaster agents, records from 2000 to 2009 rank flooding (39.86 %) the highest, followed by earthquakes (24.32 %) and landslides (17.57 %). By far, the 2004 Indian Ocean tsunami resulted in the highest death toll and level of destruction. Out of a total of 178,588 disaster casualties in that decade, 167,000 lives were lost in the 2004 tsunami, mainly in the Aceh province (Ophiyandri et al. 2010). When one and a half years later the 2006 Java earthquake hit, the tremendous destruction of the Aceh tsunami remained a close reference point for disaster management agencies, the affected communities, and the national public.

4.2.1 The Earthquake on 27 May 2006

Shortly before the 2006 Java earthquake hit, all eyes (and disaster mitigation efforts) had been directed toward Mt. Merapi, the volcano located about 27 km north of the city of Yogyakarta. Increased seismic activities had been recorded for weeks, and an eruption was expected in early March. By May 16, the highest alert level was declared, and more than 22,000 people were evacuated. Because of the threatening volcanic activity, when the earthquake hit the region on May 27, many national and international disaster management agencies were already set up in Yogyakarta, alert and prepared. The situation remained a multi-hazard scenario, because Mt. Merapi's increased volcanic activity continued for over a month, its pyroclastic flows and rock falls only decreasing in frequency and intensity after June 28.

The actual earthquake, the focus of our case study, occurred in the early morning of May 27, 2006, at 5.53 a.m. local time. It was a 6.2 magnitude earthquake, hitting the provinces of Yogyakarta and Central Java, with the districts of Bantul in Yogyakarta and Klaten in Central Java suffering the worst of it. About 300,000 houses were destroyed and another 200,000 damaged. More than 6,000 fatalities and 20,000 injuries were recorded (OCHA 2007). The high fatality rate was mainly attributed to the region's high population density of more than 1,500 inhabitants per km^2 and the lack of earthquake-resistant housing construction. However, missing guidelines in disaster management systems and a lack of preparation of the people affected have also been considered contributing factors (Bayudono 2009). A material damage of up to 3.1 billion US$ (JRF 2007) was registered, exceeding the financial damage estimates for the 2004 tsunami in Sri Lanka, India, and Thailand and comparable to those of the 2001 Gujarat, India, and 2005 Pakistan earthquakes (Leitman 2007). The damage was unusually concentrated in the housing, social, and production sectors, whereas infrastructure damage and losses were limited. The disaster had a significant socioeconomic impact, affecting living conditions and workers' revenues in small and medium enterprises. Households and private companies without any insurance coverage were particularly impacted by the disaster (Subagyo and Irawan 2008).

The damage caused by the earthquake was further aggravated by a series of subsequent disasters. In July 2006, another 7.7 magnitude earthquake caused an 8 m high tsunami wave, striking the southwestern coast of West Java and claiming over 650 lives. Most fatalities occurred around the tourist resort of Pangandaran, about 240 km west of Yogyakarta (Bird et al. 2011). The Bantul region was additionally affected by a minor earthquake in September 2007. The volcanic activities of the "ring of fire" continued. During our research, on 26 October 2010, Mt. Merapi had its largest eruption in over 100 years, killing nearly 400 people and displacing at least 300,000 (Surono et al. 2012).

4.2.2 Politics of Disaster Management

Compared to other disasters in the region, the 2006 post-earthquake disaster management had two unique characteristics. First, aid organizations were prepared to respond to an expected eruption of Mt. Merapi. Second, many international and national organizations had been involved in the post-tsunami emergency and recovery process in Aceh and were keen to apply the lessons learned (JRF 2007).

Many international, national, and local organizations were involved in the 2006 post-earthquake emergency and recovery process, including all relevant UN agencies[11], about 127 international, and 248 national NGOs (Wilson and Reilly 2007). The National Coordinating Board for the Management of Disaster (BAKORNAS PB) along with its provincial- and district-level branches[12] had a leading role in coordinating emergency response on the ground (OCHA 2006). The most influential

---

[11] The Office for Coordination of Humanitarian Affairs (OCHA), the United Nations Development Program (UNDP), the United Nations International Children's Emergency Fund (UNICEF), the Food and Agriculture Organization (FAO), and the International Organization for Migration (IOM) (MacRae 2008).

[12] The National Coordinating Board for the Management of Disaster (*Badan Koordinasi Nasional Penanggulangan Bencana,* or BAKORNAS PB) was chaired by the vice president. The equivalent coordination unit on the provincial and lower administrative levels is SATKORLAK PB chaired by the governor and SATLAK PB chaired by the mayor or head of district. Official responsibilities include formulating and stipulating policies in disaster management, coordinating the implementation, monitoring activities in disaster management, and rendering guidance and direction on disaster management. Later in 2008, the national structure was re-organized and the BAKORNAS PB was

body of international agents was the Inter-Agency Standing Committee (IASC). Implementing a direct lesson learned from the 2004 Aceh tsunami, the IASC pursued a cluster approach to coordinate humanitarian relief efforts, an approach which later became a model for more effective humanitarian response (WHO 2011). The disaster relief efforts were divided into thematic clusters or sections, and international, national, and local organizations coordinated their activities within each thematic section. The clusters were defined in accordance with corresponding UN agencies and included water and sanitation, livelihood, food, agriculture, education, health, and shelter (MacRae 2008).

With regard to shelter, responsibilities were clearly divided between the international and local agencies focusing on emergency and later temporary shelters, and the national governmental action was directed at the reconstruction of permanent housing. The government announced its reconstruction program within a week after the earthquake, though preparations for its implementation took months. Aid agencies were concerned about the upcoming rainy season. After some hesitation, the Indonesian Government agreed to allow the (I)NGOs to launch a temporary (short T-Shelter) program. This was despite earlier plans to avoid such a program, as had been recommended by international policy standards (OCHA 2007). The T-Shelter program and the construction of permanent housing were merged under the *Roof First* policy issued in August 2006.This policy stipulated that temporary shelter should have roofs that could also be used for permanent shelter. After these types of planning issues were resolved, the construction of temporary shelter began in September 2006. In order to foster the shelter reconstruction, the multi-donor Java Reconstruction Fund (JRF) was founded in October 2006[13], and its priority tasks were to build temporary shelter, assist with the formulation of earthquake-resistant building standards, and supplement the governmental reconstruction program by focusing on vulnerable groups and the rebuilding of livelihoods.

The government program for permanent reconstruction relied on a community-based approach instead of contractors. In preparation for this program, 11,426 community groups (called *kelompok masayarakat* or in short *pokmas*) were founded in August 2006, each consisting of 10–15 members (Bayudono 2009). Officially the reconstruction phase began on 5 October 2006, with its first payment cycle followed by two more over the next months (Hamengku Buwono X 2008). The entitled amount of money depended on damage assessments. BAKORNAS PB determined the criteria of four categories: totally collapsed, heavily damaged, partially damaged, and lightly damaged. The official village heads carried out the assessments.[14] Earthquake survivors could decide on the model of house, the time plan, and

---

replaced by the National Agency for Disaster Management (Badan Nasional Penanggulangan Bencana, BNPB), which today is responsible for the formulation of disaster management policies, for operational coordination of internal disaster management activities and for managing foreign donations.

[13] The JRF was pledged by the European Commission, the Netherlands, the United Kingdom, Canada, Finland, Denmark, and the Asian Development Bank.

[14] In Yogyakarta Province, a maximum of 15 Mio IDR (about 1600 US$) was paid for totally collapsed and heavily damaged houses, 4 Mio for partially damaged and 1 Mio for lightly damaged

the building material independently within their respective *pokmas* groups, as long as standards for building earthquake-resistant housing were met (Bayudono 2009; ALNAP 2008). The reconstruction budget, however, had only been calculated to include building materials. According to the official policy, the labor force was expected to be provided through mutual assistance (*gotong royong*) instead of paid labor.

Various disaster management policies were put into place. For example, it was assumed that using a community-based approach instead of a contractor-based approach for reconstruction would result in better quality housing construction, accountability, and beneficiaries' satisfaction, in addition to building social capital (Ophiyandri et al. 2010). Instead of implementing "cash for work" programs (as had been the case in Aceh), unpaid work contributions were expected. They referred to the tradition of *gotong royong* or mutual self-help (Wilson and Reilly 2007). The regional and national governments further promoted a discourse emphasizing the need to avoid dependencies, calling instead for local wisdom and local capital to be used. The Sultan warned people not to beg for help (Hamengku Buwono X 2008) and the Indonesian government did not want to accept aid that would increase foreign debts (Bayudono 2009). Posters were hung on the streets with slogans such as "donation doesn't flow forever, it is time to get back to work and "It gets worse if you just surrender, it gets backward if you just wait" (GYSP 2008, p. 25.2). The Sultan and governor appealed to the Bantul region to be a good example for the rest of the nation, as had been the case during the historical independence war against the Netherlands.

Overall, the disaster management of the 2006 earthquake is often portrayed as a positive example of a relatively fast recovery. The government's ability to quickly mobilize people, the tradition of *gotong royong*, the wide diversity of responders providing support, and the availability of trained and experienced staff from Aceh have been identified as factors contributing to the success of the response (see Wilson and Reilly 2007).The international response integrated local building practices, for example, the use of bamboo for T-shelters, even though this material had usually been used by the poor. The Bantul region's location near Yogyakarta city whose infrastructure had not been affected by the quake, contributed to relief and reconstruction efforts. Many local NGOs reside in the city of Yogyakarta. The affected villages in Bantul were rich in social resources, that is, they were equipped with active community groups, the tradition of *gotong royong*, and craftsmen and building material were available on site. Furthermore, the national government wanted to prove better disaster management after bad publicity during the Aceh aftermath (MacRae and Hodgkin 2011), so resources were more easily available.

Despite these contributing factors of success, challenges certainly remained. In the immediate aftermath of the disaster, Bayudono (2009) describes chaos, rumors (such as an approaching tsunami), overloaded hospitals, and an underequipped medical system. The structures of the local governments often collapsed, because its state officials were personally affected by the disaster and unable to simultaneously serve

---

houses (Hayashi et al. 2008). In the Central Java province, however, a maximum of 20 Mio IDR was disbursed.

the public (Bayudono 2009). Early relief efforts were further characterized by a lack of coordination. All agencies (international, national, and local) were focusing on logistics and started to compile their own needs assessments, without coordinating with one another. According to MacRae (2008) and Wilson and Reilly (2007), some regions received a lot of aid, while others were left out entirely and had to organize for themselves. These problems led to conflicts and generated dependencies on aid.

MacRae (2008) further criticizes that neither staff from local NGOs nor representatives from the affected communities participated in the international human response system. International NGO staff collected information and forwarded it to their superiors. Contact with the affected people was rare, MacRae referring to it as "planet INGO" (p. 194). The implementation was top-down, i.e., locals did not participate as partners but were hired to implement decisions that had been decided upon by others (MacRae and Hodgkin 2011). This approach is diametrically opposed to a cultural-specific standpoint:

> It is an array of universal techno-management expertise, dispersed globally, deployed and organised short- or medium-term anywhere and everywhere, in terms of its own logic, in English. Understanding of local context and communication with local people are the very things such a system is least equipped to achieve; yet their importance is blindingly obvious to anyone on the ground. (MacRae and Hodgkin 2011, p. 263)

Efforts for documentation and bureaucracy were immense. Another problem concerned the communication and transparency of the national government; policies were either not published at all or already-published plans were later changed, thus invoking insecurity and disappointments as promises were not kept. For example, the reconstruction payments were bound to specific regulations and amounted to a maximum of 15 million Indonesian Rupiah in Yogyakarta Province and 20 million in Central Java Province, instead of the promised 30 million (MacRae and Hodgkin 2011).

Summarizing key features of the professional disaster management response to the 2006 Java earthquake, Leitmann (2007) evaluates:

> Relief and recovery efforts will be more effective if they identify, use, and strengthen existing social capital (community-based skills, programs, and networks). The community-driven approach to post-disaster recovery, which builds on this social capital, requires significant investments of time and human resources but has results in greater client satisfaction, more rapid disbursement, and local empowerment. (p. 147–8)

4.2.3 Current Trends

The disaster management experiences of the 2006 Java earthquake became a valuable reference for disaster management and disaster management legislation in Indonesia, just as the evaluation of the Aceh/Nias tsunami recovery had affected the disaster response strategies in Java in 2006. Local capacities and integration of multiple stakeholders remained important directions for Indonesia's national disaster management. In 2007 the Indonesian parliament passed a new Disaster Management Bill

(Law No. 24),[15] which emphasizes coordination between different governmental bodies (Hamengku Buwono X 2008). The bill promotes an integrative approach to disaster management, demanding equal participation for all parties involved, from the private sector, civil society, and the local and national governments. It strengthens the role of the community in disaster risk management. Focus is put on development, prevention, empowerment, and avoiding harm alongside the provision of help. The law paved the way for the *National Action Plan for Disaster Risk Reduction* (NAP-DRR) 2006–2009, which is designed to integrate risk reduction and development planning on all administrative levels (PDRSEA 2008).[16] For the first time, a gender perspective was also taken into account (Sastriyani et al. 2008).

4.3 Selection and Characteristics of our Research Sites

When selecting our research sites, we aimed to include a variety of community characteristics into our study. We started with a list of criteria for theoretical sampling drawn from relevant literature, and further developed our criteria during the process of village selection. These criteria covered three major characteristics: diversity of economic and sociopolitical community characteristics, scope of disaster impact, and extent of external recovery resources. The choice of Mulya Sari, Sendang, and Sido Kabul as our research sites was also determined by the very practical criterion of field access. In practice it proved challenging to approach village communities for post-disaster research (see also Chap. 7). We ultimately made a compromise between the theoretical sampling criteria and the key asset of a relationship of trust between the communities and our research project. During the later process of data analysis, comparison of villages decreased, and sensitivity toward inner variances, for example, between different neighborhoods, emerged. Within the research process and the development of our concepts, the microsocial lens became much more prominent (see Sect. 5.4).

The following section recaps our key sample criteria for the villages, while introducing the research sites to the readers.

4.3.1 Economic and Sociopolitical Characteristics

Sound statistical data of our research context are sparse; however, the poverty data from the villages (one administrative unit above the respective hamlets of Mulya Sari, Sendang, and Sido Kabul) hint to a slight socioeconomic difference between our research sites. The village encompassing the hamlet of Sendang is comparatively

[15] The law is available in Indonesian language under http://www.bkprn.org/v2/peraturan/file/UUNo.24Tahun2007.pdf. Accessed 8 May 2013.

[16] Overall, NAP-DRR encompasses five priorities: First, to integrate national and local policies. Second, to identify, assess, and monitor disaster risks. Third, to increase knowledge in order to build a culture of safety on administrative and communal levels. Fourth, to reduce risks. Fifth, to strengthen disaster preparedness and adequate reactions on all levels.

Table 4.1 Indicators for Economic and Sociopolitical Characteristics

	Mulya Sari	Sido Kabul	Sendang
Population[a]	about 670	about 590	about 610
Households below poverty line (*desa*)[b]	6.01 %	10.24 %	13.35 %
Average percentage of households owning a motorbike[a]	64 %	62 %	n/a
Total number of cars/trucks per hamlet (*dusun*)[a]	5	6	3
Civil servants[a]	11	21	8
Police/Military personnel[a]	0	3	5
Religious affiliation[a]	Majority Islam 3 Christian households	Majority Islam 1 Christian household	Majority Islam 15 Christian households
Number of mosques[a]	1	1	4

[a] Village field notes 2011
[b] ESCG (2006) citing Satkorlak DIY

the poorest, with 13 % of its population living below the poverty line. This is followed by Sido Kabul, with 10 %, and the village encompassing Mulya Sari with the lowest percentage of only 6 % (see Table 4.1).[17] The livelihood in all three of our research sites was based on agriculture, supplemented by micro-businesses (see Sect. 4.1.5),[18] each with a small number of factory workers and government employees, such as civil servants, police, or military personnel. As we will discuss in Chaps. 9 and 10, civil servants not only have an elevated socioeconomic status, but also played an important role in the disaster aftermath for the acquisition of aid, since they were familiar with government procedures and formal requirements, such as proposals. Police or military personnel were often stationed outside the villages, but could mobilize aid drops or volunteer "troops" from afar. Comparing our research sites, Sido Kabul had 21 civil servant residents, more than twice the number that Sendang had (8), even though both villages were approximately the same size. Sendang, on the other hand, had five police or military employees, in comparison to Sido Kabul which had three and Mulya Sari with none. Another indicator of wealth in the villages and practical resources for emergency self-help were the number of vehicles. More than 60 % of the households (in Mulya Sari and Sido Kabul) had motorbikes, whereas the total number of households per hamlet owning a truck or a car ranged between three and six. From these figures and our qualitative data, generalizations about the socioeconomic characteristics of the three research sites are difficult, since an increased poverty rate in combination with a high number of civil servants and cars does not tell us about the average economic level in the village. It may point to

[17] Within the Bantul district these figures range from 4 to 22 %.

[18] These livelihoods and businesses are hardly captured by statistical surveys. The availability of detailed demographic data also varied between our research sites, depending, for example, on the implementation of specific vulnerability analysis programs, such as in Sido Kabul.

a gap between rich and poor; however, the indicators available seem too weak for such a conclusion.

As social criteria, we had planned to sample according to religious and political affiliation as well as cultural orientation. While data on nominal religious affiliation *(agama)* were easily attained, the varieties of Islam, as portrayed in Sect. 4.1.2, were impossible to assess or even survey. Similar difficulties in operationalization were related to other sample criteria of sociopolitical differences. In our subsequent qualitative interview data, religious or political self-positioning was mainly implicit, or simply absent. Therefore, we would only be able to position a few interviewees with regard to their religious or political attitudes, and are reluctant to formulate religious or political village profiles based on incomplete data. If relevant, we chose to indicate individual interviewee's positions in our data analysis in Chaps. 9–16.

If we compare the number of mosques in our three village sites, Sendang stands out for having four, whereas the other similarly sized hamlets had only one each. This was despite Sendang being the village with the largest Christian minority. This quantitative marker points to Sendang as an active field of competing religious leaders, especially if we consider the fact that before the earthquake, Sendang had only two mosques and one prayer house.

4.3.2 Disaster Impact

The level of physical destruction in our research sites correlates to their geographic proximity to the epicenter of the tremor. Almost all houses were destroyed (declared as uninhabitable) in Sendang and Sido Kabul, both located about 2 km from the epicenter.[19] In Mulya Sari, 10 km from the epicenter, destruction was vast, but comparably less (see Table 4.2). As the statistical data provided by the local government *(desa)* confirm, the majority of the houses were classified as uninhabitable, but about one quarter was deemed as still habitable. Subjective accounts of the level of destruction in the three villages roughly match the government-provided data. These data refer to one administrative level higher (*desa*) than the units of our research (*dusun*) and shows some (traceable) inconsistencies[20], but it can still serve as a rough indicator for comparison of our three villages. In addition to the differences in homes destroyed, the number of casualties in the villages was also affected by distance from

[19] Most houses had been simple one-story brick constructions. But size and quality of pre-disaster housing varied significantly, relative to socioeconomic status. In Sendang, for example, a wealthy government employee had lived in an impressive two-story building, the only such construction in the village. A widow's humble dwelling was described by her neighbors as a "chicken stall", worth a maximum of 300,000 IDR (about 320 US$). Only three buildings had the old iconic Javanese architecture of a *joglo*, which are strong wooden constructions.

[20] The logically impossible percentage of destroyed houses above 100 % points to the difficulties of sound statistical data in this research context. It shows that more households reported the destruction of their houses than registered to even exist. This fact probably points to incomplete pre-disaster data and the increase of household claiming reconstruction funds in the disaster aftermath.

Table 4.2 Disaster Impact and Recovery Aid

	Mulya Sari	Sido Kabul	Sendang
Distance to epicenter[a] (km)	About 10	About 2	About 2
Geographic risk zone[a]	Tsunami, earthquake	Earthquake	Earthquake
Level of destruction[a]	Medium high–high	High	High
Uninhabitable houses (*desa*)[b] (%)	77	108	106
Fatalities[a]	2	7	16
Reconstruction aid[a]	Gov. reconstruction, JRF, no further programs	Gov. reconstruction, JRF, additional programs	Gov. reconstruction, JRF, additional programs
Increase of households[a] (%)	13	11	24
Increase of households (*desa*)[b] (%)	−2.42	18.76	31.09
Livelihood recovery programs[a]	No NGO involvement	High NGO involvement	Low NGO involvement

[a] Village filed notes 2009

[b] Calculation based on data from ESCG (2006) citing Satkorlak DIY and Province of Yogyakarta Statistics Office

the epicenter. Sendang mourned 16 community members, Sido Kabul 7, and Mulya Sari 2.

The villages' geographic locations, in relation to their distances to the sea, also determined tsunami risk. Due to its geographic proximity to the sea, only Mulya Sari qualifies as a tsunami risk zone, whereas Sido Kabul and Sendang are situated much further inland. Interestingly, however, there was a rumor of a tsunami circulating in all villages.

4.3.3 Reconstruction Aid

The amount of reconstruction aid received by the three villages corresponds with the relative level of destruction of each village. Sido Kabul and Sengang received several reconstruction programs from the nongovernmental or private sector, supplementing the government reconstruction program. Mulya Sari residents could only count on the government reconstruction fund and a few additional houses provided by the Java Reconstruction Fund (JRF). The statistics further point to the side effect of an increase in households after the earthquake, which can be interpreted as an indicator for the availability of reconstruction resources (see Sect. 9.3). With regard to livelihood recovery programs, however, Sido Kabul had attracted by far the most NGOs, which not only provided funds for microcredit groups, but also pursued a transformative agenda with regard to social village structures, such as gender mainstreaming (see Chap. 16). Sido Kabul was also the only village in which disaster preparedness efforts were institutionalized through a disaster preparedness group (*kelompok tanggap bencana* or KTB).

Our three research sites have diverse village characteristics, although clear-cut characterizations prove difficult. Varieties within the villages, for example, between different neighborhood units (RT), offered insight into different social dynamics and economic resources. Our research sites were severely affected by the earthquake, with a slight gap between the coastal Mulya Sari and the further inland communities of Sido Kabul and Sendang, located closer to the earthquake's epicenter. Combined with the micro-level sampling criteria of households and persons, our data cover a significant range of structural and sociopolitical features which potentially shaped the way Bantul residents coped with the 2006 earthquake.

4.4 Concluding Remarks

Though brief and with inevitable shortcomings, this chapter attempted to cover and combine various features of the sociocultural contexts relevant for our case study, which could also be transferred on an abstract level to other research settings. The Java example illustrates how culture and discourses on cultural values and resources contain both ideological-political qualities and real-life qualities. The "Javanese" value of social harmony (*rukun*), for example, is repeatedly emphasized in political contexts and everyday community life, and different community members interpret *rukun* in their own way in a given circumstance. Thus, such a widely shared value of social harmony does not imply that the practice of everyday life is as harmonious as ideally depicted. It is a matter of how diverging interests and conflicts are negotiated rather than a matter of their absence.

We also addressed diverging religious worldviews and practices, since religion, or more generally all (including "secular") cosmologies, are key to understanding coping processes from an inside perspective of the person coping. As a particularly relevant aspect of cosmology, we have emphasized local psychologies in our review of ethnographic literature, as "Javanese" notions of self in relation to the world and understandings of inner processes. But, as with *rukun*, we are challenged to account for the shared quality and historical depth of such "Javanese" psychologies, while critically examining potentially contradicting representations of Javaneseness. In order to avoid common tendencies to essentialize particular cultural ideas, such as Javanese selves or psychologies, we need to account for the multiplicity of cultural references in our globalized world. The Islamic origin of the Javanese notions of *lahir* and *batin* would be a good example, just as the more recent discursive adaptations of *trauma* (see Chap. 13). Beyond such sociocultural features, disaster coping is simultaneously embedded in the physical and macrostructural context of the hazard impact itself and the disaster management efforts related to it. In the case of the Java 2006 earthquake, these efforts were characterized by a comparatively quick response and a strong emphasis on the cultural resources of the mutual self-help tradition *gotong royong*. Politicians on the national and regional level further appealed to the "Javanese" values of effort and self-reliance. However, in a socioeconomic context where most people have precarious livelihoods with very limited access to social security systems, such appeals to community capacities, effort, and self-reliance can be interpreted as both empowerment of disaster survivors and deference of state responsibility.

Acknowledgments The editors would like to thank Elise Serbaroli for her assistance in editing this chapter.

References

Active Learning Network for Humanitarian Practice (ALNAP) (2008). Responding to earthquakes 2008; Learning from earthquake relief and recovery operations. London: ALNAP. http://www.alnap.org/pool/files/ALNAPLessonsEarthquakes.pdf. Accessed 10 May 2013.

Anderson, B. (1990/1972). *Language and power. Exploring political cultures in Indonesia*. London: Cornell Univ. Press.

Antlöv, H. (2005). The social construction of power and authority in Java. In H. Antlöv & J. Hellman (Eds.) *The Java that never was. Academic theories and political practices* (pp. 43–66). Münster: LIT.

Antlöv, H. & Hellman, J. (Eds.). (2005). *The Java that never was. Academic theories and political practices*. Münster: LIT.

Badan Pusat Statistik (BPS) Republik Indonesia (2011). Data Sensus Penduduk 2010. http://sp2010.bps.go.id/index.php/site/index. Accessed 30 June 2013.

Bayudono, T. I. (2009). Disaster management post earthquake in Yogyakarta, Indonesia. *Science Without Borders, 3,* 338–348.

Beatty, A. (1999). *Varieties of Javanese religion: An anthropological account*. Cambridge: Cambridge Univ. Press.

Bird, D. K., Chague-Goff, C., & Gero, A. (2011). Human response to extreme events: A review of three post-tsunami disaster case studies. *Australian Geographer, 42*(3), 225–239.

Boellstorff, T. (2002). Ethnolocality. *The Asia Pacific Journal of Anthropology, 3*(1), 24–48.

Bowen, J. R. (1986). On the political construction of tradition: *Gotong-Royong* in Indonesia. *Journal of Asian Studies, 45*(3), 545–561.

Bråten, E. (2005). Resurrecting "Java": A call for a "Java"nese Anthropology. In H. Antlöv & J. Hellman (Eds.), *The Java that never was. Academic theories and political practices* (pp. 21–42). Münster: LIT.

Cribb, R. (2002). Unresolved problems in the Indonesian killings of 1965–1966. *Asian Survey, 42*(4), 550–563.

Emergency Shelter Coordination Group (ESCG) (2006). Gap analysis. Summary by location 26/06/2006. http://img.static.reliefweb.int/sites/reliefweb.int/files/resources/C215962B0C4B2B34C1257199004ADCBA-ifrc-idn-26jun.pdf. Accessed 25 June 2013.

Geertz, C. (1960). *The religion of Java*. Chicago: Univ. of Chicago Press.

Geertz, C. (1973). Thick description: Towards an interpretative theory of culture. In C. Geertz, The interpretation of cultures (pp. 3–30). New York: Basic Books.

Government of Yogyakarta Special Province (GYSP) (2008). Reconstruction based on local wisdom (Saiyeg Saeko Kapti). In D. Karnawati (Ed.), *The Yogyakarta earthquake of May 27, 2006* (pp. 25.-1–25.-8). Belmont: Star Publishing Company.

Hamengku Buwono X. (2008). Learning from the 27 May 2006 earthquake. In D. Karnawati (Ed.), *The Yogyakarta earthquake of May 27, 2006* (pp. xi–xviii). Belmont: Star Publishing Company.

Hayashi, T., Hokugo, A., Shigemura, T., Yamazaki, Y., & Yamaguchi, H. (2008). A study on residents' strategy for housing reconstruction after the 2006 Central Java Earthquake. http://www.earoph.info/pdf/2008papers/5–6.pdf. Accessed 21 May 2011.

Henley, D., & Davidson, J. S. (2008). In the name of Adat: Regional perspectives on reform, tradition, and democracy in Indonesia. *Modern Asian Studies, 42*(4), 815–852.

Heryanto, A. (2004). The debris of post-authoritarianism in Indonesia. In F. Quadir & J. Lele (Eds.), *Democracy and civil society in Asia* (pp. 65–85). New York: Palgrave Macmillan.

Howe, L. E. (2005). *The changing world of Bali: religion, society and tourism*. London: Routledge Chapman & Hall.

Jan Breman, J. (1980). *The village on Java and the early Colonial State*. Rotterdam: CASP, Erasmus University Rotterdam.

Java Reconstruction Fund (JRF). (2007). One year after the Java earthquake and tsunami: Reconstruction achievements and the results of the Java Reconstruction Fund. http://siteresources.worldbank.org/INTINDONESIA/Resources/226271-1168333550999/ReportJRF.pdf. Accessed 4 Feb 2010.

Koentjaraningrat (1960). The Javanese of South Central Java. In G.P. Murdock (Ed.), *Social Structure in Southeast Asia* (pp. 88-115). Chicago: Quadrangle Books.

Koentjaraningrat (1961). *Some social-anthropological observations on Gotong Rojong practices in two villages of Central Java*. Ithaca: Cornell University Press.

Koentjaraningrat (1985). *Javanese culture*. Singapore: Oxford Univ. Press.

Leitmann, J. (2007). Cities and calamities: Learning from post-disaster response in Indonesia. *Journal of Urban Health, 84*(1), 144–153.

Li, T. M. (2000). Articulating indigenous identity in Indonesia: Resource politics and the tribal slot. *Comparative Studies in Societies and History, 42*(1), 149–179.

MacRae, G. (2008). Could the system work better? Scale and local knowledge in humanitarian relief. *Development in Practice, 18*(2), 190–200.

MacRae, G., & Hodgkin, D. (2011). Half full or half empty? Shelter after the Jogjakarta earthquake. *Disasters, 35*(1), 243–267.

Magnis-Suseno, F. (1981). *Javanische Weisheit und Ethik: Studien zu einer östlichen Moral*. München: Oldenbourg.

Magnis-Suseno, F. (1989). *Neue Schwingen für Garuda*. München: Kindt.

Meyer, B. (2006). *Religious sensations. Why media, aesthetics and power matter in the study of contemporary religion*. Amsterdam: Vrije Universiteit.

Mulder, N. (1983). *Mysticism & everyday life in contemporary Java: cultural persistence and change* (3rd ed.). Singapore: Singapore Univ. Press.

Mulder, N. (1990). *Individuum und Gesellschaft in Java: Eine Untersuchung zur kulturellen Dynamik*. Saarbrücken: Breitenbach.

Office for the Coordination of Humanitarian Affairs (OCHA) (2006). Indonesia earthquake 2006. Jakarta: United Nations. http://www.undp.or.id/earthquake/docs/earthquake%20response%20plan.pdf. Accessed 8 May 2013.

Office for the Coordination of Humanitarian Affairs (OCHA) (2007). Cluster approach: Lessons learned: Yogyakarta and Central Java earthquake, Indonesia. http://star-tides.net/node/2081. Accessed 8 May 2013.

Ophiyandri, T., Amaratunga, D., & Pathirage, C. (2010). Community based post disaster housing reconstruction: Indonesian Perspective. http://usir.salford.ac.uk/9761/1/536.pdf. Accessed 8 May 2013.

Partnership for Disaster Reduction—South East Asia (PDRSEA) (2008). Monitoring and reporting progress on community-based disaster risk reduction in Indonesia. http://www.adpc.net/v2007/Programs/CBDRM/INFORMATION%20RESOURCE%20CENTER/CBDRM%20Publications/2008/final_crindonesia_23nov.pdf. Accessed 8 May 2013.

Pemberton, J. (1994). *On the subject of Java*. New York: Cornell University Press.

Ricklefs, M. C. (1979). Six centuries of Islamization in Java. In N. Levtzion (Ed.), *Conversion to Islam* (pp. 100–128). New York & London: Holmes and Meier.

Ricklefs, M. C. (2008). Religion, politics and social dynamics in Java: Historical and contemporary rhymes. In G. Fealy & S. White (Eds.), *Expressing Islam: Religious life and politics in Indonesia*. Singapore: Institute of Southeast Asian Studies.

Rigg, J. (1994). Redefining the village and rural life: Lessons from South East Asia. *The Geographical Journal, 160*(2), 123–135.

Sastriyani, S. H., Herminningsih, N., Susilowati, H., Listiandri, Y., & Sumarah, T. S. (2008). Langkah-langkah pengintegrasian gender dalam penanganan bencana di Daerah Istimewa Yogyakarta. Yogyakarta: BIGRAF.

Schlehe, J. (2006). Nach dem Erdbeben auf Java: Kulturelle Polarisierungen, soziale Solidarität und Abgrenzung. *Internationales Asienforum, 37*(3/4), 213–237.

Schlehe, J. (2011). Cultural politics of representation in contemporary Indonesia. *European Journal of East Asian Studies, 10*(2), 149–167.

Schweizer, T. (1989). Economic individualism and the community spirit: Divergent orientation patterns of Javanese villagers in rice production and the ritual sphere. *Modern Asian Studies, 23*(2), 277–312.

Stange, P. (1984). The logic of *rasa* in Java. *Indonesia*, 38, 113-134.

Stange, P. (1991). Deconstruction as disempowerment: New orientalisms of Java. *Bulletin of Concerned Asian Scholars, 23*(3), 51–71.

Subagyo, B., & Irawan, V. (2008). Building local governments and communities that are more resilient to hazards. In D. Karnawati (Ed.), *The Yogyakarta earthquake of May 27, 2006* (pp. 23.1–23.8). Belmont: Star Publishing Company.

Surono, J. P., Pallister, J., Boichu, M., Buongiorno, M. F., Budisantoso, A., Costa, F., et al. (2012). The 2010 explosive eruption of Java's Merapi volcano. A '100-year' event. *Journal of Volcanology and Geothermal Research, 241/242,* 121–135.

Torrente, E., Zhang, J., & Le-Huu, T. (2008). Regional experiences on institutionalization of CBDRM in South East Asia. http://www.adpc.net/v2007/programs/CBDRM/INFORMATION%20RESOURCE%20CENTER/CBDRM%20Publications/2008/final_cbdrminstitutionhires_23nov.pdf. Accessed 8 May 2013.

Wilson, P., & Reilly, D. (2007). Report CARE, Catholic Relief Services, Save the Children and World Vision Indonesia. Joint evaluation of their responses to the Yogyakarta earthquake. http://www.crsprogramquality.org/storage/pubs/me/yogyakarta.pdf. Accessed 18 June 2013.

Woodward, M. R. (1989). *Islam in Java. Normative piety and mysticism in the Sultanate of Yogyakarta*. Tuscon: The University of Arizona Press.

Woodward, M. R. (2011). *Java, Indonesia and Islam. Muslims in global societies* Series 3. Dordrecht: Springer Netherlands.

World Health Organisation (WHO) (2007). Humanitarian Health Action. The Cluster Approach, Annex 7. http://www.who.int/hac/techguidance/tools/manuals/who_field_handbook/annex_7/en/index.html. Accessed 8 May 2013.

Chapter 5
Methodological Basis of a Culture-Specific Coping Approach

Silke Schwarz, Tri Hayuning Tyas and Johana E. Prawitasari-Hadiyono

5.1 Introduction

In mainstream psychologies, rather specific research perspectives on coping with disaster dominate (see Chap. 1). The discipline mainly focuses on using quantitative methods to increase knowledge about the *mechanisms and conditions* by which disasters affect mental health. A further interest lies in determining *how many* people are affected by mental health problems following a traumatic event (that is, the prevalence of post-disaster psychological problems). In her article on disaster research methods, Norris (2006), for example, discusses how to apply sophisticated methods from epidemiology (such as representative sampling strategies and longitudinal designs) and, more recently, she has extended this work to include trajectories of resilience through complex designs, such as latent growth mixture modeling (see Norris et al. 2009). In these types of studies, statements are based on aggregated results and are made as independently as possible from particular cases in order to formulate general laws (Flick 2009). The major unit of analysis refers to individual differences in terms of stress, related coping strategies, and intervention outcomes (Norris et al. 2009). Bonanno et al. (2010) broadened this individualistic perspective

S. Schwarz (✉)
International Academy for Innovative Pedagogy, Psychology and Economics gGmbH
at Freie Universität Berlin, Malteserstr. 74-100, 12249 Berlin, Germany
e-mail: silke.schwarz@fu-berlin.de; silgnschwarz@yahoo.de

T. H. Tyas
Department of Clinical Psychology, Faculty of Psychology,
Universitas Gadjah Mada, Jl. Sosio Humaniora No. 1, 55281 Yogyakarta, Indonesia
e-mail: t.h.tyas@ugm.ac.id

J. E. Prawitasari-Hadiyono
Center for Research and Community Service,
Christian University of Krida Wacana,
Jl. Tanjung Duren Raya No. 4, 11470 Jakarta, Indonesia
e-mail: jeprawitasari@ukrida.ac.id

Universitas Gadjah Mada, 55281 Yogyakarta, Indonesia

M. Zaumseil et al. (eds.), *Cultural Psychology of Coping with Disasters*,
DOI 10.1007/978-1-4614-9354-9_5,

in their work on weighing the costs of disaster by examining the influence of disasters on families and communities. The authors reviewed the relatively low number of existent multivariate and prospective studies in order to identify universal predictor variables for disaster outcomes. They concluded that it is a combination of risk *and* resilience factors that informs disaster outcomes. In addition, they evaluated different clinical intervention methods to treat or to prevent mental health problems after disasters. Studies of variations over the course of recovery are presented that identify causal effects and control for variations in variables deemed important for the recovery process. Developing generalizable and, potentially, universally applicable models is a major research interest in all of these mainstream psychological approaches.

The mainstream approach is important for investigating the ways in which people cope with disasters. However, we focus in this chapter on research strategies that help to attain a more local, specific, and contextualized picture of the situation after a disaster. We discuss in detail what we present as mainstream psychology and related limitations, such as a lack of generalizability to other specific contexts. Finally, we present the methodological approach used in our case study of the May 2006 earthquake in Java, Indonesia (see Chap. 4) to illustrate cultural-psychological alternatives to mainstream research traditions.

5.2 Moving Cultural Approaches Beyond Mainstream Psychological Approaches

Mainstream psychological approaches and their corresponding quantitative studies are limited when the research question is "how does culture shape the experience of disaster stress?" (for example, see Norris 2006). Research methods that capture culture-specific ways of coping with disasters need to transcend an individualistic, Western focus by expanding the unit of research to include family and other relations, and critically address power issues in order to avoid culturalizing inherently political-economic phenomena (Pemberton 1994).

5.2.1 Allowing for Cultural Specificities

Recently, an important shift in disaster risk reduction research has led to the recognition of the potential of indigenous knowledge[1] to reduce vulnerability (Jigyasu 2002; Dekens 2007; Mercer et al. 2007, Mercer 2012). Indigenous knowledge is defined as a body of knowledge existing within or acquired by people over a period of time

[1] Indigenous knowledge is often referred to in different ways, including local knowledge, traditional knowledge, indigenous technical knowledge, peasants' knowledge, traditional environmental knowledge, and folk knowledge (Sillitoe 2010).

through the accumulation of experience, society–nature relationships, community practices and institutions, and generational transfer (for example, Brokensha et al. 1980; Sillitoe 2010).

Accounting for cultural specificities related to coping with adversity requires broadening common psychosocial-theoretical frameworks as we argued in Chap. 3. Instead of looking for universal ways of handling disasters, a cultural psychology of coping with disasters needs to grasp locally specific meanings of events, experiences, and actions after a disaster. It is essential to develop a grounded understanding of how meanings are formed in social interaction and broader discourses, as well as how they change and are modified by interpretation.

Cultural-psychological approaches in disaster-coping research sometimes examine conditions leading to mental health or illness. More often, however, they focus on a situated understanding of human agency, human experience, and meaning-making after a disaster at a given place and in a given sociocultural context (Priya 2004). In contrast, mainstream approaches usually follow a quantitative logic. They investigate trajectories of psychological impairment after a stressful event and hypotheses about causal relations are developed and tested, in order to make more accurate predictions and interventions (Norris 2006). Research tools are usually standardized instruments considered to be universally valid regardless of the cultural context. In cross-cultural psychology, for example, researchers test the generality of existing psychological theories in diverse cultural contexts to develop universal models to predict behavior. Quantitative approaches to cross-cultural psychology usually operationalize culture as an antecedent or an independent variable. The sociocultural context is considered separately from psychological phenomena and studied as an index rather than a process (see Berry et al. 2011).

Our goal is not to develop theories of mechanisms and conditions that generalize across cultures and contexts. Instead, our aim is to discover a specific way of understanding and representing the culturally, socially, and materially embedded situation after a disaster and the constraints and possibilities of human agency. We theorize this situation and the related horizon of agency in sociocultural terms (see Chap. 3).

5.2.2 *Rethinking Research Units*

Mainstream psychological approaches to disaster mainly focus on variations in human ways of thinking, behaving, and feeling with the individual as the unit of analysis. Analysis refers to how situations and contexts influence the person's behavior, thought, and feeling (for example, Berry et al. 2011). Most research on meaning-making and benefit-finding focuses on individual experiences of bereavement and illness (Pakenham 2011; Folkman 1997). As a result, human knowledge and experience are confined to individual mental processes.

In order to grasp individual *as well as* communal coping processes, we need to use larger units of analysis, such as households and communities. The investigation of inner conflict may be expanded to explore social conflicts and burdensome forms of interaction. Incorporating the analysis of discursive arenas, communal actions and collective emotions must be reflected in the formulation and implementation of research questions throughout the research process.

Another aspect refers to the understanding of persons and contexts. In cross-cultural psychology, for example, eco-cultural and sociocultural contexts are examined in terms of antecedent conditions that influence psychological variables such as values, attitudes, and behavior, which are, in turn, treated as outcome variables (see Berry et al. 2011). A further example is provided by the Pargament et al. (2000) study which used questionnaires to measure religious coping. Pargament et al. (2000) tried to identify universally applicable elements of religiosity and religiously inspired coping styles and determine how these factors are then correlated to measurements of health, illness, and well-being across world religions (Pargament 2011).

However, cultural-psychological approaches assume a co-constitution of individuals and their contexts. Intra-psychic dynamics are permeated by cultural forces and vice versa (Berry et al. 2011). As we have shown in our theoretical chapters, our aim is to transcend an individualistic focus and understand persons as contextualized social beings. The question is at which level does the mutual constitution of the psychological and sociocultural take place. Kleinman and Erin (2007) have developed a suitable concept of experience for this purpose:

> Experience, then, has as much to do with collective realities as it does with individual translations and transformations of those realities. It is always simultaneously social and subjective, collective and individual. (p. 53)

5.2.3 *Including Analyses of Resource and Power Differentials*

Situating the experience of a disaster in communal power structures further deepens a multidimensional understanding of coping with adversity. This approach is not inherently cultural-psychological, but rather follows a critical line of thinking (Markard 2010) that we consider a necessary addition to any cultural psychology of coping with disasters.

A review of the literature of mainstream psychological work in this area, however, reveals a lack of critical research that includes an analysis of power in the subjective perspectives of those who undergo and experience catastrophic events along with their corresponding relief efforts (for example, studies based on Lazarus's approach, which was introduced in Chap. 2). Hobfoll's approach to stress provides a basis for psychological coping theories that is aware of power differentials. Specifically those people with power, status, and privilege encounter developmental conditions that Hobfoll (2011) calls *caravan passageways*, and these effectively exclude those who lack power, status, and privilege. Considering the material and structural dimensions of coping processes allows researchers to contextualize research data within political-economic practices instead of conforming with dominant cultural interpretative biases (see Antlöv 2005).

In addition, we consider it crucial to reflect upon the process of producing knowledge and related power dynamics. A fruitful approach has been developed in the field of feminist research (see Acker et al. 1991; Behnke and Meusser 1999; Wohlrab-Sahr 1993; Clarke 2005). Attempting to critically relativize universal claims, we follow Kenneth Gergen's line of questioning: "Who benefits and who loses in such efforts? What are these predictions used for? Who is the knowledge empowering, and who is eliminated from view?" (Cisneros-Puebla 2008, p. 41). The research team's position within current power structures and the ethical implications of that position need to be disclosed and critically reflected upon. Reflexivity and analysis of power constellations relate to one's own situation and to the way in which one's own work is embedded and enmeshed within institutional requirements and restrictions; critical reflection on this positioning also has implications for the situation in the research area.[2] It should include an analysis of the research project history in order to create awareness of one's own (and the research team's) involvement in the requirements of institutional frameworks and power structures.

In sum, we consider the dialogic process of mutual exchange between researcher and research participant as well as between the research team and research field to be a crucial ingredient of a thorough, robust, and reflexive cultural-psychological research approach. Emerging ethical challenges mirror this co-constituting process. The (self-) positioning of researchers in the field can never be neutral. Researchers depend on local authorities to gain access to the field and they need to gain trust and access to the various groups of actors within the field. For example, the researchers need to position themselves in relation to expectations of help from them and the status as locals or international researchers that they bring to a rural setting. Research participants may ask about social assessments and evaluations as well as push the researchers to present ways of reducing risk or ways for a community to achieve certain social or health-related goals.

5.3 Fruitful Methodological Tensions

Cultural psychology has an inherent (though not exclusive) affinity for qualitative methodologies (see Ratner 2008): access to culturally situated knowledge, meanings, emotions, and practices related to disaster coping can be derived from inductive methodologies that allow for differences and uniqueness. However, we believe that a focus on methodological plurality that relies on triangulation that combines a mixture of quantitative and qualitative as well as performative approaches would best allow researchers to grasp the kaleidoscope of emic coping dynamics.

---

[2] Chapters 6–8 aim to fill this common gap in the research accounts of mainstream psychological approaches in this area. In these chapters, we address the issue of researchers' critical self-reflection about their own context.

5.3.1 Complexity Versus Simplicity

Birkman and Wisner (2006) have presented several challenges that arise when scholars from contrasting disciplines and paradigms conduct research on the "unmeasurable" (p. 3) concept of vulnerability in the context of disasters; these include different assumptions about fundamental issues like the nature of science and what constitutes an explanation. The same problem can be said to occur with the blurry concept of culture-specific ways of coping with disasters. Different assumptions, however, can also lead to creative tensions and new insights.

Socioculturally specific forms of practice, in local history and globally intertwined economic as well as political structures and processes, contribute to the complex and fluid construct of coping. It is difficult to sort out these interacting, overlapping features in a clear manner. A historical and global perspective along with a postmodern (that is, relativistic and postcolonial) standpoint may best grasp the features related to local specificities. Instead of generalizing theories or concepts developed in the North to encompass the behavior of people in the South, this hybrid perspective can account for locally specific power differentials that are historically rooted and globally intertwined. Furthermore, oversimplifications in the sense of linear, cause-and-effect assumptions are obsolete and have been replaced by complexities, differences, heterogeneities, and rather complex co-constitutions between situational elements (Clarke 2005).

In contrast, policy makers, disaster-management organizers, donors, and other actors in the landscape of a specific disaster response strive for mathematical parsimony and seek relatively simple prediction models in order to mitigate negative (mental health) outcomes. Decision makers tend also to look for firm answers or clear options rather than nuanced understandings; unanimity is always preferable to looking for patterns in a diversity of meanings, responses, and goals (see Birkman and Wisner 2006).

Which methodologies and research designs are best suited to answer the needs of the people most affected by a disaster when evaluating data about the effectiveness of a given or multiple, potentially overlapping responses? We argue that a community struck by a disaster cannot speak with one voice. Diverse experiences, interests, or claims (modulated by the availability of different resources due to various positions of those affected within complex power structures) require a response that accounts for polyphony. Furthermore, in studying a complex, long-term response to a disaster, it is difficult to untangle the response to the disaster itself and the response to experiencing relief efforts and their related injustices. Therefore, it is imperative to describe the phenomena from many perspectives using a plurality of data collection methods in order to describe thoroughly the thoughts, feelings, and behaviors of the people most affected in relation to the disaster and emerging topics such as subsequent aid-related injustice.

5.3.2 Controversies About Research Aims

Research in the context of coping with disasters ranges between the poles of

1. inductively understanding specific ways of dealing with adversity—ideally through common discovery—and
2. deductively implementing predefined research agendas or intervention programs.

The challenge for the first approach is how to transcend initial descriptions to arrive at more in-depth understandings and how to conceptualize the relations between these reconstructed subjective experiences and actions. In relation to the second approach, ethical considerations are important such as whether informed consent is ever really achieved. Moreover, many survey methods of data collection (especially scales and questionnaires) delimit the complexity and meaning of research participants' potential responses and reduce them to responding "subjects" of the research. Especially when people become research objects, who are subjected to research in top-down research projects or interventions instead of participants and active agents, problems arise. For example, social conflict can emerge when responsible authorities do not take responsibility for any long-term processes they trigger. Researchers should rather ask: "Are there not winners and losers in any intervention into the risk-scape of a locality?" (Birkmann and Wisner 2006, p. 14). In Chap. 1, we highlighted the shortcomings of such prescriptive intervention programs. The problem of preset goals, however, is partially reduced by the fact that some intervention programs are the direct outcomes of rapid assessments to gather information about requests for the programs that affected people need.

Participatory research strategies range between the two poles described above by mixing joint discovery processes with an orientation toward (preset) goals through intervention. Participatory vulnerability analysis (PVA), for example, is a systematic process that involves communities and other stakeholders in an in-depth examination of their own vulnerability, at the same time empowering or motivating them to take appropriate action (Chiwaka and Yates n.d.). A collective realization process that involves researchers and "co-researchers" in close communication is central (Kemmis and McTaggart 2005). In this process, research participants act as collaborators in the research team. As noted by Bergold and Thomas (2012), "the common aim of these approaches is to change social reality on the basis of insights into everyday practices that are obtained by means of participatory research" (paragraph 6).

The term "participation" originates in democracy theory and thus has a normative political basis. Habermas (1981) connected the idea of participation with the possibility of arriving at decisions and implementing them collectively or through appropriate delegation of authority. Accordingly, this collective process requires an analysis of and reflection upon power structures—above all, institutional ones. This does not automatically lead to overcoming (let alone eliminating) power structures, since the potential to create drastic change seldom lies within reach of those who practice participatory research. It seems possible, however, that collective reflection can expose these structures for the duration of the discursive practice and "give voice" to those who otherwise would not be heard; of course, giving voice by itself can be naïve and do harm if one fails to account for power differentials on the communal level, for example. A participatory approach enables those involved to become part of the public sphere. This can occur through performative techniques such as arts and media, which broaden the latitude for creative action and can reveal concealed shared rules (Wulf and Zirfas 2001; Haseman 2006; Prawitasari-Hadiyono et al. 2009).

However, even if participatory research succeeds in transcending a merely descriptive level, it is unclear whether the reconstruction or exact understanding of subjective perspectives contributes to a better understanding of actions. According to Bourdieu (2005), an individual's practice is determined by his or her habitus, about which he or she can give no information; the vantage point in question represents a self-evident worldview of which the individual is not aware. Relationships of dominance and the assumption of positions within a social structure can belong so self-evidently to a person's habitus or identity that their transparency or ability to be changed consciously only exists under particular circumstances. Actors can only come close to being a "subject" to the extent that they consciously control their relationship to their own dispositions (Bourdieu and Wacquant 1996, p. 171). Farnell (2000) claims that Bourdieu, in his assertion that habitus is closed to consciousness, reproduces Cartesian body–mind dualism. She argues that when we see body and mind as a unity, we *know* more than we can communicate. Bourdieu, therefore, perpetuates the fundamental misconception of dualism by stating that thought occurs only in the brain, separate from bodily activities, and by assuming a lack of awareness rather than a lack of discursive facility.

Only when we presume the possibility of self-reflexivity and reasonably justified change on our own or in collective action does the feedback provided by research results make sense. Moreover, we argue that through such feedback and by stimulating and supporting reflection about events and actions in the past and in relation to the future, we can inspire and document change. Researchers would not, then, bring this change into communities from the outside and impose it upon them in a prescriptive manner; instead, communities would generate changes themselves by becoming more aware through their involvement in the research process itself. This reflexive awareness may or may not lead to genuine and sustainable behavioral change.

The systems of values, ideas about the world, principles of conduct, shared practices, relevant societal structures, and political and economic relations guide and orient people toward their worlds and symbolize a given social order without enabling them to be fully conscious about it. This perspective helps us to understand why social change, even in the face of dramatic, unusual events—such as disasters—may only be moderate. However, underestimating agency may be an artifact of the method, too. Research methods that are not limited to verbal communication such as performative approaches are extremely useful in this area. For example, using photographs taken by community members can facilitate expression of current, past, and future life experiences (see Lykes 2001a, b).

Disasters and subsequent reconstruction efforts pose an unusual, even extraordinary situation in which many people reflect upon essential matters in their lives (see Schlehe 2006; Oliver-Smith 1998; Schwarz 2012). The interview situation, either one-on-one or in a focus group, encourages individuals to examine their experiences and actions at a greater distance. However, it is not easy for a person to reflect upon the conditions of his or her own perspective and actions. Moreover, this is true for the people who experienced the disaster, and not only for those who were there and tried to help but also for us as researchers. An assumption here is that we are limited in the extent to which we can think about why we perceive things the way we do, determine how we do things, and reflect on what leads us to act. Often, we never discover the real reasons for doing what we do but rather attribute certain motivations to our actions post hoc. The ways in which we account for our actions are often subject to the demands of the current context and relate to subjective plans that are projected forward as future actions.

As strangers to a culture and as interpreters of complex data, foreign researchers probably experience greater astonishment at what they observe than interpreters do because the sociocultural context is entirely familiar to the latter. This presents a particular danger that, for example, German researchers may impose their own Western categories on what they hear and see. There is a danger also that Westerners' own habitus-determined viewpoints and power relations, which they tend to replicate in countries of the Global South, will be concealed in reporting what they believe to have been discovered. Problems like this have led to a deep crisis in cultural anthropology, a science marked by a prior colonial history (see Clifford 1988; Berg and Fuchs 1993). In psychology, recognition of these limitations has stimulated the emergence of indigenous psychologies (see Kim 2000; Zaumseil 2006b) and the development of a distinct research standpoint that questions the universalizing demands of the "Western" gaze in psychology. The opportunity to draw on the strength of the external gaze—without misusing its biases and entangling oneself in historical pitfalls—lies in dialogue between both foreign and local researchers as well as with those who are being researched.

5.3.3 Transferability Versus Generalizability

Cultural-psychological approaches challenge the research goal of finding universal regularities and focus instead on culturally specific features of personal and social life. The main goal is to find meaningful categories to analyze and describe how people relate to the past, present, and future. By examining narratives and producing analytically ordered descriptions of situations, cultural-psychological approaches create contextualized, ideographic knowledge rather than establishing law-like statements and predicting outcomes through the pursuit of nomothetic objectives. Developing generalizable and potentially universally applicable models is not the main research aim. Researchers first need to reconstruct, as precisely as possible, the research participant's meaning (that is, his or her perspective) and then interpretatively deconstruct the positions that this meaning and its corresponding actions represent in the situation, working in a comparative manner to produce transferable knowledge. In making these comparisons, researchers can identify locally common viewpoints in connection with local power relations and property ownership. Following Charmaz's (2006) constructionist view, we do not presume to discover categories that inhere in data and an external world separate from our own. Instead, as researchers we construct grounded theories from interpretive interaction with the field, using constant comparative methods and developing standpoints and opportunities for engagement. In the interpretation and comparison of cases—within the framework of grounded theory in coding and developing categories (Strauss and Corbin 1990)—researchers develop theoretical connections that are closely linked to the data. Here, they can be theoretically *sensitized* by the various approaches to coping without directly *applying* theoretical propositions to the data.

When engaged in interpretive work, it is important to ask to what extent the findings can and should be transferred to other contexts. It is questionable to support a unified approach to any culture. Such an assumption is not tenable especially in Java, Indonesia, as many scholars have documented a formidable diversity of beliefs and ways of life on the island (above all in terms of religion, see Beatty 1999 for example). Moreover, this variety seems to be undergoing a process of change. The idealized depiction of Javanese village life, with the central elements of mutual assistance (*gotong royong*), joint decision making (*musyawarah*), respect (*hormat*), harmony and togetherness (*rukun, kebersamaan*), combined with mysticism (*kebatinan*), has arguably served to secure the domination of those in power, and, under the national leadership of former Presidents Sukarno and Suharto, has been used to justify a state ideology, according to which peace, orderliness, and compliance were supposedly rooted in "Javanese culture" rather than in the elite's claims to power (Antlöv 2005). Many anthropologists have contributed to this ideology, although it has subsequently been called into question by some and has been described by Pemberton (1994) as the culturalization of politics. The daily reality of village life is also characterized by tension and conflict despite dominant ideologies of harmonious village life. Conceptions of power, subordination, and village democracy are also very diverse (Antlöv 2005). Thus, we have to understand that accounts of Java contain interests and idealizations that obscure points of conflict and diversity; failure to reflect upon these can hinder us in our generation of power-critical representations of post-disaster reality.

5.3.4 Epistemological Controversies

Quantitative approaches suggest a positivist or post-positivist outlook and claim objectivity in presenting the research results as tangible numbers and graphs. They assume the realist position that "'things exist only in the real world' and, therefore, anything that cannot be observed through the senses is of no consequence" (Crowe and Shepphard 2010). Validity, reliability, and generalizability are crucial for quantitative approaches. For some scientists who take a quantitative research approach, qualitative designs still tend to be deemed unreliable, compared to surveys that use representative samples with valid and reliable scales or experimental designs using randomized controlled trials.

Often, theories developed in high-income countries are assumed to be applicable elsewhere, including in middle- or low-income countries (see Kalayjian et al. 2002).[3] In order to avoid the nonreflective transfer of Western theories onto other cultures, cultural psychology needs qualitative approaches and metatheoretical reflection (Priya 2010; Cisneros-Puebla 2008).

Compared to quantitative research, qualitative approaches are rather interpretative and subjective in presenting the context of the research findings. Qualitative research draws on symbolic interactionism (Mead 1934; Blumer 1969), which was elaborated by Strauss (1978) in research about social worlds and developed as the grounded theory approach (Glaser and Strauss 1967; Strauss 1987; Strauss and Corbin 1990; Glaser 1992). Research styles and epistemologies subsumed under the label of grounded theory are diverse. We follow Charmaz (2006) and Clarke (2005) in their constructionist approach. Constructionists assume that scientific observations cannot reveal the "true" character of reality since observations are always verbally mediated and point to their socioculturally specific context of emergence. Glaser (1978) overemphasizes the discovery of such an "objective" world, while Strauss (1987) and Strauss and Corbin (1990) place too much emphasis on the technical-procedural aspects of analysis. Charmaz (2006), however, looks at interactions throughout the entire interpretative research process:

> Your grounded theory journey relies on interaction emanating from your worldview, standpoints, and situations, arising in the research sites, developing between you and your data, emerging with your ideas, then returning back to the field—or another field, and moving on to conversations with your discipline and substantive fields. To interact at all, we make sense of our situations, appraise what occurs in them, and draw on language and culture to create meanings and frame actions. (p. 179)

Currently, there are only a few examples of constructionist disaster psychology research. One impressive approach has been developed by the Indian psychologist Priya (2004, 2010, 2012), who conducted research on the experiences of suffering and healing among the survivors of a 2001 earthquake in India. Priya (2010) describes the formation of the research relationship as a tool for acquiring knowledge. The process of gaining knowledge coincides with dynamic transformations on the part of both the researcher and the research participants, engendering a genuine co-construction. By and large, critical self-reflection (where the self is the individual researcher *and* the research team) is required to disentangle the constructions produced by both the researchers and those being researched (see Chaps. 6–8). The viewpoints or constructions of disaster-affected persons represent their idiosyncratic experiences. At the same time, discourses and discursive practices in their sociocultural contexts (such as conversations with neighbors or family members, discussing newspaper stories, listening to government announcements, etc.) also shape these experiences. Using a social constructionist approach, it is possible to investigate the

[3] In Chap. 2, we have shown possible ethnocentric and androcentric fallacies that accompany such universalistic presumptions.

relationships between these idiosyncratic constructions and collectively shared discourses, norms, and practices. Individual and collective features may be in conflict or may complement each other, affirm each other, and so on.

In contrast to social constructionism, realism is based on the following assumption:

> A distinctive feature of a realist philosophy is that ontology (the theory of being, which has strong implications for the conceptions of reality) is seen as distinct from epistemology (the theory of knowledge), which means that scientific theorising is based on the assumption that there exists a mind-independent reality. (Wikgren 2004, p. 12)

Therefore, realist approaches apply quantitative methods that can validly represent "reality", looking for causal mechanisms in order to make appropriate—that is, objective—explanations and predictions. Meanwhile, strong versions of social constructionism radically relativize claims of knowledge: "There are no transcendentally privileged accounts of what we take to exist" (Gergen and Gergen 1997, p. 32). Social constructionism implicitly contains an appreciation of local knowledge, a posture of reflexive deliberation toward different constructions of the world, which invites dialogue (Gergen 1999). Engler (2004) shows how the different conceptions of "constructionisms vary in several ways: according to the kinds of objects or ideas analysed as constructs; by the scope and degree of relativism; along a spectrum from descriptive through normative to activist; and by a theoretical focus on contingency, nominalism or stability" (p. 296). He argues that constructionism is not necessarily antirealist. However, like Winter (2010), we believe that the role of the body in these constructions and the contribution of the material world are missing. Clarke (2005) suggested a materialist constructionism, which we concur with and extend to create what we call a *sociocultural materialist constructionism*. This expanded form of social constructionism serves as the epistemological basis for our cultural psychology of coping with disasters (see Chap. 3).

Within this philosophical framework, we consider some universals about human nature to be valid, such as the social character of human beings. Accordingly, the social context rather than the individual should be the starting point for analysis. This approach was developed by the cultural historic school (Vygotsky 1985) and in symbolic interactionism (Mead 1934). Meanings not only emerge from what is said but are also represented in the practices, material objects, ways of conduct, and (ritual) performances that researchers encounter in local contexts. Researchers have to interpret these local meanings and practices against the backdrop of social and economic structures and inequalities in power and property. In sum, we try to strike a balance between understanding the actions and meaning-making of our research participants on the one hand, and the structures of the social and material context on the other.

5.4 Example of a Cultural-Psychological Research Project

The main features of our case study design are its process-based character and its exclusive use of qualitative research methods without preset intervention goals.

5.4.1 Process Orientation

In order to grasp what is locally specific while also allowing for the emergence of unexpected findings, research cycles need to adapt to changing contexts and unpredictable interests. The research process and its findings are the product of an open process rather than the implementation of a strict research plan (Charmaz 2006). Naturally, an open process stands in stark contrast to the structural restrictions of funding, time, and human resources. The following sections and subsequent reflective chapters (Chaps. 6–8) will touch on several of these constraints and how they were dealt with.

Any long-term research design that aims to reconstruct communal dynamics against the backdrop of possible conservation and transformation following a disaster must critically ask which changes are actually associated with the disastrous event. The disaster and its attendant interventions challenge the current state of existence of a community and intensify or catalyze the processes of change. For instance, changes in economic relationships and forms of subsistence can occur, as well as changes in power relations, gender relations, religious beliefs, and feelings of security. Such shocks and possible changes can be reflected in the data gathered during the period of research that started two years after the earthquake. For this study, we did not have data antecedent to the disaster that would provide a comparison; rather, the assumed changes are retrospective evaluations or reconstructions produced in the process of inquiry between the researchers and research participants. However, there are some official statistics and reports that can be interpreted in order to triangulate issues of preexisting problems (for example, income levels and distributions, see Chap. 4).

The extraordinary experience of an earthquake divides time into *before* and *after* and, thus, constitutes a mark by which change can be measured. Therefore, it is possible that changes are merely ascribed to the earthquake, which would actually be attributable to other influences entirely (see Rabinow 2007). Thus, it is important to view the 2006 earthquake in Java, Indonesia, against the backdrop of other changes that have occurred in the post-Suharto era in Java (see Manning and van Diermen 2000). These changes include a post-dictatorial political shift in national leadership style (Beittinger-Lee 2009), the implementation of democratization processes, a questioning of old structures and elites, significant decentralization reforms (see Holtzappel and Ramstedt 2009), modernization, and the continuing spread and diversification of Islam (see Chap. 4). Moreover, the embedding of the research process in ongoing community dynamics means that a critical analysis of communal, small-scale contexts is also paramount.

Figure 5.1 illustrates relevant time markers in the village community of Sido Kabul[4] (see Schwarz 2012). Following the disastrous earthquake in May 2006, several recovery programs were initiated, the biggest being a 1-year program of seven

[4] All names of research participants and research sites used in this book have been changed to ensure anonymity.

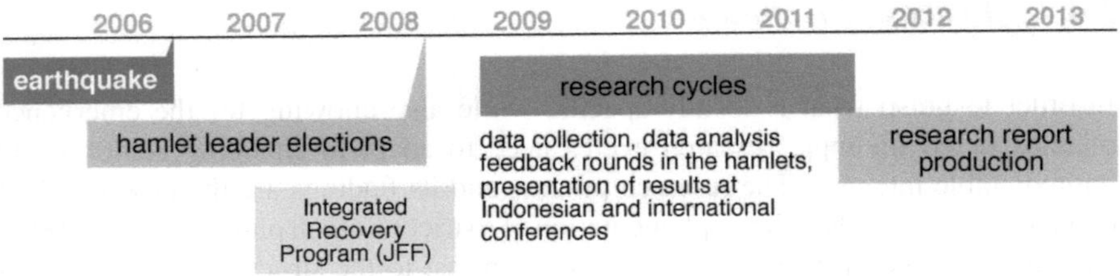

Fig. 5.1 Overview of Dynamics in Sido Kabul

nongovernmental organizations (NGOs) working together in a network called *Jejaring Ford Foundation* (JFF) from May 2007 until April 2008. In spring 2008, elections for a new hamlet leader took place. We collected, analyzed, provided, and gathered feedback, and presented the data from November 2008 to September 2011 in various research cycles. The research report production process that overlapped with the end of the research cycles lasted until mid-2013.

5.4.2 Research Dynamics: Changing Aims and Methods

In our case study on Java described in Chap. 4, we used qualitative interviews (narrative and guideline-supported interviews), focus group discussions, participant observations, and, in the final period, participatory research. Ongoing field stays of about 2 weeks were complemented by multiple short field visits, which provided information on the hamlets. Later, feedback sessions at the hamlet and regional levels provided an additional set of data that were analyzed as new data in the overall research cycle. We interviewed villagers and observed their daily lives, discussed issues with them, and equipped them with cameras so that they could record what they perceived as important to describe their own behavior. In addition, in the last phase of research in 2011, villagers themselves collected data and presented their results in various forums (see Chap. 8).

The research project was based on a long-term collaboration between the two main research applicants, Prof. Manfred Zaumseil of the International Academy for Innovative Pedagogy, Psychology and Economics gGmbH (INA) in Berlin and Prof. Johana Prawitasari-Hadiyono of the Universitas Gadjah Mada (UGM) in Yogyakarta, as well as Dr. Gavin Sullivan, formerly of Monash University, Melbourne and currently working at Leeds Metropolitan University. Funding was granted by the German Thyssen Foundation with financial responsibility for the research resting with the German team. Prof. Prawitasari-Hadiyono was responsible for implementing the research project in the field. From the beginning, there was close cooperation with the local NGO Institute of Community Behavioral Change (ICBC), a practice and research institution associated with Prof. Prawitasari-Hadiyono. The ICBC already had well-established field contacts that were developed during the delivery of the Ford Foundation recovery program (see Chap. 16) and as a result of an attached participatory project using traditional forms of theater that was conducted at the setting (see Prawitasari-Hadiyono et al. 2009).

Data were collected in the local language (Javanese) or the national language (*Bahasa Indonesia*) mainly by Indonesian researchers (due to their language skills), while the German researchers were mostly responsible for the analysis (due to their greater time resources, since the Thyssen Foundation financially supported two part-time positions for German research assistants). However, throughout the research process, shifts in roles and a process of mutual learning occurred. In the beginning, the international research team held joint workshops on techniques of data collection and analysis in culturally diverse contexts. The goal was to find out how to adapt the methods mentioned above to local conditions and the local forms of conduct. A close cooperation unfolded through role-play exercises, and a process of mutual learning helped the foreign researchers tune in to local ways of feeling und understanding. For example, it was essential for the German researchers to grasp the meaning and importance of the community embeddedness of coping. We discussed at length issues of field access and research ethics, as well as criteria for a theoretical sampling of the villages (see Sect. 4.3) and the persons to be interviewed (see later).

In the first research period, from 2008 to 2009, data collection was predominately carried out by the Indonesian team while the German team focused on the preliminary data analysis. German researchers often accompanied the Indonesian interviewers in the hamlets in order to familiarize themselves with the reality of village life.[5] It was paramount to immediately share and discuss preliminary data analyses in joint team meetings, in order to become aware of culturally bound interpretations and worldviews. This can be described as a mutual process of transformation in which the German researchers aimed to get closer to the villagers' habitus and local meanings, and the Indonesian researchers aimed to look at what seemed to be usual and familiar from the perspective of an unfamiliar gaze. Later, in 2010, the Indonesian researchers developed their own research questions, collected relevant additional data, and presented their results at the conference of the International Association for Cross-Cultural Psychology in Australia and other conferences in Indonesia. Meanwhile, the German team continued analyzing the data and compiling results. During the participatory research period in 2011, the Indonesian research team was responsible for the overall implementation, while the German researchers were available for reflection and planning sessions. The project culminated in a visit by the Indonesian researchers to Berlin to present the participatory research project in a joint workshop at the Wissenschaftszentrum Berlin für Sozialforschung (WZB; Berlin Social Research Center). This book constitutes a collaborative report of the funded research, although the distribution of authorship reflects the structural research imbalances indicated earlier.

Overall, the 3 years of research represented a process of mutual change in views, conceptualizations, and methods, resulting in a transformation to a more participatory approach. The transformation included the researchers on a personal level, the

[5] The data analyzed in Chap. 16 were collected by Silke Schwarz over the course of her dissertation research, for which she also conducted field stays.

organization of responsibilities and distribution of tasks and funds, as well as the representation of the project in local and international forums.[6]

From 2008 to 2010, 167 interviews and 19 focus group discussions took place.[7] The research team used digital voice recorders to record each interview and group discussion in its entirety. Recorded interviews and group discussions lasted approximately 60–90 min each. Some villagers (that is, those who might offer theoretically interesting insights) were interviewed several times in order to achieve a more comprehensive understanding. The main criterion in selecting our sample referred to the interviewee's current place of residence within the boundaries of a given hamlet. Our sample portrays the diversity of village inhabitants and purposive sampling maximized participant variation for age, marital status, gender, occupation, money and other possessions, and educational background. The vast majority of our interviewees originated from Central Java, with only a few having migrated from other parts of Indonesia, mostly after marriage. Almost all villagers officially endorsed Islam; only a very few Christians were living in the rural area and could be involved in our research. We interviewed formal and informal hamlet leaders who were designated "key persons" because they could provide detailed accounts on communal life and dynamics, both before and after the earthquake. Examples were hamlet and neighborhood leaders or the leader of a PKK[8] group as well as influential and respected village figures like *kyais* (that is, villagers with expert knowledge of Islam). Collective representations of stories about the hamlet were also elicited by conducting focus group discussions with ordinary villagers (Morgan 1997).

In order to formulate research questions on the level of "cases" (rather than using individuals as units of analysis, even though an affected person might be the central figure of interest), it was important to determine what constituted a case. We considered a case to be dependent on the life situation of the affected individual, which presents a definable, micro-social context that includes family members, neighbors, and significant others. It was useful to extrapolate the structure of a "case" from the multiple perspectives of different persons.[9] We included "cases" of people and their families who were bereaved as a result of the loss of a significant other or long-term impairments resulting from earthquake-related injuries. We also interviewed

---

[6] International examples were: 19th International Congress of the International Association for Cross-Cultural Psychology (IACCP), Bremen, Germany; 20th International Congress of the International Association for Cross-Cultural Psychology (IACCP), Melbourne, Australia; 1st International Conference of Indigenous and Cultural Psychology, Yogyakarta, Indonesia; 2nd International Conference of Indigenous and Cultural Psychology, Denpasar, Indonesia. Local forums included village celebrations or workshops and presentations at the Universitas Gadjah Mada, Yogyakarta.

[7] Data were mainly collected by Lucia P. Novianti, Nindyah Rengganis, Tiara R. Widiastuti, Yohanes K. Herdiyanto, and Silke Schwarz, with support from Ratri Atmoko Benedictus, Budi Rahmat Riadi, David Hizkia Tobing, Christoph Uhle, Jeane A. Indradjaja and Mechthild von Vacano.

[8] PKK stands for *Program Kesejahteraan Keluarga*, the Program for Family Welfare that is a government program to improve family welfare within hamlets. PKK groups are governed by the wife of the hamlet, an arrangement that represents hierarchical structures in village life and reinforces a gender-separated distribution of tasks. All PKK participants are married women and their activities relate to increasing family income and improving health.

[9] In the context of another investigation on Java, Zaumseil (2006a) reported that it was useful to have eight narrating informants including the individual who was personally affected.

individuals and their families without such extreme coping challenges in order to provide a range of long-term perspectives on pre- and post-earthquake village life. For Chap. 13, we sampled people who could be described as cases of "trauma" or similar long-term psychological effects, and included interviews with people who were close in terms of their social surroundings or network such as core and extended family members, as well as neighbors. For Chap. 14, the main sampling criterion was whether interviewees were involved in aid distribution processes as a distributor or receiver and her or his response of complaining or keeping silent about irregularities in the distribution process. Native speakers transcribed the interview data verbatim into MS-Word documents. During the participatory research phase in 2011, 50 villagers organized into nine community groups were involved in developing interview guidelines and organizing group discussions to gather data.

For data analysis, the German research team used Clarke's (2005) grounded theory approach to progress from a more descriptive analysis of the data and local concepts in the field to theory building.[10] We[11] used the computer program Atlas.ti developed by Thomas Muhr to support data evaluation and theory building. From the beginning, the process of building concepts and categories evolved in close dialogue between the research field and our disciplines. We used coding to search for theoretical concepts to describe the patterns of results emerging from the data and to identify units of meaning. Building on the results—and always maintaining close contact with the empirical data—we then searched systematically for new instances that refined the initial codes and provided rich examples of phenomena and their contexts, in order to identify larger units of meaning, categories, and interrelations within the categories. This creative reconfiguration and rediscovery of theory by using theoretical sensitivity (Glaser 1978) entailed an awareness of specialized scientific theories and concepts, but did not involve acceptance of or use of these models. Thus, theories such as those generated by quantitative methods formed part of an initial set of tools that could be critically deconstructed, ready to be used in new creative combinations (Zaumseil 2007).

Initially, we developed *situational maps* closely based on the data. As described by Clarke (2005) these "lay out the major human, nonhuman, discursive, historical, symbolic, political and other elements in the research situation of concern and provoke analysis of relations among them. These maps are intended to capture and discuss the messy complexities of the situation in their dense relations and permutations" (p. xxxv). In these maps, relations between the elements found in the situation were laid out and critically discussed. In a second step of theory building, the preliminary descriptive findings were mapped and linked to different theories

[10] For the implementation of practical research, Clarke (2005) developed a fruitful approach to the social scientific analysis of complex situations. Based on grounded theory and exceeding the boundaries of that framework, Clarke's approach creates links among disciplines and various scientific viewpoints.

[11] The impersonal "we" used hereinafter mainly refers to the German research team as analysts, while the Indonesian researchers' perspectives were included through discussion and feedback rounds.

(for example, the appraisal-based model of coping). Third, we tried to map the results of the descriptive analysis onto other theoretical models, such as the Crunch and Access-to-Resources Model (Wisner et al. 2004), to see what was missing and what needed to be fleshed out. In this way, we brought various insular disciplinary approaches into contact with one another. Using a critical analytical stance, we focused on the limitations of existing theories by identifying any untenable universalist assumptions and looking for where an account of social dimensions would improve our understanding. This flexible attitude toward existing disaster and coping theories helped us advance the theoretical structure by highlighting what needed to change in order to be compatible with the data, and where the model did not yet fit. We critically questioned the usefulness of the various coping models, and debated the implicit assumptions hidden in the models in order to suggest further theoretical developments (see Chaps. 3 and 17) warranted by our findings (see Chaps. 9–16). The theories presented in Chaps. 1 and 2 were used to determine how to decode the data and to offset the potential for multiple, plausible interpretations within different frameworks with different theoretical assumptions. With this attention to theoretical sensitization, a four-dimensional framework for coping with disasters (Chaps. 9–12) was formulated. A range of themes found in the interviews and the field observation data were identified and grouped with the dimensions. We consider this structure of themes to be congruent with the data because the villagers spontaneously focused on specific topics and wanted to discuss them in detail. Research participants were, of course, positioned by our ways of posing questions as well as directing the interviews and focus groups, but the research team was also vigilant for signs of resistance to this agenda and variations that disconfirmed emerging themes (but still needed to be incorporated and explained).

The research project was free of any intention to initiate an intervention based on the results. Rather, it is a documentary description of coping with the consequences of a disaster on the level of daily practices and related discourses. It aimed to develop categories that could grasp locally specific details as well as categories that could transcend the case study and may be—at least partially—transferable to other contexts. Due to the shortcomings in theory thus far (see Chaps. 1–3), we wanted to examine the cultural specificities of coping with a disaster.[12] How did affected people make sense of the event in the long term, and how did they interpret the experienced disaster aid and the resulting social changes and social conflicts created in their hamlets? Which emotions were evident in the discursive practices and narratives of the people involved? Furthermore, we were interested in the emotions, expectations, interpretations, and behaviors that might be connected to disaster-related threats in the future. Another focus centered on the relationship between the meanings and feelings shared by communities and the meanings and feelings experienced by individuals and families.

With regard to coping, it is important to note that our criteria for distinguishing between "successful" and "unsuccessful" coping were not based on appraisal-orientated

[12] More detailed research questions can be found in the relevant empirical chapters.

stress theories (for a critique, see Zaumseil 2006a), but rather followed resource-orientated theories (see Hobfoll 2001) supplemented by the addition of emotional coping. In this regard, the criteria for "successful" and "unsuccessful" coping correspond to the everyday concepts of a "happy" and "unhappy fate" of each affected person and family. Criteria for both were developed on a case-by-case basis, according to the principal of theoretical sampling alternating with data analysis throughout the research process (see also Chap. 13).

Overall, we evaluate our applied methodological approach as a partially successful dialogic process of mutual exchange between the Indonesian and German researchers as well as between the researchers and the research field. This process only became more balanced after a certain level of trust had been established. However, we argue that an equality of perspectives and related legitimacy claims was only partially achieved in the end. During field visits, for example, the researchers—especially those from Germany—continuously had to reiterate our inability to provide money or, for instance, a tractor that a group of farmers in Sido Kabul repeatedly requested. We were further forced into the position of experts when villagers asked for social assessments and evaluations and urged us to present risk reduction methods or ways for the community to achieve gender justice. Further reflections on our joint research process, such as issues of informed consent and ethics, are dealt with in Chaps. 6–8.

The German researchers reformulated the villagers' perspectives, transcending and partially restructuring their voices, probably even violating emic experiences at times. We counterbalanced a stark culture-bound perspective through feedback rounds in the hamlets, during which we crosschecked whether our analysis offered deeper insights about their lives and worlds. Another strategy entailed intense discussions within the international research team. Yet, an actual balance between German and Indonesian perspectives was limited by structural power imbalances within the research design because the German research team had access to greater financial and time resources.

Drawing on a social constructionist version of grounded theory, we did not aim to develop a model of causal links for further testing but rather to reconstruct emic perspectives. The huge amount of data gathered over time contained a diversity and large quantity of positions, adding merit to our claims made in the empirical chapters of this book (Chaps. 9–16). We linked our arguments to direct quotations as much as possible to increase credibility, highlighted liminal and unstable, taken-for-granted meanings, and deliberately employed a power-critical perspective in order to draw links between larger collectives or institutions and individual lives, when the data so indicated (see Charmaz 2006). We were looking for fresh categories that offered new insights that could overcome the theoretical shortcomings identified in Chap. 3. The challenges that our multidimensional framework of coping poses to current ideas, concepts, and practices are summarized in the concluding remarks section of each empirical chapter and in the book's conclusion (Chap. 17).

5.5 Concluding Remarks

In this chapter, we have clarified the methodological basis for our culture-specific coping research approach. Our conception focuses on the analytical unit of contextualized persons (cases) and communities. Personhood is located in and informed by social interactions, symbolic meanings, actions, and material artifacts. In Chap. 3, we acknowledged that subjectivity and agency are always contextualized, and can appear in locally specific forms of coping with events such as disasters. Therefore, the main objects of study are not technical features, social structures, organizational forms, or institutional and political processes after a disaster. Rather, these issues are treated as broader contexts of interest, since research participants referred to these contexts and were embedded within them. Within a cultural-psychological framework of coping, the research interest encompasses people's culture-specific rather than universally applicable understandings of traumatization, descriptions of suffering and impairment, healing practices associated with a disaster, and the relevance and meaning they ascribe to this suffering and healing. The analytic focus is on their everyday and disaster-related discursive practices in their particular cultural settings.

The main challenge facing culture-specific approaches is the relative difficulty of transferring research results to other contexts. It is possible that, for instance, findings reported in Parts III and IV may apply more generally to culture-specific coping responses in the event of an earthquake, but not to other catastrophes—for instance, volcanic eruptions, tsunamis, floods, fires, civil wars, or the suffering that occurs when someone falls ill with cancer. Yet, developing culturally adequate research methods in the context of coping with a specific disaster deepens the field of disaster research in general. For this purpose, previously restrictive epistemological approaches to coping with disasters need to be broadened by rethinking and expanding the units of investigation, allowing for complex interrelations and resisting oversimplification, as well as being process-oriented and including power-critical examinations.

Postcolonial thinking and a postmodern standpoint may best grasp the features of interest when focusing on local specificities because this entails not generalizing theories or concepts developed in the North to the behavior of people in the South and instead, accounting for historically produced, global power differentials. This hybrid perspective can account for locally specific power differentials that are historically rooted and globally intertwined. The use of a participatory qualitative approach helps to explore coping with adversity and simultaneously to encourage the research participants to participate actively in generating data about their perspectives and experiences; this, in turn, allows researchers to better understand the complexity of the topic.

Acknowledgment The editors would like to thank Sophie Perl for her assistance in editing this chapter.

References

Acker, J., Barry, K., & Essveld, J. (1991). Objectivity and truth. Problems in doing feminist research. In M. Fonow & J. Cook (Eds.), *Beyond methodology. Feminist scholarship as lived research* (pp. 133–153). Bloomington: Indiana University Press.

Antlöv, H. (2005). The social construction of power and authority in Java. In H. Antlöv & J. Hellman (Eds.), *The Java that never was. Academic theories and political practices* (pp. 43–66). Münster: LIT.

Beatty, A. (1999). *Varieties of Javanese religion. An anthropological account*. Cambridge: Cambridge University Press.

Behnke, C., & Meuser, M. (1999). *Geschlechterforschung und qualitative Methoden. Qualitative Sozialforschung 1*. Opladen: Leske+Budrich.

Beittinger-Lee, V. (2009). *(Un)civil society and political change in Indonesia*. Milton Park, Abingdon, Oxon; New York: Routledge.

Berg, E., & Fuchs, M. (1993). *Kultur, soziale Praxis, Text*. Frankfurt am Main: Suhrkamp.

Bergold, J., & Thomas, S. (2012). Participatory research methods: A methodological approach in motion [110 paragraphs]. *Forum Qualitative Sozialforschung/ Forum: Qualitative Social Research*, 13(1), http://nbn-resolving.de/urn:nbn:de:0114-fqs1201304. Accessed 12 Dec 2013.

Berry, J., Poortinga, Y., Breugelmans, S., Chasiotis, A., & Sam, D. (2011). *Cross-cultural psychology. Research and applications (3rd ed.)*. Cambridge: Cambridge University Press.

Birkmann, J., & Wisner, B. (2006). *Measuring the un-measurable. The challenge of vulnerability*. Bonn: Publication Series of UNU-EHS No. 5.

Blumer, H. (1969). *Symbolic interactionism: Perspective and method*. Englewood Cliffs: Prentice-Hall.

Bonanno, G. A., Brewin, C. R., Kaniasty, K., & La Greca, A. M. (2010). Weighing the costs of disaster: consequences, risks, and resilience in individuals, families and communities. *Psychological Science in the Public Interest, 11*(1), 1–49.

Bourdieu, P. (2005). *Die männliche Herrschaft*. Frankfurt am Main: Suhrkamp.

Bourdieu, P., & Wacquant, L. (1996). *Reflexive Anthropologie*. Frankfurt am Main: Suhrkamp.

Brokensha, D., Warren, D., & Werner, O. (Eds.). (1980). *Indigenous knowledge systems and development*. Lanham: University Press of America.

Charmaz, K. (2006). *Constructing grounded theory: A practical guide through qualitative analysis*. London: Sage.

Chiwaka, E., & Yates, R. (n.d.). Participatory vulnerability analysis. A step–by–step guide for field staff. Actionaid International. http://www.actionaid.org.uk/sites/default/files/doc_lib/108_1_participatory_vulnerability_analysis_guide.pdf. Accessed 27 March 2013.

Cisneros-Puebla, C. A. (2007). The deconstructive and reconstructive faces of social construction. Kenneth Gergen in conversation with César A. Cisneros-Puebla. With an introduction by Robert B. Faux [83 paragraphs]. *Forum Qualitative Sozialforschung/ Forum: Qualitative Social Research*, 9(1). http://nbn-resolving.de/urn:nbn:de:0114-fqs0801204. Accessed 6 Jan 2013.

Clarke, A. (2005). *Situational analysis. Grounded theory after the postmodern turn*. Thousand Oaks: Sage.

Clifford, J. (1988). *The predicament of culture*. Cambridge: Harvard University Press.

Crowe, M., & Sheppard, L. (2010). Qualitative and quantitative research designs are more similar than different. *The Internet Journal of Allied Health Sciences and Practice, 8*(4). http://ijahsp.nova.edu/articles/Vol8Num4/crowe_8_4_.htm. Accessed 26 Jan 2013.

Dekens, J. (2007). Local knowledge for disaster preparedness. Kathmandu: International Centre for Integrated Mountain Development (ICIMOD). Online: http://preventionweb.net/go/2693. Accessed 10 May 2013.

Engler, S. (2004). Constructionism versus what? *Religion, 34*(4), 291–313.

Farnell, B. (2000). Getting out of the habitus: An alternative model of dynamically embodied social action. *Journal of the Royal Anthropological Institute, 6*(3), 397–418.

Flick, U. (2009). *An introduction to qualitative research*. London: Sage.

Folkman, S. (1997). Positive psychological states and coping with severe stress. *Social Science & Medicine, 45*(8), 1207–1221.

Gergen, K. J. (1999). *An invitation to social construction*. London: Sage.

Gergen, K. J., & Gergen, M. M. (1997). Toward a cultural constructionist psychology. *Theory & Psychology, 7,* 31–36.

Glaser, B. G. (1978). *Theoretical sensitivity*. Mill Valley: Sociology Press.

Glaser, B. G. (1992). *Basics of grounded theory analysis*. Mill Valley: Sociology Press.

Glaser, B. G., & Strauss, A. L. (1967). *Discovery of grounded theory*. Mill Valley: Sociology Press.

Habermas, J. (1981). *Theorie des kommunikativen Handelns*. Frankfurt am Main: Suhrkamp.

Haseman, B. (2006). A manifesto for performative research. *Media International Australia incorporating Culture and Policy*, theme issue Practice-led Research (no. *118*), pp. 98–106. http://eprints.qut.edu.au/3999/1/3999_1.pdf. Accessed 16 Feb 2013.

Hobfoll, S. E. (2001). The influence of culture, community, and the nested self in the stress process: Advancing conservation of resources theory. *Applied Psychology, 50*(3), 337–421.

Hobfoll, S. E. (2011). Conservation of resources theory: Its implication for stress, health and resilience. In S. Folkman & P. E. Nathan (Eds.), *The Oxford handbook of stress, health, and coping* (pp. 127–147). New York: Oxford University Press.

Holtzappel, C., & Ramstedt, M. (2009). *Decentralization and regional autonomy in Indonesia*. Singapore, Leiden, Netherlands: Institute of Southeast Asian Studies; International Institute for Asian Studies.

Jigyasu, R. (2002). Reducing disaster vulnerability through local knowledge and capacity. http://ntnu.diva-portal.org/smash/get/diva2:123824/FULLTEXT01. Accessed 6 June 2013.

Kalayjian, A., Kanazi, R. L., Aberson, C. L., & Feygin, L. (2002). A cross-cultural study of the psychosocial and spiritual impact of natural disaster. *International Journal of Group Tensions, 31*(2), 175–186.

Kemmis, S., & McTaggart, R. (2005). Participatory action research: Communicative action and the public sphere. In N. Denzin & Y. Lincoln (Eds.), *Handbook of qualitative research* (pp. 559–604) (3rd ed.). Thousand Oaks: Sage.

Kim, U. (2000). Indigenous, cultural, and cross-cultural psychology: A theoretical, conceptual, and epistemological analysis. *Asian Journal of Social Psychology, 3*(3), 265–287.

Kleinman, A., & Erin, F.-H. (2007). The experiential basis of subjectivity: How individuals change in the context of societal transformation. In J. Biehl, B. Good, & A. Kleinman (Eds.), *Subjectivity. Ethnographic investigations* (pp. 52–65). Berkeley: University of California Press.

Lykes, M. (2001a). Activist participatory research and the arts with rural Maya women: Interculturality and situated meaning making. In D. L. Tolman, & M. Brydon-Miller (Eds.), *From subjects to subjectivities: A handbook of interpretive and participatory methods* (pp. 183–199). New York: New York University Press.

Lykes, M. (2001b). Creative arts and photography in participatory action research in Guatemala. In P. Reason, & H. Bradbury (Eds.), *Handbook of action research. Participative inquiry and practice* (pp. 363–371). Thousand Oaks: Sage.

Markard, M. (2010). Kritische Psychologie: Forschung vom Standpunkt des Subjekts. In G. Mey & K. Mruck (Eds.), *Handbuch Qualitative Forschung in der Psychologie* (pp. 166–181). Wiesbaden: Verlag für Sozialwissenschaften.

Manning, C., & van Diermen, P. (Eds.). (2000). *Indonesia in transition: Social Aspects of Reformasi and Crisis*. Singapore: Institute of Southeast Asian Studies.

Mead, G. H. (1934). *Mind, self, and society*. Chicago: University of Chicago Press.

Mercer, J., Dominey-Howes, D., Kelman, I., & Lloyd, K. (2007). The potential for combining indigenous and western knowledge in reducing vulnerability of environmental hazards in small island developing states. *Environmental Hazards, 7*(4), 245–256.

Mercer, J. (2012). Knowledge and disaster risk reduction. In B. Wisner, J. C. Gaillard, & I. Kelman (Eds.), *The Routledge handbook of hazards and disaster risk reduction* (pp. 97–108). London: Routledge.

Morgan, D. L. (1997). *Focus groups as qualitative research (2nd ed.)*. Thousand Oaks: Sage.

Norris, F. H. (2006). Disaster research methods. *Journal of Traumatic Stress, 19*(2), 173–184.
Norris, F. H., Tracy, M., & Galea, S. (2009). Looking for resilience: Understanding the longitudinal trajectories of responses to stress. *Social Science & Medicine, 68*(12), 2190–2198.
Oliver-Smith, A. (1998). Disasters, social change, and adaptive systems. In E. L. Quarantelli (Ed.), *What is a disaster?* (pp. 231–233). London: Routledge.
Pakenham, K. I. (2011). Benefit finding and sense making in chronic illness. In S. Folkman & P. E. Nathan, (Eds.), *The Oxford handbook of stress, health, and coping* (pp. 242–268). New York: Oxford University Press.
Pargament, K. I. (2011). Religion and coping: The current state of knowledge. In S. Folkman & P. E. Nathan (Eds.), *The Oxford handbook of stress, health, and coping* (pp. 269–288). New York: Oxford University Press.
Pargament, K. I., Koenig, H. G., & Perez, L. M. (2000). The many methods of religious coping: Development and initial validation of the RCOPE. *Journal of Clinical Psychology, 56*(4), 519–543.
Pemberton, J. (1994). *On the subject of Java*. New York: Cornell University Press.
Prawitasari-Hadiyono, J. E., Paramastri, I., Suhapti, R., Novianti, L. P., Widiastuti, T. R., & Rengganis, N. (2009). Social artistry, lokales Wissen und Konflikte nach einem Erdbeben. *Zeitschrift für Psychodrama und Soziometrie, 8*(2), 277–295.
Priya, K. R. (2004). Survivors' suffering and healing amidst changing socioeconomic forces in two years of post-earthquake Kachchh. *Psychology & Developing Societies, 16*(1), 41–60.
Priya, K. R (2010). Research relationship as a facilitator of remoralization and self-growth: Post-earthquake suffering and healing. *Qualitative Health Research, 20,* 479–495.
Priya, K. R. (2012). Social constructionist approach to suffering and healing: Juxtaposing Cassell, Gergen and Kleinman. *Psychological Studies, 57,* 211–223.
Rabinow, P. (2007). Anthropological observation and self-formation. In J. G. Biehl, B. J. Good, & A. Kleinman (Eds.), *Subjectivity. Ethnographic investigations* (pp. 98–127). Berkeley: University of California Press.
Ratner, C. (2008). *Cultural psychology, cross-cultural psychology, and indigenous psychology*. New York: Nova Science Publishers.
Schlehe, J. (2006). Nach dem Erdbeben auf Java: Kulturelle Polarisierungen, soziale Solidarität und Abgrenzung. *Internationales Asienforum, 37*(3–4), 213–237.
Schwarz, S. (2012). *Eine kritische und kultursensible Sicht auf das Mainstreaming von Gender in einem Katastrophenkontext: Umstrittene Gendergerechtigkeitsvorstellungen, ein heuristisches Modell sozialen Wandels und Strategieprozessvorstellungen. Betroffenen- und AktivistInnen-sichtweisen*. Doctoral Dissertation, Fachbereich Erziehungswissenschaften und Psychologie, Freie Universität Berlin.
Sillitoe, P. (2010). Trust in development: Some implications of knowing in indigenous knowledge. *Journal of the Royal Anthropological Institute, 16,* 12–30.
Strauss, A. L. (1978). A social worlds perspective. *Studies in Symbolic Interaction, 1,* 119–128.
Strauss, A. L. (1987). *Qualitative analysis for social scientists*. Cambridge: Cambridge University Press.
Strauss, A. L., & Corbin, J. (1990). *Grounded Theory: Grundlagen Qualitativer Sozialforschung*. Weinheim: Beltz Psychologie Verlags Union.
Vygotsky, L. S. (1985). *Thought and language*. Cambridge: MIT Press.
Wikgren, M. (2004). Critical realism as philosophy and social theory in information science. *Journal of Documentation, 61*(1), 11–22.
Winter, R. (2010). Sozialer Konstruktivismus. In G. Mey & K. Mruck (Eds.), *Handbuch Qualitative Forschung in der Psychologie* (pp. 123–135). Wiesbaden: Verlag für Sozialwissenschaften.
Wisner, B., Blaikie, P., Cannon, T., & Davis, I. (2004). *At risk: Natural hazards, people's vulnerability and disasters (2nd ed.)*. London: Routledge.
Wohlrab-Sahr, M. (1993). Empathie als methodisches Prinzip? Entdifferenzierung und Reflexionsverlust als problematisches Erbe der „methodischen Postulate der Frauenforschung". *Feministische Studien, 11*(2), 128–139.

Wulf, C., & Zirfas, J. (2001). Das Soziale als Ritual: Perspektiven des Performativen. In C. Wulf, B. Althans, K. Audehm, C. Bausch, M. Göhlich, S. Sting, A. Tervooren, M. Wagner-Willi, & J. Zirfas (Eds.), *Das Soziale als Ritual* (pp. 339–347). Opladen: Leske+Budrich.
Zaumseil, M. (2006a). Der alltägliche Umgang mit Schizophrenie in Zentral-Java. In E. Wohlfart & M. Zaumseil (Eds.), *Transkulturelle Psychiatrie. Interkulturelle Psychotherapie – Interdisziplinäre Theorie und Praxis* (pp. 332–360). Berlin: Springer.
Zaumseil, M. (2006b). Beiträge der Psychologie zum Verständnis des Zusammenhangs von Kultur und psychischer Gesundheit bzw. Krankheit. In E. Wohlfart & M. Zaumseil (Eds.), *Transkulturelle Psychiatrie. Interkulturelle Psychotherapie – Interdisziplinäre Theorie und Praxis* (pp. 3–50). Berlin: Springer.
Zaumseil, M. (2007). Qualitative Sozialforschung in Klinischer Kulturpsychologie. *Psychotherapie und Sozialwissenschaft, 9*(2), 99–116.

Chapter 6
Research Ethics: Between Formal Norms and Intentions

Lucia Peppy Novianti

In 2008, I had the opportunity to be involved in a research project as part of an Indonesian team in close cooperation with a German team. At the time, I had just finished my undergraduate studies and was beginning a graduate professional program in psychology. I felt that I had received a great chance to build on my theoretical knowledge and get direct and practical research experience while gaining necessary skills toward becoming a practitioner in psychology. I was very enthusiastic because the goal of this research was to understand the dynamics of people's coping processes after the Bantul 2006 earthquake disaster, of which I was one of the survivors.

In the first year, the Indonesian team participated in a research workshop and learned skills in preparation for becoming qualitative interviewers. From the very beginning, I was interested in issues focusing on how a researcher should behave and work to maintain the well-being and convenience of research participants. Even after 3 years of involvement in this research, the topic of how we, as researchers, need to pay attention to the perspectives and psychological condition of the survivors continues to interest me the most. In this chapter, I would like to share the ethical research issues that I faced and describe how, as a researcher *and* as a part of the community of research participants, I was able to consider and act in relation to these ethical issues while carrying out the task of collecting data.

The consideration of ethical issues in research processes aims to guarantee a balance between the aims of the research and the well-being of participants (see Kazdin 1992). Some topics discussed with regard to ethical research issues are informed consent, efforts to respect participant anonymity and confidentiality, and issues around publishing of research findings (Flick 2002, Bowling 2002). These topics have also become issues in experimental research (Kazdin 1992) but they take on an added complexity when the researcher yields control over their research environment and goes into the field to collect data. The essence of these discussions focuses on minimizing any disadvantage or harm to participants in the research process. I found

L. P. Novianti (✉)
Institute for Community Behavioral Change,
Jalan Ki Mangunsarkoro 27, Pakualaman, 55111 Yogyakarta, Indonesia
e-mail: lucia.peppy@gmail.com

M. Zaumseil et al. (eds.), *Cultural Psychology of Coping with Disasters*,
DOI 10.1007/978-1-4614-9354-9_6,

that adhering to ethical standards was often difficult or challenging in practice due to some of the social values in the research setting. For example, I was confronted with the paradoxical effect of confidentiality guidelines: My insisting on an undisturbed confidential one-on-one interview situation might have negative consequences for the interviewee, since such a secluded conversation would be perceived as secretive and could raise suspicion among the village elite and community members toward my interviewee. This is similar to Riessmann's (2005) experience of research in South India where she found that trying to comply with the code of confidentiality resulted in problems between participants and their families. The social norms, as well as community practices, interfered with the implementation of the ethical standard of confidentiality.

In my experience, minimizing harm to research participants not only is an ethical obligation but also creates a favorable atmosphere and allows one to access deeper data. I was very much concerned about causing no additional harm, as my interviewees were survivors of a severe earthquake and I wanted to prevent any additional suffering. I aimed at a relationship based on respect toward one another that could positively influence achieving the research goals, while at the same time benefitting the research participants. After 3 years of research, I would argue that research ethics are about building relationships and maintaining well-being on both sides.

6.1 Evoking Negative Experiences: How to Avoid Hurtful Topics

Throughout the research process, I experienced an internal conflict about evoking community members' memories of their unpleasant experiences. The 2006 earthquake was a horrible disaster that caused great stress among survivors. Being an earthquake survivor myself, I could understand this condition very well. I shared the sociocultural orientation and customs of the people in the study. However, I did not live in the Bantul district but in a neighboring urban region that was less severely affected by the quake. Even if the destruction was less in comparison to Bantul, the aftermath had a terrible impact. Having experienced it myself, I sometimes had the urge to share my experience with colleagues or friends, but sometimes sharing my own experience evoked feelings of anxiety as they remembered the earthquake. If I experienced these feelings of anxiety, then what about the survivors from the Bantul area who were perhaps still haunted by memories of the earthquake?

I started interviewing for the study approximately 2 years after the 2006 quake. As I had been, many people were still enthusiastic about sharing their incredible experiences of the earthquake, especially with new people or strangers, but I wondered whether or not this could become a negative or harmful experience. The thought that reliving the events could cause harm to these people made me feel uncomfortable. Yet, this research aimed at obtaining data about the survivors' experiences that would help understand what lessons had been learned and, also perhaps, alleviate the suffering of others in the future. These conflicts dominated my thoughts.

The interview guidelines given by the German team recommended approaching the topic of suffering slowly and indirectly; however, it was necessary to explain the research topic and aims right in the beginning, since we as interviewers were obligated to ask the subjects for informed consent. The procedure of obtaining informed consent brought us straight to the hot topic, the 2006 earthquake. In my cultural context, people tend to discuss only the positive and are discouraged from discussing the negative. Therefore, relating negative memories can make them feel uncomfortable. I was afraid to undermine the condition of my interviewees through a sensitization process, because it might have forced them to choose between telling the truth and following the norm of discussing only positive topics.

In our research team, we discussed the possibility that remembering past adverse or uncomfortable feelings could create an unfavorable psychological condition in participants, even though the process could also have therapeutic effects, much like the process of exposure therapy. According to Feske (2008), such prolonged exposure can lead to the improvement of post-traumatic stress disorder (PTSD) symptoms. We thus equally considered whether talking about these feelings could actually have a positive impact and allow people to demonstrate their resilience and ability to cope.

In order to deal with this dilemma of immediately bringing up the subject of suffering in order to obtain informed consent, I felt it would be better to start the interview encounter with more comfortable conditions and conversations. Before obtaining the subject's informed consent, I chose to chat and converse in a relaxed manner until I felt more "at ease" to begin the discussion about their earthquake experiences. I did that to build a general rapport, but I was also following the ethical code of the Indonesian Psychology Association, Himpunan Psikologi Indonesia (HIMPSI). HIMPSI guidelines stipulate that the psychologist, as a researcher, should attempt to maintain participants' well-being, referring to psychological aspects of well-being, such as emotions or social life. It also offers information regarding keeping the data-gathering process safe and providing comfort to the participants.

Personally, I used my own indictor of feeling "at ease" and found that I did not have any barriers when communicating about the research with the participants. This resulted in the participants feeling more comfortable in discussing the earthquake experiences early on. I believe that it is effective for researchers to use their own emotions as a personal indicator of the unease of participants. An empathetic attitude while carrying out research helps in understanding the readiness of research participants to speak about topics that are part of the researcher's agenda. Empathy can be described as a researcher being able to find the right time to bring up the sensitive research topic. However, using the emotional state of a researcher as an indicator of the participant's condition (or process of mirroring) also has the potential to lead to misinterpretations or early judgments (and even collusion in avoiding particular topics on the basis of a shared background).

During the research, I learned how to handle the process of mirroring in order to minimize misinterpretations or early judgments. It is crucial to be sensitive to the bodily and emotional reactions of the participant and continue to monitor both throughout an interview. Rechecking what I felt or sensed during the interaction could help in ensuring the real, authentic, or factual condition of both the interviewer and the interviewee. The process of understanding bodily reactions and then rechecking was reinforced by the basic condition that the participants and I came from the same cultural background. In rechecking, I was interested in achieving a better understanding of participants' feelings, opinions, or initial ideas as they emerged in my interaction with them. It allowed me to dig deeper into the emotional or psychological condition of the participants and the feelings evoked by our interaction while maintaining a sense of a social connection as the interview progressed.

In retrospect, excessive emotions such as crying, bodily reactions, or anxiety were not evoked. This may have been caused by two things. First, villagers had been habitually exposed to research due to the experience of this natural disaster. As survivors, the exposure of their stories sometimes resulted in a kind of reward, for example, the presence of aid or a feeling that they were the focus of attention. Second, the local people had actually undergone a process of recovery; most of them had been able to accept the unpleasant experience positively. I understood this acceptance due to the sociocultural values of the local people, mainly a submission (*pasrah*) and resignation (*nrimo*) to one's fate . This response of acceptance subsequently became a special discussion in this book about the concept of coping among the Javanese people (see Chaps. 11 and 12).

The process of relating their difficult experiences became a process of release and healing. Most subjects told their stories easily, though some subjects needed a few minutes before they were able to continue calmly. In my opinion, an important issue to consider while conducting research in a disaster setting is that of excessive emotions. Excessive emotions can act as an alarm for the research team, which should assist in minimizing harm. In this case study based in Bantul, for example, this topic was considered because of the cultural tradition of avoiding or hindering extreme emotions.

6.2 The Problem of Informed Consent Versus Developing Closeness

Informed consent is a "compulsory element" of ethics (my own term) in the practice of psychology, both in providing individual services and complying with ethical research procedures (see HIMPSI 2010; APA 2002). The concept of informed consent originates from biomedical treatment procedures but has become normative in many research procedures, including social science research. Informed consent aims to ensure that the purpose and impact of the research procedure have been explained to the subject and permission to participate in the research process has been given. For research participants, informed consent is useful in order to understand the context, topic, and aims of the research, their rights and obligations as participants, and also the risks as well as any compensation involved. For researchers, informed consent usually guarantees that participation was voluntary and engaged in without duress (Riessman 2005; Jackson 2003; Bowling 2002; Flick 2002; Kazdin 1992; Fowler 1988). I was concerned about complying with the ethical rule that informed consent be in written form because this procedure had the tendency to be misunderstood in the context of our research. After the disaster, there had been cases of misuse of aid and issues about fairness that had resulted in some of our interviewees misinterpreting signatures as giving consent to use what they said as witness statements against other villagers.

Among the Indonesian researchers, we discussed the concrete detail of participants' consent statements in order to make them more contextual. In discussion between the Indonesian and German teams, we agreed that informed consent emphasized obtaining permission and statements of willingness from the research subjects. We also talked about the ethical constraints involved and that it was important that these were genuinely understood by participants. Finally, we reached an understanding that consent could be given verbally and that an audio recording of the statement before the interview was conducted would be sufficient. Stressing the formal and official procedure of using written documents would have resulted in mistrust, due to the above-mentioned history. There was, in fact, one refusal of an interview because the potential interviewee believed that the interview would be used to prove the misconduct of other villagers. Understanding the context of the participants' experiences greatly influenced decisions about the best means by which participants could give their free and informed consent.

6.3 Maintaining Confidentiality: Anonymity in the Context of a Communal Society

The research participants continue to live in a communal–collectivist culture, which is traditional to Javanese life. This communal–collectivist character is found in daily habits, such as families living as extended families rather than as nuclear families, which is also very apparent during celebrations such as marriages, births of new family members, or funerals (see Chap. 10). There are various values and related practices that reinforce this communality or togetherness, such as *gotong royong* (voluntary work together in the community) and some common phrases, such as *mangan ora mangan asal kumpul* (the main thing is being together, even when there is no food, because the most important thing is the togetherness). People know each other very well, for example, when I first began to seek out one or two villagers to be interviewed (based on certain criteria), and the person was not at home, a neighbor would explain to me where that person had gone, with whom, and could even predict how long that person would be away. Not surprisingly, the line between private or personal space is often unclear. Having been brought up in this type of environment, I was able to fully understand the importance placed on being involved in the daily life of and caring for each other and one's neighbors in the villages we investigated.

In the context of these communal bonds, there appeared to be potential for contradictions in response to the need for anonymity in research. For example, it was often very difficult to convince an interviewee to participate in an interview alone, in a private place without any neighbors or members of the extended family present.

Being interviewed alone made some participants uncomfortable, as indicated by the subjects themselves saying that there was nothing they were trying to hide. This condition was also experienced by Riesmann (2005). In these contradictory circumstances, I felt blocked but when interviewing villagers in the presence of others, forms of social control also inhibited respondents to talk openly (at least negatively) about members of the village elite and the village committee. In this type of interview context, topics such as irregularities in aid distribution were avoided. However, if I had insisted on conducting the interview in private, suspicion might have arisen and I could potentially have exposed the interviewee to negative consequences or punishment by powerful people in the village.

My response was to move my interviews in the direction of chatting. To protect my interviewees, I even tended to delay the interview and avoid certain topics. After the initial meeting, I would propose a new appointment, hoping to be able to meet him or her in a private setting with no one around, and to be able to explain the concept of informed consent.

Control of the situation varied between the different villages; for example, in one village we experienced control exerted by the village committee. In this context, the Indonesian research team tried to influence the conditions in the villages. The attempts to maintain anonymity focused on not only making the research participants more assertive but also deterring the village committees from intervening and thereby threatening the anonymity of the participants. In order to achieve this, we took on the role of educating and raising awareness about anonymity in the context of research with people in rural villages. We were aware that we could not change the hierarchical power structures in the villages. An important point for us was to understand the meaning of anonymity from the participants' perspective within the sociocultural context of the villages in our study.

6.4 Research Data: Usage and Ownership Issues

This research resulted in interviews and observation data. There were some secondary data used including village demographics and other information from the village or subdistrict administration, institutions or departments, and also from the media. Through the process of obtaining informed consent, the research data actually become the researcher's property, though special permission is needed if the data will explicitly show the subject's identity (for example, in photos or videos) (Van den Eynden et al. 2011). There was an instance in which a survivor who had been physically disabled as a result of the earthquake initially refused and then subsequently gave permission to use a photograph of him in a publication. In this case, I learned how important it is to understand the context within which a person refuses or gives permission. The respondent had been disappointed by a reconstruction helper who had not shown him respect and had made him feel left behind. Because of a discussion of this past event of not having been respected by the helper, he helped me understand the reasons behind the initial refusal of permission to use his photo.

An in-depth conversation on this previous experience was crucial for the subsequent permission. Participants have their own world of experiences and perspectives that affects their decisions.

Another interesting experience was related to conducting participatory research with the community in the third year. What is the property or ownership status of research data produced in a participative manner? The participatory research conducted in the third year included research cooperation between the research team and the villagers. The research data "property rights" became an ethical topic of special interest: as the villagers were the ones doing the research and the role of the Indonesian team was more to assist the process, the real primary owner of the data was actually the village researchers. Interestingly, the village researchers felt that they were not researchers, but rather just people who were involved in this program. They felt that the research belonged to us, the professional researchers from the Indonesian/German research team. I believe we have to realize that in conducting participatory research, the researchers consist of two parties and this means that research results are owned by both parties with equal rights and obligations. As researchers, we need to maintain ethical practices, namely by encouraging the people to own and to have power over their research results. Building awareness of their rights and empowering them to own the research data that they help to create are two of our central responsibilities as researchers.

6.5 Concluding Remarks: Lessons Learned

This chapter has given me the chance to reflect on the ethical concerns involved in my interactions with participants as a researcher during the 3 years of the research project. The most basic insight resulted from reflecting upon variations in distance and closeness between my research participants and me, in the roles of researcher, fellow survivor, and fellow Javanese. The well-being of both researcher and participants could benefit from these insights. Reflecting on ethical, moral, and power issues may also create uncertainty that leads to internal conflicts. However, becoming aware of one's own position in the research field affects the power relationship between the researcher and subject because it enables the researcher to act differently.

Another issue arose around concerns about ethical conduct according to Western or international perspectives. The Indonesian Psychological Association (HIMPSI 2010) tried to make guidelines for Indonesian professional conduct to conform with Western rules. However, when actually applying these adapted rules to a sociocultural context, such as a post-disaster rural setting, local conditions (and knowledge) must be taken into consideration. If it is crucial to maintain the subjects' well-being, then it is important to build a positive, respectful relationship with the participants based on mutual trust and an empathetic understanding of their situation. Researchers can do this by understanding the main ideas for ethical research practice beyond the formalized techniques and rules by adapting these ideals and aspirations to local practice. The goal is not just to reduce the complexities of ethical conduct in the data-gathering process, but also to bring a positive feeling to the researcher as well as the participants. The combination of an Indonesian team in a position of closeness to the research field and a German team's outsider perspective resulted in many productive discussions.

Some suggestions regarding ethical practices for future research in disaster or Indonesian contexts include:

- To be aware of and open toward the special characteristics of participants. The researcher should not only consider the ideas or information that would be beneficial for analysis (as a background for research to be conducted) but should also adapt views of ethical conduct to the specific sociocultural context.
- It is an advantage to have the perspectives of insiders and outsiders in a research team, particularly when the team is international. International collaboration when conducting research offers the opportunity to better understand the participants in their context. This not only benefits the research data, but also helps maintain the well-being of participants. A "local researcher" who is close to the world of the participants is crucial in the transformation of perspectives of "outsiders" and helps in reducing bias and producing valid interpretations .

Acknowledgments The editors would like to thank Elise Serbaroli for her assistance in editing this chapter.

References

American Psychological Association. (2002). Ethical principles of psychologists and code of conduct. *American Psychologist, 57*(12), 1060–1073.

Bowling, A. (2002). *Research methods in health. Investigating health and health services* (2nd ed.). Buckingham: Open-University Press.

Feske, U. (2008). Treating low income and minority women with posttraumatic stress disorders: A pilot study comparing prolonged exposure and treatment as usual conducted by community therapist. *Journal of Interpersonal Violence, 23*(8), 1027–1040.

Flick, U. (2002). *An introduction to qualitative research* (2nd ed.). London: Sage.

Fowler, F. J. (1988). *Survey research methods. Applied social research methods series* (1. Rev. ed.). Thousand Oaks: Sage.

Himpunan Psikologi Indonesia (HIMPSI). (2010). *Kode Etik Psikologi Indonesia*. Ciputat: Himpsi Jaya.

Jackson, W. (2003). *Methods doing social research* (3rd ed.). Toronto: Pearson Education.

Kazdin, A. E. (1992). *Research design in clinical psychology* (2nd ed.). Massachusetts: Allyn & Bacon.

Riessman, C. K. (2005). Exporting ethics: A narrative about narrative research in South India. *Health, 9*(4), 473–490.

Van den Eynden, V., Corti, L., Woollard, M., Bishop, L., & Horton, L. (2011). Managing and sharing data. Best practice for researchers. UK Data Archive. http://www.data-archive.ac.uk/media/2894/managingsharing.pdf. Accessed 10 June 2013.

Chapter 7
Reflections of an Earthquake-Survivor Researcher

Nindyah Rengganis

When we first met, Manfred Zaumseil asked me what the most important event in the past 5 years of my life was. I answered, "the earthquake," and then elaborated why. It was 2008 and Manfred had come to visit the Institute for Community Behavioral Change (ICBC), the nongovernmental organization (NGO) I was working with. My colleague and friend Edward Theodorus sat next to me and interrupted, "Didn't you just get married? Wasn't that important?" Only then did I realize that I had positioned the 2006 earthquake as more important than my 2007 wedding, and I began to wonder why.

Coming from the Bantul region, when the earthquake occurred, I lived approximately 7 km from the earthquake's epicenter near Bantul city. The day had started as a bright morning, but suddenly the air filled with the dust of collapsing houses as people panicked and screamed. Later, when the rumor of a subsequent tsunami spread, we fled north. Some of my close family members, living in one of the villages included in our study, were affected too. I have first-hand experience of what it means to be an earthquake survivor. I prefer the term "survivor" over "disaster victim,"[1] because Bantul residents continued to live their lives in spite of the loss and destruction they faced. "Victim" can be used to refer to anyone struck by disaster, regardless of whether they have died or survived. I am more than just a survivor. In the immediate aftermath, I volunteered to provide first aid and to clear debris in my own community. Later, I worked for a disaster recovery program as an NGO activist, since ICBC had joined a network of 12 local NGOs that distributed additional reconstruction funds. In the context of this program, we were one of the many donor organizations that surveyed the needs and entitlements of the affected villages.

---

[1] The term "survivor" came to Indonesia in the context of international post-tsunami recovery programs. It then spread among activists and academics who introduced the Indonesian version of survivor: *penyintas*. This new terminology has found its way into official government language. Among villagers, this relatively new term is only beginning to spread and most still refer to themselves as "victim" (*korban*).

N. Rengganis (✉)
Institute for Community Behavioral Change,
Jalan Ki Mangunsarkoro 27, Pakualaman, 55111 Yogyakarta, Indonesia
e-mail: nrganis@yahoo.com

M. Zaumseil et al. (eds.), *Cultural Psychology of Coping with Disasters*,
DOI 10.1007/978-1-4614-9354-9_7,

When I was first approached to join the research team as a psychology graduate, my initial feeling was that I would be studying my own neighbors. Skepticism made me voice several reservations against such a research endeavor.

In 2006, the people of Bantul had already been the center of attention. Immediately after the earthquake, Bantul attracted crowds of outsiders. Within the first few days after the quake, roads in the region were jammed and the police had a difficult time managing traffic. Vehicles carried survivors' family members or friends, people bringing aid, or people who merely wanted to "look around." It was as if Bantul had become a tourist attraction, the physical destruction drawing outsiders' attention. This phenomenon has been dubbed a culture of "disaster tourism." The media coverage accentuated this effect, always in search for "a good story." Besides media professionals, citizen amateur journalists also came to the villages to interview survivors. Simultaneously, donor agencies conducted surveys in affected areas, asking people about the event, the number of casualties, the damage that occurred, and the aid needed. Working for the NGO recovery program, I had been one of the people conducting these surveys. With all of these different actors involved, Bantul residents were not always fully informed about what questions they were answering and what would happen to all the data. Some surveys had no clear follow-up. All of this attention brought relief goods and programs to the villages, which sometimes led to conflict.

7.1 Initial Skepticism

Against this background, I wondered why anyone would conduct research in the midst of such an unsettled, postdisaster situation where many aid programs were still in place, potentially causing conflicts within the community and where any "survey" would be closely associated with these aid programs. What were the research aims and topics? What was so appealing in studying a disaster from a psychological perspective? From a survivor's perspective, the main priority was to recover from the physical damage and casualties. The disaster had taught me how important it was to keep on doing things and not spend too much time thinking.

My main concern was the question of benefit and burden. I doubted that the benefit of this study would be for the communities. Instead of helping people in need, research can constitute a burden as it usually consists of many inquiries. When we first approached the village communities to introduce our research agenda, they were well aware of this aspect and critically asked about any benefits for them and the purpose of the research. I asked myself if it was appropriate to study a disaster at a moment when people were just beginning to recover. People were motivated to carry on with their lives, to go back to school, go back to work, and rebuild their homes. Slowly, they were able to forget the horrific impact of the disaster as they were faced with other challenges. Housing and social structures were being reestablished, and people's lives were returning to normal.

As the research process continued, my initial skepticism faded. The study intended to document how the community was dealing with the disaster. Their experiences and perspectives were key to this study and they were valued as meaningful and important. I experienced a similar acknowledgment when the German research counterparts addressed me as an expert. An expert, in our society, is considered to be someone who dedicates her or his time to science and knowledge and is well educated and experienced in research. Experts are usually met with a great deal of respect for their expertise and social status, especially by villagers. Neither as a bachelor graduate of psychology nor as an earthquake survivor had I considered myself an expert. Being addressed as one was an empowering experience that changed my way of thinking. I realized that knowledge is everywhere and that everyone can be the source of it. Everyone can be an expert.

7.2 International Research Collaboration

When I was offered the opportunity to join the international research team, I was addressed not only as a survivor-expert but also as a young academic. At first, the other graduate students and I were asked to assist the German team with data collection. We were trained in qualitative interviewing techniques and then expected to conduct structured guideline interviews with respondents in the three research villages. During our first meeting, my assumptions about such a collaboration were challenged. I had expected the first meetings to be technical and educational, conveying research techniques in a top–down style to us, the Indonesian graduates. To my surprise, the German team, at that time consisting of Manfred Zaumseil, Silke Schwarz, and Jeane Indradjaja, posed questions instead. They asked about our own experiences of the earthquake, about the arrangement of our meetings, and how to approach the villagers as a stranger and how to start the study. When I asked Manfred, as the official principal investigator, what his plan was, he just answered, "I am not your boss." But who was then, I wondered, and would there really be no boss at all? My thinking was so used to top–down team structures that this experience disturbed me deeply.

Over the 3 years of cooperation, I learned to "cope" with this kind of team structure. We all learned through cooperation, conflict, and reflection. In a process of transcultural exchange, we developed a mutual understanding for our ways of working, including suitable ways of organizing our meetings and communication. Within this process, the Indonesian team influenced the German team and vice versa. Despite nonhierarchical intentions, responsibilities, resources, and status were still unequally distributed within the international team. When I reflect back on this, my own role expectations were influenced by internalized power structures. For one, Manfred was a professor and I was only a graduate. Additionally, Manfred was a White European from Germany and I was an Indonesian. So, without doing or saying anything, Manfred had a much higher social status than I considered myself to have as an Indonesian researcher. In this respect, my mind was still enslaved by the experience of a formerly colonized person. At first, I perceived myself only as a "native" that could be asked for her opinion, and despite the fact that ICBC had delegated me to participate in the research to learn about research through my involvement, I still felt passive within the large research team officially headed by Manfred. When I realized through our conversations and discussions that we as Indonesian team members were not expected to be rigid in fulfilling our tasks and that we could speak our minds, I began to experience a sense of self-worth (as it should be), and, for sure, I felt respected by the German team.

Our roles as Indonesian researchers changed over the 3 years of cooperation. In the first year, we were six student research assistants collecting data; four of us continued in the second year, while our status changed to junior researchers. Sidelining the overall research process, each of us developed her or his own miniresearch, according to our own interests, to be presented at the International Association for Cross-Cultural Psychology (IACCP) conference in Melbourne, Australia. Having the opportunity to present my own findings to an international audience was an empowering experience. We as Indonesians really could do research in our own context. In the third year, three of us remained and were responsible for the implementation of the participatory research process under the institutional roof of ICBC. Especially in the participatory research phase, we had multilevel cooperation where my two colleagues, Tiara R. Widiastuti and Lucia P. Novianti, and I were somewhere in the middle, between the German team (as leading researchers supervising the extended ICBC team), and facilitating the community researchers. The interaction between these three levels (villagers, Indonesian research team, and German research team) was a precious experience to me, although not free of conflict. When I reflect on the process, I recognize moments of empowerment on different levels.

7.3 Negotiating Closeness and Distance

Positioned in relative closeness to the field, my Indonesian colleagues and I provided important knowledge of the research context, which was very helpful in minimizing transcultural disturbances in the overall process. For example, when approaching village residents to join our study, we blended in well with the local social structures and were probably seen less as intruders than our foreign German research colleagues. Most of our respondents felt more comfortable expressing themselves in their local language, Javanese, rather than the national language, especially when sharing emotional experiences and inner thought processes. Our fluency in Javanese was therefore an important aspect in enhancing familiarity in the interview situation and promoted an understanding of the local context. My own knowledge of local meanings and traditions provided me with rich resources to interpret what the interviewees were saying. My German colleagues did not immediately understand what the locals meant, for example, when prayer was referred to as a form of "disaster preparedness" or how people, soon after the earthquake, started to accept (*nrimo*) their situation even when they had lost a loved one. As a Javanese Indonesian researcher, I could translate and mediate between the village setting and the international research perspective. However, being so close to the field also misled us to assume that we would already know and understand it, as if there were no further questions to ask. If we asked villagers questions, they did not elaborate much because they assumed we had the same experience and could understand without the need for further explanation. In such situations, we might have gained more information if they had been interviewed by members of the German team.

Research transforms the common into the extraordinary and important. Such a transformation requires an analytical distance from the ordinary. It is like fish in an aquarium that can neither see nor appreciate their surroundings, since it is the only thing they know. Only those outside the aquarium are able to see and appreciate it. However, will those on the outside ever know what it feels like to swim in the aquarium? Or how the world looks through water and glass? I would therefore rather not privilege the position of distance over the position of closeness, because both can be a curse and a blessing. Emotional attachment to the research field means that we have a complex connection to what we study and that the connections we have include a wide range of connotations. For example, I felt ambivalent about the wider use of the term *trauma*. People in Bantul were using it so lightly, which contradicted my academic understanding of it. Our relational position to the field influences not only how we see things but also what we see. Thus, "insiders" and "outsiders" are best combined to complement each other.

7.4 Empowerment Through Research

Due to our multilevel team structure, we had various insider and outsider perspectives in the research process. In the Indonesian research team, we were positioned somewhere in between. From the German team perspective, our ICBC team was "local," with the label "local" indicating our relative closeness to the research field. From the perspective of the Indonesian team, the community researchers of our participatory research were the "local" researchers. Because of the reflective potential of research communication, both the researcher and the research subject learned from the interview process. An example of the type of insight that a research participant might gain is indicated by my previous example of when Manfred had asked me about the most important event of the past 5 years of my life. Obviously, the earthquake had had a profound effect on me, perhaps more so than the private event of my wedding, even though marriage was a much more permanent life change. It was the collective experience of the earthquake affecting the lives of our whole community that seemed most relevant to me. Reflecting on my answer, I realized how communal we, as Indonesians, are.

Throughout the research process, there were many other situations where I came to see the ordinary in a new light, and I am grateful to have had the opportunity to see my own community from the inside and outside. For example, in our interviews on emotional aspects of coping with the earthquake, respondents used several Javanese concepts to describe their experience, such as acceptance (*nrimo*) or sincerity *(ikhlas)* (see Chaps. 11 and 12). By having to describe their own coping processes, which were usually taken for granted, respondents could reflect upon their own emotions and actions. Recounting their earthquake experiences was like putting the pieces of the puzzle of their life together, a process of reframing supported by us as researchers. When discussing these findings later in the international team, our Javanese ways of coping became even more apparent. When trying to explain these Javanese concepts to our German colleagues, we as Indonesian researchers learned a lot about our culture, our nation, and ourselves. To me, this interactive learning process was empowering, as we learned about our own cultural resources in facing disasters. Similarly, the villagers reflected on their own capacities by communicating with the researchers.

Besides these important insights, the research itself was an empowering experience. In one particular situation within our participatory research phase, this aspect became particularly clear to me. I remember one meeting with the community researchers from the village youth group when we were compiling the group's interview data. Mody, one of the youth group members, had been smiling to himself; then he spoke up and shared this thoughts:

> I am so glad that we have gained input from the villagers, and that I can hear what people have to say. So, I think if I want to get some input from other villagers about our youth group activities, we could assess it through a research like this, couldn't we?

By joining our participatory research process, he felt inspired and empowered to do research on other topics more relevant to himself, namely on people's perceptions of the youth group's activities. By gaining a valuable new skill, he directly benefited from the research. Research is a key to knowledge, and Mody's experience that night shows that the experience of being able to carry out research is empowering, as it opens up new possibilities to gain knowledge. I also experienced this when conducting research in the second year of our international project. The opportunity to explore my own research questions boosted my confidence. I learned from both the content of the research and the experience of carrying out the research. That night, Mody reminded me of myself. From my perspective, it is an important capital for Indonesian people to know and realize our potentials through research, especially since it is often *bule*, White foreigners, who come to study us Indonesians. Later, we have to read about the Indonesian context in a book written in English. By learning how to carry out research, we can initiate our own projects, even with simple means.

7.5 Dealing with Closeness as a Survivor–Activist–Researcher

Becoming a survivor-expert and survivor–researcher was an empowering experience for me and an important contribution to our international research constellation. I was close to the field as a Bantulese myself, as an earthquake survivor, and as a former NGO relief worker. In comparison with my other Indonesian colleagues, I was particularly close to two of our research sites; in one of the research villages, I had close family ties, and in another one, I had been involved in a reconstruction program. In both cases, I experienced the limiting aspects of being too close to the research. At first, interviews proved difficult. People knew me, and I could sense them feeling uncomfortable answering all the questions on my interview guideline. Even as an "outside" researcher, I was too much of a community "insider" for respondents to talk to me openly about certain village dynamics.

My role as a researcher was also complicated by the fact that people still perceived me as an aid worker. For example, when I visited a villager in Sido Kabul, he automatically assumed that I had come to monitor his spending of the reconstruction funds. I was concerned that my presence in this village would raise people's hopes about receiving further relief funds. To avoid such potential miscommunication and subsequent disappointment, I refrained from researching in this particular village and focused instead on the third village.

7.6 Concluding Remarks

Looking back on our research process, the multilevel cooperation was an invaluable experience for me, full of new insights and moments of empowerment, especially in the third participatory phase of research. By the third phase of our cooperation, our roles had changed and we explicitly clarified our understanding of our mutual roles. This whole process was an expression of our common reflection on the previous years of research. An important precondition had been to hand over the research role to members of the community. These shifting roles enhanced my whole understanding of research as an interactive process, as I have elaborated upon above. I learned how essential the reflection of one's own role in research can be and how important it is to reflect upon one's own position and closeness in respect to every party involved in the research process. I also learned that there always needs to be a certain distance between myself as a researcher and the rest of my viewpoints and roles. In order to carry out good research, it is necessary to balance my triple role as researcher, activist, and community member.

Acknowledgments The editors would like to thank Elise Serbaroli for her assistance in editing this chapter.

Chapter 8
Reflexive Comments on the Process of Participatory Research

Tiara R. Widiastuti

Complementary to our qualitative research approach, we integrated an element of participatory research in the final stage of our research process. We encouraged community members to investigate their own social context using the overarching question "how do villagers perceive their future?" This alternative research approach challenged previous roles, and new research dynamics emerged.

As a member of the Indonesian research team, together with my colleague, Nur Khorifah (later referred to as Khori), I was responsible for facilitating the participatory research process in Sido Kabul. This process started with an assessment phase, during which we spoke to the village representatives, participated in community meetings, and consulted with villagers informally in order to explore potential groups for involvement in our research. Due to time constraints, we chose to approach existing groups and offered them the opportunity to become research teams. In a second "informing" phase, we introduced our idea to the groups as a basis for them to decide whether to join the overall process or not. In the end, we had three different community groups involved in Sido Kabul. Each of them conducted their own research. Over the course of several workshops, members of these groups were trained to become community researchers. Each group designed their own research, which consisted of formulating the research question, deciding on the research methods, and carrying out the final result. Each group was offered the opportunity to conclude their research process with a media product in order to record their findings and make them accessible for others. In this chapter, I would like to share and reflect upon my own experience in facilitating such a participatory research process, of plunging into the field and interacting with the villagers. I will first discuss the implementation of participatory research and, then, reflect more deeply on the implementation of "participation" in research practice and the challenges faced during the research process.

T. R. Widiastuti (✉)
Institute for Community Behavioral Change,
Jalan Ki Mangunsarkoro 27, Pakualaman, 55111 Yogyakarta, Indonesia
e-mail: tiarawidiastuti@yahoo.com

M. Zaumseil et al. (eds.), *Cultural Psychology of Coping with Disasters*,
DOI 10.1007/978-1-4614-9354-9_8, © Springer Science+Business Media, LLC 2014

I begin with an example of my interaction with Nur, a community researcher from a women's group in Sido Kabul. She lives with her husband and daughter. Her husband owns a small piece of land, which she helps to cultivate. Together they produce pottery as a subcontract manufacturer to larger factories. As an side job, Nur sells snacks and beverages to support her family economically. In her village, Nur is a member of several community associations, such as the female farmers group and the Damai group, which are facilitated by a Yogyakarta-based NGO. In our first assessment phase, we identified Damai as a potential group to involve in our research and Nur, one of the group members, as a potential community researcher. To her neighbors Nur was known as a humble, hard-working, friendly, popular, and active member of the village, and she had shown a high level of interest in the research. Nur and two other members of Damai agreed to join our process as community researchers.

When we conducted our first introductory workshop with the community researchers of the Damai group, Khori and I had a hard time explaining the nature of participatory research and the roles of community researchers within our research team. At that time, Nur stepped up and helped. To describe the cooperative relationship between the research team and the community researchers, she introduced the metaphor of a gun and its bullets. Khori and I were the shooting gun because we facilitated community researchers to learn about research and eventually enabled them to conduct research on their own. Community researchers were like bullets since they were the ones who would interact directly with the other villagers as research participants. This analogy helped her peer researchers understand their different roles in the research process, which Khori and I had less successfully tried to convey.

During discussion sessions, Nur often contributed helpful ideas about the focus of the research and specific issues such as the design of the questionnaire. Moderating the group discussion on the final research product, I was concerned that the conversation could swerve "off-grid" when one of the community researchers suggested establishing a health-care center for the elderly. When I realized where the discussion was heading, I tried to highlight once more the limitations of our research and gently refused her idea. After listening to my explanation, Nur came up with the idea of writing a book. She suggested it because some of the women had previous experience writing such a book. She convinced everyone that this would be a more feasible product and would also benefit the group, because, through that book, they could speak their mind and share their hopes.

When collecting data, Nur patiently sat next to the respondents filling in the questionnaires. On several occasions, she sought clarification and asked important questions about participants, written answers. Once Nur told me how a female villager had requested to be included in the questionnaire research because she was hoping for some financial compensation. The woman needed money to pay her daughter's school fees. Nur explained to her that there was no financial compensation, as the purpose of this study was not to survey people's need for assistance, but to understand the future based on villagers' perspectives. Nur further explained to me that there had been many donation programs in the village after the 2006 earthquake. Through this experience, villagers had learned to associate strangers doing surveys as either a part of donation programs or college students doing their community development participation (CDP)[1].

Community researchers struggled with status-related challenges, since most were common villagers with relatively less education and low economic status. The various difficulties they faced lowered their self-confidence throughout the research process. They felt tremendously disappointed when only one out of 15 questionnaires was returned from one of the neighborhood units. The fact that the person who had distributed the questionnaires was considered to have the highest level of education among them added to these feelings. It almost made them give up and quit the research. I was also shocked. I had never anticipated such a low response rate. At that moment, we all—the community researchers, Khori, and me—had doubts. Nevertheless, I felt responsible for continuing this research and motivating the group. What kept me going at that point was the visualization of a book as our final product. I shared this vision with the group, hoping that it would lift their spirits as it had lifted mine.

8.1 Dynamic Processes of Participation

Within the participatory research phase, I understood my role as a facilitator for community researchers to conduct their own research. The overall process included an introductory workshop on the research process, data collection and analysis, and, finally, creating and launching a final media product to represent the research result. Another one of my responsibilities was, on a more strategic level, communicating the overall process of the participatory research phase to the community leaders so that the whole process was officially approved and could run smoothly.

As illustrated earlier, there were times when I felt obligated to intervene in the community researchers' discussions, feeling the need to draw the line between realistic and unrealistic ideas. However, there were also moments in the research process when I positioned myself as an equal to the community researchers. For example, in creating the final media product, it seemed to me that labor and workload were shared equally among all of us. All of these experiences made me wonder if what I was doing through the research process had fulfilled the criteria and the principles of 'participation'.

In order to reflect on this question, Arnstein's ladder of participation proved helpful to me. Instead of a simple, dichotomous understanding of participation or nonparticipation, Arnstein (1969) suggests a gradual understanding, distinguishing different levels as rungs of a ladder of participation. She identifies eight such rungs, categorizing them into three major levels of participation. The first level is called nonparticipation and consists of two rungs, *manipulation* and *therapy*. The second level is called tokenism, which includes three rungs, *informing*, *consultation*, and

[1] All university students in Indonesia are obligated to do community development participation (CDP) as part of their university curriculum. This program is called *Kuliah Kerja Nyata* (KKN).

placation. The third and highest level of participation is called citizen power and it is made up of the rungs of *partnership*, *delegated power*, and *villager control*.

In applying Arnstein's categories to the situations discussed earlier, the first situation of explaining about research and participatory research methods could be classified as *informing*. The community researchers were primarily receiving the information from Khori and me, though they could still openly express their ideas, as Nur demonstrated. When I dismissed the idea of establishing a health-care center for the elderly, I acted as a decision maker and that form of participation could be called *placation*. In the data-collecting phase, however, the community researchers, Khori, and I planned collaboratively and divided tasks and responsibilities. The community researchers determined the number of respondents, methods, time, and duration of data gathering. Based on the questionnaire data, we all took the decision on which participants would be asked to participate in the in-depth interviews. Meanwhile, Khori and I were assigned to provide the equipment. This stage of the process could be considered as collaborating in a *partnership*.

The level of participation shifted dynamically throughout the process. It depended not only on the particular activity of each research phase but also on the motivation of the community researchers themselves and on the quality of the interaction between them and us. Motivation to learn was a basic component throughout and this motivation was relatively independent of the education level of participants. The community researchers themselves decided how deeply they wanted to get involved and what they wanted to learn or find out. My co-facilitator, Khori, and I played a part in this dynamic process; that is, in order to facilitate community researchers to develop their own creative research, our role included providing information, feedback, advice, and space to explore for themselves or just listening to their experiences. Within our international team, we called this general attitude the "midwife strategy," because our role was that of assisting the community researcher to "give birth" to their research. There are many ways to put the midwife strategy into action in the field. I would not say that I chose a particularly fixed role or degree of participation from the beginning of the process. Rather, I adjusted my role in an interactive process with the community researchers and chose the appropriate response for specific situations so that the process could keep going. Due to the very dynamic and interactive nature of the participative research process, facilitators of any participatory research should be prepared for various levels of participation from different groups they are facilitating within the same research phase. We were the facilitators of three groups in Sido Kabul and experienced three different levels of participation within the same research phase.

8.2 The Problem of Tacit Assumptions

Nur explained to me that because people in the village had been the target group of post-disaster recovery programs, they had become sensitive toward the presence of new people in their village. If the residents spotted strangers strolling around their village and taking notes or asking questions, they expected them to be surveyors for some donation programs. If they saw unfamiliar young people visiting residents' houses, they would assume those young people to be university students doing their CDP. I wondered why hardly anybody perceived us as researchers or as research facilitators. This question bugged me for quite a long time, until we realized that the villagers had had prior experiences, which were influencing the way they perceived us. Their experiences with the surveyors and donation programs, as well as the CDP university students, influenced the way villagers interpreted the presence of strangers. Perception psychologists explain this as the priming effect (Kunda 1999). In practice, both assumptions presented Khori and me with difficulties. Each assumption was associated with certain expectations. The "donation program" assumption led people to demand material aid in the form of either money or goods, whereas the "student program" assumption raised people's expectations about the provision of skill training programs, such as cooking and Koran lessons for their children. Miscommunication emerging from these assumptions consumed time and energy, especially at the beginning of the research process. In planning and implementing our participatory research program, we needed to account for and try to counter these assumptions. If inaccurate assumptions were not corrected from the start, they could potentially create misunderstandings about the expected outcome of the research process. Villagers might expect donations, money, or the like. We were therefore very cautious in informing the villagers about our research and explaining that the sole purpose of our activities was research. If villagers echoed our explanation, it was an indicator that we had succeeded in communicating our intentions. We figured that if some villagers had understood, then they could explain it in their own words to others, as Nur did on several occasions.

8.3 Maintaining Motivation

Undoubtedly, motivation is a key element in participatory research processes, not just for the research facilitators but also for the community researchers who take up this role. The motivation of everyone involved is an important factor influencing the success of participatory research (Leach and Wallwork 2003; Trujillo 2007). In reflecting upon my own motivation during the implementation, I would say that my motivation levels fluctuated during the research process. I wondered how the community researchers experienced the process. I thought it likely for them to have similar changes of motivation since what we were doing was outside of their usual or everyday activities. Motivational aspects are communicated verbally and nonverbally. In order to account for motivational dynamics, facilitators of participatory research need to observe carefully. Facial expressions, gestures, and voice intonation all offer clues. As an integral part of motivation dynamics, facilitators need to be self-aware and honest about their own feelings. Whenever I felt exhausted during the research process or when I sensed a lack of self-confidence, tiredness, demotivation, and even despair in the community researchers, I addressed my observations openly and sought a discussion with them. I found it was important to check on our own perception of what was happening. If my impression was right, we could decide to take a break from the research process. Sometimes we needed only one or two days of rest, but sometimes we needed a week. As a facilitator, I assisted the research teams in adjusting their time schedule to their needs and obligations.

Another aspect that I came to realize was that it was much easier to interact with expressive people rather than those who were reserved. This became most relevant while communicating states of motivation or emotional experiences. I experienced this kind of a challenge during my earlier interactions with Dika, one of the community researchers from the Muda Budaya group. Dika, a teenage, vocational school student majoring in computing came from a middle-class family. His parents make starch flour for a living. According to his mother, Dika had always been a quiet child. Dika joined the Muda Budaya group, in which school-aged teenagers are educated about hosting guests according to Javanese traditional manners and culture.

I first met Dika at a regular Muda Budaya meeting during the assessment phase. He stood out, not because he was active but because he rarely spoke or even responded to what was happening around him. He just smiled occasionally when his friends were laughing. I could barely hear his soft voice from across the room when he introduced himself to the group. When I spoke to the group about the research, he just stared at me. I saw him occasionally whisper to the friend sitting next to him and right after that, the friend would raise his hand and ask me questions. Observing that, I became certain that beneath his silence, Dika was paying close attention to what I was saying. Nevertheless, I was disturbed by his quiet behavior, because it left me wondering. I was unsure if he understood my elaborations or whether he truly agreed on our plan. I sometimes even asked myself if he really wanted to participate. In the beginning, such questions often frustrated and demotivated me because they indicated my limited understanding of the group's dynamic. At one point, I realized that I was working in a team and I could share these questions with my team members. Regarding my insecurities toward Dika, another community researcher from the Muda Budaya group who had been friends with Dika was able to help me. Apparently, Nika and Dika, the two friends, had their own system to motivate and cheer each other up.

Additionally, Dika's own development within the research project taught me a valuable lesson. At first, he seemed to prefer to observe quietly rather than to participate actively in discussions. However, after a while he began to speak his mind more often, especially when the researchers were asked to write down their ideas on cards prior to oral presentations of their contributions. His voice became louder with every new session. We did several exercises to prepare the community researchers for collecting data. They learned how to conduct interviews and guide group discussions. Dika learned quickly in these exercises. In interview situations, he probed and paraphrased interviewees' answers. When he facilitated a group discussion, he first became insecure and sought my eye contact for reassurance. I simply smiled and, through body language, encouraged him to continue. I signaled him to take a deep breath, which he did, and then he continued. After listening to his friends' answers for a while, he managed to paraphrase the answers and smoothly related them to the next question. This experience with Dika reminded me of how people can be different and how everyone has a different way of learning new things. As a facilitator, I needed to acknowledge these differences and account for distinct needs.

The final media product from the Budaya Muda group was a slideshow of the results. For the public event, Dika had initially refused to present and chose to operate the presentation file instead. After being motivated by his Muda Budaya trainer and Khori and me, he agreed to present it, together with his friend Nika. The presentation turned out to be a complete success for the group and for Dika, personally. He seemed well prepared and calmly talked the audience through his slides. His friends and trainers were surprised and took turns congratulating him. Dika felt happy with his own progress, having confidently spoken in front of a group of people.

8.4 The Multiple Benefits of Participatory Research

As elaborated upon earlier, participatory research is a demanding challenge for everyone involved. Since community members become researchers themselves, they are asked to invest more time and effort in the research than conventional research methods would require. When my own role changed from being a researcher to being a research facilitator, it brought a whole new range of responsibilities and challenges. It is, thus, important to reflect on the benefits of participatory research.

Advantages for the Community Researchers According to Puoane et al. (2004), community researchers can gain benefits from their roles as well as through interacting with external research facilitators and informants in the field. I had moments of doubt if the community researchers really benefitted from the research process because most of the community researchers I met said that they mostly wanted to help the (international) research team do the research. This statement somehow made me feel guilty about having bothered them. However, during our concluding evaluation session, the community researchers themselves articulated several benefits they had gained from their involvement in this participatory research. I have summarized a few as follows:

Gaining Experiences and Acknowledgment Most of the community researchers had never done research before, especially the older participants; it was a completely new experience for them. Since most of the community researchers were common villagers, their involvement in this research made them well known and helped them gain the respect of other villagers, especially when they could present their final products as a book or a film.

Gaining Knowledge The elderly community researchers appreciated gaining an understanding of what their children or grandchildren do at school. Those community researchers still in school evaluated their participation in this research as helping them with their school tasks. They could better understand what their teachers had explained to them about research. Beyond the experience of being a researcher, the answers from respondents had enriched their knowledge of village life.

Improvement of Self-Consciousness As the research results were made accessible through the final media products, they offered a helpful tool for self-reflection for those involved as well as for their groups and villages. Some felt that it was as if they were standing in front of a mirror, able to see their own reflections, including the good and bad sides.

Learning and Developing New Skills The example of Dika exemplifies this point. At the beginning, Dika was a passive person whose soft voice could barely be heard from across the room. Through training and encouragement, he used this research process to become more assertive and learn to speak in front of peer and community fora.

Advantages for the Community Within the team of Indonesian researchers, we further discussed the benefits of our research for the participating communities (i.e., in our case, the villages involved). We came up with the following points:

Encourage Self-Improvement Through the final media products, research results were made publicly accessible to the village. After seeing or reading the media products, people were often motivated to improve themselves. The movie of a youth group from Sendang, for example, raised the issue of village development and health in simple everyday situations; it offered input for discussing these issues at a village level.

Fostering Intergenerational Understanding The fact that the groups of community researchers within each village represented different age levels further stimulated an intergenerational exchange of perspectives. The media product offered a way to express distinct generational perspectives and communicate different aspirations for the future. The research process thus fostered cross-generational understanding in both directions; older people could learn about the younger people's concerns and vice versa.

Advantages for the Overall Research Project Last but not least, we discussed benefits for the international research team. By facilitating the community researchers' process, I gained a new kind of access to the research topic. I was able to learn how community members would approach a topic like 'the future', and what questions and concerns seemed relevant for them to include in their research. Finally, the multiple and various activities provided our overall project with a deeper understanding of the research context itself, as seen through the eyes of our community researchers.

Applying participatory research in a community is certainly a challenge. It not only requires an understanding of the method itself but also an understanding of its basis in community dynamics and social interaction. This method can be very fruitful if it is used appropriately not only because of its flexible nature and the rich data gathered during the process but also because it will generate answers to research questions from a whole new perspective.

Acknowledgments The editors would like to thank Elise Serbaroli for her assistance in editing this chapter.

References

Arnstein, S. R. (1969). A ladder of citizen participation. *Journal of the American Institute of Planners, 35*(4), 216–224.

Kunda, Z. (1999). *Social cognition: Making sense of people*. Cambridge: MIT Press.

Leach, G., & Wallwork, J. (2003). Enabling effective participation, negotiation, conflict resolution and advocacy in participatory research: Tools and approaches for extension professionals. Conference proceeding, Apen 2003 forum, Hobart.

Puoane, T., Sanders, D., Ashworth, A., Chopra, M., Strasser, S., & McCoy, D. (2004). Improving the hospital management of malnourished children by participatory research. *International Journal for Quality in Health Care, 16*(1), 31–40.

Trujillo, C. A. (2007). Building internal strength, sustainable self-esteem, and inner motivation as a researcher. *Journal of Research Practice, 3*(1), 1–9.

Part III
Multidimensional Coping Framework

As a result of the co-influencing process of synthesizing an interdisciplinary theory and analyzing our Indonesian case study, we were able to develop a four-dimensional analytical framework for a cultural psychology of coping with disasters, while the formulation of four (instead of three or five) dimensions of coping was determined by the researchers.[1] The framework encompasses material, social, religious, and life conduct dimensions. A playful and critical attitude towards theory helped us to question the usefulness of the various concepts and models presented in the previous theoretical chapters. These theoretical sensitivities contribute to a specific focus on how to analyze the data. With these conceptual sensitizations in mind we have extracted a range of themes within the four dimensions. And yet, the structure and particularly the contents of the main themes are also congruent with the data because the villagers themselves often focused on special themes in a socioculturally unique way.

Productive tensions between universal patterns, theory-based and Western-inspired concepts and sociocultural specificities including experience-based and emic insights are evident throughout the following chapters. In an ostensibly paradoxical manner, these four dimensions simultaneously untangle and represent the complexity of coping processes. The complex nature of coping is revealed in the tensions between symbolic and material, as well as between individual and social realms. Instead of thinking of these dimensions in terms of a hierarchical importance, we understand these dimensional analytical perspectives to complement each other and to overlap in understanding coping processes. Using a metaphor of photo camera settings, this framework helps to zoom in and to back out again. Each dimension provides a peculiar lens to look at the complex phenomenon of coping. While we may lose a comprehensive vantage point in the process, nevertheless all four dimensions are necessary in order to grasp the overall phenomena of coping with disasters. Accordingly, the distinctions we make are for analytical purposes and may therefore appear to be artificial.

---

[1] The general outline of our multidimensional coping framework was developed in a collaborative process involving the whole research team, in particular between German researchers. Chapters 9–12 were written in intense exchange of ideas and transfer of data examples between the authors Schwarz and von Vacano.

Each dimension and specific constellation of referential contexts (see Chap. 3) is relevant in different ways for different individuals. Apart from these personal idiosyncracies within a specific sociocultural context, coping processes are modulated by what actually needs to be coped with. In our Indonesian case study, many losses and challenges were produced by the earthquake: material destruction of a place of living and livelihoods, personal injuries and disabilities or that of significant others are of mention in this respect. Problems were also produced and intensified by a shattering of daily routines with the further result that a sense of security and meaningful world view needed to be reestablished and renegotiated. When taking a long-term post-disaster perspective, that is when analyzing data gathered several years after the earthquake, further problems that villagers have to cope with become visible. For example, there are long-term consequences of having to cope with the way official organizations handle the relief and recovery phase. Family structures and responsibilities may change due to economic hardship or disability and the position within communal structures of relationships and power may decrease along aid distribution processes. These possible strains not only are experienced differently by different persons, but may vary due to histories of social arrangements particular to a given village.

The temporal features of the research are of paramount concern because the search for dynamics of transformation in relation to conversation occurs through retrospective evaluations. As the subjective representation of time and the nature of memory are not chronologically structured, we were concerned not to create an ostensibly objective timeline of developments based on people's recollections of post-disaster coping. For example, the villagers themselves mostly differentiated between life *before* and *after* the disaster. This is seen in relation to other important communal and family events, such as elections of the head of the hamlet, child bearing and marriage. Accounting for transformations and dynamics is a way to integrate a power-critical perspective; it enables the search for continuities and for irregularities and possibilities for change. It goes hand in hand with our dynamic understanding of culture.

The Material Dimension (Chap. 9) refers to the biophysical side of disaster coping, which includes perceptions of physical destruction, rescue, relief and reconstruction efforts, and the subjective experiences of these. The material dimension points to the tangible objects, to dynamics of physical forces, or to everything that is exosemoitic, or extradiscursive. But humans only have access to material reality mediated through interpretations and practices. Accordingly, this relation of biophysical context to humans *being in the world*—their worldviews, subjective experiences, social practices and structural settings—lies at the very heart of the material dimension of coping.

The Social Dimension (Chap. 10) highlights coping as a social phenomenon which extends traditional social support dynamics in mainstream psychology. Communal coping efforts, power dynamics and the renegotiations of sociocultural specific values and practices are all examined to explore the dynamics of a village struck by disaster. In times of adversity and scarcity, the collectivization of private property, a solidarity ignoring issues of rank and class, and social conflicts and bitterness are the dynamics that have been found in Peru, Poland and elsewhere in the world. This chapter traces the locally specific referential contexts and experience frames. By this thorough contextualization, the double-edged character of social features is accounted for and an unbiased approach to social benefits and burdens along coping processes is developed.

The Life Conduct Dimension (Chap. 11) emphasizes the intertwining of sociocultural features with personalized, enacted codes of conduct. Furthermore, coping with current challenges or problems is influenced by prior developmental successes; that is, the extent to which individuals have gained competencies in practicing locally valued codes of conduct. And yet, the potential for further development is influenced by effective management of current stresses and challenges. Local concepts of self and related control patterns differ strongly from Western ideas of a goal-striving, intentional individual. These dynamics of socioculturally specific and valued developmental trajectories are vital to an adequate understanding of assimilative and accommodative processes in the context of disaster.

The Religious Dimension (Chap. 12) is based on a broad anthropological understanding of religion as cosmology, practice and lived experience in which people connect with a metaempirical sphere (see Chap. 4). In disaster contexts, religion is an important resource for meaning-making which helps people to find metaphysical explanations of events as well as their personal significance. However, religion is more than meaning as it includes spiritual practices and community experience. For believers, religion can be a pervasive way of being in the world while also offering a broad range of coping resources.

The multidimensional framework is used to present our case study and may be transferred to other contexts as an analytical tool for a cultural psychology of coping with disasters. When applying the framework to other sociocultural contextual constellations, however, certain dimensions may lose of their importance and others may become more important to those people affected by disasters.

Chapter 9
The Material Dimension of Coping: Socioculturally Mediated Biophysical Process

Mechthild von Vacano

Common images of disasters involve destruction, injuries, rescue work, or the provision of food, shelter, and medicine to survivors. All of these elements can be subsumed as biophysical objects and processes or the material dimension of coping. With respect to coping with disasters, this material dimension seems to be overemphasized and understudied simultaneously. Applied disaster management has been criticized for its excessively narrow focus on material responses to crisis and risk. Despite being challenged by participatory or local knowledge approaches, hegemonic disaster management practice still proclaims the universal validity of its technocratic solutions, which are designed to reduce objectively calculated disaster risks. Disaster management thus has a universalist and objectivist bias, being based on the assumption that "the material" is objectively given and that function and meaning inhere in objects themselves. Subjective experiences of material constellations, if any, find their way into disaster aid evaluation reports whenever the question of adequacy is raised. In coping theories, conversely, we find the opposite tendency to de-emphasize the material aspects and overemphasize (individual) subjective appraisals. This inclination can be explained with reference to the disciplinary location of coping theory in psychology and has been the subject of criticism from within the discipline itself. Calling for a clearer reference framework for coping theories, Hobfoll (1989) has developed what he calls the "conservation of resources" theory to provide a sociocultural and socioeconomic contextualization of coping processes. Disaster psychology has been criticized for neglecting the material aspects of disaster impacts. Freedy et al. (1992) point out that most psychological studies of disaster only measure disaster exposure in terms of the mental distress evoked by "threat, terror, or horror," and disregard exposure to correlated (material) post-disaster adversities like food scarcity and property damage.

The resource-based approach of Hobfoll (1989) offers a valuable starting point for a cultural psychology of disaster, as its aim is to synthesize the concerns of disaster management with psychological coping theory (see Sect. 2.3.1). However, Hobfoll's

M. von Vacano (✉)
Institute for Social and Cultural Anthropology,
Freie Universität Berlin, Landoltweg 9-11, 14195 Berlin, Germany
e-mail: m.vacano@fu-berlin.de

M. Zaumseil et al. (eds.), *Cultural Psychology of Coping with Disasters*,
DOI 10.1007/978-1-4614-9354-9_9,

aim was to link an objective reference frame back to appraisal-based coping theory by accounting for object resources and energies, which include time or money. However, from an epistemological perspective caution is required if inherent qualities of objectivity and definiteness are projected on to material features. If we distinguish analytically between the object itself, our perception of it, and the functions and meanings attributed to it, constructivist approaches suggest that our epistemological access is limited to perception and interpretation, because any access to the object itself is inevitably mediated by social construction processes.[1] Nevertheless, biophysical objects are more than purely discursive or social phenomena, as we have argued in Chap. 1, with respect to the exosemiotic forces of nature (Oliver-Smith 2002). As biophysical aspects shape social contexts and condition the way humans engage with them through their specific material qualities, we follow Clarke's (2005) suggestion and adopt a *materialist* social constructivism.

The material aspects of coping are embedded in interpretative patterns and worldviews, as well as in social practices and settings. A cultural psychology approach to material resources must therefore account for its contextual qualities and dynamics. Economics is much more than just survival and necessity, as utilitarists claim: economic anthropologists have emphasized that despite being the foundation of survival, economic activity is always a cultural practice in itself and, as such, is embedded in sociocultural contexts which provide normative settings for livelihood strategies, construction practices, or consumption (see Rössler 2006). Similarly, housing is not just about the basic need for shelter, but constitutes a cultural practice involving aspects such as status expressions, lifestyle choices, norms and limits, or emotional attachments. Threatening lives and destroying physical surroundings, disasters often expose the interrelations of material and sociocultural life (Oliver-Smith 2002) because, in the aftermath of disaster, the physical world is rebuilt and losses as well as resources are (re)evaluated.

The following analysis aims at developing an understanding of the complex dynamics of (material) coping and disaster aid "on the ground." The mostly qualitative account of material features of disaster coping serves to eliminate the interrelations between subjective coping processes, social dynamics, and material conditions. By highlighting the subjective experience of these material features, such as emotional responses, ascribed values and meanings, and strategies and attitudes, my aim is to expand on prevailing disaster management perspectives. The first three sections of this chapter are organized in a roughly chronological order and trace the dynamics of material resource loss through the earthquake to compensation or gain in its aftermath. I begin with an analysis of survivors' initial assessments of their physical environment and then proceed to discuss emergency relief and long-term recovery, understanding both of these disaster management phases, not as strictly temporal but rather as managerial and analytical. I will conclude by turning to the narrative and interpretative level of material coping, pointing to interrelations with other coping dimensions, such as life conduct, social and religious features. Balancing the requirements of

[1] Our interview data provide us with a first-degree interpretative account of these material features, while a second-degree interpretation of qualitative research analysis is presented here.

comprehensiveness and in-depth analysis, I have chosen to highlight the aspects of food, livelihoods, and shelter, while setting aside others here, such as infrastructure.

9.1 Initial Assessment of the Physical Environment

> At first, when it happened, nobody realized that this was an earthquake. Because we heard the sound of an awful explosion. [...] and then, it became dark, [...] because of all the dust. Ya, 'bler' and all of a sudden everything ... was razed to the ground. Like after a bomb attack. (Pak Ahmad, Sendang)

For most of the villagers, when the earthquake struck, it represented an unexpected and direct interruption to their daily lives. When it began at 5.55 a.m., only a few people were still asleep, and most were already following their morning routines. The onset itself is often reported as a strange sound from underneath the earth, suddenly followed by the ground trembling. Subsequently, everything collapsed into ruins, causing vast amounts of dust to spread. The limited visibility reinforced an overall sense of disorientation: What had just happened? The immediate response was that everyone was concerned with securing their own survival, locating family members, and rescuing those trapped in the ruins. The overwhelming extent of the disaster demanded spontaneous prioritizations, and most people chose to care for their own families first before assisting their neighbors (see Chap. 10). Soon villagers started to improvise medical treatment, sought food, water, and shelter, and proceeded to bury the dead.

However, only a few hours later, rescue activities were interrupted by the rumor of a subsequent tsunami. Panic spread fast, as most people instantly recalled horrifying media images of the Aceh/Nias tsunami of 2004. Depicting a general atmosphere of fear and chaos, most respondents recall their instant response being to flee. However, fleeing posed difficult dilemmas: Should we leave our property unsupervised? Should I locate all my family members prior to fleeing? Or should I at least save the one child who is with me? Should we run to survive, but leave the weak and injured behind? Should we abandon the corpses? Confronted with these questions, several families decided to stay despite their fear. Others followed the mass movement toward the north, until hours later, government officials successfully corrected the misinformation and encouraged people to return to their villages. By official standards, only the area of Mulya Sari qualifies as a tsunami risk zone because of its proximity to the sea. However, the panic had spread far inland, beyond all our research sites up to the city of Yogyakarta, which is located over 25 km from the coast and is 100 m above sea level (Schlehe 2006). However, few respondents in Sido Kabul and Sendang reported that they resisted the rumor and critically assessed its basis, with some of them referring to the risk calculation of the geographical area, while others sought confirmation from relatives living on the coast or inspected the water level of the nearby river.

Apart from this wave of panic, the emergency was further intensified by adverse weather conditions and aftershocks. The first night especially is often described as a horrifying scenario, in which a constant level of perceived threat prevailed until the next morning. A region-wide power blackout had left the villages in total darkness:

> After the earthquake, there was no food for one day and one night—it was totally dark. Off and on "yeeg, yeeg", another earthquake came. Not as awful as the original one, but approximately every five to ten minutes there was an earthquake, day and night. It was raining heavily; we had no electricity; it was totally dark. Everyone sought shelter with whatever they could find. There was no food, no food at all. (Pak Daryono, Sendang)

No external aid had yet reached the villages, and communication with the outside world was extremely limited.[2] In an atmosphere of disorientation, fear, and despair, people fearfully asked themselves what would happen next. Some felt that the world might be coming to an end, that doomsday (*kiamat*) had come. Interpretations like this need to be analyzed against the (discursive) presence of three geological hazards—volcanic eruption, earthquake, and tsunami—as well as the adverse weather conditions. People were exposed to a combination of (perceived) natural forces, and even though there was no tsunami, through the power of rumor, fear of it became an integral part of the disaster situation itself and shaped people's perceptions and responses. The effects of this collectively perceived threat, as well as the frightening experience of the first night, need to be analyzed as interrelated sources of extreme emotional distress and hence as elements of disaster exposure.

Crisis behavior was adjusted to how survivors assessed their physical environment. There was initial confusion concerning the agent of the destruction, even though minor tremors are a common occurrence in the area. This was because, prior to the earthquake, experts had mobilized the public for an imminent volcanic eruption of Mount Merapi, located 27 km north of Yogyakarta city, far enough for Mulya Sari, Sido Kabul, and Sendang not to count as risk zones. Overwhelmed by the sensual–emotional experience of the destructive tremor, people only gradually developed an understanding of the situation (see Sect. 11.3). At first, they could only guess at the extent of the destruction as their perception was impaired physically by the dust and psychologically by an emotional state of shock and confusion. If we look at the extremes, some respondents initially assumed that the destruction was minor and that only their house or village had collapsed, while others speculated the whole world coming to an end. These immediate presumptions represent different instant interpretations of the situation, which were later amended. Quite a few respondents mentioned a feeling of relief when they first realized that not only their own house had collapsed but that their entire neighborhood was in ruins. This runs counter to the quantitative logic of material resources, according to which rebuilding a single house seems much easier than rebuilding a whole village or region. However, in contrast, respondents found solace in sharing their loss and facing the same challenges as their neighbors. As members of the local community, they feared being singled out in suffering: Neighbors could talk and speculate about the self-induced reasons for such a collapse, from bad construction to sinful behavior. On the other hand, the household that had lost its home would need to ask everyone else for help, without being able to

[2] Communication networks reportedly did not break down immediately, and some mobile phones could be used on occasion to contact relatives or the emergency services.

pay them back any time soon; the reciprocity of long-term relationships was at stake. In this regard, the social dynamics attached to resource transfers overshadowed the pragmatic short-term logics of resource quantities (also see Chap. 10). However, this effect of relief was limited to the community as the unit of reference because the psychological burden increased for those who learned that not only their village but also the whole region had been affected. Being exposed to such a landscape of destruction and suffering was overwhelming, and it also decreased the hope that there would be effective assistance from outside. The most intense notion of destruction was apocalyptic (*kiamat*), a feeling that the entire world was about to end. This interpretation was clearly proved wrong by the limited extent of the destruction, both spatially and temporally. However, when other (less holistic) large-scale assumptions were refuted; people implicitly questioned why their region had been affected and not another one, and respondents reported feelings of disappointment and injustice.

Fluctuating assessments of a situation represent an emotional process, which reveals contextually specific dynamics of stress. The examples draw attention to the complex relationship between material loss and psychological burden, which cannot be understood solely in terms of a quantitative logic. The burdensome effects of loss are not immanent in total material resource loss, but are moderated socioculturally.

9.2 Crisis Responses of Rescue and Relief

The earthquake caused the immediate loss of material resources by devastating infrastructure, houses, and possessions, which resulted in the breakdown of basic supply systems, such as water, transportation, electricity, and communications, and it overloaded the health system. Collapsing houses threatened people's lives and health, destroying their possessions and food stocks or leaving them inaccessibly buried. To cope with the emergency and immediate aftermath, people in the villages had to mobilize their self-help capacities because outside aid arrived only after 1–3 days.[3] Early assistance came mostly through informal support mechanisms of relatives and friends. Government agencies or international nongovernmental organizations ((I)NGOs) needed 2–3 days to find their way to the villages (see Chap. 10; Wilson and Reilly 2007; Kusumastuti et al. 2010).

9.2.1 Supply of Food and NonFood Items

Recalling the days when villagers had to rely solely on themselves, respondents shared narratives of destitution, improvisation, and solidarity. As most of them were too scared to retrieve groceries and household items from the ruins, alternative strategies were required. People ate whatever they could find, harvesting the natural resources around them, mostly bananas which were not always ripe to eat. Alternatively, some of the small village shops (*warung*) selling food and other

[3] Memories of the arrival of external aid vary between villages, neighborhoods, and individual households.

supplies were collectivized (i.e., shared among the community members without expectation of payment). Such shops are usually constructed lightly, and thus even after collapsing they were still easily accessible. However, these self-help strategies depended on the resources available (collectively), which directly correlated with socioeconomic factors: While some neighborhoods had bananas, others fed themselves collectively from their chickens, goats, and other livestock.

When the first relief goods arrived from outside, the scarcity of supply still required rationing and, for some recipients, to be prioritized. Many adults recalled the absence of any feeling of hunger—possibly as a bodily symptom of shock and anxiety—but as parents, they were concerned for the well-being of their children. In Sendang, sufficient food supplies were reported from the fourth day onward, a situation that soon changed into a temporary oversupply, a "flood" of wrapped rice meals (*nasi bungkus*).[4] In these early days, political leaders set up coordination posts (*pos koordinasi*, abbreviated to *posko*). As the term indicates, the primary function of a *posko* is the coordination of crisis management, but with the village infrastructure in ruins, most *posko* served multifunctional purposes (see Andayani and Koentjoro 2008), as collective emergency shelters, community kitchens, distribution centers, and storage facilities. *Posko* units, in general, correlated with neighborhood units (RT, abbreviation for *rukun tetangga*), managed by a committee of neighborhood leaders.

After the immediate distress was relieved, further flows of relief goods depended on villagers' own initiatives. Yet again, neighborhoods differed in their resources and particularly in their social capital. Being in the military, one neighborhood leader was well acquainted with administrative procedures, had the necessary connections, and started to write proposals immediately after the crisis. Another, particularly poor, neighborhood had no resident government employees at all, so people compensated through collective effort and formed a committee, gathering their infrastructure resources (i.e., transport and communications), which were mainly motorbikes and mobile phones[5], to search for aid. Information on available assistance was centralized, and proposals were drawn up collectively, in writing, for the village youths to deliver. Sometimes alternatively the young people just appealed randomly to potential donors.

Just as randomly, some NGOs drove through the affected areas to drop their goods in any of the villages they encountered, usually at the central *posko* for further distribution by village personnel. People soon discovered how crucial the strategic positioning of their *posko* was in benefiting from these relief drops. Sometimes even aid addressed to a particular village was intercepted and the transport persuaded to drop its supply on the spot, or one neighborhood of the same hamlet would hijack the aid addressed to a neighboring RT. In reaction, some *posko*s were moved or secondary *posko*s set up. Remote neighborhoods compensated for their unfortunate locations by actively conducting their own searches. Besides writing proposals to formal aid

[4] These accounts mirror Wilson and Reilly's (2007) consternation over the insufficient coordination of agencies, especially in the emergency phase, leading to both oversupply and shortages.

[5] In general, telecommunication lines were back to normal after 5 days (GYSP 2008). However, because the power network took 3 weeks to be restored, people had to wait in long queues to charge their mobile phones in neighboring villages or the next field hospital.

agencies, people activated their informal networks, especially if they thought them capable of mobilizing financial or logistic resources (see Chap. 10).

With the exception of the initial scarcity in the emergency period, relief goods[6] were generally regarded as positive, and some interviewees referred to the aid as a blessing (*berkah*), which promoted their prosperity (*makmur*). In our interview data, we frequently found narratives of an abundance of food, particularly instant noodles, while narratives of shortage were almost absent. Excess instant noodles could even be resold in exchange for other food items. In this way, shortages of fresh products were addressed, and storage problems reduced. Overall, unlike with reconstruction aid, we hardly found any complaints about the quantity or quality of relief goods.[7] Accounts of discontent and conflict appear, rather, to relate to problems within the respective communities (see Chap. 14).

Narratives of the emergency period usually describe an emotional turning point in suffering and despair when the external aid unexpectedly arrived, as Pak Daryono remembered:

> Before the earthquake, I never imagined there could be help like this [...] The first one, two, three days, I didn't think of anything like that. I was concerned whether I could ever rebuild my house again or not, but I never thought of aid. [...] Finally we could eat, and I am grateful (*sykur*) that we could survive like that. (Pak Daryono, Sendang)

The arrival of aid had a profound psychological impact: People interpreted it as a sign of hope, reviving their spirits and promoting positive feelings of calm (*ketentraman*) and comfort (*kenyamanan*). In addition, the mere fact that outsiders cared and were willing to share was consoling. Some respondents framed these acts of solidarity as religious acts: God had sent humans with relief, the arrival of aid was therefore perceived as a sign of divine presence and care. Pressing worries about the future remained, but were reduced by such experiences of relief and hope.

9.2.2 Emergency Shelter

The unfavorable weather conditions made shelter an urgent issue. To seek protection from the rain, people gathered under banana trees or erected emergency tents from any materials available. Some neighborhoods owned a larger tent for community celebrations, which could be used as a collective emergency shelter, at least offering protection to some of their residents. Personal networks also provided tents or tarpaulins before official aid agencies could supply them more comprehensively, at least for collective community shelters.

---

[6] Relief goods consisted of food, including baby milk and drinking water, as well as nonfood items such as clothes, blankets, towels, lamps, cooking equipment, first-aid kits and medicine, and toiletries, including gender-specific products. People further received religious supplies, such as women's hijabs and prayer mats. To enable self-help activities, tools and cleaning-up kits were distributed.

[7] However, this retrospective evaluation needs to be interpreted with caution as it is highly selective with respect to relief items, with a strong emphasis on food items. Further, the interview context may have fostered the reproduction of a culturally normative positive bias.

Only a few villagers chose to leave temporarily and seek shelter with relatives who had not been affected. In rare cases, entire families evacuated to avoid the immediate emergency. However, men especially felt the need to stay on site in order to start clearing away the debris and recover buried belongings. Systematic cleaning began after 1 or 2 weeks, using unpaid labor (cf. Wilson and Reilly 2007). Families were sometimes helped by external volunteers; a few neighborhoods introduced a rotating system of community work (*gotong royong*). Clearing efforts were directed at constructing shelters on family land, but the actual timeline for the transition from a collective to a family shelter varied dramatically. Some families were lucky enough to have their own shelter from the very first night, while others remained in collective shelters for up to 3 months. Within the same village, whole neighborhoods could show different dynamics, depending on the average level of wealth. Similar differences applied to households. As a general rule, families preferred to set up their emergency tent separately on their own plot as soon as they could do so.

The official shelter policy in the case of the Yogyakarta earthquake was based on the provision of transitional shelters (T-shelter) by (I)NGOs, to bridge the time span until the Indonesian Government could provide funds for permanent reconstruction. In timeline terms, the first T-shelters were erected in September (MacRae 2008), roughly 3 months after the earthquake, whereas the first payments from the reconstruction program were made in October 2006 (HamengkuBuwono X 2008). Different agencies were in charge of supplying T-shelters coordinated by the International Federation of the Red Cross. Despite coordination efforts, even within one village, different agencies might be at work. Here, again, different distribution policies were followed and the shelter models differed accordingly, though most designs incorporated local materials and construction techniques, similar to the bamboo houses of poor people (MacRae and Hodgkin 2011). Whether or not T-shelters were erected through community labor depended on donor guidelines and community practice. As with all collective efforts to provide individual housing, one major challenge was to agree on the order of construction—whose shelter would be erected first and whose last—as those at the bottom of the list had to trust that their *gotong royong* unit would support them the same way they had supported everyone else. However, as most T-shelters could be built quickly, the time gap was not very long and the *gotong royong* system often worked.

In our data, the transition from advanced emergency shelters, mostly tents, to T-shelters and from T-shelters to permanent housing was indistinctly described. Obviously, donor agencies' categories of shelter differed from subjectively relevant stages of post-disaster shelter provision experienced by affected villagers. Important subjective indicators were the return to one's own plot of land and a certain degree of comfort and family privacy. In many accounts, the transition from community shelters into family units marked an important moment with a calming effect. As Wicaksono recalled:

> For some days we had been living in a [collective] emergency tent, just made from a mat used to sun-dry the rice harvest. At the time we were not yet calm (*tenang*). But when we [. . .] were able to erect our own tent, on our own land, we started to feel calm (*tenang*). (Wicaksono, Sendang)

Some individuals even continued sleeping in their tents or T-shelters, despite their houses having been rebuilt because they were afraid of being buried again under a collapsing house—a fear often explained as *trauma* (see Chap. 13). In this regard, the lightly constructed, nonpermanent shelters were perceived as safer than the new permanent brick houses. Thus, people had to learn to relate to their houses again as places of safety.

9.2.3 Medical Services

> When I ran out the house, I didn't know where my children were. I even didn't know where I was. After I had reached the street, I asked someone for help: "Would you please take me to the hospital?" But nobody helped me. Everyone just thought about their own survival. (Kyai Abdul, Sendang)

The most dramatic accounts of the absence of aid were articulated with reference to first aid and medical services. After community members had freed injured people from the ruins, they found that official medical services were beyond reach. One woman recalled how she tried to call an ambulance from the nearest public health center, but the system was overloaded and no ambulance was available. Therefore, people again relied on alternative strategies of self-help. Stretchers were improvised using doors and traditional herbal medicines were administered. One man in Sendang, who had a reputation as alternative healer (*sebangsa alternative*) and, apparently, also owned a stock of biomedical medicines, distributed his remedies throughout the village as first aid. Not every medicine he offered was suitable for the person's condition, but he chose to administer at least some pills for their placebo effect.

For some medical treatments, mobility became a question of survival. If people managed to carry the injured to the main road, they had a good chance of being picked up by the Indonesian Red Cross in the afternoon. However, official transportation did not reach villages off the main road until the following day, and villagers tried to organize alternative transportation, which depended on vehicles being available. For the severely injured, motorbikes were not an option, but only the richest families owned cars, a total of three, five, or six in each of the villages we studied (see Sect. 4.3). Economic disparities and the potential for social conflict became strikingly evident. Regardless of a car owner's willingness to help, not every car was accessible; the keys, for example, might be buried in the ruins. However, such practical reasons given by car owners were often not accepted; instead, interviewees complained about their egoism and voiced deep feelings of disappointment at this alleged refusal to give assistance to people who were dying. In addition, even if transport was available, roads were hardly passable and gasoline was scarce. If all these obstacles were removed, people still lacked reliable information regarding which of the regional health facilities were operational, if at all, and which had been destroyed.

Initially many of the injured were brought to emergency field hospitals set up at the village level (*desa*). However, in these field hospitals only the most urgent injuries were treated due to shortage of resources and staff, while those needing operations were referred to proper hospitals. Accommodation in tents was reserved for people with severe or medium injuries, while those with minor injuries were sent away without treatment. Even with these strict prioritizations, the capacities of these field hospitals were still overstretched, and people died of their injuries while waiting in the rain to be treated. The situation in and around the hospitals was similar. Tents were set up outside in the streets, but due to hospitals being severely overloaded, medical treatment to them was not guaranteed either (see Bayudono 2009). Respondents who had been treated at such health facilities or who had accompanied relatives there often saw people dying in large numbers while waiting without hope for any treatment. Kyai Abdul recalls his experience at a local doctor's office: "All along the road in front of the house people were dying, and nobody could do anything, there were so many of them!"

9.3 Returning to a New Normalcy

"All but three houses were leveled to the ground," Pak Riyadi told us, describing the post-disaster situation in Sendang. According to official statistics nearly all the houses in Sido Kabul and Sendang were classified as uninhabitable, while in Mulya Sari at least one quarter were still deemed functional (see Sect. 4.3.2). Most of the village infrastructure had been damaged, and many households had lost their livelihoods. Learning from previous mistakes in Aceh, the Indonesian government had chosen a community-based reconstruction approach for Yogyakarta, where survivors were provided with the means to rebuild their houses on their own, managed by community groups (Sect. 4.2.2). With all agencies focusing their efforts on housing, livelihood recovery was given less priority, while village infrastructure was rehabilitated through community initiatives and community work. The overall recovery process lasted for more than 2 years, although it is difficult to determine when the process ended, especially with regard to the restoration of livelihoods.

9.3.1 Housing Reconstruction[8]

Apart from injuries and bereavement, loss of housing constituted one major burden in respondents' outlook on the recovery. Most could not imagine how to rebuild using only their own resources because earlier houses had often been constructed through a long and slow process. The earthquake had shown quite clearly how rapidly such long-term investments can be turned to dust. Pak Daryono recalls: "After many years of saving I was able to build my own house, though it was small. But actually, it took just one minute, and everything was gone."

Hence, when about a week after the earthquake, the vice president announced government reconstruction funds of 30 million IDR (about US$ 3,200) per house, his promise alone lifted people's spirits by nourishing new hopes for the future and

[8] Reconstruction-related issues of distribution and social conflict are treated in Chap. 14.

increasing the motivation to clean up. However, hope was, at the same time, moderated by a deep distrust of government promises. People tended to remain skeptical and prepared mentally for anything to happen. Wicaksono, for example, anticipated personal disappointment by thinking: "Maybe everyone else will [receive the funds], but not me." When reconstruction payments were actually made, emotional relief reached another level. However, the skeptics were proved right nonetheless because, of the 30 million IDR promised, only 15 million was ultimately paid.[9]

As the first payments were only made in early October 2006, more than 4 months after the earthquake, those who could afford it had already started reconstruction. The privileged group of employees in the government or private sector could use improved credit opportunities offered by their companies or the public banking sector. An even smaller group of people could tap their financial reserves or mobilize the financial support of family members. In the latter case, these were mostly adult children who had migrated in order to find work and were able to send money to their parents. However, most households did neither possess any savings nor have relatively well-earning family members. In these cases, the government announcement at least prevented them from selling land or motorbikes, thereby reducing the potential for secondary long-term effects on their livelihoods.

Households that had owned a house prior to the earthquake and whose members were registered as local residents were entitled to government reconstruction aid. Two guidelines applied to the reconstructed houses. First, they were to have dimensions of 6-by-6 m, with a standard layout of one guest room, one living room, and two bedrooms (Hayashi et al. 2008). However, most importantly, they had to meet the construction standards for earthquake-resistant housing. As long as these basic guidelines were met, residents could decide on the construction model, time frame, and materials themselves (Bayudono 2009). Community groups (*kelompok masyarakat), pokmas*, consisting of 10–15 households were responsible for the local implementation of the reconstruction program. These *pokmas* administered their funds independently, transferred in two payment cycles by the central government. According to our interviewees, *pokmas* members decided on the form, order, and timeline of the distribution of funds. Ideally, all these questions were agreed on through a process of mutual deliberation (*musyawarah*). In determining the order of payment, official guidelines required that priority be given to those who had lost close family members and to the elderly or injured and families with small children. However, as almost everyone in the village met at least one of these criteria, determining need was a delicate matter of the public negotiation of people's plight (see Sect. 9.4). Those last in the line for the payments were disadvantaged not only with regard to time but also because of the persistent uncertainty whether the funds they were entitled to would still exist at the end of the payment process. As with the government

[9] Entitlement depended on the level of destruction, measured in four categories, as issued by the National Coordination Body for Disaster Management. In Yogyakarta province, 15 million IDR were paid for totally collapsed and heavily damaged houses, 4 million for partially damaged, and 1 million for lightly damaged houses (Hayashi et al. 2008). Figures varied in Central Java province, where a maximum of 20 million IDR were allocated.

announcement, the factor of trust in official institutions and their procedures needs to be taken into account in government communications about reconstruction aid.

Government reconstruction aid was supplemented by other programs offered by international aid agencies or the private sector. Some of these programs provided additional houses, while others retrofitted houses or gave minor amounts for making improvements to the houses. Private-sector programs, in particular, were restricted to certain villages, thus creating unequal access to additional reconstruction funds even between neighboring villages. Because each program had specific regulations and requirements with regard to participation and implementation, lack of knowledge of these requirements posed a serious access barrier for common villagers. Instead, the distribution of information usually depended on local political village elites.

The timing of reconstruction also differed significantly depending on the available funds. As described earlier, few households could afford to begin reconstruction prior to the receipt of government funds—which the majority of families had to wait for. Generally, therefore, the timing of house reconstruction depended on these centralized payments and the official period allocated for the building process (Subagyo and Irawan 2008). These time constraints determined the region-wide reconstruction process, causing the prices of building material to soar and creating a shortage of skilled crafts persons (Subagyo and Irawan 2008). In addition, the demand for unskilled labor usually exceeded the capacities of most villages, making the procurement of external workers necessary. Contrary to idealized official reports, permanent housing reconstruction was hardly carried out by *gotong royong*; this principle instead was only practiced to help particular people in need, such as widows. Not a single *pokmas* was known to have organized their regular reconstruction process through *gotong royong* in any of the three villages studied.[10] Villagers usually agreed that *gotong royong* did not meet the requirement to rebuild as quickly as possible because it would have meant rebuilding houses one by one and a further wait for those in line for reconstruction. Interviewees complained that neither problem was accounted for in the governments' allocation of 15 million IDR for newly built houses of 36 m^2, because building materials were more expensive compared to normal times, and reconstruction labor had to be paid for at about 30,000 IDR (about US$ 3) per person per day in contrast to unpaid *gotong royong*. Hence, supplementary funds from other agencies were perceived as necessary for adequate reconstruction to take place.

The criteria of entitlement to reconstruction funds created certain necessities and incentives, inducing a change in community patterns. Larger multi-generational households were forced to split because reconstruction funds were granted per household, regardless of their former size. At 6-by-6 m, the new houses were relatively small. However, because various programs offered reconstruction funds to married couples, regardless of whether they had earlier possessed an individual house or not, there was a surge in new households of mostly young married couples. Some programs required land titles for building plots to be issued in the name of the applicants. To meet this criterion, many older people divided their land and left or bequeathed some of it to their children. Reconstruction criteria thus favored a certain

[10] Our findings concur with Hayashi et al. (2008), who found that, if at all, *gotong royong* was resorted to for construction of T-shelters.

family norm and fostered family nuclearization, with an unknown potential impact on family structures in the long term. However, one might also argue that these new resources only accelerated ongoing changes to village life. After all, the young families welcomed their newly established households as an opportunity that they would not otherwise have had for a long time.

Overall the degree of satisfaction with and gratitude for reconstruction funds depended on comparisons with one's previous housing conditions. New households perceived the aid as a blessing, while those who had previously owned large houses complained about the insufficiency of the funds. The government decision against compensatory reconstruction payments and in favor of the equal provision of basic housing reduced differences in housing quality within the village communities especially concerning size and materials, though economic differences were still visible in the additional building measures and the finish of some houses.

9.3.2 Recovery of the Household Economy

The earthquake affected people's livelihoods in many ways as a complex combination of loss and gain of resources. The extent of losses and their compensation depended on the extent of household vulnerabilities and resilience. For most households, livelihoods even before the disaster were insecure and fragile. Most households can be characterized as flexible family economies based on the multiple economic activities of its members. In general, the majority of households in the three villages we studied had sufficient income to cover their daily needs, but had little scope for any investment beyond these everyday expenses (see Chap. 4).

Economically, home industries were most severely affected. Because in these cases, the production facilitis and assets had been destroyed together with the collapsing houses. In the agricultural sector, fish-farming ponds had been destroyed with all fish stocks lost, while rice farming was affected by the enormous damage to drainage systems (see BAPPENAS 2006). Furthermore, livestock and shop inventories had been reduced dramatically due to the destitution of the emergency phase. However, a few businesses profited from the earthquake, especially those working in the construction sector, including those mining sands on the nearby riverbanks. Employment conditions for the few factory workers or civil servants were hardly affected as their incomes remained stable and most were even offered housing credits. In some cases, family income was jeopardized by the death or long-term injury of the main income earner. Other households suffered from secondary economic loss, such as when families were forced to sell productive assets or use their reserves to cover medical bills, pay reconstruction costs, or invest in the recovery of their businesses.[11] Others took even longer to recover as they lacked the funds for necessary investments, such as purchasing new seeds or livestock. Some had recourse to other

[11] According to a joint study by the United Nations Development Programme (UNDP) and the United Nations Coordination Center (UNCC), more than 70 % of micro- and medium-size enterprises invested their savings, borrowed money, or sold valuables to restore their businesses (quoted in Subagyo and Irawan 2008, p. 23.6). In liquidating these capital reserves, recovery increased vulnerability to other possible risks.

general strategies of capital mobilization and departed as labor migrants. For households that had had one of their members hospitalized, the government's coverage of immediate hospital bills was important in absorbing financial burdens, at least to some degree, and in preventing households from divesting their livelihood assets. However, medical treatment for long-term injuries was not covered, and this posed a heavy burden on affected households, as health insurance is extremely rare in rural areas.

While the disaster management literature generally treats the Bantul case as a positive example of housing reconstruction, livelihood recovery is seen in a rather critical light. MacRae (2008) notes the slow recovery of livelihoods, while Wilson and Reilly (2007) describe all resources being focused on reconstruction before people sought to recover their livelihoods. The obligations of the *gotong royong* system of infrastructural construction further committed residents' labor for many of the months that followed and prevented them from resuming their usual livelihood activities. This neglect of livelihoods was only possible because relief supplies were provided for over 6 months. Compared to reconstruction efforts, livelihood recovery programs were minor: if such programs were implemented at all, they often focused on certain villages or economic sectors and typically provided micro-credits to be administered by community groups. Of the three research sites, Mulya Sari attracted the most funds from livelihood recovery programs (also see Chap. 16).

According to the National Planning and Development Agency, the persistence of fear inhibited clearance and reconstruction activities and the resumption of livelihood activities in some communities (BAPPENAS 2006). In contrast, our interviewees highlighted an opposite tendency: The resumption of regular work was experienced as a helpful distraction that reduced negative thoughts. Some respondents also found solace in their restored ability to provide for themselves and their families, despite such adverse circumstances. This motivation derived from role responsibilities, as Mbak Kusmini recalled: "At that time I just worked to provide for our basic needs, [. . .] for food, for my child, and that is what got me back on my feet (*membangkitkan*)." This spirit of recovery was driven by a work ethic and the pursuit of independence, all of which are key elements in the general life capacities discussed in Chap. 11. They also blended well into the official slogan to encourage Bantul residents to act: "Bantul, get on your feet!" ("*Bantul bangkit*!")

In talking about economic prospects and concerns, respondents usually distinguished between everyday needs, mainly food, and extraordinary costs, such as medical bills or long-term investments in housing construction, school education, or transportation and productive assets. For most households any extraordinary investment posed a difficult challenge, even in normal times. For most, their houses represented accumulations of financial and labor investments over a long period of time, which had been annihilated in a matter of seconds. Prior to the announcement of reconstruction aid, the question of how to rebuild houses caused great anxiety. Pak Subarkah from Sendang had seen his plans for the future come to nothing. He had built his house by gradually saving and had finished it only a few months before the earthquake. After this long-term investment in housing, Subarkah had planned to fund the education of his two children. Seeing his house in ruins, he felt like he was starting again from scratch. In the end, reconstruction aid buffered his losses but what his example illustrates is how all extraordinary costs compete in normal times, and even more so in times of crisis: Sudden medical bills might jeopardize children's education or the family's mobility, for instance, if the motorbike is sold to cover such unexpected expenditures. Much of the economic hardship, which followed the earthquake was therefore an accumulation of familiar challenges rather than a disruption of financial security; strategies to face these problems thus derived equally from usual crisis management strategies, such as budget reallocation, income flexibility, the activation of family networks, or labor migration.

9.4 Narratives of Material Loss and Destitution

Just as external aid had material and symbolic significance, everything involved in coping with the massive physical destruction had a "hard" and a "soft" side. Narratives of loss and of coping with loss help us understand the symbolic level of disaster coping and its interrelation with the material level. When respondents spoke about their earthquake losses, most pointed out how relatively insignificant property loss and material values were in general (see Chap. 11). For once, property loss was weighed against survival and physical integrity. Such threats to survival were mainly perceived at the time of the earthquake itself and its immediate aftermath. As soon as the aid system and emergency shelters had been established, material worries mostly related to life quality issues, such as concerns about inconveniences, status, and the prospect of an economically secure future. Under these prevailing circumstances, people arranged themselves in relation to their post-disaster living conditions by differentiating their needs. In a rhetoric of modesty, many reduced their needs to an existential core.

> So we just accepted (*terima*) our condition, because what else could we do, except accepting (*terima*) our condition? We didn't need to expect good [quality], we didn't need anything fancy... As long as we were healthy, we survived and there was some place to stay, we were OK. (Bu Ngatini, Sido Kabul)

Bu Ngatini's distinction between basic supply or protection and "anything fancy" can be analyzed as the instrumental value of physical or object resources as opposed to their symbolic or acquired value (Hobfoll 1989). According to this distinction, a house provides shelter (instrumental value), but also indicates social status (acquired value). Narratives of modesty, as deployed by Bu Ngatini, strip these object resources down to their instrumental value while rendering their acquired value as secondary. The relativity of material values is thus negotiated on the level of acquired values as long as people think that their basic needs are covered. On the other hand, the value of property is weighed against religious or social values. The most fundamental relativization is certain when property loss is reevaluated as a matter of worldly life as opposed to the afterlife. According to this perspective, any worldly experience or hardship fades in the light of the afterlife. Respondents of different religious orientations commonly viewed material goods as given by God and accepted them as His to take. Believers should therefore respond with acceptance and trust in some form of divine compensation (see also Chap. 12). Following this rationale, Pak Subarkah, who had lost half a million Rupiahs in cash in the ruins, explained:

> What we can do is be patient (*sabar*) and accept (*menerima*) anything that happens. [...] Later, if there is an opportunity, Allah will give us something else. That is why, whenever we lose something, we only refer to Him who owns everything (*Yang memiliki*). (Pak Subarkah, Sendang)

Accepting that material loss and gain is beyond human control was regarded as a strategy to counter psychological distress. The divine is entrusted to reward human patience and effort in material or immaterial terms. Some respondents ultimately saw reconstruction aid as just such a positive reward.

In general, very few respondents complained about or mourned over their material losses in our interviews; this finding could be interpreted as a relatively low degree of material suffering or as relative success in coping. However, the normative preconditions of our interview settings need to be considered as well: We have to ask how subjective levels of (material) loss could be expressed in the normatively structured context of our interview situations. All social norms that promote a positive and encouraging attitude, and that might be supportive in the coping process, have to be interpreted as ambivalent factors, because they make it harder for people to voice subjective experiences which may contradict these ideals. Any comparison which puts material loss into perspective with other forms of loss—any expression of modesty or highlighting of immaterial values—conforms with normative limits about what can be expressed. Such discourses shape the way material loss can be mourned. Overall respondents did not acknowledge property loss as a source of long-term stress except where they offered pejorative comments such as a story about how a woman from the neighboring hamlet was supposedly still traumatized (*trauma*) by the loss of her valuable house.

Expressions of need and destitution were also aggravated by the normative setting. Respondents saw any request for financial assistance as a matter of potential humiliation and shame, because it amounted to admitting one's inability to support one's own family. Pak Daryono anticipated becoming a subject of gossip, as everyone knew about his plight and that he had asked for help. Against the high normative value placed on acceptance, patience, and strain, any public admission of destitution can be interpreted not only as a revelation of one's plight but also as a proof of a limited capacity to bear and face adversities as opposed to normatively prescribed attitudes. In contrast, receiving unsolicited aid is culturally charged and regarded very positively because it is considered an expression of compassion and care. The receiving party feels that his or her plight is being recognized and thus that there is no need to feel ashamed or to fear negative gossip. Asking for aid (*meminta*) and being given aid (*dikasih*) were explained as two very distinct transactions, both socially and emotionally. These sociocultural norms in the communication and expression of destitution influenced *pokmas* groups in deciding the order of reconstruction payments. In this setting, deciding between competing needs was intense because almost everyone met one or the other criteria for prioritized treatment as laid down by the

National Coordination Body for Disaster Management. At the time of our interview, Pak Basuki was still deeply disappointed and hurt that nobody in his group had suggested that he should be prioritized for reconstruction, despite having lost a child (in the earthquake) and his responsibility to care for the younger, surviving sibling. Basuki never spoke up, hoping that others would recognize his suffering, but nobody did. Others, particularly members of the elite, were less humble and shy in advocating their needs. Ending up last on the list, for example, Pak Basuki was hurt that his plight had been disregarded by the group.

9.5 Concluding Remarks

Loss of lives, injuries, and physical destruction are at the core of what the earthquake challenged people to cope with. In our interview data, the challenges of the earthquake experience were narrated in relation to people's exposure to the event itself, living through the precarious period of its aftermath, and coping with the long-term recovery from economic losses. About 2 years later, it was the interviewees who had been bereaved, in particular, who were still struggling to cope. The physical reconstruction of houses and the village infrastructure had progressed far, though livelihoods were still recovering. Apart from the sentimental valuing of houses or other lost objects, physical destruction could be made good by material resources, when they were available. Relief supplies and reconstruction programs provided significant assistance in the form of monetary and nonmonetary resources, and simultaneously had a symbolic impact, as their initial promise and especially their actual distribution provided hope and promoted a spirit of recovery. The early announcement of a government reconstruction program eased survivors' worries about how they would rebuild their houses (which had mostly been built through long periods of resource accumulation). However, this hopeful prospect was also undermined because people generally tended to mistrust such political promises. External assistance communicated the acknowledgment of survivors' plights, providing a sense of being cared for and hope for recovery. However, government officials and the village elite voiced the concern that outside aid could create long-term dependencies, thus weakening communities' resilience. Slogans like "*Bantul bangkit*!" appealed to people's pride in being able to mobilize their capacities for self-help (see Chap. 11).

The policy of community-based reconstruction matched this discourse, putting the survivors in charge of managing housing reconstruction themselves. Given certain limits, such as construction guidelines and time constraints, survivors could organize the construction of their new houses according to their own needs. However, the community-based approach had anticipated that reconstruction would be carried out by *gotong royong*, that is, as unpaid community work. The entire calculation of the government's reconstruction payments relied on these community resources, leading to the amount of aid being reduced to the costs of building materials. Conveniently, the government discourse of self-help as empowerment coincided with considerations of cost efficiency. However, village reality proved *gotong royong* incapable of coping with the extent of the destruction and the simultaneous urgency of the desire to rebuild. In addition, the principle of unpaid community work was applied to the reconstruction of village infrastructure, and residents reported how these commitments, combined with the reconstruction of their own houses, prevented them from returning to their main livelihoods for over a year. However, economic resources reduced the impact of community commitments and the few villagers in stable employment were able to fulfill their *gotong royong* obligations by making payments rather than entering into work commitments. Community-based reconstruction placed decisions regarding implementation in the hands of the *pokmas*, which required survivors to negotiate priorities of need. Prioritization guidelines proved difficult to apply to village contexts, where almost everyone had been severely affected, as they left some community members hurt and disappointed that others had not recognized their plight sufficiently. The issue of aid raises further questions about how destitution and material needs can be articulated. Sociocultural patterns of communication, reputation, and social relations shape the way people express their needs and experience help. In the community contexts of our study, pride was rated highly in relation to suffering; people hesitated to ask directly for help, but rather hoped to receive it and to be cared for. Expectations regarding government institutions differed, however, because respondents felt entitled to their assistance (see Chap. 14).

Despite the relative sufficiency of relief aid and the broad range of reconstruction programs, for most households these material resources were not enough to compensate for their physical losses, let alone the sentimental value placed on lost objects. However, compensatory strategies were applied on different levels: Specifically, the common discourse of property loss heightened the symbolic aspects of material objects, thus relativizing physical damage in relation to social and religious values. Any analysis of the material dimension of coping, therefore, requires that we account for the physical *and* symbolic qualities of material objects and processes.

Acknowledgments The editors would like to thank Robert Parkin for his assistance in editing this chapter.

References

Andayani, B., & Koentjoro (2008). Social and psychological management of post disaster trauma. In D. Karnawati, S. Pramumijoyo, R. Anderson & S. Hussein (Eds.), *The Yogyakarta earthquake of May 27, 2006* (pp. 21.1–21.8). Belmont: Star.

Badan Perencanaan Pembangunan Nasional (BAPPENAS) (2006). Preliminary damage and loss assessment. Yogyakarta and Central Java natural disaster. http://www.undp.or.id/earthquake/docs/Damage%20Assessment.pdf. Accessed 2 June 2013.

Bayudono, T. I. (2009). Disaster management post earthquake in Yogyakarta, Indonesia. *Science Without Borders, 3,* 338–348.

Clarke, A. (2005). *Situational analysis. Grounded theory after the postmodern turn.* Thousand Oaks: Sage.

Freedy, J. R., Shaw, D. L., Jarrell, M. P., & Masters, C. R. (1992). Towards an understanding of the psychological impact of natural disasters. *Journal of Traumatic Stress, 5*(3), 441–454.

Government of Yogyakarta Special Province (GYSP) (2008). Reconstruction based on local wisdom Saiyeg Saeko Kapti: Revive with independence, cultural resilience and solution for the future. In: D. Karnawati, S. Pramumijoyo, R. Anderson & S. Hussein (Eds.), *The Yogyakarta earthquake of May 27, 2006* (pp. 25.1–25.8). Belmont: Star.

HamengkuBuwono X (2008). Remarks of the Governor of Yogyakarta Special Province. Learning from the 27 May 2006 earthquake. In: D. Karnawati, S. Pramumijoyo, R. Anderson, & S. Hussein (Eds.), *The Yogyakarta earthquake of May 27, 2006* (pp. xi–xviii). Belmont: Star.

Hayashi, T., Hokugo, A., Shigemura, T., Yamazaki, Y., & Yamaguchi, H. (2008). A study on residents' strategy for housing reconstruction after the 2006 Central Java Earthquake. http://www.earoph.info/pdf/2008papers/5–6.pdf. Accessed 21 Mai 2011.

Hobfoll, S. E. (1989). Conservation of resources. *American Psychologist, 44*(3), 513–524.

Kusumastuti, R. D., Insanita, R., & Wibowo, S. S. (2010). Relief logistics practices in Indonesia: A survey. The Fifth International Conference on Business and Management Research (ICBMR), University of Indonesia, August 4th, 2010. http://ssrn.com/abstract=1681217. Accessed 16 June 2013.

MacRae, G. (2008). Could the system work better? Scale and local knowledge in humanitarian relief. *Development in Practice, 18*(2), 190–200.

MacRae, G., & Hodgkin, D. (2011). Half full or half empty? Shelter after the Jogjakarta earthquake. *Disasters, 35*(1), 243–267.

Oliver-Smith, A. (2002). Theorizing disasters: Nature, power, and culture. In S. M. Hoffman & A. Oliver-Smith (Eds.), *Catastrophe & culture: The anthropology of disaster* (pp. 23–48). Santa Fe: School of American Research Press.

Rössler, M. (2006). Wirtschaftsethnologie. In B. Beer & H. Fischer (Eds.), *Ethnologie. Einführung und Überblick* (6th Rev. ed., pp. 101–124). Berlin: Reimer.

Schlehe, J. (2006). Nach dem Erdbeben auf Java: Kulturelle Polarisierungen, soziale Solidarität und Abgrenzung. *Internationales Asienforum, 37*(3/4), 213–237.

Subagyo, B., & Irawan, V. (2008). Building local governments and communities that are more resilient to hazards. In D. Karnawati, S. Pramumijoyo, R. Anderson & S. Hussein (Eds.), *The Yogyakarta earthquake of May 27, 2006* (pp. 23.1–23.8). Belmont: Star.

Wilson, P., & Reilly, D. (2007). Report CARE, Catholic Relief Services, Save the Children and World Vision Indonesia. Joint evaluation of their responses to the Yogyakarta earthquake. http://www.crsprogramquality.org/storage/pubs/me/yogyakarta.pdf. Accessed 18 June 2013.

Chapter 10
The Social Dimension of Coping: Communal Negotiations of Social Benefits and Burdens

Silke Schwarz

Coping dynamics in mainstream psychology have been described as individual processes of appraisals and actions, while the social features and collective dimensions of coping have been neglected. Recently, the phenomenon of social support has been incorporated into coping theory, that is, when others help person A to cope with his or her stressor (Schwarzer and Knoll 2007). The main focus stays on person A. In contrast to this tendency in mainstream psychological approaches to restrict analysis to the level of the individual and the immediate context, we argue for the need to examine larger analytical units. In community psychology and sociology, for example, social units can be regarded as actors. Social capital is defined as the central element in the agency and coping efforts of a community. If the social capital of a community is high and robust, the community's capacity for problem solving is also considered to be high (see Chap. 2). We follow this broadened perspective and focus our analysis on contextualized persons and communal features, that is, on neighborhood- and village-wide dynamics and interactions. Only brief references are made to issues that extend beyond local surroundings, to translocal networks that are Java-wide, Indonesia-wide, or even worldwide.

If individual and social features of psychological phenomena are understood as co-constituting and permeating each other and if the starting point is the contextualized person, coping itself becomes a social phenomenon. Moreover, we conceptualize the social dimension of coping as a field permeated by power structures, values, and discourses that influence agency. Smaller and bigger social units are—as actors—located within these fields; they negotiate or rework and co-constitute their social contexts alike (see Chaps. 1–3). We assume that changes in one person will affect the states of other group members and that individual coping efforts have an impact upon social structures and dynamics. Lyons et al. (1998) coined the term *communal coping* and noted that the main difference between this and social support

S. Schwarz (✉)
International Academy for Innovative Pedagogy, Psychology and Economics gGmbH
at Freie Universität Berlin, Malteserstr. 74-100, 12249 Berlin, Germany
e-mail: silke.schwarz@fu-berlin.de; silgnschwarz@yahoo.de

M. Zaumseil et al. (eds.), *Cultural Psychology of Coping with Disasters*,
DOI 10.1007/978-1-4614-9354-9_10,

is in the fact that a cooperative problem-solving process is triggered, as the stressor is perceived to be a collective problem instead of an individual one. This is especially the case when community events such as earthquakes affect whole populations.

Community-based disaster risk reduction approaches—which have become prominent in international disaster management—build on this collective dimension of coping. Their aim is to promote community resilience in the long run, wherein the community is usually an inherently positive concept in which civil participation and empowerment are highlighted. However, this paradigm has been criticized for its neglect of possible community exploitation and a romanticized view of communities (for an overview, see Delica-Willison and Gaillard 2012). Accordingly, we understand the social dimension as both a resource that may foster coping processes and as a source of resource loss that can hamper coping processes.

In order to highlight coping processes as a social phenomenon, we ask: What meaning and function do social features and dynamics have for coping processes? How does a community, struck by disaster, handle this experience? How do people use their social networks and connections in times of crisis? How do the social dynamics and structures of everyday practices change or adapt in times of crisis? Who is involved in communal coping processes? And finally, how do people react to the dynamics of exclusion and inclusion?[1] This chapter starts with an overview of the multiple agent groups (or agents) involved in the coping process and the types of resources that circulate in social networks. Socioculturally specific ideals and practices are highlighted to explore the communal dynamics of a village struck by a disaster. Communal coping efforts, power dynamics, and the renegotiations of social values and practices are all examined. The chapter closes with narratives about the conservation and transformation of communal resources.

10.1 Village Communities in Crises

During disasters, numerous actors are involved in coping with the consequences and the scale of events. Different or new agents can become more relevant than in times of daily and routine existence. Conversely, formerly active agents can disappear because they are not available anymore, either permanently or temporarily, to share and exchange resources. In our case study, villagers described the following agent groups as relevant for coping endeavors: core and extended family members, as well as ancestors;[2] friends and acquaintances; colleagues and employers; members of religious communities, politicians, and entrepreneurs; neighbors; unskilled volunteers; and professionals, which included soldiers, craftsmen, medical personnel, local civil servants, and (inter)national disaster management teams.[3]

---

[1] The topic of social conflicts, potentially or actually arising out of aid distribution processes, will be covered in Chap. 14.

[2] Occasionally, deceased ancestors were described as being supportive by providing advice and strength via dreams.

[3] In Chap. 9, the appearance and disappearance of specific agent groups over time are highlighted.

Several resource types can circulate through social networks. In our case study, these were: financial transfers and tangible objects such as blankets, tents, drugs, kitchenware, corrugated steel, food, means of transportation, cigarettes, a place to sleep and live, and building material. In addition, the instrumental help described included helping to free people who had been buried under rubble, cleaning up together, guarding property, caring for the injured and sick, coordinating tasks, cooking and eating together, providing information, and rebuilding together. Moreover, the emotional and motivational aspects of social encounters were emphasized, such as hope or despair and a sense of togetherness.[4]

10.1.1 Harmony and Togetherness as Value and Practice

Before tackling the characteristics of communal interactions and their social arenas during crises, we describe the culturally specific social peculiarities that seem to be central to local coping processes. According to the historian Bankoff (2007), certain social structures develop due to specific contexts such as disaster-related hazards and poverty. These contexts provide critical life-recovery factors during times of crisis. Socioculturally specific ideals and practices may support or hinder a process of collective meaning-making and the emotional processing of extreme events, as well as collective problem-solving efforts.

10.1.1.1 The Ideals of Harmony (*rukun*) and Togetherness (*kebersamaan*)

In public discourse, togetherness and harmony[5] are declared to be part of "local wisdom" (see Chap. 11), and the earthquake experience is described as a test of this wisdom (for example by the Sultan, Hamengku Buwono X 2008, p. xiii). This ideal is used to relativize material losses and to counteract egoistical tendencies:

> Whether eat or not, togetherness is more important. (The Government of Yogyakarta Special Province 2008, p. 25.4)

According to villagers, the concepts of harmony and togetherness depict communal relationships, in contrast to familial relationships in daily routines and in times of crisis. The concept, however, is closely linked to family metaphors, as Bu Zamroni from Sido Kabul explains: "We treat our neighbors the same as our relatives *(saudara)*."

---

[4] This list does not express disparate categories: for example, receiving money secures one's livelihood, mitigates financial worries, and thus has an emotionally calming effect, as well as signifying being cared for.

[5] The abbreviated term *harmony-ideal* will be used synonymously with *ideal of harmony and togetherness*.

This ideal expresses social expectations[6] and translates into the virtues of cooperation and solidarity being social commitments (*rasa sosial*). Being respectful, being polite, and being in harmony are contrasted with individualistic and arrogant stances. Therefore, *rukun* describes the quality of social relationships as harmonious and consensual (*akur*). *Rukun* is said to foster the code of conduct of being understanding and compassionate as well as the code of conduct of love (*rasa cinta, rasa sosial*), instead of any uncomfortable feelings such as hate, envy, or disappointment:

> Harmoniouness (*rukun*) means that we feel what our neighbors feel. So we're one, how can I put it, so we're united. When we're harmonious, we don't feel uneasy. No hatreds, no uneasy feelings. (Pak Nurdin, Sido Kabul)

We assume that this ideal of harmony fosters the making of communally shared narratives and social meanings, while at the same time the "local wisdom" of harmony and togetherness is maintained by the "doing of" collectively shared narratives (that is "the doing of local wisdoms") (see Chap. 11). Individual stances can have multiple relations to collective ones: supporting them, adding new features, or even contradicting them (Hermanns and Hermanns-Konopka 2010). In the context of our research site, we needed to take into account the strong normative pressures to accept and conform to collectively shared presentations in public. A nonconfrontational manner of interaction and narrating, that is, a conflict-avoiding attitude, was dominant (see Chap. 14).[7]

10.1.1.2 Harmony and Togetherness as Practice (*gotong royong*)

In normal times, the values of harmony and togetherness imply cooperative actions, that is, having a common goal and shared interests and responsibilities, a willingness to work together, and actually working together to achieve this goal. This practice is referred to as *gotong royong*, mutual assistance, communal self-help efforts, or "being united in carrying out one's responsibilities," as the villager Pak Zamroni from Sido Kabul explained. Engaging in these cooperative actions also expresses the propensity to follow norms and traditions:

> *Guyub rukun*. That's Javanese language, [. . .] *guyub* means following what is regularly done in a society, like what are the customs here. [. . .] *Guyub rukun* means being harmonious in working with other people. (Mas Bambang, Sido Kabul)

In the daily routines of many Javanese villages, discussion forums take place during which a consensus ought to be achieved about what should be done in a village community and how, involving whom, etc. This type of communal decision-making is called *musyawarah*. Community leaders have the function of initiating these forums,

---

[6] Exchange rules and related expectations are strongly linked with subjective concepts of what is socially just, a topic we will further examine in Chap. 14, with regard to aid distribution dynamics and in Chap. 16, with a focus on gender relations.

[7] This contrasts with a Western view that each individual has the right to express his or her unique standpoint and opinion.

in which the male elite (*tokoh*) usually participate as formal and informal leaders, and only sometimes does the broader (male) community.[8] The extent to which there are inclusive and open democratic and gender-just structures is, therefore, very questionable.

In general, there are different types of communal practice, mainly differing along the dimensions of what, who, and how.

The question of *what* relates to the subject of cooperative practices and to appraisals of *our* (public, in Javanese *umume*) or *your* (private) problem. For example, helping to repair village streets or participating in night watches (*ronda*) are activities on the public level, indicating that the village infrastructure or village security are shared tasks. According to most villagers, helping a neighbor to build a house describes an activity on a private level and indicates how securing shelter is an individual matter even if an entire hamlet has been razed to the ground by an earthquake.

Another dimension relates to *who* is expected to be involved: the neighboring houses in closer proximity, the entire neighborhood (RT) or even the hamlet (RW, *dusun*), or preexisting groups such as communal night-watch groups (*ronda*). For example, there is an obligation for a household representative to help clean up the streets within one's own neighborhood (RT). The gender dimension is another example of distinguishing who should be involved and by doing what (see Chap. 16).

The question of *how* is a matter of whether labor contributions are paid or unpaid. Some villagers refuse to call activities involving payment *gotong royong* because this would contradict the "true nature of *gotong royong*," as the villager Pak Kartono from Sido Kabul explained, while others consider payment to be a normal development of modern times.

In sum, the following practices have been depicted as cooperative actions:[9] road construction and regular cleaning efforts, graveyard maintenance, night watches (*ronda*), cooking together, conducting communal feasts and rituals called *slametan* or *kenduri*, group meetings (such as newly founded microcredit groups, as well as existing informal rotating savings and credit associations called *arisan*), monthly meetings of the PKK,[10] visiting the sick, religious activities, house (re)construction, and finding solutions through discussion forums called *musyawarah*.

---

[8] The broader community was denoted as *orang awam*, literally meaning layman, and *orang kecil*, literally meaning little people.

[9] Cooperative actions on a communal level were called *gotong royong*, *kerja bakti* (literally, *devoted work*), *sambatan* (derived from Javanese, depicting mutual assistance), and *sumbangan* (literally, *contribution*).

[10] PKK stands for *Program Kesejahteraan Keluarga*, the Program for Family Welfare, which is a government program to improve family welfare within hamlets. PKK groups are governed by the wife of the hamlet head, an arrangement that represents hierarchical structures in village life and reinforces a gender-separated distribution of tasks. All PKK participants are married women and their activities relate to increasing family income and improving health.

10.1.2 Communal Coping Efforts During Crises

In our case study, communal coping efforts during crises need to be seen in the context of the socioculturally specific ideal of harmony and togetherness. The "matching" between socioculturally mediated and individually held expectations and actual interactions is crucial to experiencing social encounters not as burdening but as facilitating the coping process. In any case, power dynamics are decisive in the access to and control over valuable material and symbolic resources that symbolizes inclusionary and exclusionary social dynamics. Accordingly, concepts such as bonding, bridging, and linking social capital are useful tools here for analyzing coping efforts (Grootaert et al. 2004).[11]

10.1.2.1 Coping Efforts Transcending Communal Dynamics

In the aftermath of a disaster, communal systems can crash (at least temporarily). In our case study, volunteers and soldiers (and later on increasingly professionals too) were alerted to assist communities by broadcasts in the local mass media, government orders, and policies, and the high level of needs of survivors along with the lack of community resources to respond. Volunteers possessing instrumental resources such as technical skills were expected to use their respective competencies within socioculturally ascribed roles consistent with their professional or informal identities. According to most villagers, physically strong men ought to help clean up debris and female volunteers were expected to organize and distribute food. Above all, institutionalized and professionalized forms of help—that is, disaster management entities such as local or central government civil servants and medical personnel—were vital in framing the coping efforts of insiders, that is, of those people directly affected by the disaster (Wright et al. 1990). For example, official guidelines for aid distribution and housing reconstruction greatly influenced the problem-solving capacities of affected communities.[12]

Altogether, expectations toward strangers seemed to be lower than toward those whom an individual already knows. However, being helped by, for example, a close relative was experienced as more consoling. Furthermore, support received from strangers was rarely returned. If so, the expectation referred to reciprocation at a general and public level, not necessarily a personal one. For example, people from Bantul, who received help from residents of the Northern regency, Sleman, after the earthquake in 2006, provided support to Sleman residents in 2010 and 2011 when the northern volcano, Mt. Merapi, exploded. Earthquake survivors prepared food and gathered other urgently needed goods such as blankets for those who had formerly provided assistance to them in times of despair and sorrow. The ability to

---

[11] Another possible—but apolitical—conceptualization of social coping dimensions refers to the quantitative and qualitative characteristics of social networks (Barth 1998).

[12] For villagers' expectations directed toward the government as a provider of aid in times of adversity, see Chaps. 14 and 15.

repay the kindness that people had experienced was described as a moment of pride and gratitude alike.

In the aftermath of the earthquake in 2006, family members and relatives living outside the disaster area helped when the communal support system failed. The degree of kinship and gender ascriptions decisively moderated the enacted coping efforts. Core family members had a greater obligation to provide resources than extended ones, and women tended to have reproductive obligations (such as caring for the sick ones) while men rather fulfilled tasks such as helping to clean up debris. Friends and acquaintances can also be distinguished with regard to their degree of closeness: the closer the acquaintance,[13] the higher the probability that one is involved in the coping process. The types of resources accumulated (in the sense of bonding, bridging, and linking social capital) make a major difference to coping processes. For example, Pak Siswanto from Sido Kabul was able to involve friends living as far away as Jakarta, who donated money to him and his community. In general, the direction of contact can flow both ways: earthquake-affected people proactively activated their networks and, conversely, outsiders motivated by worries about the well-being of family members or friends contacted those who had been affected by the disaster. Therefore, proactive actions by both insiders and outsiders initiate, maintain, and direct communal coping efforts.

10.1.2.2 Communal Coping Efforts within a Village Struck by Disaster

> On the first day, I helped to evacuate the earthquake victims. The second day I worked hard together with others to bury the dead. The next day I worked hard to build the post for collecting aid goods. (Pak Wagimin, Sedang)

Villagers spoke of working together to rescue earthquake victims who had been buried; they described cleaning up and rebuilding together, chatting with each other, indicating care for one another, as well as informing each other (for example, about how to access aid). Moreover, villagers jointly organized necessary tasks, produced an assessment of what needed to be done, and jointly took decisions, such as how to organize vehicles as ambulances and how to coordinate the night watch (*ronda*). Collective emergency shelters and communal emergency kitchens were established, and social movements transcending geographical or administrative hamlet boundaries emerged, for example, to demonstrate against electric power companies (see Chap. 14).

These responses indicate that the earthquake recovery was, at least partly and temporarily, experienced as a shared responsibility. These acts may be described as acts of solidarity, altruism, charity, reciprocity, and empathy (Prainsack and Buyx 2012). Before outside help arrived, villagers described a collectivization of private property and human resources, and a solidarity neglecting issues of rank, gender, and class. This implies certain valued principles of life conduct such as generosity and solidarity. Typically, this sort of communal coping (that is, living, cooking,

[13] Expressed in Indonesian by *sahabat* (close friend), *teman* (friend), etc.

and eating together) was limited in time to several weeks only or was otherwise described as having had rather negative impacts on individuals and families (for example, contributing to a lack of privacy and to work overload).

Rituals and collective memory work are further forms of communal coping efforts (Bhandari et al. 2011). For example, funeral rituals were described as guiding people through the grieving process. Collective annual prayers called *tahlilan* were conducted in some hamlets for up to 5 years after the disaster. *Tahlilan* may be described as a religious and sociocultural ritual in order to work toward a better life and to reflect upon the past while facing an uncertain future (see also Chap. 15).

10.1.2.3 Power Dynamics and Resource Differentials

With regard to coping endeavors, it was commonly acknowledged that everybody may contribute to communal coping efforts in times of crisis in accordance with their resources. Some villagers predominantly provided support (some providers expected something in return and others contributed out of charity), while other villagers predominantly received support, a phenomenon that is captured by the concept of social support. Many villagers worked together toward a common goal, a phenomenon that illustrates collective or joint coping dynamics and appraisals of challenges as "ours" instead of "yours" or "mine."

Limited time resources, power dynamics, and related resource differentials within a hamlet moderate the communal coping processes. A villager's socioeconomic position within the communal network of power relations determines what types of resources can be accessed and controlled. For example, not all members of a community share the same interests, goals, and values, and not all people can or want to participate in communal coping dynamics or receive the same quantity of outcomes of communal coping efforts.[14] Interviewees usually differentiated between the "village elite" (*tokoh*) and the "ordinary" or "common people" (*orang awam, orang kecil*), the former being formal and informal leaders; that is, they acknowledged a village cadre consisting of religious, respected, and well-educated community figures as well as the wealthy, all of whom had a higher social ranking compared to ordinary people.

The elite were attributed with organizing and decision-making functions. The typical tasks and responsibilities of official leaders within political village structures, that is, the chiefs of the neighborhood (Pak RT) and hamlet (Pak Dukuh), included organizing medical treatment for the injured, communicating with aid institutions, organizing and distributing the necessary aid, and providing advice to community members. In contrast, ordinary people (*orang kecil*) were depicted as the implementers of plans. Therefore, hierarchical structures in village life impede democratic and balanced dynamics in communal coping efforts. The elite usually have quite resource-rich networks, that is, bridging and linking social capital. For

[14] In order to offer this power-critical assessment, our analysis, therefore, emphasizes a timeline perspective that highlights these (complex) processes instead of states.

example, one respected village figure described how he managed to acquire help through his personal translocal networks, which even reached as far as the Netherlands. In addition, he had the highly valued ability to write proposals to solicit for institutionalized (inter)national aid.[15]

If official leaders were not able to fulfill their political roles,[16] conflicts and dilemmas were described as arising, such as: Should I accompany my injured wife to the hospital or instead leave her unattended and organize the clean up in my neighborhood? Unfulfilled leading roles and a bad leadership performance contributed to disappointments, discomfort, and sometimes even turmoil within a community. Moreover, some ordinary villagers felt burdened by the lack of influence:

> I invited the RT leader to help me to build a tent so that all the sick people could be brought there and would receive good treatment. [. . .] But since I am not well educated, the people here neglected my suggestion. They thought that I don't know anything, even though my advice was good. Javanese people said that my suggestion was still raw. That kind of suggestion was supposed to be said by the richer people or well-educated people, not me. (Pak Wagimin, Sedang)

Social positions within current power structures influence coping processes, as they impact on abilities, chances to negotiate sociocultural norms, and issues of access to and control of resources (see Christensen and Larsen 2008).

10.1.2.4 (Re)Negotiating Social Values and Communal Practices in Turbulent Times

Villagers described temporary shifts in social reference units, which were altered by places of refuge and changed communal structures. In the aftermath of the disaster, coordination posts (*posko*) for the receipt of disaster-aid goods became a central reference unit. These posts encompassed several neighboring houses, several neighborhoods (RT), an entire hamlet (*dusun*), or even village (*desa*). Expectations of who ought to help whom in times of disaster seemed to adapt to these changed circumstances and shifting dynamics.

Shifting dynamics may translate simply into altered units or into shrinking or expanding social reference units. For example, three families came together for several months after the disaster to eat together, live communally, and share in caring for the injured family members. For the most part, however, expectations and felt obligations were primarily channeled to one's own family during the crisis.

However, how are the interests of one's social reference unit negotiated with regard to collective needs? What position do the most underprivileged occupy? It was broadly accepted in retrospect that people should satisfy the needs of their own social group first—usually the family, sometimes and usually only temporarily also

[15] Whether these privately acquired aid goods were distributed privately or publicly, made a difference to perceptions of injustice (see Chap. 14).

[16] The reasons given were old age, a lack of linguistic competence in Indonesia needed in order to communicate with donors, injury to oneself, fulfilling caring tasks for (injured) family members, and fear.

larger units such as the three families described above or the inhabitants of a collective emergency shelter—before passing on resources to wider networks. Personal obligations, such as looking after cattle, were valid excuses for living alone with one's family instead of joining with others in emergency camps. Even though a self-referential or selfish stance is devalued in Java, the chaotic and burdensome situation legitimated nonattendance at the otherwise routine social occasions such as funerals. Activities for self-support in a crisis were not considered to contradict principles of life conduct such as generosity, understanding, compassion, and solidarity.

In essence, during the interviews, villagers extolled the maxims of sharing with and caring for each other in times of adversity only and always in accordance with one's capacities. Need, on the other hand, justified expecting and receiving aid and support from others, as Pak Nurdin from Sido Kabul explained:

> Which one needs to be given precedence? It is clear, the house which is not collapsed and those who still have a complete and healthy family should help those who need more help. [...] As a Moslem, we must help each other.

Understandings of who is in greatest need were reworked in the face of disaster: The elderly, the widowed, children, women, the injured, the traumatized, and poor households were prioritized to receive support. Javanese and Islamic references go hand in hand here to support solidary acts in times of crisis and criticism of their absence in retrospect. Evaluations of need are made by different stakeholders in different contexts and for different purposes, sometimes invoking conflict dynamics. In one context, evaluations of toughness indicated psychosocial well-being and the capacity to handle enduring aftershocks. Usually, family members were assessed by other family members. Those who were considered "vulnerable" or "traumatized" were then evacuated to relatives and friends living outside the disaster-affected area. Another context for evaluating need referred to the aid context, where aid agencies carried out appraisals accompanied by the village elite (indicating a material need).

Some family members were not capable of providing emotional or instrumental support, as they were preoccupied in making sense of their own burdensome experiences. This lack of familial support could be compensated by feelings and practices of a communal solidarity that were triggered and reinforced by referring to the "local wisdom" of harmony and to metaphors of family, that is, by extending the concept of "brothers and sisters" (*saudara, kekeluargaan*) to persons with whom one had no genetic connection and even to strangers. For example, people from the northern regency, Sleman, who came to help clean up the debris, were described as *saudara*.

In the final analysis, prioritizing communal needs was rare and usually confined to elite discourses. During the interviews, many formal leaders reinforced a shared sense of communal mastery and produced a positive and proud image of their community. In this way, "local wisdoms" were reinforced and images of a local identity fostered (see Chap. 11). However, discourses of communal mastery do not necessarily correspond to applied practices.[17]

[17] Bowen (1986) describes impressively, how discourses of communal self-help were instrumentalized politically during Suharto's "New Order".

In the Yogyakarta earthquake, a community-based approach was applied to implement housing reconstruction efforts. In the international disaster management evaluation literature, the quick recovery in Yogyakarta is partly ascribed to the fact that existing community social structures were left intact (Manfield 2007). As noted in the previous chapter, community-based reconstruction groups (*pokmas*) were formed based on self-reliant communal coping efforts that, in normal times, are called *gotong royong*. According to Ophiyandri et al. (2010), the applied group approach created better housing quality, accountability, and greater satisfaction, as well as increasing social capital.

According to our data, these groups usually received the necessary building materials but the reconstruction process itself was not carried out through mutual assistance. Some villagers saw the group principle as a burden. Every member had to fulfill certain standards; if one failed, the entire group would be made accountable for it. If one member fell behind, all the others would need to wait for him to catch up and would not receive any further money to buy building materials. From a critical standpoint, disaster management responsibilities were shifted from government entities to communities, partly resulting in additional burdens for those affected and had to rebuild, resume their livelihoods, and deal with emotional unrest, simultaneously. The distribution of government money, which arrived only about 6 months after the disaster, also hampered earlier efforts to strive for self-reliance. Furthermore, the amount provided by the government for reconstruction was not sufficient. In an interview in 2010, the regent of Bantul (Pak Bupati) explained that this did not result in greater financial burdens, as the costs of paying craftsmen could be saved by reverting to the practice of *gotong royong*. During the clean-up phase, however, the actual lack of a joint neighborly agency had to be compensated for by the work of volunteers and relatives, while during the reconstruction phase, professionals and relatives stepped in whenever possible and if their labor was affordable. Those lacking access to financial and human resources struggled in their reconstruction efforts, often took longer to complete their work, or they were not able to complete reconstruction (for example, still having concrete floors instead of ceramic tiles), or achieve aseismic building standards.

The following prerequisites for conducting successful communal practices in a crisis such as an earthquake were described by the interviewees in our study:

1. The availability of sufficient time and manpower was depicted as crucial (from the perspective of a person helping others). Otherwise, helping others may result in additional burdens, which are likely to hinder one's own ability to cope.
2. Being in a psychologically stable state was declared by some villagers to be a necessary prerequisite to help cleaning up after an earthquake; that is, having a certain level of toughness and following the code of conduct described in Chap. 11 were deemed crucial.
3. Presence in the hamlet was decisive: If a person had left the area to live with family members outside, she or he could not participate in *gotong royong*.
4. The possibility of reciprocating help fostered acceptance of help from others (from the perspective of a person to be helped). In comparison, being compassionate

(*kasihan*) and sincere (*ikhlas*) instead of taking an egoistical stance was said to foster helping others (from the perspective of a person helping others):

> Mutual cooperation is conducted by our free will (*keikhlasan*). We don't ask for payment when we do it. We do it by our own free will and from the heart (*keikhlasan dari hatinya*). For example, there's a new neighbor here building a house. We can help him or her to indicate the harmony here. (Pak Jiyo, Sido Kabul)

5. A certain level of harmony (*rukun*) within one's neighborhood or hamlet was identified as supporting solidary acts (and the other way round).
6. The level of conflict or harmony was related to the performance of the elite and their degree of social commitment. They were described by villagers as having a great impact on the enactment of communal practices.
7. Finally, material and physical conditions do make a difference. For example, the availability of meeting rooms fosters the type of communication that is needed to initiate, coordinate, and maintain communal practices such as mutual self-help.

Overall, communal coping efforts decreased in the hamlets that we studied in times of adversity compared to normal times and despite the elite's discourse of successful communal coping. In this respect, it is important to acknowledge that the community-based reconstruction program initiated by the national and local government failed to foster self-help efforts.

10.1.3 Functions and Meanings of Social Features During Crises

This section will examine the beneficial as well as burdensome functions and meanings of social settings, structures, and interactions in times of disaster.

10.1.3.1 Possible Benefits

Perceptions of a shared fate (called *senasib* by interviewees) after learning about the extent of the destruction (see Chap. 11) and a sort of solidarity in suffering with other earthquake survivors were reported by several interviewees. This solidarity had a consoling effect in which people felt that, since everybody had been affected, the earthquake had made everyone equal. Being in company with others also had the effect of distracting villagers from their surroundings and suffering. Fears were reported as calming down simply as a result of chatting or watching television (TV) programs, such as the World Cup, together. Feelings of solidarity also had motivating effects, as described by Pak Kartono from Sido Kabul:

> I took everything lightly. Since we were all struck (*senasib*) by the disaster, we were in togetherness.

Feeling solidarity with others implied shared responsibilities and encouraged collective action. In other words, solidary acts such as cooking together can ease the burden for individuals. This can be an extraordinary benefit during a crisis when collective action provides instrumental as well as emotional relief. Villagers joined in boosting each others' "hearts" and easing each others' pain and grief about losses, in addition to exchanging important information. Solidarity also implies that an ingroup is formed and distinguished from an outgroup, although the social reference units of an in- and outgroup may vary depending on, for example, whether scarce aid goods were distributed among several families only or whether the group of disaster survivors decided to demonstrate against the local government.

Working together, such as jointly building a graveyard wall, provided a forum for exchanging different perspectives and for increasing mutual understanding. Because being solidary, understanding, compassionate, polite, and respectful are highly valued in "Javanese" culture, being able to conduct oneself accordingly has positive impacts on the self and the community. Moreover, when you help someone else with a personal problem that is not considered a shared one but *yours*, this is said to increase merit for the afterlife according to Islam.

Some disaster survivors were afraid of aftershocks and the possibility of a tsunami and thus lived with relatives outside the disaster area. This was reported as restoring feelings of safety. Injured villagers could be cared for until they were able to return to their homes. Physically well relatives were responsible for caring for injured disaster survivors and accompanying them to obtain medical treatment.[18] Closer and more distant acquaintances and relatives provided food and clothes, goods that were greatly needed in the immediate aftermath, before the official aid agencies became active. This mitigated financial worries and even led to increases in socioeconomic status for some disaster survivors in the longer term. Young and physically active family members and friends helped to rebuild temporary and permanent shelters, providing their manpower, money, or materials. People who had not experienced the traumatic earthquake themselves were able to show their bravery by, for example, rescuing material from the debris.[19]

Overall, this analysis implies that some problems can only be solved with the involvement of several people, implying a social responsibility that may be expressed in the following motto: "even though it is your problem, we will work together to resolve it." Collectively doing something and helping one another was said to have a uniting effect and benefit the provider as well as the receiver or the entire group, providing instrumental relief as well as invoking feelings of being socially embedded and of being proud to live in a community full of *gotong royong* spirit. From a pragmatic perspective, communal or joint coping efforts often are the only means by which village development can occur, as Pak Zamroni from Sido Kabul explained.

Lastly, the construction of collective narratives and the making of shared meanings, as well as the discovery of socially understood benefits, were crucial in our research site. A dominant position in the collective narrative was that villagers had

---

[18] This indicates shared (but age- and gender-differentiated) responsibilities for family members in need, as it was the younger generation or women who were usually responsible for providing this type of assistance.

[19] Other relatives and friends who were expected to help, however, were not available due to other responsibilities such as work. Their inability to attend in person could be compensated for by money, a common strategy also applied in ordinary daily routines.

developed greater social awareness, leading to an increased appreciation of communal relationships. This was invoked by being reminded of the finiteness of life and the view that humankind is weak and is therefore dependent on others as well as on God in times of adversity. Additionally, a greater appreciation of social bonds was described due to becoming aware that losing a loved one can be painful (which many interviewees witnessed in other families). Furthermore, the earthquake set down a marker, which was said to enable a common new beginning "from zero," as 24-year-old Mbak Kusmini from Sido Kabul explained on a family level:

> I really felt that I got closer to my family. Got closer to them because it is like as if we restarted our life again from zero (*nol*). [. . .] After the earthquake, I realized that in fact it hurts to lose someone we love a lot. I began to realize it when I saw my neighbors who lost one of their family members. It is clear that I am really grateful (*bersyukur*). Really *alhamdulillah* [Arabic for expressing gratefulness], because all members of my family were safe and healthy. That is why I became closer to my family. [. . .] We share, chat, tell our experiences and what we will do in our future. [. . .] I rarely talked with my family before the earthquake. I could be talkative when I was speaking with others but not with my family. I couldn't change it because it's the way I was. But, after the earthquake, I talked more frequently with my family.

10.1.3.2 Possible Burdens

Not being alone, however, can also hinder coping processes. For example, rumors can spread easily in social networks due to misinformation. This was the case with the tsunami rumor, which provoked panic and a mass flight to the north, away from the southern coast.[20]

The bigger the social network, the more social support is provided, as well as requested, which can itself become a source of stress. Therefore, being solidary with others due to shared identities (in the course of assuming a shared fate called *senasib*) can have controversial effects.[21] Even though being together with others had calming effects in the hamlets we studied, it prevented some people from evacuating in the face of the expected approaching tsunami. Some villagers described their dilemma in ways such as the following: How would it be if only I survived and all my family members were taken by the tsunami? Many villagers talked about how distressing it was to consider such possibilities. In the end, it was usually the family that was prioritized above one's own survival.[22] Furthermore, community-wide rituals, such as *tahlilan* in memory of the deceased, were considered by some interviewees to be just as troubling; specifically, several villagers refused to participate because the

[20] Hobfoll (1986) called this phenomenon *rumor mills*.

[21] Hobfoll (1986) called a similar phenomenon the *pressure cooker*, that is when people tend to exchange experiences of a terrible event due to their same background experience.

[22] Rescuing oneself at the expense of others was reported by some interviewees as having troubling effects. For example, a son described rescuing his injured father from the debris and protecting him from the sun by covering him with a coconut leaf. However, when he had to leave him behind to escape from the expected tsunami, troublesome feelings of guilt followed.

rituals were too confrontational and participation would reawaken feelings of loss and suffering.

Receiving support in general can also affect feelings of self-reliance, which is a highly valued attribute according to the code of conduct at our research site. Feelings of uneasiness and confusion were reported when in need to receive or ask for help. Furthermore, a lack of privacy sometimes was in conflict with other normative features of selfhood and identity. Some villagers were said to be preoccupied with their own personal thoughts and feelings and to find it disturbing (feeling uneasy, *tidak enak*, and feeling puzzled, *karuan*) not to have any privacy or self-reliance. For example, one widow described feeling burdened when living with relatives, not feeling at home, not feeling self-reliant, and even feeling compelled to depend on others.

Living in an affected village can lead to social comparisons with the more fortunate cases that, in turn, can result in decreased feelings of solidarity, accompanied by emotional and motivational problems. For example, several villagers reported comparing their progress in cleaning up and rebuilding temporary or permanent shelters with neighbors and others in their surroundings and some became demotivated after they realized that they had been left far behind.

The limited resources of one's social reference unit may also result in a tendency to isolate oneself from others and a stance expressed in the motto "first me, then my family, only then others." A relative scarcity of resources can lead to competition and produce social conflict (for more details see Chap. 14).

If expectations remain unfulfilled and necessary support is not forthcoming—for example, when one has to free buried family members all alone—this can be extremely burdening:

> I had shouted for help until I could not talk [. . .]. All of the people around me were thinking of their families. [. . .] Yes, I cleared it [the debris to free his buried wife] myself. I asked for help until I was husky. Nobody helped. (Pak Geno, Sido Kabul)

For many family members, friends, and acquaintances, not being able to be with those who were affected by the disaster also led to psychosocial suffering. For example, Mbak Kusmini from Sido Kabul could only return to her home village 8 months after the earthquake as she had to finish her work contract as a domestic worker in Malaysia. She felt extremely troubled when comparing her living situation in Malaysia, where she had a place to sleep and sufficient food, with the condition of her family who were dependent on aid because their house and the entire village infrastructure had been destroyed. She compensated for her inability to attend in person with numerous phone calls to check on her family's well-being. She also sent money and necessities such as clothes. She explained that she used further strategies to cope, such as sharing her troubles with friends, distracting herself by focusing on her work, and communicating with God. After about 5 months, she started to find inner peace.

Last but not the least, help provided by others may be seen as nonsupportive. The work performance of strangers, relatives, or neighbors compared with those of professionals was partly judged as unsatisfactory and uncertain. Several villagers complained about volunteers, as they caused further damage rather than treating remaining building and household materials carefully so that they could be used again. Furthermore, having many strangers around also led to a tendency to separate in- and outgroup members, with strangers being suspected of possibly stealing property. The thieves discourse (a rumor, as no accounts of actual thefts could be found in our data) was very dominant in the aftermath of the disaster (see also Schlehe 2006). The idea that there might be thieves in or coming to a village endangered communal peace and harmony. At the same time, bonds between communal insiders were strengthened as they had to guard the community, for example, in night-watch rounds (*ronda*), against possible thieves. This links with a very common finding from high- and low-income research settings; it is usually associated with a condition where people cannot live on the site of their former home and they are concerned about losing items, etc. from damaged or destroyed houses (see, for example, Frailing 2007).

The chapter closes with narratives about the conservation and transformation of communal resources.

10.2 Narratives About the Conservation and Transformation of Communal Resources

What is of interest in this section is the locally specific way in which villagers construct both continuity and change with regard to the social features of communal and familial life after the disaster.

> In addition to personal danger and fear, they [disasters] destroy and disrupt the arrangements of everyday life. (Gordon 2009)

Disasters are often presented as events that threaten the social fabric of societies and can cause social structures and power dynamics to "totter." In our interview data, we found a variety of positions on the impact of the earthquake and other factors on social and power structures. Some villagers declared the disaster to be the crucial force for change; others attributed changes to more general developments such as the global financial crisis or the rising national unemployment rate. And yet others described the type and quality of village politics including the process of aid distribution and reconstruction programs as the crucial motor for change.

According to several villagers, after only about 2 years, the practice of communal assistance (*gotong royong*) had returned to "normal," pre-earthquake levels. These reports did not contain any further criticism or reworking of social norms and practices in this area of village life. Besides, an increase in social and religious gatherings was described by many interviewees (both depicted as *gotong royong* practices). These gatherings increased communication among the villagers in each hamlet. Additionally, the earthquake experience itself resulted in an increased feeling of dependence on one another. All of these experiences and changes were described as contributing to communal harmony (*rukun*) and togetherness (*kebersamaan*). This broadly shared narrative of eventual disaster-related communal benefits and collective pride countered the critical narrative mentioned below. It indicates that social capital and communal coping efforts increased due to the earthquake experience and produced new groups in the long run.[23]

However, several villagers did report that the nature of *gotong royong*, in general, had changed or decreased. The way they talked about this change indicates normative renegotiations. Comparing arrangements from before the earthquake to several years after it, *gotong royong* began to be paid for and was only used for public rather than private purposes. Changes were attributed to an increasingly materialistic orientation, as well as to a decrease in social harmony (due to aid-distribution conflicts and increasingly individualistic orientations of some villagers). Some villagers presented this materialistic development as neutral, accepting it as a part of normal developments of "modern times." Mostly, however, it was described negatively as a sign of social deterioration. For instance, marginalized villagers used the discourse of a decline in mutual assistance to criticize a widening gap between the rich and the poor.[24] This gap was said to have deepened, especially as those who were close to the village administration had gained in social standing and financial wealth after the earthquake. Corruption, fraud, and nepotism were impeached by several villagers (see Chap. 14). Conversely, the poor were said to have become even poorer as they did not have enough additional resources to rebuild their homes or because they participated in one of the newly initiated micro-credit programs, which pushed them into debt. In Sido Kabul, the temporary hamlet leader, during the relief and reconstruction phases, was strongly criticized by his fellow villagers for increasing his own wealth in the aftermath of the earthquake. Emotions associated with these injustices were said to have endured for a long time; for some, this included the time up to the end of our research presence in that hamlet. In 2008, the election of a permanent head of the hamlet took place. Many claimed that conflicts were greatly intensified around the time of the election. The current hamlet leader was close to the temporary one and also criticized for profiting from the disaster aid. Furthermore, opponents of the current hamlet head accused him of election fraud by bribing villagers with Indonesian Rupiahs 50,000 (around US$ 5.35) per vote. They complained that elections did not have secret ballots and people who did not elect the current hamlet leader were not invited to social and political events in the aftermath of the elections. Moreover, opponents were said to have been denied access to government poverty programs due to their "disloyalty."[25]

Overall, the social fabric of village life was said to have changed due to processes of aid distribution after the earthquake. Some claimed that everyone has become more

---

[23] For example, new *pengajian* groups to recite the Quran were formed in several hamlets. In Sido Kabul, new micro-credit groups (*arisan*) were established in accordance with the types of business involved. Women in the same business, but not necessarily from the same neighborhood (RT), started to meet and established new connections.

[24] A neighborhood head (Pak RT), on the other hand, discussed these changes within an alternative discourse that invoked the social responsibilities of the rich toward poorer community members and an appeal to the rich to be generous.

[25] Supporters of the current hamlet head, however, claimed that opponents would feel hurt as their candidate lost, and thus they would withdraw socially. No connection to corruption or attempted bribery was claimed.

equal than before the earthquake, has grown closer, and has a better socioeconomic standing. One materialistic indicator of increased equality often referred to was that all houses are now built with stone (rather than bamboo, which is not used anymore) and most of them now have ceramic tiles rather than concrete floors. However, others did claim to feel more distanced from the village elite because the elite defrauded them of disaster aid and because the reconstruction money provided by official agencies was not sufficient, which led to further impoverishment of the poor, as explained earlier.

With regard to family life, the most commonly reported changes were positive.[26] Parents presented themselves as having learned how to become better caregivers for their children through being more affectionate. This contrasted with descriptions of being indifferent or strict before the earthquake. Increased mutual understanding and closer relationships were described, in general, as the quotation by Mbak Kusmini in Sect. 10.1.3. illustrates. However, becoming more protective can be experienced as restrictive and nonsupportive from the perspective of children and adolescents. Mbak Sujati, a 17-year-old teenager from Sido Kabul, for example, badly wanted to go to a school located further away from her parent's home village. After the earthquake, her parents forbade her to go to this school as they feared that their daughter would not be informed in time if anything should happen to her parents, for example, if another earthquake occurred.

10.3 Concluding Remarks

This chapter has highlighted the social dimension of disaster coping dynamics. We argued for a permeating co-constitution of collectively shared and idiosyncratic features in coping processes. What is collectively shared may be located in the self as a stance or an attitude (in the form of partly individualized "local wisdoms" or socioculturally specific principles of life conduct), as well as in collectively shared sentiments such as local pride and solidarity, in public discourses, and in observable joint activities and social interactions.

Consistent with Kagan et al. (2011), we understood a village community mostly in geographical terms, that is, as a space where people live, which in our case study referred to the administrative village units (*dusun*, RTs).[27] Because sharing material goods bonds people together, sometimes smaller geographical units, such as a coordination post (*posko*) and its surroundings, temporarily became more important. Moreover, we acknowledged that social identities are constructed around a community and presented the emotional and symbolic dimensions of what it means for villagers to live within their communities. Finally, we argued in favor of including the

[26] Problematic or challenging transformations were hardly reported, usually only in the context of long-term effects of injury and extreme suffering (see Chap. 13).

[27] The term *communal* used in this chapter, therefore, does not denote a religious community, a school community, or a political community.

dimension of social structures and related power dynamics of inclusion and exclusion when examining disaster-affected communities. In doing so, we counterbalanced the tendency in mainstream psychology to focus exclusively on the emotional dimension of communities (as does the concept of a *sense of community* described in McMillian and Chavis (1986)).

It is generally recognized that disaster-affected people develop spontaneous feelings of solidarity with one another, a phenomenon called a *brotherhood of pain* by Oliver-Smith (1999a).[28] Similar to Kaniasty and Norris' (1993) *social support deterioration model*, we found processes of the collectivization of private property, a solidarity ignoring issues of rank and class, followed by social conflicts and bitterness. This is a typical dynamic in times of adversity and scarcity and has been found in Peru (Oliver-Smith 1999b), the USA (Kaniasty and Norris 1993), and elsewhere in the world. However, our main interest related to the cultural specificity of our research site. We examined whether the experience or nonexperience of solidarity and existent relational references and experience frames were fundamentally different in our research site in comparison to universalistic patterns. To tackle these questions, it was helpful to closely examine the social features of communal and familial dynamics during daily routines. It was important to understand what is expected and considered as "normal" in order to represent clearly the socioculturally specific resources and burdens as well as hopes and disappointments experienced in a community during adversity, because the matching of or failure to match expected and received support influences the experience of stress. General concepts such as collectivism and individualism are too general and abstract to depict the specificities that matter and that make a difference to a given community. Therefore, we highlighted the concepts of harmony and togetherness, *rukun* and *kebersamaan*, as well as related communal practices often referred to as *gotong royong*, in order to capture local dynamics accurately. With regard to future research, we further suggest accounting for the double-edged character of the social dimension of coping by developing an unbiased approach to social benefits and burdens and to consider in a balanced manner the dynamic relations that encourage as well as burden people. We reiterated our belief that this can be achieved by a thorough contextualization of the research itself. From this analysis, the question arises of how to increase community resilience in a socioculturally adequate manner. Chapter 15 highlights several possibilities and associated potential difficulties.

When accounting for socioculturally specific features and dimensions of social life, it is crucial to account for the political and economic impacts on coping dynamics as well. These (inter)national macrostructures influence the possibilities of local agency enormously. A macro-level approach translates into a historical as well as power-critical socioculturally specific standpoint that helps to contextualize discourses and research phenomena further. For example, it is important to consider

[28] Although Oliver-Smith originally referred to disaster-affected people only, the concept can be broadened to include a universal tendency to provide support to others in times of disaster. It then depicts a solidarity that increasingly turns global, with mass media and its emergency appeals to raise money for disaster survivors.

the feudal origins and political instrumentalizations of *gotong royong* and *rukun* (see Bowen 1986) and to analyze the perspectives of ordinary villagers (*orang kecil*) in relation to those of the village elite (*tokoh*). This standpoint made it possible to create a critical account of the highly praised community-based approach which was used during reconstruction efforts but which failed in terms of collective action.

Acknowledgement The editors would like to thank Robert Parkin for his assistance in editing this chapter.

References

Bankoff, G. (2007). The historical geography of disaster: 'Vulnerability' and 'local knowledge'. In G. Bankoff, G. Frerks, & D. Hilhorst (Eds.), *Mapping vulnerability* (pp. 25–36). London: Earthscan.

Barth, S. (1998). Soziale Netzwerke und soziale Unterstützung. http://www.stephan-barth.de/Homepage-Aufsaetze/Soziale%20Unterstuetzung.pdf. Accessed 27 May 2011.

Bhandari, R. B., Knottnerus, J. D., & Okada, N. (2011). Urban ritual events and coping with disaster risk: A case study of Lalitpur, Nepal. *Journal of Applied Social Science, 5*(2), 13–32.

Bowen, J. R. (1986). On the political construction of tradition: Gotong-royong in Indonesia. *Journal of Asian Studies, 45*(3). 545–561.

Christensen, A. D., & Larsen, J. E. (2008). Gender, class, and family: Men and gender equality in a Danish context. *Social Politics – International Studies in Gender State and Society, 15*(1), 1–26.

Delica-Willison, Z., & Gaillard, J. C. (2012). Community action and disaster. In B. Wisner, J. C. Gaillard, & I. Kelman (Eds.), *Handbook of hazards and disaster risk reduction* (pp. 711–722). London: Routledge.

Frailing, K. (2007). The myth of a disaster myth: Potential looting should be part of disaster plans. *Natural Hazards Observer, 16*(4), 3–4.

Gordon, R. (2009). Community impact of disaster and community recovery. http://www.psychology.org.au/inpsych/community_impact/. Accessed 27 Feb 2013.

Grootaert, C., Narayan, D., Nyhan, J. V., & Woolcock, M. (2004). *Measuring social capital. An integrated questionnaire*. Washington, D.C.: The World Bank.

Hamengku Buwono X. (2008). Learning from the 27 May 2006 earthquake. In D. Karnawati (Ed.), *The Yogyakarta earthquake of May 27, 2006* (pp. xi–xviii). Belmont: Star Publishing Company.

Hermanns, H., & Hermanns-Konopka, A. (2010). *Dialogical self theory: Positioning and counter-positioning in a globalizing society*. Cambridge: Cambridge University Press.

Hobfoll, S. E. (1986). *Stress, social support, and women*. Washington, D.C.: Hemisphere.

Kagan, C., Burton, M., Duckett, P., Lawthom, R., & Siddiquee, A. (2011). *Critical community psychology*. West Sussex: Blackwell.

Kaniasty, K., & Norris, F. H. (1993). A test of the support deterioration model in the context of natural disaster. *Journal of Personality and Social Psychology, 64*(3), 395–408.

Lyons, R. F., Mickelson, K. D., Sullivan, M. J., & Coyne, J. C. (1998). Coping as a communal process. *Journal of Social and Personal Relationships, 15*(5), 579–605.

Manfield, P. (2007). Java Earthquake 2006/7: Part I: Early recovery. Jakarta: UN Humanitarian Coordinator/Resident Coordinator's Office. http://www.humanitarianreform.org/humanitarianreform/Portals/1/cluster%20approach%20page/Evaluation/Evaluation%20for%20Early%20Recovery%20in%20Java%20v5.pdf. Accessed 27 Aug 2008.

McMillan, D. W., & Chavis, D. M. (1986). Sense of community: A definition and theory. *Journal of Community Psychology, 14*(1), 6–23.

Oliver-Smith, A. (1999a). The brotherhood of pain: Theoretical and applied perspectives on post-disaster solidarity. In A. Oliver-Smith, & S. M. Hoffman (Eds.), *The angry earth* (pp. 156–172). New York: Routledge.
Oliver-Smith, A. (1999b). Peru's five hundred year earthquake: Vulnerability in historical perspective. In A. Oliver-Smith, & S. M. Hoffman (Eds.), *The angry earth* (pp. 74–88). New York: Routledge.
Ophiyandri, T., Amaratunga, D., & Pathirage, C. (2010). Community based post disaster housing reconstruction: Indonesian perspective. http://usir.salford.ac.uk/9761/1/536.pdf. Accessed 05 Oct 2011.
Prainsack, B., & Buyx, A. (2012). Understanding solidarity (with a little help from your friends). Response to Dawson and Verweij. *Public Health Ethics, 5*(2), 206–210.
Schlehe, J. (2006). Nach dem Erdbeben auf Java: Kulturelle Polarisierungen, soziale Solidarität und Abgrenzung. *Internationales Asienforum, 37*(3–4), 213–237.
Schwarzer, R., & Knoll, N. (2007). Functional roles of social support within the stress and coping process: A theoretical and empirical overview. *International Journal of Psychology, 42*(4), 243–252.
The Government of Yogyakarta Special Province (2008). Reconstruction based on local wisdom (*saiyeg saeko kapti*). In D. Karnawati (Ed.), *The Yogyakarta earthquake of May 27, 2006* (pp. 25.1–25.8). Belmont: Star Publishing Company.
Wright, K. M., Ursano, R. J., Bartone, P. T., & Ingraham, L. H. (1990). The shared experience of catastrophe: An expanded classification of the disaster community. *American Journal of Orthopsychiatry, 60*(1), 35–42.

Chapter 11
The Life Conduct Dimension of Coping: Local Wisdom Discourses and Related Life Orientations

Silke Schwarz

In mainstream psychology, individual differences between personality types are considered central to different coping trajectories. Carver and Connor-Smith (2010), for example, stress the relevance of the personality traits known as the Big Five. Their work and that of many others demonstrates the dominance of biological and goal-based views of human nature. Generally speaking, coping theorists highlight person-centered constructs such as self-efficacy expectations, optimism, a person's sense of mastery, and hardiness (Hobfoll 2002). We do not challenge the existence of such individual differences in coping styles, but we do advocate abandoning the much vaunted binary opposition between person and context, with its individualizing biases.

Instead, we assume a mutual constitution and blending of sociocultural, ecological, and personal features. Unlike many mainstream psychological approaches, we do not look for causal or correlational relationships between *external* sociocultural and *internal* psychological variables. Following Markus and Hamedani (2007), we assume not only that contexts shape forms of psychological processes but also that people actively engage with multiple contexts at the same time. In this way, a dynamic mutual constitution of sociocultural and psychological features becomes crucial. In this chapter, we aim to understand the referential connections within a web of meaning that is produced by this mutual constitution and embedded in a symbolically mediated praxis (Straub and Thomas 2003; Markus and Hamedani 2007). We follow Ortner's (2006) position that culture—or more generally speaking, contexts—constructs people and their respective agency. At the same time, she argues that people transform and reproduce culture or contexts through their variable practices in everyday life. This transforming and at the same time stabilizing character of culture and context is central. Ortner (2006) refers to Giddens (1979),

S. Schwarz (✉)
International Academy for Innovative Pedagogy, Psychology and Economics gGmbH
at Freie Universität Berlin, Malteserstr. 74-100, 12249 Berlin, Germany
e-mail: silke.schwarz@fu-berlin.de; silgnschwarz@yahoo.de

M. Zaumseil et al. (eds.), *Cultural Psychology of Coping with Disasters*,
DOI 10.1007/978-1-4614-9354-9_11,

who sees actors as partially knowing subjects with, according to her, a consciousness that is "always ambiguously part of people's personal subjectivities and part of the public culture" (Ortner 2006, p. 111). Accordingly, local wisdom discourses, which will be introduced in Sect. 11.1, are understood as orienting frameworks rather than as structural determinants of people's agency. Local wisdoms provide advice on the directions that humanity should be developing and striving toward and on how to live one's life accordingly to normative expectations, both in one's daily life and in times of crisis. People's agency is (un)consciously structured by these local wisdom discourses and strongly influenced by socioculturally specific principles of life conduct. Simultaneously, the way people embody and enact these codes of conduct in everyday life can be very diverse—sometimes confirming and sometimes completely renegotiating them.

We understand personalized and practiced codes of conduct as fundamental pragmatics of life, that is, as context-specific resources. These resources are used for individual, familial, and communal functioning in daily lives, as well as for overcoming stressful events such as an earthquake. However, what happens if one cannot or does not want to adhere to highly valued sociocultural ideals? Certainly, normative pressures to conform to socioculturally valued ideals can be at work, underlining possible disadvantages of "resources."

In brief, this chapter deals with the following questions: What are the locally specific fundamental pragmatics of life (Baltes and Kunzmann 2004) after a disaster; that is how do socioculturally informed life orientations, beliefs, positions, values, attitudes, competencies, and abilities affect the way people handle an adverse situation? This leads to more detailed questions such as: How do socioculturally distinctive features contribute to the process of meaning-making? What is the relationship between accommodative and assimilative action orientations in this socioculturally specific context when coping with disaster? What are the possible disadvantages of these codes of conduct? Overall, this chapter aims to capture the mechanisms and trajectories of these processes, focusing on valued and practiced codes of conduct in times of crisis. The chapter starts with a presentation of local wisdom discourses. An overview is provided of socioculturally specific and valued developmental trajectories, socioculturally adequate understandings of assimilative and accommodative processes, the range of life conduct orientations, and relevant strategies for fostering these codes of conduct. The functions of these principles of life conduct for disaster coping are also reported.

11.1 Local Wisdom Discourses as Orienting Frameworks

Our understanding of individuals as sociocultural beings calls for ways of understanding how sociocultural features intermingle with personalized codes of conduct. As stated above, the concept of "local wisdom" (*kearifan local*) is appropriate for this purpose. Instead of Baltes and Kunzmann's (2004) universal understanding of wisdom as "a body of expert knowledge about the meaning and conduct of life" (p. 294), we highlight sociocultural particularities and related practices.

What is central is not a focus on the form and content of knowledge itself, but rather the notion that wisdom serves the fundamental pragmatics of life, that is, "knowledge and judgment about the meaning and conduct of life and the orchestration of human development towards excellence while attending conjointly to personal and collective well-being" (Baltes and Staudinger 2000, p. 122). Overall, the concept of wisdom used in this chapter encompasses several features and functions. Local wisdom translates into local knowledge (see Chaps. 1–3) that is historically grown, collectively shared, and partly unconscious, similar to Bourdieu's (2002) concept of habitus. In this understanding, local wisdom produces practice and is itself formed by social practices. Local wisdom is also embodied. Related discourses convey information about valued human characteristics, virtues, stances, gestures, emotional socialization, and observable behavior or what we call principles of life conduct. These principles are evident in accepted manners of, for example, resolving conflicts and regulating one's own and others' actions, thoughts, and emotions. Local wisdom discourses serve as an orienting framework, providing valued developmental goals and legitimizing certain behaviors in specific contexts. These principles of life conduct and associated ideals and practices are continuously being reworked in social interactions and through sociocultural activities such as *wayang kulit*, the Javanese shadow puppet play (Keeler 1987). Similar to Ortner's (2006) understanding of culture, we assume the existence of ongoing negotiation processes (alongside certain stabilities in form of power structures) in the sense of "doing local wisdoms".[1]

Furthermore, local wisdom discourses convey moments of sociocultural pride and confidence by imparting positive images of one's own social reference group. It is the active, positive reframing of local pride and reworking of "Javanese" identity discourses that encourages collective self-confidence and fosters or maintains collective agency. Local wisdom stands for an expressible awareness of one's sociocultural background in comparison to others while valuing one's own reference group usually more highly than others.

In our case study, the term "local" was usually understood in geographical terms and referred to Southeast Asia in general, to Indonesia, to the island of Java, to the regency of Bantul, or merely to a village. For example, the Regent of Bantul (Pak Bupati) compared Aceh's tsunami recovery process to the recovery after the Bantulnese earthquake. The Bantul case was declared as a great deal more efficient and successful due to Bantul's specific sociocultural capital. A code of conduct expressing solidarity was emphasized, while the civil war history of Aceh and its influence on reconstruction efforts was entirely ignored.

From a critical perspective, local wisdom discourses can be analyzed for the way they serve to restore or undermine the status quo. These discourses were often (but not exclusively) used by the elite and in public arenas after the Bantul earthquake.

[1] This is similar to Hörning and Reuters' (2004) understanding of culture in the sense of "doing culture" or "culture as praxis". See also the concept of "doing difference" in West and Fenstermaker (1995).

For example, huge posters with brief folk wisdom phrases and slogans were hung up in the streets:

> Help will not arrive for ever
> Now it is time to work
> If you give up, it gets worse
> If you wait, you will not improve (Sairin and Marah 2008, p. 124)

In 2007, the National Technical Team published a book titled *Living in Disaster-prone Area Relying on Local Wisdom.* In this book, government responsibilities for reconstruction were partly shifted on to communities by referring to "Javanese" virtues of self-reliance and solidarity. The resulting additional burdens for disaster-stricken communities were neither criticized nor openly discussed. Instead, positive reframings were common:

> This redevelopment period had run so well due to the people's strong resolve, hard work, perseverance, and their spirit of *gotong royong* (working together). (National Technical Team 2007, p. 147)

Conversely, local wisdom discourses can be used ironically as a subversive strategy. They are not consistent, and like any discourse, they encompass contrasting features that can be strategically deployed, as in the context of corruption:

> Some of the money went into the pockets of those in charge. What puzzled me was that the reason they gave for cutting the aid was local wisdom (*kearifan lokal*). (Mas Zaki, Sido Kabul)

11.2 Developmental Trajectories

Local wisdoms provide advice on the directions that humanity should be developing and striving toward and on how to live one's life accordingly to normative expectations, both in one's daily life and in times of crisis. These socioculturally informed and individually lived distinctive features have an impact on coping trajectories.[2]

Earthquake-affected villagers described an urge to restore normality as soon as possible (often justified by an obligation of good role fulfillment) and aimed for progress (with references to an ideal of lifelong refinement). Two necessary steps were highlighted: (1) know your rightful place in the worldly and cosmic order (therefore, introspection is needed, which is related to the code of conduct of awareness; see following text) and (2) fulfill your role the best you can, that is, refine yourself in fulfilling your role. This maxim translates into a principle of personal responsibility. Being responsible for oneself originates in the idea that one has a predestined place

[2] From a long-term or developmental psychology perspective, these dynamics and the constant doing of local wisdom become visible in people's life course. In general, development can be understood as a stepwise upward trend, moving from one stage to the next, more refined one (for example, similar to Colby and Kohlberg's 1986 and Piaget's 1969 phase model of development). Lately, development trajectories have been understood in a more neutral sense, as capturing both progressive and regressive changes as well as stabilities (see Norris et al. 2008).

in the world, a personal fate (*takdir, nasib*), and that one should do one's best to fulfill this role. Fulfilling one's role or fate and attempting to improve oneself in one's role fulfillment is associated with being socially accepted and maintaining a positive self-image. Some villagers also considered this a form of religious service (*ibadah*).

In a disaster, this maxim seems to ensure and foster agency due to its motivating effects. Furthermore, it seems to counteract or even prevent negative emotions such as feeling distressed, because fulfilling one's role can have a distracting effect. For example, focusing on income-generating activities was often described as helpful in order not to dwell on things and not to deepen one's sadness, but instead to focus one's attention and efforts in another direction. Another example is the importance of parental obligations: many villagers emphasized that children can be a motivational force in the reconstruction process.[3] Conversely, not being able to fulfill one's duties (for example, because of earthquake-induced physical injuries) can be experienced as extremely burdening. Felt discrepancies between a current condition ("Is-state") and personally desired and socioculturally valued alternative conditions ("Should-be-states") can result in one experiencing challenges as stress (see Leipold and Greve 2009).

Fundamentally, coping with current challenges is influenced by prior developmental successes, that is, by the extent to which individuals have gained competencies and come to embody and practice valued codes of conduct. Moreover, the potential for further development is influenced by how effectively a person manages current strains (see Leipold and Greve 2009). Besides these biographical contexts, developmental trajectories appear to depend on what has to be coped with: whether one has lost loved ones, whether one has to deal with a disability resulting from an injury (or injuries), or whether resource losses are exacerbated because of social conflicts over distribution processes—all these make a difference to coping and developmental processes (see Part III Multidimensional Coping Framework).

The majority of interviewees reported experiencing rather constant developmental processes supported or enhanced by the earthquake experience. For example, many stated having been patient and modest ever since. However, because of the earthquake experience and the consequent scarcity of goods in the aftermath of the disaster, they learned to become even more modest and more patient.[4]

[3] The ascription or assumption of the "appropriate" role is socioculturally mediated by dimensions of difference (or power) such as gender, age, socioeconomic status, etc. (see the concept of "doing difference" in West and Fenstermaker 1995). For instance, women in our case study especially referred to the well-being of their children and to the importance of economic rehabilitation, while men rather highlighted housing and safety issues.

[4] This generally positive trend in our data may be due to our sampling strategy. A bias may be produced by the fact that participating in our research was voluntary. Moreover, the social situation of the interview may have hindered villagers from expressing the burdensome aspects of their lives as lamenting and complaining is frowned upon in "Javanese" culture. Even though criticism was still possible in the interviews, it was often indicated in more subtle and indirect ways (see Chap. 14).

Some disaster survivors reported having experienced skewed developmental life courses. They encountered several difficulties during the coping process in the first instance and only later had a sense that some kind of progress was being made.

Bu Suprapti, a 31-year-old mother from Sido Kabul with a precarious economic background when compared with the rest of her hamlet, lost her 10-year-old daughter to the earthquake. For months, she described lacking motivation (*putus semangat*). She just did what was necessary, that is, caring for her other three children, who survived the disaster. Her feeling of being obliged to fulfill the "role of a good mother" seemed to help her remain capable of acting, at least minimally. During this time, she explained, she had not yet been sincere and not accepting of these events and her losses "from the inside" (*batin*).

Indicators that she was struggling included her lack of motivation to complete practical tasks (such as cleaning up and rebuilding like the others), frequent bouts of crying, protesting against God, and comparisons with more "fortunate" others that were of little benefit to her. She asked why it was her daughter and not herself who was taken by the earthquake. She asked why it was her family, not others, who had to deal with the loss of a child, as her family had always been economically worse off compared with her neighbors. She distanced herself from God, not praying anymore and even being angry (*marah*) with him. Constant conversations with her husband were described as consoling. As a religious person, her husband was able to reconcile her with Islam again and solace her by relativizing the here and now with the afterlife and by instilling the hope that she will meet her daughter again in the afterlife.

At the time of the disaster, Bu Suprapti was pregnant and her feeling of being responsible for her unborn child as well as her obligation to fulfill her role as a mother well motivated her to regain a sense of agency. Gradually, she asked God for forgiveness and pleaded to be reconciled with him, while also trying to focus on the present and to come to terms with her past. This triggered a search for meaningfulness (*hikmah*): Was the newborn child a replacement for her deceased daughter? Is this child possibly even better than the deceased one? She gradually adopted a humble position, accepting the finiteness of human life, limitations in humans' control over the span of human life, and that death is in God's hands. This acceptance helped her also to feel that she had become more sincere. Her reflections ended with a positive conclusion, acknowledging personal refinements as her personal benefits of the earthquake experience and as "meanings made" derived from this "bitter test" (*cobaan pahit*). She described herself as having become more modest, more religious, more aware (by practicing introspection instead of being arrogant), more loving to her children, and reported having more inner peace (instead of strong emotions such as anger):

> The meaning (*hikmah*) for me, I just love my children more, and I'm much... more, well, yeah, in my opinion, the deeper meaning (*hikmah*) is that I'm better than before.[...] I've realized (*sadar*) it just recently, Mbak! Back then I didn't, I just followed my emotions! I was mad, cursing, like that. I didn't understand the reason behind it (*bakalan belakangnya*). In sum, now I just focus on my efforts in sending my children to school, and to be able to recite the Koran.

Narratives of these disrupted life's trajectories were more common when one needed to cope with the loss of a loved one or with long-lasting bodily impairments (one's own or others), and when trust and hope in a higher power and one's own or one's community's capabilities were reported to have been temporarily reduced or shattered. Sometimes, enduring deteriorations were depicted as relating to changes in inner peace (see Chap. 13 for an example).

Still more interviewees, especially adolescents, presented the earthquake event as a turning point in reevaluating their previous life journey and as a chance for improvement.[5] Some disaster survivors also described experiencing no developments. In such cases, the stable existence of valued ideals was implied: for instance, solidarity was often presented as an everlasting practice and value. Constructions of stability may give these codes of conduct a greater sense of legitimacy.

11.3 The Triad of Understanding, Positive Reframings, and Finding Benefits

In most cases, the experience of the earthquake as well as its narration during the interview situation itself triggered villagers to reevaluate themselves or their circumstances. This dynamic process can be subdivided analytically into a number of phases that overlap: an initial understanding of what is happening and why, followed by retrospective identification processes of personal and collective meanings and benefits.

In the disaster situation itself, people are abruptly taken out of their normal existences. They need to adapt to the new situation in order to survive initially and, eventually, to thrive. Acute reactions to the extreme event, such as disorientation and bewilderment (what will happen next?), despair (why is no one helping?), sorrow, fear, and financial worries, were described as temporary in nature. A phase of overwhelming emotion can merge into an active quest to understand *what* is happening and *why*. Making things comprehensible and arriving at an overview was described to be crucial in our case study. In general, people used different sources of information to increasingly make the unexpected and thus also incomprehensible make sense. Villagers reported using the following sources for assessments of their current situation in the immediate emergency: observations, previous experiences (for example, eruptions of Mt. Merapi), stories from elderly people, third-person accounts, and the mass media. Socially informed assessments or appraisals of current circumstances were also important, as the reactions and emotions of other people served as cues to the level of destruction.

Initial assessments, such as becoming increasingly aware of the scale and extent of the destruction, convey information about the *need* to act and the *possibility* to

[5] However, these developments must not necessarily be consistent with socioculturally valued ideals or local wisdoms and may lead to exclusionary processes in a community. This was the case with an Islamic family in Sido Kabul who was perceived as becoming too "fanatical" (*fanatik*) within his village because he prioritized religious rules over harmonious community life (see Chap. 12).

do so, thus allowing crisis management such as rescuing others and organizing the medical care and transport required. After learning how extensive the earthquake-affected area was, a spontaneous feeling of solidarity was usually described to have emerged (see also Chap. 10). Furthermore, having an overview of what has happened can have a calming effect when this provides information about the safety of loved ones (for example, after being separated in the turmoil and panic of the earthquake and the subsequent tsunami rumors) and any subsequent risks. Conversely, having an overview can also have a troubling effect, as one is now aware of the extent of the destruction, human suffering, and financial and material loss :

> When I got to the streets, I saw the condition of the people, you know, *Masya Allah*[6]... I saw those people, I was crying, Oh my God... I thought it was only me who got the disaster. But it struck so many people. (Pak Ratman, Sido Kabul)

Our data tell us how people (re)evaluated their experiences several years after the incident. One crucial and probably universal feature of these quests for meaning is translating the earthquake experience into a chance for developmental progress and enhancement, an opportunity to refine one's code of conduct (see later). Socioculturally specific codes of conduct nurtured the tendency to make positive reframings of adverse experiences. Both transcendental and socioculturally discursive frames mediated these processes. Beliefs such as the existence of fate (*takdir, nasib*), the almightiness of God or a higher power, the existence of an afterlife (and *karma*), humans' limited ability to understand, deeper, initially hidden meanings (*hikmah*) that need to be found by human introspection and other practices, and about suffering as an integral part of life (the metaphor of the *Wheel of Life*) were all broadly shared frames that fostered a positive transformation of initially negative experiences. They helped those affected regain hope and trust, providing resources to encourage optimistic and trustworthy outlooks on the future.

> Life is *cokro manggilingan* (life should continually roll on from time to time in search of perfection), as the cycle of life that must be experienced by human being. Sadness and happiness is a must-experience part of the circle of life. Forget bitter memories, and revive soon to improve yourself. (The Government of Yogyakarta Special Province 2008, p. 25.1)

The content and quality of "meanings made" indicate the degree and success of one's coping efforts, as well as changes in developmental pathways. Positive meanings were described as being associated with calming effects, counteracting negative emotions, and fostering acceptance, all of which indicated that benefits had been found and that positive developmental trajectories had occurred. Meaning outcomes can also be neutral (that is, no personally relevant meaning is found) or have negative associations:

> For me, I felt that (2 sec.), basically, I felt really destroyed by the earthquake. So I don't feel that the earthquake provided a good meaning to me. (Mas Bambang, Sido Kabul)

For the most part, negative connotations were said to have endured only temporarily. In retrospect, interviewees generally reported having become more aware of their

---

6 An Arabic expression of surprise.

own capacities and local wisdoms.[7] The reported benefits relate to all four dimensions. Material benefits encompassed an increased awareness of the relativity of the material world, that is, material wealth is less important than survival, social moralities, and religious values, and material possessions can easily be lost. Additionally, an improvement in the village infrastructure and in family finances and the increased socioeconomic status of certain villagers were highlighted. Verbalized benefits relating to social features included an increased awareness of the equality of all humans, as everyone will have to die sooner or later; moreover, rich and poor villagers alike were affected by the disaster. Also reported were the broadening and diversification of social networks, as well as shifts in power structures and fairer gender relations (due to gender mainstreaming programs). An increased awareness of social moralities was emphasized; this included the need to help others in their shared misery and an increased appreciation of familial and social relationships. Furthermore, the need to maintain social harmony (*rukun*) and to avoid social conflict (that is, not to be annoyed and angry and not to bear grudges in cases of conflict) was highlighted. With regard to the principles of life conduct, increased awareness and practice of valued codes of conduct were addressed. Last but not least, gaining skills and competencies concerning aid distribution, reconstruction, and emergency management of earthquakes were declared by several villagers to be a useful benefit.[8]

11.4 Principles of Life Conduct

Principles of life conduct are associated with action orientations between accommodative and assimilative dynamics in the course of coping. Instead of referring to related culture-bound Western ideas, this section describes sociocultural distinctive features in these coping dynamics.

11.4.1 Balancing Accommodative and Assimilative Processes

In our case study, the maintenance of equilibrium and refinement in general seem to be more relevant for many villagers than reaching personal goals and exerting personal control.[9] This relates to socioculturally specific understandings of the outer

[7] There appears to be a universal human tendency to reevaluate the past as having positive outcomes and to formulate lessons learned, while the content seems socioculturally specific. Whether these benefits are only cognitively represented and verbalized or whether they are also practiced cannot be answered here. This is due to our methodological approach, which highlights verbal expressions instead of behavioral observations.

[8] For transcendental benefits, see Chap. 12.

[9] In Western coping theory, assimilative coping has been distinguished from accommodative coping; the former is characterized by persistently adhering to goals, whereas the latter depicts self-regulatory aspects, that is, not further pursuing or devaluing blocked goals (Brandstädter 2011). Self-regulation is usually understood as an effort on the part of the human self to alter any inner states

(*lahir*) and inner (*batin*) self which differ from "Western" ideas of the inner and outer, of private and public. *Batin* refers to the inner dynamics, to subjectivity and to feelings and thoughts that are considered capable of being kept secret from others or which others may not directly grasp. In contrast, *lahir* refers to the outside world, that is, to the outer appearance and to observable behaviors, speech acts, gestures, and the expression of emotions. The inner is seen in correspondence to a higher power, to the cosmos, and to one's social and physical surroundings. In extreme situations, an imbalance can occur that one is then motivated to change in order to restore an equilibrium and to enhance refinement ultimately. The ideal state of *lahir* and *batin* is balanced or refined. In extreme situations, an imbalance can occur that one is then motivated to change.

Inwardly directed actions help to regain and maintain an inner balance through a form of inner management, that is, controlling one's thinking and emotions (*menata hati*).[10] They can also serve the purpose of bringing oneself more into alignment with transcendental goals and sociocultural morals, such as being more in harmony with the cosmos. An inner balance and refined state foster agency and allow one to act reasonably instead of in a panic. Trust becomes important for being able to accept something rather negative and remain capable of acting. Trust may refer to trust in God, trust in other people, or simply trust in good luck. Trust and acceptance are associated with feelings of being responsible for fulfilling one's life path and destiny. Only if the situation is experienced as incapable of being influenced by human beings, as was the case in the immediate emergency situation when the unsettling tsunami rumor circulated, did villagers describe a position of immediate acceptance without any outwardly directed attempts to act.[11]

Examples of outwardly directed, that is, observable actions that manipulate the outside environment, were improvised survival strategies such as attempting to rescue others, free oneself or others from the rubble, organize medical treatment, food, instruments, and tents, clean up, resume income-generating activities, search for social support and rebuild the destroyed village communities, as well as trying to influence the benevolence of a higher power by prayers.

This basic distinction between *lahir* and *batin* allows for actions that aim to influence both the inner *and* the outer realms[12] and thus fosters an (un)conscious process

---

or responses (Vohs and Baumeister 2004). Accommodative coping corresponds to secondary control (Heckhausen 2002) and emotion-focused coping (Lazaraus and Folkman 1984). Assimilative coping is similar to primary control and to problem-focused coping and is associated with conscious intentions to act. Although often denied, the primacy of primary control or problem-focused coping over secondary control or emotion-focused coping is implied in many research reports (see Leipold and Greve 2009).

[10] Here, the inner is not to be understood as an individualistic subjectivity separated from its context, but rather as permeated by sociocultural features.

[11] The term *immediate acceptance* may invoke images of passivity, control loss, or fatalism. However, interviewees did not seem to apply such categories to themselves. Immediate acceptance was often combined with turning to God, which can be interpreted as exerting control and influence in the transcendental realm.

[12] The distinction between inwardly and outwardly directed action is analytical in nature. In daily practice, these processes are intermingled.

of balancing between inwardly and outwardly directed agency. The distinction of both realms enables a person to stay positive from the *batin* and psychologically healthy when one has limitations or weaknesses related to the *lahir* (for example, the inner acceptance of an inevitable approaching death, instead of panicking in the face of a tsunami). In general, neither is a mere benefit nor a sole hindrance to successfully coping with psychological strain. The dynamic interplay of both (that is, the flexibility of agency) seems more important. In sum, habitualized consideration of inwardly and outwardly directed agency results in acting in accordance with sensed capabilities.

The consideration of inwardly and outwardly directed agency is done against the background of partly unconscious and partly also conscious cost–benefit calculations, whereas having to deal with such costs can still be rather strenuous. For example, Bu Suprapti from Sido Kabul described the following situation as a "difficult dilemma" (*buah si malakama*), because each alternative came with costs. One of her four children was buried by debris during the earthquake. She wanted to stay near the house, waiting for her child to be freed from the debris and checking on her well-being. This would have meant endangering her remaining three children, as a tsunami was expected. She decided on a rather "assimilating" alternative, that is, to rescue herself and her children instead of staying and applying inwardly directed calming strategies. She explained that she would have felt sorry if her buried daughter emerged from the rubble dead and her other children had been swept away by the tsunami as well.

Habitualized evaluations of whether current experiences and actions fulfill socioculturally and personally relevant needs may result in a nagging sense that something is not right, thus motivating people to change the situation or themselves (see Joseph and Linley 2005). The balancing between inwardly and outwardly directed agency is embedded in sociocultural maxims (such as "strive for the best in even adverse situations" and the ideal of lifelong refinement as this is socially and morally obligatory and being rewarded by God) as well as reflecting certain life philosophies (such as the idea of *karma* and personal fate). The quotation below illustrates this merging of oneself with the outside world, the cosmos, and others.

> The most important thing is to pursue a good goal. Good deeds will be answered positively. And bad deeds will have bad effects. Like killing a person, even though the killer can escape today, but later, he or she will suffer the consequences of the deeds. [...] That's the belief. (Pak Kartono, Sido Kabul)

11.4.2 Overview of Codes of Conduct

The principles of life conduct presented below connect means to end, as they shape enacted coping strategies. If a person is humble, modest, and grateful, for instance, it seems more likely that she or he will find meaning and benefits. Furthermore, the enactment of these codes of conduct can be understood as providing information about the success of coping attempts. However, not all principles are themselves beneficial for the process of coping. For example, a greater awareness about personal wrongdoings in the past may have troubling effects. This insight, however, can be counteracted by striving for enhancement and refinement. In general, these principles express socioculturally valued human development goals. As a result, they also pose an end in themselves, and striving for and enacting these codes of conduct can be understood as an active endeavor to influence the course of one's life. Table 11.1 gives an overview of these principles, which are closely interwoven, as the following quote illustrates:

> Anyway, I faced [the troubles, that is caring for my injured mother] by being grateful (*syukur*) that I was still given a chance to stay alive. I faced everything in a relaxed (*santai*) way. (Mbak Ratmini, Sido Kabul)

The enactment of these codes of conduct can serve several functions. First, being able to enact these virtues contributes to the development of positive images about the self, the family, and the community, as it indicates being on the right track in one's conduct of life. For example, striving for self-reliance was presented as crucial. Resuming income-generating activities signaled diligence in role fulfillment and was contrasted with morally and normatively condemnatory discourses of laziness (*malas*). Resuming work can be regarded as an indicator that one is successfully coping, as it demonstrates good functioning in the occupational area of life. It also supports the coping process itself, as focusing on work can have a distracting effect and provides one with urgently needed income.

Second, the enactment of these principles allows and restores repose instead of distress. Being relaxed, that is, having an inner balance, repose, or inner peace, circumscribes an ideal developmental goal that humans should strive for. Even in adverse situations, that is, when outer realms (*lahir*) are not peaceful—for example, when there are environmental threats—one should strive for inner peace. Accepting something adverse can restore an inner balance. For example, during enduring adverse situations such as aftershocks, many villagers described practicing patience and acceptance. Sincerely accepting something adverse that cannot be changed, however, can take some time and be a rather exhausting journey for those affected, whereas toughness fosters or enables this sincere acceptance (compare case description of Bu Suprapti given previously).

Last but not least, these principles enable individual, familial, and communal functioning. The (un)conscious consideration of and balancing between inwardly and outwardly directed agency allows one to balance accommodative and assimilative processes adequately. Especially in enduring adverse situations, a mixture of acceptance, patience, and toughness can help one remain optimistic and capable of acting. In the following quotation, practicing patience is seen as allowing one to bounce back instead of giving up. Bu Nurdin described searching for medical treatment for her mortally injured child:

> Did they lack medical personnel? Or was it because it took time for the doctors to treat the patients? [. . .] What could I do then? I was trying to ask the nurses. [. . .] So I had to wait until the next day. [. . .] I was trying (*berusaha*), and I had to be patient (*sabar*). (Bu Nurdin, Sido Kabul)

Table 11.1 Overview of Codes of Conduct

Toughness	The capability to face something adverse in an active manner instead of giving up, or succumbing to passivity and hopelessness. Similar to being hardy, resilient, and even obstinate. Described sources of experiencing toughness were faith, social support, and embeddedness in the community, and local discourses of pride
Awareness	An increased level of awareness (*kesadaran*) about socioculturally informed and personally relevant developmental goals, that is, having recourse to local wisdoms. The process of detecting a deeper, that is, hidden meaning behind events. Process is supported by experiencing human limitations during the earthquake and dependence on others in the aftermath of the disaster. Awareness is also enhanced by being reminded of the finiteness of life and through the idea of the afterlife and related merit systems
Acceptance	The acceptance of (past, present, or future) conditions and events that are experienced as uncontrollable and inevitable or regarded as a matter of personal fate (*nasib*, *takdir*). It is a point of local wisdom that fate is not to be fought against but needs to be accepted (was expressed with: *pasrah*, *nrimo*, *sudalah*), otherwise several dysfunctions may result
Sincerity	Sincerely (*ikhlas*), that is, authentically accepting something adverse, in contrast to an artificial acceptance only displayed on the outside (*lahir*). Sincerity is often located in the heart (*hati*), an organ attributed with several symbolic functions. Sincerity also describes the quality of social interactions, for example, when helping others or working together
Self-reliance[a]	The position that a person ought to be self-reliant in his or her conduct of life or role fulfillment instead of depending on something or someone else: "do not wait for help and do not depend on others, but help yourself." Reported preconditions for being able to strive for self-reliance included a certain psychological well-being or toughness, embeddedness in the community, and a relative lack of alternative resources or trustworthy sources of aid. Meanings made influenced striving for self-reliance as the quotation by Pak Siswanto from Sido Kabul shows: "It was a trial (*cobaan*). If we just waited, development would be stopped. It was destiny (*takdir*). Rebuilding was our fate"
Patience and serenity	Practicing patience (*sabar*) and serenity or equanimity (*santai*) translates into conducting oneself carefully and with awareness, as well as doing something persistent instead of doing something hectically and instead of being worried or troubled. These stances are used instead of being worried or troubled. Being able to practice patience and serenity in an adverse situation, such as enduring aftershocks, can be understood as an indicator of a strong mental state or as an absence of "trauma" (see Chap. 13). Reported sources were trust in God, in oneself, and in others; it was fostered when a person can understand *what* is happening and *why* it is happening
Gratitude	Becoming and being grateful (*bersyukur*) describes a generally positive stance toward life, fostering benefit-finding processes. Being grateful can also be seen as the emotion that results after finding positive features in rather negative experiences. Villagers described being grateful for, for example, being spared injury or death, the survival of others, the aid they received, and for rather unspecific things such as the beauty in life: "But Alhamdulillah [Arabic for expressing gratefulness], I am still given a long life until now to witness the beauty of this world" (Mbak Prapti, Sido Kabul)

Table 11.1 (continued)

Humility, modesty, and generosity	Modesty (implying the reception of material resources) and generosity (implying the provision of material resources) both entailed a voluntary foregoing of resources, mostly when one's own reference group had sufficient resources. Both are rewarded by God, besides being socially reinforced as alternatives to being greedy or egoistic. And yet, humility can develop when no resources are available. The socioculturally specific stance of humility, or what interviewees called *prihatin*, is related to belief in the almightiness of God, the limitations of human capabilities, and that suffering constitutes an integral part of human life
Understanding and compassion[b]	This orientation touches upon two features. First, it can translate into a stance of not being reproachful, accusatory, or depreciatory. Related discourses have normative and regulatory effects. They are mainly legitimized by means of the ideal of conflict avoidance, with references to God or social morals. In other words, being understanding and empathetic supports harmonious relationships. Interviewees reported that social conflicts were associated with inner imbalances that are to be avoided. Secondly, it describes a state that contrasts with indifference. In this understanding, it fosters providing social support for others who are evaluated as needy
Solidarity	Solidarity can refer to relationships with formerly unknown people, with neighbors or the wider community, as well as to familial relationships, although the latter were distinctively characterized by loving or close relationships. It contrasts with being egoistic, greedy, unsupportive, angry, harsh, etc.
Politeness and respect	Politeness and respect ensure and maintain harmonious relationships. This refers to observable behaviors and speech acts, that is, to the *lahir*. It can function as an indicator of knowingly acting in accordance with social norms and hierarchies. The separation of *lahir* and *batin* allows for social harmony to be maintained by respectful observable behavior, even when one experiences dislike of another person from the inside. If one is not being "polite and respectful" of others, it threatens the ideal of harmony and might lead to social sanctions extending to exclusionary practices (see Chap. 14). Solidarity, politeness, and respect can be legitimized by religious norms about how to be a good human being as well as by social norms

[a] We understand the self not just as an isolated individual but as a contextualized part of the family, the neighborhood, and the community as well

[b] The stances described above mostly convey information about ideal social interactions implicitly. The last three categories convey information rather explicitly about how to be a good member of society and the family

11.4.2.1 Strategies Fostering Code of Conduct Orientations

Villagers described several strategies that foster the codes of conduct after experiencing adversity.

The active search for finding benefits instead of pondering and dwelling on the negative along with processes of reframing is fostered by different *types of beneficial comparisons*. Inter-comparisons can be made with imagined or real others or situations that are more negative. Moreover, intra-comparisons of oneself now with oneself in the past while comparing these dynamics with locally specific principles of life conduct are possible. Identified comparisons usually resulted in the conclusion that one is lucky to be only disabled instead of dead, that one has only been injured instead of disabled, etc. Nonbeneficial comparisons, however, resulting from a discrepancy between one's capabilities and (imagined) demands (or wished outcomes), between one's capabilities in an emergency situation and those in normal times, or between oneself and others, can be experienced as burdening:

> I was very shocked. I felt that I was in the worst situation compared to others. It seemed that others weren't injured. This trial (*cobaan*) felt too hard for me. (Mbak Ratmini, Sido Kabul)

Villagers often described an *inner shifting of priorities*. A rather negative experience—be it the immense material loss or the threat of the earthquake itself—is relativized by bringing other values to the fore. Negative aspects can be counterbalanced by positive ones. Referring to an afterlife was used to balance a variety of experiences including the earthquake itself, the suffering after losing a loved one, or the material destruction and social injustices associated with aid distribution. This type of relativization constitutes one aspect of local wisdom or regional pride and self-respect that was often used by the elite:

> Losing property means losing nothing. Losing soul means losing some. Losing faith means losing everything. (The Government of Yogyakarta Special Province 2008, p. 25.1)

Besides emphasizing transcendental issues, villagers also preferred to speak of social cohesion (for example, instead of stressing material goods). Again, this stance was reinforced in public discourses:

> Although the reconstruction is done for physical building, it should go with social reconstruction to mend and improve social relation. A closer social relation is the soil of recovery from bitterness. (Hamengku Buwono X 2008, p. xiv)

Overall, material and financial losses can be relativized in relation to survival and physical integrity, religion and social moralities.[13] Shifting priorities is practiced when alternatives exist between securing oneself or one's property, for example. As described in previous chapters, in the immediate emergency situation of the earthquake, a rumor of a tsunami spread, causing a panic reaction and mass flight. Many had to decide whether to stay behind and protect their properties or to rescue themselves and others. In this situation, most of the villagers described putting aside their worries about their material possessions. Moreover, the destructive earthquake can be relativized through a positive, materialistic reframing, for example, by appreciating material gains acquired in the aftermath of aid distribution as a gift, as a blessing (*berkah*), and as providing a deeper meaning:

> Yes, there is also wisdom (*hikmah*) in it, Mbak. Those without houses can have houses. (Bu Jiyo, Sido Kabul)

[13] The immense financial loss due to the destructive earthquake was not only and not always coped with through an inner shifting of priorities but also by beneficial comparisons (such as downward social comparisons). Furthermore, outwardly directed actions (such as improvised survival strategies) were crucial in this regard.

A *humorous way* of presenting and looking at a rather negative experience can increase acceptance and provide an inner calm. A humorous way of narrating burdensome memories that many interviewees displayed is a narrative coping style that supports emotional distancing while talking about negative experiences.[14]

Villagers described the human ability to forget as a blessing. A *general present orientation* was depicted as encompassing this "art of forgiving,"[15] that is, exercising capacities to come to terms with one's past, to stay focused on the here and now, and to avoid pondering uncertain futures:

> The most important thing for me was that we could provide what was needed for a day, then I could be stress-free (*udah tenang*). (Pak Jiyo, Sido Kabul)

Adopting this stance necessitated accepting what could not be changed and the ability to practice stopping one's thoughts from racing, that is to think one step at a time. This strategy was often narrated in emergency situations, when thinking might prevent one from functioning or when one's inner peace is threatened (for example, when financial worries become more and more dominant). It translates into the maxim "do it instead of pondering." For example, a 29-year-old mother of four children, Mbak Prapti from Sido Kabul, described running outside her house as soon as the earthquake stopped and rescuing her children one by one. One had been severely injured and needed immediate medical treatment, which is why she organized transportation with her husband. However, help arrived too late, and her child died in hospital. In the interview, she explained not having thought of anything in these moments, just acting in a step by step manner and accepting things as they are, without asking why. Obviously, this strategy has a calming effect and ensures agency in times of sorrow, chaos, and panic.

Besides this present orientation, a tendency toward *future-oriented thinking and doing* was described by many villagers.[16] Coming to terms with one's past fosters this future orientation. It also prevents one from ruminating about past losses or missed opportunities, as one villager described it: "We didn't think about now, but we thought about the long-term" (Pak Murjiyo, Mulya Sari). In the context of suffering, such as the loss of a loved one, the following belief is implied in a future orientation: "time will heal." A future orientation can also be optimistic or rather realistic. The villager Pak Murjiyo illustrates an optimistic outlook:

> Everything has something negative and something positive. But what predominates are the positive aspects. Well, the negative—if there is any—will be felt only for a few minutes.

---

[14] We caution against the conclusion that a humorous way of (retrospectively) narrating negative stories indicates the capacity for coping, however. The strong normative pressure on Java to stay (at least) positive from the *lahir*, that is, the outer, observable appearance, could contribute to a biased representation in this regard.

[15] The idea of forgiveness contrasts with a state of ongoing conflict and feelings of having sinned. In general, humans can forgive other humans or God can forgive humans.

[16] Generally speaking, a future orientation can refer to this life or the afterlife (see also Chaps. 12 and 15).

A realistic stance is derived from the sociocultural idea that suffering is an integral part of life (the *cokro* or Wheel of Life metaphor). Villagers described this stance, that is, being happy in sorrow and being worried in happiness (*prihatin*), to be part of "Javanese" wisdom.[17] A realistic future outlook enables agency while avoiding disappointments due to unrealistic expectations and hopes. It triggers a sort of preparation for future disasters as well.

11.5 Concluding Remarks

Socioculturally specific understandings of principles of life conduct in times of crisis were investigated in order to avoid reproducing the Western overemphasis on person-centered constructs and on a goal-based human nature linked to ideas of self-regulation, conscious control over agency, and rational calculation. Local concepts of self[18] and related control patterns differed strongly from Western ideas. In Europe, an autonomous, independent self that aims at individual enhancements and the conquest of new domains is highly valued. The person is considered to be in charge of his or her life course, and intentions are emphasized. Therefore, primary control, that is, when one alters outside realities such as manipulating the stressor or self-directed behaviors (such as controlling one's eating behavior in times of food scarcity), is highly valued. The goal is to bring the environment into closer alignment with one's personal preferences. Social aspects are not so important (that is, social bonds are less valued; see Morling and Fiske 1999).

In our research site, however, the following motto appeared to be more dominant: "be flexible and accomplish your goals without acting towards them." The dynamic interplay between assimilative *and* accommodative processes was crucial in this respect.[19] By ignoring or denying resource losses, their relevance could be decreased, and attention could be focused on aspects that were sensed as being subject to influence. Instead of locating resources for agency (and agency itself) only in the individual, which happens with constructs like self-efficacy or self-perceptions of locus of control, collectively shared and transcendental realms proved to be at least as relevant for villagers at our research sites. Morling and Fiske (1999) developed a concept they called *harmony control*, which "stresses a holistic world view and a flexible understanding of the control that resides in contextual [spiritual] or social forces" (p. 380). Whether the term "control" fits emic perspectives or not is questionable for the context of our research site.

---

[17] This is similar to the stance that has been described in empirical work on emotion as the experience of positive *and* negative or dialectical emotions (Miyamoto et al. 2010).

[18] Compared with mainstream concepts of self, a socially interconnected self and the independent or autonomous self (see Markus and Kitayama 1991) are both represented in our data (see also Hobfoll et al. 2002).

[19] As stated above, the concepts of *batin* and *lahir* differ from "Western" ideas of the inside and the outside, of private and public, and therefore of accommodative and assimilative processes.

Interviewees emphasized that humans should give their all within the limits of their capacities, while the results of these attempts remain unpredictable. The fundamental pragmatics of life or codes of conduct described in this chapter serve as context-specific resources, as an orienting framework, or as "local wisdom" for adequate functioning, in order to foster a positive image of the self, family, and community as well as to fulfill one's role in a positive manner or maintain inner balance. To enact these codes of conduct when confronted with a crisis situation is a different coping strategy than directly attacking a problem in a goal-directed manner. Such virtue orientation is an indirect way of approaching challenging situations and thus requires that the anthropological assumptions of common coping theories are reworked.

These codes of conduct are not static qualities of a person. Rather, they represent desired developmental trajectories toward personal refinement (*kehalusan*). From a power-critical perspective, however, these coping strategies need to be put into their political, historical, and economic contexts, as they might contribute to the structurally manifested powerlessness of particular social groups (see Chap. 14). We assume a general positive bias in "Javanese" culture, that is, a tendency, at least verbally, to present things from a positive angle. Furthermore, "Javanese" discursive frames tend to be more rigid and less diverse compared with other sociocultural contexts (in which one can find more individualized meanings with less socially normative pressure to integrate the collectively shared aspects). Some villagers who were interviewed referred to these frames quite superficially, such as reading the earthquake as a reminder, without translating them into a personally relevant meaning. This indicates that there are certain meanings—in the sense of boundary objects (Star and Griesemer 1989)—circulating in social units that are available to individuals. Because of normative pressures, people adhere to them, while at the same time there are always ways to transform them personally by relating to them in a unique way (that is "doing culture").

Last but not least, we must caution that the relationship between these principles of life conduct, psychological well-being, and functioning is not based on firm empirical foundations. Rather, our presentation here is phenomenological in nature instead of theoretical in the sense of detecting preconditions, effects, etc. Little is known about how to foster these forms of life conduct in therapeutic or other interventions (Tedeschi and Calhoun 2004), so it is important to be cautious in interpreting our findings. Furthermore, our data were collected several years after the incident, which could give a false impression of the capacity for coping at the time of the disaster. Different methodical approaches would be needed that concentrate on the lived and practiced features of people's everyday lives, rather than focusing solely on what can be expressed verbally in interviews and group discussions.[20] Moreover, the question remains of how to operationalize well-being in our case study. Indicators of successful coping implying a sort of psychological well-being were expressed in socioculturally valued ideals such as inner peace (*tenteram*). In Chap. 13, we will deal with this question more thoroughly.

---

[20] A similar point has been made by Hobfoll et al. (2007), who redefined the concept of posttraumatic growth as *action growth*.

Acknowledgment The editors would like to thank Robert Parkin for his assistance in editing this chapter.

References

Baltes, P. B., & Kunzmann, U. (2004). The two faces of wisdom. *Human Development, 47*(5), 290–299.

Baltes, P. B., & Staudinger, U. M. (2000). Wisdom: A metaheuristic (pragmatic) to orchestrate mind and virtue toward excellence. *American Psychologist, 55*(1), 122–136.

Bourdieu, P. (2002). Habitus. In J. Hillier, & E. Rooksby (Eds.), *Habitus: A sense of place* (pp. 27–34). Aldershot: Ashgate.

Brandtstädter, J. (2011). *Positive Entwicklung. Zur Psychologie gelingenden Lebens*. Heidelberg: Springer/Spektrum Akademischer Verlag.

Carver, C. S., & Connor-Smith, J. (2010). Personality and coping. *Annual Review of Psychology, 61*(1), 679–704.

Colby, A., & Kohlberg, L. (1986). Das moralische Urteil: Der kognitionszentrierte entwicklungspsychologische Ansatz. In H. Bertram (Ed.), *Gesellschaftlicher Zwang und moralische Autonomie* (pp. 130–162). Frankfurt a. M.: Suhrkamp.

Giddens, A. (1979). *Central problems in social theory: Action, structure, and contradiction in social analysis*. Los Angeles: University of California Press.

Hamengku Buwono X. (2008). Learning from the 27 May 2006 earthquake. In D. Karnawati (Ed.), *The Yogyakarta earthquake of May 27, 2006* (pp. xi–xviii). Belmont: Star Publishing Company.

Heckhausen, J. (2002). Developmental regulation of life-course transitions: A control theory approach. In L. Pulkkinen, & A. Caspi (Eds.), *Paths to successful development: Personality in the life course* (pp. 257–280). Cambridge: Cambridge University Press.

Hobfoll, S. E. (2002). Social and psychological resources and adaptation. *Review of General Psychology, 6*(4), 307–324.

Hobfoll, S. E., Schroder, K. E. E., Wells, M., & Malek, M. (2002). Communal versus individualistic construction of sense of mastery in facing life challenges. *Journal of Social and Clinical Psychology, 21*(4), 362–399.

Hobfoll, S. E., Hall, B. J., Canetti-Nisim, D., Galea, S., Johnson, R. J., & Palmieri, P. A. (2007). Refining our understanding of traumatic growth in the face of terrorism: Moving from meaning Cognitions to doing what is meaningful. *Applied Psychology, 56*(3), 345–366.

Hörning, K. H., & Reuter, J. (2004). Doing culture. Kultur als Praxis. In K. H. Hörning, & J. Reuter (Eds.), *Doing Kultur. Neue Positionen zum Verhältnis von Kultur und sozialer Praxis* (pp. 9–15). Bielefeld: transcript-Verlag.

Joseph, S., & Linley, P. A. (2005). Positive adjustment to threatening events: An organismic valuing theory of growth through adversity. *Review of General Psychology, 9*(3), 262–280.

Keeler, W. (1987). *Javanese shadow plays, Javanese selves*. Princeton: Princeton University Press.

Lazarus, R. S., & Folkman, S. (1984). *Stress, appraisal and coping*. New York: Springer.

Leipold, B., & Greve, W. (2009). Resilience: A conceptual bridge between coping and development. *European Psychologist, 14*(1), 40–50.

Markus, H. R., & Hamedani, M. G. (2007). Sociocultural psychology: The dynamic interdependence among self systems and social systems. In S. Kitayama, & D. Cohen (Eds.), *Handbook of cultural psychology* (pp. 3–39). New York: Guilford.

Markus, H. R., & Kitayama, S. (1991). Culture and the self: Implications for cognition, emotion, and motivation. *Psychological Review, 98*(2), 224–253.

Miyamoto, Y., Uchida, Y., & Ellsworth, P. C. (2010). Culture and mixed emotions: Co-occurrence of positive and negative emotions in Japan and the United States. *Emotion, 10*(3), 404–415.

Morling, B., & Fiske, S. T. (1999). Defining and measuring harmony control. *Journal of Research in Personality, 33*(4), 379–414.

National Technical Team. (2007). *Living in disaster-prone area relying on local wisdom. The post earthquake rehabilitation and reconstruction program for Yogyakarta and Central Java. A guideline for decision makers and program managers*. Yogyakarta: National Technical Team.

Norris, F. H., Stevens, S. P., Pfefferbaum, B., Wyche, K. F., & Pfefferbaum, R. L. (2008). Community resilience as a metaphor, theory, set of capacities, and strategy for disaster readiness. *American Journal of Community Psychology, 41*(1–2), 127–150.

Ortner, S. A. (2006). *Anthropology and social theory: Culture, power, and the acting subject*. Durham: Duke University Press Books.

Piaget, J. (1969). *Nachahmung, Spiel und Traum*. Stuttgart: Klett.

Sairin, S., & Marah, R. (2008). *Bantul bangkit. Songsong peradaban baru*. Yogyakarta: Pemerintah Daerah Bantul.

Star, S. L., & Griesemer, J. R. (1989). Institutional ecology, 'translations' and boundary objects: Amateurs and professionals in Berkeley's Museum of Vertebrate Zoology, 1907–39. *Social Studies of Science, 19*(3), 387–420.

Straub, J., & Thomas, A. (2003). Positionen, Ziele und Entwicklungslinien der kulturvergleichenden Psychologie. In A. Thomas (Ed.), *Kulturvergleichende Psychologie* (pp. 29–80). Goettingen: Hogrefe.

Tedeschi, R. G., & Calhoun, L. G. (2004). Posttraumatic growth: Conceptual foundations and empirical evidence. *Psychological Inquiry, 15*(1), 1–18.

The Government of Yogyakarta Special Province. (2008). Reconstruction based on local wisdom (*Saiyeg Saeko Kapti*). In D. Karnawati (Ed.), *The Yogyakarta earthquake of May 27, 2006* (pp. 25.1–25.8). Belmont: Star Publishing Company.

Vohs, K. D., & Baumeister, R. F. (2004). Understanding self-regulation: An introduction. In R. F. Baumeister & K. D. Vohs (Eds.), *Handbook of self-regulation: Research, theory, and applications* (pp. 1–12). New York: Guilford.

West, C., & Fenstermaker, S. (1995). Doing difference. *Gender Society, 9*(1), 8–37.

Chapter 12
The Religious Dimension of Coping: The Roles of Cosmologies and Religious Practices

Mechthild von Vacano and Silke Schwarz

This chapter was written by the first author, based on her conceptual work and in-depth analysis of the data. The second author's contribution to the chapter lies in the preliminary analysis of data on this same subject.

> When the dust settles over a ruined landscape, for survivors it is religion and the sacred that become exceptionally important. (Islam 2012, p. 209)

Confronted with destruction and loss, many disaster survivors turn to religion, seeking to derive meaning from religious cosmologies and looking for support from the divine or the religious community. However, mainstream disaster and coping theories have both neglected the role of religion. Candland (2000) goes so far as to detect an anti-religious bias in the social sciences for their tendency to devalue religion as an obstacle to "reasonable" responses and as a source of violent conflict. In coping theories, as Pargament (1997) claims, religion has been associated with "acquiescence and lethargy" (p. 177). Countering this bias, Pargament and others have elaborated an approach to religious coping (see Sect. 2.2.3). However, these studies of religious coping still reproduce other aspects of the ethnocentric bias of appraisal-based theories (see Sect. 2.4.1). In the context of disaster research and management, religion similarly was either disregarded (Gaillard and Texier 2010) or viewed as an obstacle to the reduction of vulnerability or as a "lack of resilience rather than an expression of a constructive engagement with (the forces of) nature" (Islam 2012, p. 210). As in mainstream psychology, religion tends to be associated with fatalism (Oliver-Smith 1996; Islam 2012). Such presumed fatalism runs counter to the explicit and implicit cultural values of hegemonic approaches to disaster: human control, which is

M. von Vacano (✉)
Institute for Social and Cultural Anthropology,
Freie Universität Berlin, Landoltweg 9-11, 14195 Berlin, Germany
e-mail: m.vacano@fu-berlin.de

S. Schwarz
International Academy for Innovative Pedagogy, Psychology and Economics gGmbH
at Freie Universität Berlin, Malteserstr. 74-100, 12249 Berlin, Germany
e-mail: silke.schwarz@fu-berlin.de; silgnschwarz@yahoo.de

M. Zaumseil et al. (eds.), *Cultural Psychology of Coping with Disasters*,
DOI 10.1007/978-1-4614-9354-9_12,

grounded in a technocratic ideal of safety (see Chap. 1). Dismantling the stereotype of religion as fatalism, several authors assert the potential of religion as a resource in disaster contexts (see, for example, Gaillard and Texier 2010; Chester et al. 2012; Islam 2012). Others, such as Schlehe (2008, 2010), have realized how religious discourse on disaster enables individuals and social groups to articulate their critical views on society, thus contributing to a "hermeneutics of disaster" (Campbell-Nelson 2008).

As opposed to universalist approaches to religion developed in mainstream religious coping research, any *cultural* psychological approach needs to account for the sociocultural embeddedness of religion (see Gaillard and Texier 2010), including local forms of globalized religions such as Islam or Christianity. Further, in Chapter 4 we argued for a broad anthropological understanding of religion which encompasses diverse experiences, practices, or expressions of humans relating to "a meta-empirical sphere that may be glossed as supernatural, sacred, divine, or transcendental" (Meyer 2006, p. 6). Javanism or *kejawen* is thus analyzed as religion, even though it contains a broad ethical frame (Mulder 1990), which is not just related to the meta-empirical sphere. The religious practice of the majority of people in Java can be established as a religious variety (Beatty 1999) oscillating between Islam and *kejawen*. Our research sites reproduce such variety: most of our respondents refer to a more or less *kejawen*-inspired Islam, while a minority adheres to Christianity. Our interview data indicate diverging prioritizations of more "Islamic" or more "Javanese" values, though most respondents did not fit into such a binary classification.[1] While adherence to Islam or Christianity was easily known, substantial differences between Muslim and Christian respondents appeared to be secondary to common interpretative frames of Javanese concepts and values.

This religious plurality showed in the various ways in which the divine was addressed: most commonly used were the words *Allah*, *tuhan* (Lord, God) or *Yang kuasa* (Javanese: *Sing Kuoso*), which literally means, "Who has/have power."[2] Despite the different connotations of these words, which might have hinted at a certain religious positioning, such as *Allah* to Islam or *Yang Kuasa* to *kejawen*, the empirical use of these terms underscored the ambiguity of the field. In order to maintain this ambiguity, we chose to refer to the divine as an overarching or general category that encompasses all these connotations, while using the more specific terminology when analyzing respondents' statements.

This chapter will place a special focus on religious meaning-making and the cosmological understandings on which religious coping efforts were based. This emphasis is due to the strengths and weaknesses of our qualitative interview data,

[1] More in-depth interview material on religious matters might have provided us with a clearer picture, though a certain degree of indistinctiveness may be a characteristic of the field itself, as Beatty (1999) has argued for Banyuwangi.

[2] As indicated by this literal translation, the emic term is grammatically ambivalent, designating either a singular divine being or plural divine beings. *Yang kuasa* might be imagined as one or many, leaving interpretative flexibility to contestations of pantheistic and monotheistic perspectives (see Beatty 1999).

which provided us with 2-year retrospective accounts and interpretations of the event, where religious meanings and general values were elaborated more broadly than distinct religious practices. The performance of religion enters the final section on the vertical and horizontal relations of religion, though it requires further research.

12.1 Religious Meaning-Making

In the immediate aftermath, the earthquake survivors assessed their situation, trying to understand what had just happened. In the further course of coping, people continued to make sense of and adjust their earlier interpretations. The data of our study provide us with information on retrospective interpretations or (re)evaluations 2–3 years after the event. Such processes of meaning-making potentially involve all aspects of life, among which religion provides a fundamental resource endowing the disaster with meaning (for intersections with other dimensions, see Sects. 9.1 and 11.3). Meaning is a fuzzy concept. In order to sharpen it, Davis et al. (1998) breaks meaning-making down into sense-making, which reflects the fit between the ways in which the world is expected to work and the actual event, and benefit-finding, where the event is (re)evaluated in terms of its positive effects and its significance for one's own life. But sense is at least made in regard to two different aspects of explanation: physical explanations answer the "how" question, while metaphysical explanations respond to the ultimate question of "why" (see Macamo and Neubert 2004). Metaphysical explanations allow personal significance or benefit to be found. Seeking to illuminate the processes of meaning-making in coping, Park (2010) introduced the distinction between situational and global meanings. According to her psychological meaning-making model, coping processes only succeed if congruence between them is (re)established. Transferred to religious meaning-making, we therefore ask how religious meanings that are attributed to the disaster itself (situational meanings) relate to general views on life and the world (global meanings)?

12.1.1 Physical and Metaphysical Explanations

Asked about the meaning attributed to the earthquake, the majority of respondents answered in terms of religion, interpreting the disaster as divine test (*cobaan*, *ujian*) or admonishment (*peringatan*). Only singular voices referred to the earthquake in terms of divine punishment (*hukuman*) or wrath of God (*murka Allah*). All of these frames suggest a divine purpose behind the occurrences, which can be deciphered as communication from the transcendent realm. But they differ with regard to the question of human misconduct or blame. Explicit attributions of blame were only articulated by the two respondents who respectively interpreted the earthquake as a punishment and coming from the wrath of God. According to Pak Susilo from

Sendang the earthquake came as a punishment from the Higher Power(s) (*Yang Kuasa*) and was provoked by human exploitation of nature. Conversely, Pak Nurdin from Sido Kabul concluded that human sin had incurred the wrath of Allah, and he supported his interpretation by referencing a quote from the Quran: "Corruption has flourished on land and sea as a result of people's actions and He will make them taste the consequences of some of their own actions so that they may turn back" (Quran 30: 41; Oxford World's Classics edition 2004). Susilo and Nurding both ascribe the cause of the disaster to prior human misconduct, thus following a logic of punishment. Susilo deploys more of a "Javanese" frame, while Nurdin argues through Islam.

Much more common was the frame of admonishment (*peringatan*), which implies divine criticism of human conduct and calls for change or improvement. But other than punishment, the notion of admonition does not necessarily imply unusual misconduct or specific sins. The notion of admonishment suggests human imperfection and carries the idea that any believer requires such reminders in order to (further) improve her or his faith.[3] Another religious frame, mostly mentioned in accounts of the initial event, is the Islamic and Christian concept of doomsday *(kiamat)*. Inherent in the concept itself, this interpretation is tied to a specific moment in time, namely the ongoing crisis, and does not qualify as producing long-term meaning: if the world did not end, it could not have been the end of the world. Thus some villagers shifted to the concept of "little doomsday" (*kiamat kecil*), which functions as a reminder of the actual doomsday (cf. Akasoy 2009) and enhances people's awareness of their duty to "do good." In that sense, the idea of "little doomsday" is semantically close to the meanings of reminder, warning, or admonition (*peringatan*).

Yet another notion is communicated in the popular frame of divine testing (*cobaan, ujian*), because testing implies challenge rather than criticism or even punishment. The believers' faith is tested through crisis and can be proved in the process of coping. Schlehe (2008) documents an interview with a representative of the modernist Muslim organization Muhammadiyah, who expressed this very interpretation of the Bantul earthquake as a divine testing and quoted yet another Quranic verse: "We shall certainly test you with fear and hunger, and loss of property, lives, and crops. But [Prophet], give good news to those who are steadfast, those who say, when afflicted with a calamity, 'We belong to God and to Him we shall return.' These will be given blessings and mercy from their Lord, and it is they who are rightly guided" (Quran 2: 155–157). The frame of a divine test is thus directed less at the pre-disaster past and more at the present and future (cf. Akasoy 2009).

Ultimately, all of these religious frames share the interpretation of the temporal worldly disorder as a divine reminder of a superior transcendent order, by which humans are positioned in relation to the divine. Suffering is perceived as instrumental to the divine purpose, as Chester et al. (2012) describe it as a common characteristic of Islamic interpretations. Notions of divine purpose or divine message provide

---

[3] The Indonesian term *peringatan* even literally translates as "reminder". Accordingly, Schlehe (2006) has chosen the German translation *Erinnerung*.

believers with personal significance. However, the content of the divine message is interpreted in various ways, depending on individual context.

In our interview data, although such metaphysical understandings of the disaster are widely represented, interpretations referring to physical or material causality were rarely articulated. However, this finding does not allow us to conclude that these were less important to our respondents, because our interview guidelines explicitly addressed the metaphysical explanatory level of ascribed meaning while neglecting the "how" question.[4] Only a few respondents addressed the physical level, mostly by referring to standard geological explanations, framing the earthquake as a natural disaster (*bencana alam*) caused by the movement of tectonic plates. However, such references to science were complemented by religious interpretations. Thus science and religion were not perceived as mutually exclusive cosmologies (see Schlehe 2008; Frömming 2006; Islam 2012). The earthquake was explained as a worldly, geographical event serving a divine purpose and containing a divine message. As Rohyati from Sendang put it, it is a matter of perspective: "According to religion, the earthquake definitively is a divine test (*cobaan*), an ordeal (*ujian*) [. . .]. But in the context of natural science (*ilmu alam*) or—how do you call it—biology or physics, then, it is different from religion." Then he continued to elaborate on tectonic plates.

Pure science-based interpretations, which rendered the earthquake explicable exclusively in terms of geology, were hardly articulated. Pak Rohman from Mulya Sari was one of the very few respondents to do so:

> It is a disaster, everything was ruined by the earthquake. Nothing remained. But it's fine. If it is supposed to happen, let it be (*ya sudah*). If people are struck by an earthquake, everyone is struck. And then those who got hurt, well, they are hurt, and those who aren't, aren't. That's how it is. (Pak Rohman, Mulya Sari)

His comparatively arid interpretation of the earthquake might originate from the fact that his elderly sister was severely injured in it. Even when further asked about the significance the event had on him, Rohman remained straightforward: "What I drew [from the event] is just that I am alive." But he still ascribed the very question of survival, injury and death, to the higher power(s) (*yang kuasa*). In a similar way, Mbak Mulyani, who lost her mother, saw the earthquake exclusively as a natural disaster and explicitly rejected any religious frame or metaphysical explanation. Obviously, she feared that such frames would ascribe guilt to her mother or family. Mulyani is a pious Christian, and despite her secular interpretation of the earthquake, she was convinced that the death of her mother itself had a divine purpose: "God had better plans for her." Opposing the interpretative frames of admonition, test, and punishment, Rohman and Mulyani attributed causality of the earthquake primarily on the physical level, leaving metaphysical interpretations aside. However, when it comes to coping with distinct injuries and death, to the painful consequences of the earthquake, both referred to a general religious frame of divine control and intent.

[4] Most interviews did not touch upon physical explanations of the event because the interview guidelines rather asked about assigned meanings (*makna, arti*) and the subjective relevance of the event rather than causal explanations.

Alternative physical explanations, or geomythologies (Chester et al. 2012), were hardly mentioned in our data, and if so were accompanied by dissociation and laughter. The head of a religious boarding school, Pak Budiman, described how children imagined that God had moved the tectonic plates by His own hands. While an elderly woman from Mulya Sari, humorously provoked by her daughter, recounted how "the ancestors" had explained earthquakes as the subterranean movement of a giant snake. Both speakers distanced themselves from these alternative "geologics" by ascribing them to either childhood imaginations or the past; both seemed keen to position themselves as modern educated persons. References to Javanese mythology were absent in our interview data, a fact that may seem striking to those familiar with Schlehe's (for example 2006, 2008, 2010) anthropological work on spiritual interpretations of the earthquake. Only when explicitly asked did the old graveyard keeper from Mulya Sari mention Ratu Kidul, the queen of the South Sea, a goddess ruling all spirits of Java.[5]

12.1.2 (Re)Evaluations of Personal Significance

By implying divine purpose, transcendent frames foster positive reevaluations of the event and encourage a process of benefit finding. Abstractly put, they transform the situation of loss and suffering into a situation of gain. Several other keywords with more or less religious connotations indicate a similar process. While the frames of admonition and test form a bridge between metaphysical purpose and personal significance, other common frames such as deeper wisdom (*hikmah*), lesson (*pelajaran*), or awareness (*kesadaran*) expressed personal significance itself. As mentioned above, the search for personal significance touches upon elements of all four of our analytical dimensions: the material, the social, life conduct, and religion. With regard to the latter, the following insights and changes were formulated:

- Being reminded of a transcendental order: of divine omnipotence versus human powerlessness and of the limited span of life on earth versus prospects of the afterlife.
- Increased faith: a deeper relationship to the divine, a realization of the requirement to surrender to the divine, or experience of one's own faith as a resource.
- Improved character: self-correction, reduction of sins, and return to the right path.
- Increased praying: increased attendance at public prayers, conducting the five daily prayers (*solat*) more regularly, and starting to pray regularly.

---

[5] Such differences call for reflections on the intersubjectivity of research: our interviews were conducted by Indonesian university students, who interviewed a range of village elite and ordinary residents. Talking to young representatives of the Indonesian academia, village residents might have elaborated on views of disaster they thought would be "acceptable" according to such standards, while neglecting others. Conversely, Schlehe might have produced the opposite tendency, as she has been researching *kejawen* mythology for many years and based her data on interviews conducted with people she specifically approached to elaborate on spiritual aspects of the earthquake in 2006 (see Schlehe 2006).

- Improved quality prayer.
- Increased charity (*amalan*).

Quantitative or qualitative improvements in prayer activities were a common theme in meaning-making. Pak Suparno, for example, deemed the earthquake a divine admonishment, which reminded humans of the finiteness of their worldly lives and the necessity to do good (*berbuat baik*):

> Actually, now, after the earthquake many people pray (*sholat*) [...] They are afraid to die, because later, they say, if you didn't conduct [yourself] well in life, you will be tortured in hell. [...] [That is why] we are improving ourselves from now on. [...] Perhaps it was the admonishment (*peringatan*) by the power of Allah that humans have to do good (*berbuat* baik). (Pak Suparno, Sendang)

Suparno refers to a general change of awareness, spiritual self-improvement, and increased prayer activity. Bu Surini from Sendang added an additional social twist to the interpretation of admonishment. For her, the very experience of the emergency situation, when rich and poor gathered together in emergency shelters, symbolized the essential equality of all humans before Allah, despite all worldly wealth and social status: "In front of Allah, even if you are president, you are just the same." A former neighborhood leader, Pak Subarkah, pondered a superior transcendental order. He emphasized how the earthquake gave humans proof of their own powerlessness and limited agency, while revealing divine omnipotence:

> What I learnt (*dapat*) from the earthquake is that we are really weak. [...] Even though we haven't yet experienced "The earthquake" (*izal zull zillaha*)[6] like in the Quran. In case of doomsday, wouldn't we feel even much weaker? [...] Where would we run to? After all, we, as believers, we should return (kembali) to the power of Allah. We should lean on Him (*semendhe*), surrender (*pasrah*). [...]. We always need to remember God's power immediately because we are religious, Islamic, pious people. [...] For if we wouldn't, we might get confused (*pusing*). (Pak Subarkah, Sendang)

From the relative weakness of humans and the absolute almightiness of Allah, Subarkah deduced that all believers need to entrust themselves to the divine. He sees this ability to surrender (*pasrah*) as a resource of the Islamic faith, which can psychologically protect humans confronted with crisis situations from confusion (*pusing*). Subarkah continued by listing further codes of conduct, all being grounded in trust in the transcendental order and providing guiding principles for emergency behavior. Skillfully mixing metaphorical with practical rhetoric, Subarkah explained how the earthquake had taught him that humans need to practice patience (*sabar*) because any hasty rescue action might have injured those being saved. We can see that he connects the value of endurance to the concept of acceptance:

---

[6] The phrase "*izal zull zillaha*" is a Javanese pronunciation of the first words of the sura, "The earthquake" in Arabic, which refers to Judgment Day: "When the earth is shaken violently in its [last] quaking, when the earth throws out its burdens, when man cries, 'What is happening to it?'; on that Day, it will tell all because your Lord will inspire it [to do so]. On that Day, people will come forward in separate groups to be shown their deeds: whoever has done an atom's-weight of good will see it, but whoever has done an atom's-weight of evil will see that." (Quran 99: 18).

> Endurance (*tabah*) means that we accept (*menerima*) whatever happens, we accept (*menerima*) any event. [. . .] [Because] to whom do we want to address our protest? Who could be blamed? (Pak Subarkah, Sendang)

The need for acceptance derives from the divine world order. Since all events are contained in divine omnipotence, any expression of protest or complaint would necessarily be directed to the divine. Protesting is thus considered unacceptable, a religious norm that Subarkah conveyed by his rhetorical question.

Such normative expectations regarding disaster coping flared up every now and then in our interviews. As a general tendency, hegemonic discourses seemed to produce a necessity to find benefit in the earthquake. Only a few maintained a long-term negative narrative of loss. Among them was Rohyadi, a sand miner from Sendang, whose relative had suffered long-term injury from the earthquake. Despite having framed the earthquake as a divine testing (*cobaan*), he calculated that there was a negative balance overall when weighing his losses against benefits, both materially and spiritually. We found a few other interviews in which religious forms of meaning-making were suspiciously absent, despite religion playing a key role in other regards. One such respondent was Pak Basuki, who at the time of the interview was still struggling with the loss of his child. He asked whether he had to blame himself for previous sins, but when it came to the benefits he derived from the earthquake he avoided any spiritual reference, referring instead to the practical acquisition of new skills as a gain.

The vast majority of our respondents described their religious benefits as a gradual change or improvement or an increase in previously known norms and values (assimilation), rather than reporting or framing the disaster as a life-changing event (accommodation). However, individual interviewees saw their lives as having changed; the earthquake had made them realize their sinful wrongdoings and had led them back to the right path, turning them from being a gambler or drinker to a supportive husband, or finding true belief and a way of living religiously, which might even exceed the religious rigidity and narrowness approved by the village community itself.

12.2 Coping Against the Background of Human–Divine Relations

Religious meaning-making refers to the embeddedness of religious coping in general cosmologies or global meaning frames (Park 2010). Elaborating on the key aspects of human–divine relations, the following section will provide a deeper analysis of these global frames, showing how they affected the way people coped.

12.2.1 Implications of Divine Omnipotence

One of the fundamental realizations attributed to the earthquake was being reminded of the existence and omnipotence of the divine. Divine omnipotence suggests divine intention behind every occurrence and thus implies a general abstract significance. As Pak Ahmad from Sendang put it: "Anything that happens through Allah certainly has a deeper meaning (*hikmah*) behind it." A person may gain insight into these intentions, or they may remain a "mystery beyond comprehension" (Adeney-Risakotta 2009, p. 239). But the general faith in a benevolent God consoled believers for such lack of comprehension: for example, though Mbak Mulyani could not find any answer to why her mother had died, she confided in God to have "better plans" for her family. Further, divine omnipotence implies not only potential risk, but also luck and happiness, as well as plight, survival, and death: "We live and die by the hand of God", as a neighborhood leader from Mulya Sari explained. Sunan, a youth from Sendang, transferred this to the risk of dying in an earthquake:

> Even if I tried to save myself by running to a mountain top, if I was meant to die that way, a landslide might occur [. . .] and I might be killed by falling rocks. [Or] Even if I was here sleeping, if I was not destined to die that way, my house might not be destroyed, or maybe it would collapse, but my room wouldn't. The key is that we believe in God (*tuhan*). (Mas Sunan, Sendang)

Despite all precautions, humans are subject to divine forces that defy human control and predictability. This does not imply that humans should not take precautionary measures such as building earthquake-proof houses. Ultimately though, humans cannot escape the divine will by taking such measures. However, through the ultimate divine power virtually everything is possible. For that reason, miracle narratives were a common element in our interviews too. Survivors were astonished by the small details that had ensured their survival. One respondent felt he had been miraculously protected when a wall collapsed in the direction of his motorbike instead of on himself; another reported how he was saved by an invisible hand pulling him aside just before his roof collapsed. Others hoped for miraculous physical recovery against the doctor's negative prognosis. Such miracles went beyond logic or science, and no university professor could explain them, as Kyai Abdul assured us. In reevaluating the past, the miracle narrative serves as a transcendent version of (hypothetical) beneficial comparisons (see Chap. 11), which is based on the idea that "it could have been worse"; in relation to people's outlook on the future it affords hope, and even against negative prognoses of science.

Through the earthquake, survivors experienced how it feels to be at the mercy of higher powers. Interpretations of these powers as natural may provide a causal explanation of "how" the destruction came about, but they do not offer much in the way of a metaphysical explanation. But being exposed to divine forces, or to natural forces mobilized by divine intention, adds a spiritual quality to the experience. Confronted with suffering and the limits of their own agency, humans could experience divine omnipotence. According to a broadly shared religious perspective, it was deemed "normal"—that is, within the horizon of expectancy—and spiritually beneficial for humans to experience their powerlessness in such a way. Though the disaster was horrifying and burdening in the way it was perceived by many participants, it did not disrupt or shatter general assumptions about the world because the world was not considered a stable and safe place—where dangers could be controlled by humans—to begin with (cf. Magnis-Suseno 1989). Through the earthquake believers could experience the transcendental order of divine omnipotence and human weakness, thus enabling believers to grow spiritually and religiously.

12.2.2 The Trinity of Acceptance, Surrender, and Effort

Because human capacities of understanding and agency are limited in the face of divine omnipotence, humans should thus accept *(nrimo)* and surrender *(pasrah)*.[7] Exposed to danger, any believer should turn to God and lean on Him *(semendhe)* in order to find an emotional relief, as Pak Subarkah elaborated above. Surrender and acceptance are considered key resources for coping with adversity. Sunan remembers the way his parents had conveyed to him how important it was to surrender and worship *(ibadah)* in any situation of threat in order to attain patience and calmness. Educated in this way, he claimed that he had kept cool and was relaxed *(nyantai-nyantai saja)* when the earthquake struck. Yet, later in the interview he mentioned that fear might arise despite surrender, but it could be reduced and he could be comforted by trust in the Almighty. In coping with the loss of his wife, Pak Priyanto found solace in his faith in the Almighty:

> It was an act of the Almighty *(Yang Kuasa)*, so if she was taken by the Almighty, I can only accept it *(tinggal terima saja)* [. . .] For those who truly believe in the Almighty, whatever happens, they surrender *(pasrah)* with a calm heart *(tenteram hatinya)* [. . .] That is my belief *(percaya)* in the Almighty, thus I don't feel bereaved. (Pak Priyanto, Sendang)

According to religious discourse, however, the responses of acceptance and surrender alone are insufficient for coping with crisis situations. Both need to be complemented by a third element, namely effort *(usaha)*. Effort refers to the human responsibility to take the initiative and shape one's own living conditions according to one's capacities. Although the stances of surrender and acceptance function to calm the mind, they only provide the precondition for outwardly directed actions (see Sect. 11.4.1), for effort *(usaha)*, as Pak Susilo elaborated:[8]

> If we only accept *(nrimo)* and surrender *(pasrah)*, there will be no development. It only serves to cool down our thoughts *(ngedem piker)*, but we also need to cultivate ways to achieve something. [. . .] We cannot only expect [external] aid, but we must make our own effort *(berusaha)*. According to our Javanese principles, food comes from the movement of our own hands. If we do not want to work, we will not eat. Although I am still young, I am fond of learning such ancestral knowledge. (Pak Susilo, Sendang)

---

[7] The concepts of surrender *(pasrah)* and acceptance *(nirmo)* are closely interrelated and commonly deduced from each other. Even though respondents used both terms almost interchangeably, in its syntactical use, *pasrah* is related to the transcendent *(pasrah sama/ kepada tuhan)*, and is therefore translated as surrender, whereas the Javanese *nrimo* or the Indonesian *menerima*, if specified by an object, refers to the acceptance of a situation *(nrimo lelakon/menerima keadaan)*.

[8] From the perspective of life conduct, the correlation between acceptance and effort is discussed as consideration of inwardly and outwardly directed agency in Chap. 11.

Susilo's emphasis on effort hints at the *relativity* of human powerlessness, as well as at the human potential and responsibility for shaping the physical world, respectively. Like other members of the political elite, Pak Susilo ties the ideal of effort to a particular Javanese work ethic, emphasizing self-reliance and warning against becoming dependent on external aid (see Chap. 11).

This triad of acceptance, surrender, and effort needs to be understood as an ideal framework for coping. From this ideal perspective, general religious values translate into coping resources: surrender, trust, and faith are perceived as the core virtues and indicators of true beliefs. These normative values transform the situational coping challenge into a more general religious challenge, by which believers are tested or admonished to prove the extent of their faith. But actual processes of coping with the disaster may assume quite different trajectories. Especially respondents who were injured or confronted with the deaths or injuries of loved ones revealed discrepancies between ideal and actual crisis responses and testified to the personal struggles of dealing with such discrepancies. Bu Sum from Sendang started to cry when she told her interviewer about the loss of her son. After rescuing him barely alive from the ruins, she had held him in her hands, leaving the situation up to God (*menyerahkan*) while pleading for a miracle. She retrospectively described this emotional state as in between despair (*putus asa*) and surrender. In another example, Pak Subarkah went so far as to admit the limits to his ability to accept. Several of his family members had barely survived the earthquake. A few days later, his 3-year-old child had fallen sick and was been hospitalized. Subarkah described his fear for his child's survival as his cracking point:

> I could accept the earthquake, but when all of a sudden my child fell sick, my heart could not accept it (*hati niku ora iso nompo*). At that point, I refused (*nolak*). I was so sad because my child had survived the earthquake without harm. And despite the fact that some other family members had been injured [in the event], I could immediately return to Allah (*kembali kepada Allah*). But [at that time], when all of a sudden [my daughter fell sick], I questioned 'What is this supposed to be, Allah?' (Pak Subarkah, Sendang)

Subarkah shared the general ideal of unconditional trust in God, but experienced a personal limit to his acceptance. Eventually his child recovered, and at the time of the interview Pak Subarkah reflected upon his temporary rejection as a human weakness, which he seemed to own up to.

12.2.3 Notions of Fate and Prospects of the Afterlife

Divine omnipotence and human weakness both manifest themselves in the ultimate question of life and death. According to the broadly shared concept of fate (*takdir*), human destiny is determined by transcendent powers:

> We are human. We just can accept it. Everything has been arranged. We just let it flow. We let God preside, whatever will be the result, whether we die or survive. (Pak Subarkah, Sendang)

If it is time to die, death is inevitable; but if someone is not yet meant to die, it is possible to survive anything by divine power. Ideally, the human fear of death resolves itself into absolute trust in the divine. Accepting death as one of God's possible plans is the ultimate state of trust and surrender. In cases of bereavement, the notion of fate provides a general sense of significance because it implies a divine purpose behind the loss (see above).

Many respondents explicitly or implicitly assumed that the human experience continues beyond life on earth to the hereafter. In comparison, worldly life—may it be pleasant or hard, long or short—is secondary to the afterlife. As Kyai Abdul explained: "We live not only a worldly life, but also in the afterlife. And the afterlife is more eternal than our worldly life." When people die, they are thus imagined as going to a (better) afterlife. Given such a prospect, the finiteness of worldly life conveys a notion of consoling truth. The afterlife also implies an extended time frame for meaning-making. The relevance of (a good) worldly life decreases because the primary aim from a religious, mainly Islamic perspective is (a good) afterlife. This expectation or promise of a good afterlife provides a certain buffer zone for hardships in one's worldly life.

The prospect of an afterlife serves as an incentive, positively providing hopes for reward, and negatively providing a prospect of punishment and suffering in hell. Ideally, humans should conduct their worldly lives in such a way that they do not need to fear even sudden death. Humans can prepare for the afterlife by acting as good persons or believers in this life. Respondents who referred to the idea of an afterlife mostly emphasized the necessity to pray, to reduce, or compensate for one's sins, not to leave behind debts, and to acquire merit (*bekal*, literally provisions). Ideally, if believers have been leading a pious life, they can face even sudden death with a profound inner calmness (*tentram*). But this notion works both ways: thus if a person doubts her or his own piety, psychological distress might increase. It is widely held that, through the confrontation would death, believers would realize whether or not they felt adequately prepared to die, or whether they needed to change their way of life. Notably, respondents tended to ascribe such revelatory experiences to others, often implying a slightly derogatory notion:

> Besides suffering (*maut*), the earthquake brought us wisdom (*hikmahnya*). [...] [People asked themselves:] "If suddenly an earthquake happened, if I died and did not acquire any merit (*bekal*), what would happen to me?" Maybe people would become afraid and start to realize (*kesadarannya*). They would start to pray on a regular basis (*solat*), so that, if all of a sudden another earthquake happened and they died, they could face it sincerely (*ikhlas*). (Bu Jiyo, Sido Kabul).

But this emphasis on religious duty and on the need to prepare for the afterlife was not shared equally among all of our interviewees. Perspectives rather oscillated between two opposite poles, as represented by Pak Nurdin from Sido Kabul and Pak Priyanto from Sendang. Nurdin presented himself as recently converted by the earthquake and as having become a strict believer in a rather "Arabic" version of Islam. According to his understanding of Islam, humans are provided with divine rules to obey, and the need to recognize and follow the right path, as set by Allah. A good believer ought to worship (*ibadah*) Allah and fulfill his or her religious duties with sincerity. Pak

Nurdin went so far as to prioritize religious rules over harmonious community life and therefore was perceived as a bit too "fanatical" (*fanatik*) within his own village. Conversely, Pak Priyanto articulated a rather *kejawen*-influenced version of Islam, underlining the need for a strong character through which humans actively live their lives and direct themselves while also emphasizing human responsibility and effort (*usaha*). According to his worldview, divine power(s) only provide humans with basic tools, leaving it up to them to lead a good life and do right, or in his own words: "You are provided with feet and foot soles, but you should not just walk ahead, you need to direct yourself."[9] Pak Priyanto derived his strong emphasis on self-guidance from Javanese knowledge, which he introduced as traditional wisdom passed down from his grandfather. Comparing the two perspectives, the idea of fate (*takdir*) may have quite different implications: while for Nurdin religion provides believers with duties, rules, and a right path to follow, Priyanto locates the religious persons' guidance in themselves, without any right path (cf. Beatty 1999).

Material loss and gain are also perceived as a matter of fate, though such notions do not imply human passivity, as the triad of acceptance, surrender, and effort has shown. Pak Siswanto framed the earthquake destruction as well as the reconstruction process as matters of fate and invoked the multifaceted notion of *rezeki,* which can be translated as either sustenance or luck. Both meanings are further implied as having been given by the divine:

> It was predetermined by fate (*sudah takdir*). And later the reconstruction was predestined as well (*sudah takdir*). [. . .] People need to look for sustenance (*rezeki*), and then they might be provided with sustenance/divine reward (*rezeki*). (Pak Siswanto, Sido Kabul)

Rezeki is an important element within the concept of fate, especially as it integrates the element of effort. *Rezeki* is a category of non-predictable material reward provided by the divine. People ought to prove their own efforts (*usaha*) and strive for economic progress (*mencari rezeki*), and they will then be rewarded. The timing and form of this reward, though, are uncertain and non-predictable, as the semantic notion of luck implies. People actively shape their course of life, but are incapable of determining it, because fate, after all, lies beyond the range of human influence. As the example of Pak Siswanto shows, this complex of fate, effort, and *rezeki* serves as an important reference in dealing with material loss and recovery (see also Sect. 9.3).

12.2.4 The Principle of Divine Lessons

Being examined by God (*cobaan; ujian*) or being taught a lesson (*pelajaran*) are common concepts not only with reference to disaster, but also in relation to negative life events in general, such as accidents, illnesses, or crimes. These frames imply a

[9] He further tied this principle of self-guidance to four key codes of conduct, presented by Pak Priyanto in yet another metaphor: "Every human alive needs reins (*kendali*). Just as animals have bridles and cars or bicycles have brakes, humans need ethical principles: patience (*sabar*), faith in the divine (*tawakal*), surrender (*pasrah*), remembering (*ingat*) [the divine]."

general worldview that integrates adverse and potentially disruptive events as challenges to the course of life. These frames suggest a global worldview, according to which uncontrollable life events are considered to be an integral part of human existence, calling for human humility and highlighting human imperfections, as well as the human potential for improvement. Despite all the suffering, these frames allow the image of the divine as benevolent to be maintained: the divine shows kindness through the examination, because it is only by being tested that humans can prove their faith. Kyai Abdul, a religious leader from Sendang, expressed this idea as follows:

> Allah or God (*tuhan*), has given us this test (*ujian*) to improve [. . .] our level of faith and piety towards God. It is comparable to schoolchildren who have to be examined. [. . .] Without tests, there wouldn't be any grades. (Kyai Abdul, Sendang)

The successful accomplishment of divine tests may be rewarded not only with grades metaphorically but also with tangible gains, measurable not least in the quantity of material aid, as received by Kyai Abdul for his religious boarding school. Bu Sulasmi deployed a similar religious logic of ambition, only for her the severity of the test constituted a distinction in itself, because Allah examines his congregation (*umat*) only according to their degree of faith: "The stronger their faith (*iman*), the harder the examination." Thus, in coping with the disaster, believers can prove that Allah was right to have challenged them through such an ordeal. Such interpretations add a transcendental motivational layer to the coping process and empower survivors to believe in their own coping capacities, since the divine challenge, however overwhelming it might seem, will not exceed their potential.

12.3 Religion as a Vertical and Horizontal Resource

The broad range of divine lessons expressed by our respondents points to a holistic understanding of the ideal human character (Fig. 12.1). According to this understanding, faith is not limited to the human–divine relationship, and even less to an institutionalized domain of religion, but is expressed as a way of life. The strength of faith manifests itself through spiritual awareness, worship and trust in God, as well as through quite general codes of conduct, such as acceptance, patience, or self-reliance (see Chap. 11), and also social awareness (see Chap. 10).

This holistic ideal of human character was broadly shared by those we interviewed, but respondents highlighted different aspects, and in this plurality mirrored general tendencies in the discourse on religion in Indonesia. In general, religion is considered to encompass both a vertical and horizontal dimension, the balance and interpretations of which are matters of debate. The vertical dimension refers to the relationship between the believer and the divine, while the horizontal relationship contextualizes the believer in her or his social environment. According to this perspective, the world is an inherently social space where religion is practiced in social cooperation and where faith constitutes a foundation for respect among humans. If we turn this discourse into an analytical lens, the transcendent dimension of coping

	divine omnipotence						
ideal	awareness of transcen-dental order	worship, prayer	surrender, trust, acceptance	sincerity, patience, gratefulness	self-reliance, effort	altruism	do good
	faith		character strength			social awareness	
anti-ideal (sin)		not praying	despair, absence of faith	impatience, ungratefulness	laziness	egoism greed, envy,	do harm
	human weakness						

Fig. 12.1 Ideals and Anti-Ideals for Humans

encompasses a vertical component of communication with the divine and a horizontal component emphasizing the community aspect of religion (cf. Pargament 1997).

12.3.1 Communication with the Divine

The vertical dimension can be framed as a communicative relationship to a "force that goes beyond the individual" (Pargament et al. 2000, p. 521), which is expressed in prayer. Prayer practices can take many shapes, from the recitation of standard texts to spontaneous individual expressions, from external verbalizations to silent internal communications. The increased piety the earthquake produced was often described as a matter of convergence with God (*mendekatkan diri pada tuhan*), which could be attained by regular individual worship (*beribadah; solat*) and attending public prayers. This strong emphasis on prayer conventions represented Islamic perspectives rather than *kejawen* ideals, which place less emphasis on formalized prayer (Beatty 1999).

In narratives on the immediate emergency situation, prayer was often described as a mediator between fear and surrender. Prayer helped to overcome, reduce, or simply deal with fear by promoting the inner process of surrender. At the same time, prayer was described as an expression of surrender, because surrender is "only" a spiritual process, while prayer is a distinct practice. In crisis situations, when people feel powerless and incapable of acting, and when they do not know what to do, prayer fills the place of agency because it provides a useful thing to do, an activity, when there is nothing else left.

> I was afraid and I surrendered (*pasrah*); what else could I have done? (laughing) [. . .] I just prayed and asked for forgiveness for all my mistakes, because humans often make mistakes [. . .] I just prayed and asked for protection. (Bu Purwanti, Sendang)

Beyond this profane occupational aspect, prayer serves as technique for emotional management. Bu Sutini described how she struggled for inner peace by appealing to Allah:

> I just kept repeating my *tasbih* [a formula invoking Allah], but I still could not overcome my fear. [. . .] I begged Allah (*gusti Allah*) to save my grandchild. [. . .] I was emotionally upset (*tidak tentram*) [. . .] I prayed as hard as I could for Allah to give peace to my heart. (Bu Sutini, Sendang)

Bu Purwanti and Bu Sutini both turned to the divine with specific requests. While Bu Purwanti asked for her own protection and forgiveness in the face of the afterlife, Bu Sutini begged for her grandchild's survival. Other accounts contained requests for recovery, practical support, inner peace, salvation in the afterlife, or a place in heaven. In times of crisis it is common to ask for divine assistance, individually or institutionalized in public prayers. Families might invite the village community to pray for the cure and recovery of a severely ill family member, as was done for Pak Rohman's disaster injuries in Mulya Sari. It is also common to pray for the deceased on regular occasions.[10] Such ritual prayers may support the grieving process. However, due to the overwhelming chaos of the post-disaster period, death rituals were often improvised or neglected. Mourning the death of his child, Pak Hadi from Sendang complained about the laxness of his coresidents and felt neglected in having to conduct these ritual payers for the deceased himself.

Altogether prayer served different purposes, which were more or less explicitly expressed by our interviewees. Some requested practical support, such as food or being rescued from the ruins. Others searched for emotional support; prayer increased inner peace, reassured survivors that they could trust in the divine, and mediated the process of surrender. Routinized forms of prayer helped to reestablish a sense of normality, while prayer as a duty to worship was perceived as preparation for the afterlife.

The collaborative quality of the human–divine relationship is determined by the degree and character of one's personal intimacy with the divine. Bu Sum, a Christian, described an intense and personalized relation to God. She perceived Jesus as a communicative counterpart in everyday life and as a partner in problem solving. Waiting to be rescued from the ruins, she had cried out to God for support. Her calls were answered by a voice which had told her to pray and later on she was rescued. Her life narrative was full of similar miracles and successful interactions with the divine. In another example, Mbak Kusmini described her relationship with God (*Yang Diatas*) as intimate, but rather casual. For emotional support she generally seemed to rely on social networks and friends, but also turned to God, sharing her feelings (*curhat*), surrendering (*pasrah*), and praying for the well-being of her family. The way Kusmini described this communication implies a comparatively nonhierarchical relationship with God, because a colloquial term like *curhat*[11] would normally be used for intimate and casual communication among family, friends, or lovers.

The case of Pak Subarkah, who had faced the limits of his acceptance, indicates how people struggled with their religious beliefs. But our data do not contain any

[10] Ceremonies for the deceased should be held after 3, 7, 40, 100, and 1,000 days.

[11] *Curhat* is an abbreviation of *curah(an) hati*, literally 'pouring out one's heart'.

cases of believers who fundamentally questioned the divine or divine benevolence. Within the dominant discourse the emphasis is rather on how faith and people's personal relationships with God were strengthened by experiencing adversity, as expressed in the common idiom of "drawing nearer to God" (*mendekatkan diri pada tuhan*).

12.3.2 Religion as Community Relations

As soon as we turn to the horizontal relationship in religious coping, overlapping points with the social dimension (Chap. 10) become obvious. Religion is an inherently social phenomenon because it consists of shared cosmologies and is expressed as individual and collective practice. In the context of our research, religion further serves as an important basis of village life. Despite the dominance of the Muslim majority, religious plurality has an important value in maintaining a harmonious village life (see Beatty 1999). Most people maintained the view that any expression of religion needs to accord with this higher value of communal life, while fanatical (*fanatik*) interpretations of religion were explicitly rejected. During a focus-group discussion with village youth in Sendang, Sunan and Restu conveyed what they had learned from a village elder:

> Sunan: Most importantly, we have to struggle (*usaha*). As long as they live, humans need to look for money and food. If people worship (*ibadah*), they should not worship all the time, that would be wrong. Restu: We need a balance between religion and our worldly lives. [. . .] Problems arise if the balance is off. It is not good to place religion above everything, because we are social people, we live with other people. [. . .] But there are people who exaggerate, we call them "fanatics" (*fanatik*), because their solidarity is limited to the people within their congregation (*jamaahnya*). Sunan: . . . and not with the community in general.

In Sido Kabul, the newly converted Pak Nurdin was regarded as such a *fanatik*. His example illustrates how "too much religiousness" was disapproved of because it was considered a threat to a harmonious community life.[12] In the above quote, Sunan also weighed the value of effort (*usaha*) against worship (*ibadah*), thus stressing a Javanese work ethic over such *fanatik* interpretations of Islam.

If we turn from these rather general issues to socio-religious coping, at least two aspects should be mentioned. First, the collective experience of praying together, for example, in the immediate aftermath, when thunder, rain, and aftershocks increased the general atmosphere of confusion and fear, helped to calm people down. In addition to the effects of prayer discussed in the previous section, the collective quality of prayer provided survivors with a comforting sense of togetherness, what Pargament et al. (2000) referred to as intimacy. Second, religious communities can be analyzed

---

[12] This case was elaborated by Tiara R. Widastuti in her presentation "Earthquake and its relief processes as triggers of social inclusion and exclusion: a case study in Bantul, Yogyakarta" at the Congress of the International Association for Cross-Cultural Psychology in Melbourne, Australia, 08.07.2010.

from the perspective of social capital (for example, Candland 2000). In our case, religious networks provided material support in the form of emergency relief and funds for reconstructing religious facilities. But the involvement of religious donor agencies led to various problems because villagers were skeptical of the potential hidden agendas of Christian organizations, or feared co-optation by Islamic political parties (see Chap. 14).

12.4 Concluding Remarks

In conjunction with other dimensions, Bantul residents experienced religion as a key resource in coping with the earthquake and its aftermath. Shared religious cosmologies that placed divine omnipotence at their core served as foundational reference for survivors to find metaphysical meaning in the event and derive meaningful insights or other benefits from it. The experience of being at the mercy of the divine power, or of nature exercising divine intent, was interpreted as a reminder of the divine order or as a challenge to the believer's faith. As our interview data have shown, people were cautious in deploying religious discourses of blame, as interpretations such as "punishment" might suggest. However, questions of self-blame and the social fear of being blamed were certainly present.

As the relative absence of explicit blaming discourses suggests, respondents rarely deployed larger political discourses in the name of religion, such as Javanism versus Islam, or tradition versus modernity (cf. Schlehe 2008, 2010), though these issues were implicitly negotiated in the values emphasized in interpretations of the disaster. Differences showed in the various emphases our respondents placed on religious, social, and general ethic values, respectively. But these differences in prioritizing religious duties and rules as opposed to community cohesiveness, self-guidance, and an appropriate work ethic were formulated as gradual variations rather than representations of opposites (cf. Beatty 1999). These values were commonly linked directly to the earthquake *experience*: the disaster became a practical challenge for everyone to prove her or his strength of faith and quality of character in handling the crisis, as well as providing an opportunity for self-correction and improvement.

At the center of the religious discourse was the triad of acceptance, surrender, and effort, which was cosmologically deduced from divine omnipotence and the relative powerlessness of humans. These notions were construed as generalizable values and tangible life principles at the same time. Transcending the reductionist fatalism–control dichotomy, this triad offers an alternative to anthropocentric and control-biased coping theories. The positive potential of spiritual surrender has been discussed by Cole and Pargament (1999), who also point out the limits of the control paradigm:

> Because people are finite, because personal resources are bounded, and because the possibilities in any situation are necessarily limited, a preoccupation with personal control will often lead to frustration and failure. [. . .] Through spiritual surrender, control is abandoned for the sake of the sacred, be it a transcendental purpose, ideal, relationship, or commitment. In the process, however, both primary and secondary control may be inadvertently enhanced. (Cole and Pargament 1999, p. 184)

Cole and Pargament define a paradoxical relationship between control and surrender, where spiritual surrender is reached by giving up a sense of control, though the actual potential for control is regained by the relinquishing of its idea. If applied to the acceptance–surrender–effort triad, the basic description of the mechanism seems to match well, though it is doubtful that the notion of regained *control* would be supported from an emic perspective. Human effort (*usaha*) implies human attempt rather than control, meaning that humans give their all within the limits of their capacities. However, where their effort will lead to is unpredictable as we have illustrated with reference to the notion of *rezeki* as sustenance and luck.

Whether or not surrender leads to a paradox is a matter of cosmological assumptions. In this regard, psychological coping theory and hegemonic disaster research share the same referential frame: both privilege human control as a way of dealing with adversity and disaster. In Chap. 1 we discussed how this control bias is closely tied to a technocratic world view which promotes a security paradigm: human control, predictability, and security are construed as the norm, whereas disaster is construed as a disruption of normality, which needs to be corrected by regaining control and reestablishing security. As an alternative to this discourse on disaster as an exceptional disruption of normality, "Javanese," *kejawen*, Islamic, and Christian cosmologies offer an interpretative frame through which such large-scale destructive events are integrated into "expected normality" because human existence itself is seen as uncertain (cf. Macamo and Neubert 2008). Religious perspectives were thus rather reaffirmed by the earthquake than disrupted. At the same time, cosmologies are always multiple and in flux, and framing disaster is still a matter of interpretation and potentially contested. Different reference frames are available among and within different cosmologies (Schlehe 2010), as our case study has shown.

As with any other of our dimensions, religious coping needs to be studied in context because religion always interacts with material, social, and political conditions. Some religious discourses may be more convenient to the ruling political elite than others; some religious interpretations may foster social exclusion, others may foster integration; some religious frames may empower people to cope, while others may increase their burden. For a cultural psychology of coping, it is crucial to link subjective experiences and agency to the larger picture of religion, and to view the broader context through the lense of such subjective experiences. With respect to meaning-making, it seems promising to combine psychological meaning-making models with the more discursive approaches of an author like Schlehe, in order to situate meanings made in relation to the subjective life experiences, and micro-social contexts in relation to macro-political ones.

Acknowledgments The editors would like to thank Robert Parkin for his assistance in editing this chapter.

References

Adeney-Risakotta, B. (2009). Is there a meaning in natural disasters? Constructions of culture, religion and science. *Exchange, 38*(3), 226–243.

Akasoy, A. (2009). Approaches to earthquakes in Islamic theology and science. In C. Mauch & C. Pfister (Eds.), *Natural disasters, cultural responses* (pp. 183–196). Lanham: Lexington Books.

Beatty, A. (1999). *Varieties of Javanese religion*. Cambridge: Cambridge University Press.

Campbell-Nelson, J. (2008). Religion and disaster. A critical reflection post Alor earthquake 2004. Institute of Indonesia Tenggara Timur Studies, Working Paper 8. http://genderandsecurity.researchhub.ssrc.org/religion-and-disaster/attachment. Accessed 12 June 2013.

Candland, C. (2000). Faith as social capital. *Policy Sciences, 33*(3/4), 355–374.

Chester, D. K., Duncan, A. M., & Sangster, H. (2012). Religious interpretations of disaster. In B. Wisner, J. C. Gaillard, & I. Kelman (Eds.), *Handbook of hazards and disaster risk reduction (pp. 109–120)*. New York: Routledge.

Cole, B. S., & Pargament, K. I. (1999). Spiritual surrender: A paradoxical path to control. In W. R. Miller (Ed.), *Integrating spirituality into treatment: Resources for practitioners* (pp. 179–198). Washington: American Psychological Association.

Davis, C. G., Nolen-Hoeksema, S., & Larson, J. (1998). Making sense of loss and benefiting from the experience. *Journal of Personality and Social Psychology, 75*(2), 561–574.

Frömming, U. U. (2006). *Naturkatastrophen: Kulturelle Deutung und Verarbeitung*. Frankfurt a. M.: Campus.

Gaillard, J. C., & Texier, P. (2010). Religions, natural hazards, and disasters: An introduction. *Religion, 40*(2), 81–84.

Islam, R. R. (2012). Believing to recover. The role of religion in the recovery phase of natural disasters. *Anthropos, 107*(1), 209–217.

Macamo, E., & Neubert, D. (2004). Die Flut in Mosambik – Zur unterschiedlichen Deutung von Krisen und Katastrophen durch Bauern und Nothilfeapparat. In N. Schareika & T. Bierschenk (Eds.), *Lokales Wissen. Sozial-wissenschaftliche Perspektiven* (pp. 185–207). Münster: LIT.

Macamo, E., & Neubert, D. (2008). Erwartung an Sicherheit. Subjektive Katastrophenwahrnehmungen und Bedingungen der Bewältigung am Beispiel Mosambiks und Deutschlands. In K. Rehberg (Ed.), *Die Natur der Gesellschaft. Verhandlungen des 31. Kongresses der Deutschen Gesellschaft für Soziologie* (pp. 858–874). Frankfurt: Campus.

Magnis-Suseno, F. (1989). *Neue Schwingen für Garuda*. München: Kindt.

Meyer, B. (2006). *Religious sensations. Why media, aesthetics and power matter in the study of contemporary religion*. Amsterdam: Vrije Universiteit.

Mulder, N. (1990). *Individuum und Gesellschaft in Java: Eine Untersuchung zur kulturellen Dynamik*. Saarbrücken: Breitenbach.

Oliver-Smith, A. (1996). Anthropological research on hazards and disasters. *Annual Review of Anthropology, 25*, 303–328.

Pargament, K. I. (1997). *The psychology of religion and coping*. New York: Guilford.

Pargament, K. I., Koenig, H. G., & Perez, L. M. (2000). The many methods of religious coping: Development and initial validation of the RCOPE. *Journal of Clinical Psychology, 56*(4), 519–543.

Park, C. L. (2010). Making sense of the meaning literature: An integrative review of meaning making and its effects on adjustment to stressful life events. *Psychological Bulletin, 136*(2), 257–301.

Schlehe, J. (2006). Nach dem Erdbeben auf Java: Kulturelle Polarisierungen, soziale Solidarität und Abgrenzung. *Internationales Asienforum, 37*(3/4), 213–237.

Schlehe, J. (2008). Religion, Natur und die aktuelle Deutung von Naturkatastrophen auf Java. In J. Schlehe & B. Rehbein (Eds.), *Religion und die Modernität von Traditionen in Asien* (pp. 207–234). Berlin: LIT.

Schlehe, J. (2010). Anthropology of religion: Disasters and the representations of tradition and modernity. *Religion, 40*(2), 112–120.

Part IV
Specific Aspects of Coping

The dimensional presentation of multiple post-disaster coping dynamics systemizes the data about the material, religious, personal and social worlds which was the product of multiple dialogues between the researchers and research participants. The dimensions are a general framework which can be used to understand the culturally specific features of coping with a disaster. Our aims were to contextualize the concepts of our specific case study and, to this end, the local coping trajectories are positioned within a space of specific material, social, personal and religious dimensions. We refer to these as referential dimensions because they are socioculturally specific relations of references within a symbolically mediated practice (see Chap. 3). These references are relevant in different ways to different individuals. The next step is then to apply these locally specific insights derived from the multidimensional coping framework to key themes that play a crucial role in international discussions about disaster management and risk reduction.

The theme of suffering in contrast to what is called disaster mental health in international and Western contexts, illustrates the difference between the locally specific approaches to suffering and a universal medicalizing and clinical–psychological perspective. Chapter 13 covers locally-specific understandings of the term "trauma" in Yogyakarta, Indonesia, related ways of manifesting and expressing extreme suffering, and possible forms of healing in terms of the coping dimensions referred to in our framework presented in Part III.

Financial gains in post-disaster situations for people with power and material resources appears to be a universal phenomenon that evokes a dramatic sense of moral offence in people without resources who also suffer personal and material losses. Chapter 14 details the locally specific sociocultural formation and handling of these individually and collectively shared forms of moral and political feelings. Cultural-specific dimensions of coping with social conflicts resulting from aid distribution processes—which have been long neglected in individualistic and apolitical psychological approaches—are highlighted.

The issue of risk management is dealt with in Chap. 15, where we show that concerns about risk and the future are rather different issues. Individual and communal futures are not necessarily discussed in terms of risks or in relation to the specific risk of and need to prepare for another earthquake. Cultural-specific lifestyles or principles of life conduct instead take precedence when communities deal with uncertainties. Such local approaches contrast with international ideas about risk management which assume an opposition between an objective explainable environment and a biased subjectivity when attempting to educate people about how to prepare themselves against possible hazards.

The thematic focus ends with a critical evaluation of gender mainstreaming issues in disaster contexts. In Chap. 16, the concept of coping is understood and presented as the capacity for societally assimilative or accommodative development rather than as an individual, subjective, intrapsychic and, above all, cognitive process. Instead of examining individuals' well-being from a value-free perspective, the chapter presents a critical inquiry into different ways of understanding justice, as well as means and ways of increasing social justice with regard to gender relations in a post-disaster village community.

Chapter 13
Suffering, Healing, and the Discourse of Trauma

Jeane A. Indradjaja and Manfred Zaumseil

13.1 Introduction

This chapter is about suffering and healing after a disaster. Building on the work of Cassell (2004), Charmaz (1999), Kleinman (1988), and Radley (2004), Priya (2012) suggests that "suffering is inherently subjective, local and pluralistic in nature" (p. 214). We think it is of critical importance to contextualize both the threat caused by stressful events and the experience of suffering. We suggest to understand suffering as a threat to personhood in the sense outlined by Cassell (2004) which encompasses the person in context: "the lived past, the family's lived past, culture and society, roles, the instrumental dimension, associations and relationships, the body, the unconsciousness mind, the political being, the secret life, the perceived future, and the transcendent-being dimension" (p. 42). Kleinman (1988) stressed that suffering may include demoralization, loss of self-esteem or self-worth in a socio-moral context; more recently, Priya (2010) has argued for a broad understanding of healing as a "reaffirmation of moral status: Gaining meaning and value or worth for one's experience through narrating how one adhered to culturally valued principles or practices" (p. 7).

In a *landscape of risk* such as the region in our study (Bantul in Central Java, Indonesia), there is a long history of handling extreme suffering. For centuries, the sense of insecurity caused by the threat of earthquakes and volcanic eruptions has been part of the everyday life of the inhabitants of this region; these types of events are not characterized by the singularity with which they might be perceived in the Western world. In our interviews, which were conducted 2–4 years after the 2006 earthquake, we encountered many facets and stories of mild to severe suffering.

J. A. Indradjaja (✉)
Berlin, Germany
e-mail: jindradjaja@web.de

M. Zaumseil
International Academy for Innovative Pedagogy, Psychology and Economics gGmbH
at Freie Universität Berlin, Malteserstr. 74-100, 12249 Berlin, Germany
e-mail: zaumseil@zedat.fu-berlin.de

M. Zaumseil et al. (eds.), *Cultural Psychology of Coping with Disasters*,
DOI 10.1007/978-1-4614-9354-9_13,

There was a strong sense of insecurity and confusion. Most individuals experienced extreme fear due to frequent aftershocks. A few suffered and felt affected by the disaster for longer periods of time.

Right from the beginning, we found that the villagers frequently made use of the term *trauma*, often in the context of a self-diagnosis: "I am still traumatized" (*saya masih trauma*). In other circumstances, this *trauma* was ascribed to others. This imported term, which is frequently used by international and local aid organizations, appears to be a new cipher or anchor for suffering and a means of gaining access to resources. To approach the topic of suffering and healing, we decided to address the newly created trauma discourse in order to develop an understanding of the way in which this term is linked to local concepts and to determine how respondents used these related concepts to communicate with interviewers about their different forms of subjective suffering and methods for handling their suffering. Our interview partners mentioned a wide array of meanings associated with the imported trauma concept. In the following, we aim to expand upon this broad spectrum of meanings. This spectrum includes ideas that range from specific local worldviews to imported meanings from disaster mental health. In addition, we gathered data on the forms of suffering for which villagers used terms other than *trauma*.

In Indonesia, unlike in Western culture, *trauma* is not viewed as an individualized, problem-focused phenomenon; the concept describes the person's overall mental state rather than localized symptoms. Because this term is relatively new in Indonesia, there is no established common understanding of the concept and those affected by the disaster tend to use the word fairly arbitrarily to describe negative mental states. The Western definition of trauma and the caring, professional approach to handling traumatized individuals as ill have only developed over the last 50 years (see Chap. 2). This definition revolves around causal ideas about the effects of external events on psychological functioning (especially memory and emotion) within disposed individuals. These assumptions and constructs are not shared in Java. The inner sphere is commonly perceived to be linked with the transcendental-spiritual world. There is no strict separation between body and mind, feeling and knowledge, and individual and social spheres. In general, people do not draw a strong distinction between physical and mental illness (see Ferzacca 2001).

Based on these views, we aim to develop a specific, local understanding of extreme suffering and responses to this suffering which complements existing understandings of *trauma*. Our investigation focuses on local principles of classification, in particular the notion of inner and outer self (*batin* and *lahir*). We attempt to preserve the specialized logic governing this local presentation; however, the chapter is artificially divided into sections based on the following different but related elements. We begin by addressing the explicit meanings of the *trauma* concept for affected villagers. We then describe the necessary criteria for defining an experience as a terrible event. Next, we illustrate the ways in which our interview partners subjectively experience and describe suffering. Finally, we address the responses to the extreme suffering caused by the earthquake. These responses, which focus on relieving or diminishing suffering, will be examined as part of the subject of coping. They include any methods which, from the perspective of the other villagers, help those who have experienced extreme suffering. This analysis is consistent with the focus on remoralization and healing described by Priya (2010, 2012).

13.2 Terminologies of Extreme Suffering

In response to the question of where and in what context they learned about the concept of *trauma*, our interviewees gave a wide range of answers. Some did not know where the word came from while others said that they learned the word *trauma* from their friends or the media. Others simply used the word—just like everyone else—without necessarily knowing what it means. Most people were familiar with the word *trauma* from such sources as recent television programs, emergency training, and external aid workers who have been in the region since the earthquake in 2006.

> It was actually during the earthquake, [I heard people say], "*trauma*" or "I have *trauma*", so I just followed the others (laughing) [. . .] There was no such term "*trauma*" [before the earthquake]. And where it came from, I don't know (laughing). (Pak Budiman, Sendang)

When we consider the concepts that are most frequently associated with *trauma*, descriptions tend to focus on ideas such as fear, shock, worry, and the memories and intrusive images connected to these emotions. This subjective experience, which is frequently shared with others, is often remembered and recounted as a response to a terrible event (such as being buried under a wall or witnessing a death). When we asked about the Indonesian term for *trauma*, respondents often mentioned the word *takut* (fear) in connection with the term *trauma*. In Javanese, the term used is *jinjau* (uncanny, dreadful), a word which Pak Priyanto described as meaning "too afraid" (*terlalu takut*). Another respondent emphasized the way in which fear and memory fed into one another and characterized this phenomenon using the Javanese word *kethentho-thento*, which means something like "recurring vague shadows or ideas."

> I think *trauma* is when someone is reminded of a previous experience. [. . .] (S)he always remembers and becomes afraid; the [same] fear reappears as at the first instance [. . .] The Javanese term is "*kethentho-thentho*." (Pak Budiman, Sendang)

When attempting to translate the *trauma* concept or define extreme suffering, fear and the intrusive memories linked to this fear are central features.

This relatively new term has most likely been influenced by meanings that have been imported by external aid workers and the media. The vagueness of the term, in the sense of a "boundary object" (Star and Griesemer 1998), suggests a number of connections to different discourses, and because *trauma* is a new concept for which there is no established understanding, it can be used in many ways and imbued with different meanings.

13.3 Description of Terrible Events

The discourse surrounding the local concept of *trauma* has developed alongside subjective descriptions of a terrible event. The villagers described the way in which they perceived the sudden, unexpected, overpowering, terrible event: they were surrounded by destruction, death, and injury; there was heavy rain, dust in the air, no electricity, and life was overcome by darkness, chaos, and wild, destructive tremors. Some believed that it was the end of the world *(kiamat)* and there were rumors of a tsunami.

> Every day there was an earthquake, rain, earthquake and rain. I was thinking: is this doomsday (*kiamat*)? I was really very horrified (*ngeri*). Everyone was panicking (*panik*), there was no one, who was not in a state of panic, because the earthquake happened in the morning, clouds came up and chaos broke out, everyone tried to escape. [...] The night felt like doomsday, [...] thunder and lightning, striking one after another. Everyone went crazy (*gila*), everything went crazy. At that time there was no electricity yet. (Pak Geno, Sido Kabul)

Mass destruction, chaos and panic, darkness, dust clouds, screaming, and shouting led to a frantic attempt to flee in fear of a tsunami or tidal wave like that which had destroyed Aceh 17 months before. Once the initial fear of a tsunami had subsided, affected individuals described their terror during the persistent aftershocks, and their fear of additional destruction, death, or injury. They were also afraid of the renewed threat of material losses and of experiencing death or being left alone during future earthquakes. They depicted their shock and horror at the things they saw and experienced, for example, seeing the injured or dead, or described, how the aftershocks during the cleanup fueled their fear of being unable to flee the situation. The panic and chaos they felt was connected with a deep sense of insecurity.

In respondents' descriptions of the event, there seemed to be no distinction between the characteristics of the event and their subjective response to it. The experience was an integral part of the context; together they formed a single unit. In the face of this extreme situation, the villagers described themselves as helpless and stunned. Their world of experiences changed suddenly and drastically. Their everyday feelings of safety and security transformed unexpectedly into insecurity, fear for their lives, and inner unrest *(tidak tentram)*. They described themselves as being in a weak, disoriented mental state[1] and articulated a broad spectrum of fear-related feelings: shock (*kaget, terkejut*), worry (*kuatir*), and fear (*takut*)—including very intense fear/horror (*takut sekali/ngeri*).

13.4 Forms of Disaster-Related Suffering

The earthquake was viewed as a collective experience that shocked everyone. According to the respondents, this meant that everyone was "traumatized." They attributed this to the continued aftershocks and indicated that the condition lasted approximately 6 months. They reported that only one or two individuals in the village were still seriously affected by the suffering they experienced during the disaster 4 years ago. In the following section, we will introduce the spectrum of suffering-related experiences that occur after extreme disasters.

---

[1] Respondents normally used the word *mental*.

13.4.1 Deep and Enduring Suffering

Bu Geno (see case study) was buried in the rubble of her house. Her husband, who was also injured, screamed for help until he lost his voice. He was ultimately forced to free her on his own and her leg was injured in the process. In our interview, she indicated that she was still "traumatized" (*trauma*). In the following, she described the images that haunt her and her attempts to cope with the experience:

> That wall behind there always reminds me of being buried. I couldn't breathe; after a while the air became thin [...] and it seemed that I was gradually dying. I couldn't breathe. Today I still remember, and when I go to sleep, I don't want to be close to a wall. [...] I am still traumatized (*trauma*) like that....it feels like it reappears (*terbayang-bayang*). I imagine that there is an earthquake, and when I am having these thoughts, my heart is upset (*tidak tentram*). It is a feeling where I cannot sleep; but if I look towards the sky, then I can sleep. (Bu Geno, Sido Kabul)

In this quotation, Bu Geno begins with the image of the wall in her house and proceeds to give a precise description of the general physical situation of a person who has been trapped or buried. Later on in the interview, she connects the wall with the concept of *trauma* (*trauma sama tembok* trauma from the wall) and relates the images to her subjective feelings, the unsettled feeling in her heart, and her difficulty sleeping. At the end of her description, she changes course and focuses on her method of coping: when she looks toward the sky, she is able to find peace, and sleep at last.

Later in this chapter, we address the complex relationship between the part of the person directed at and attributed to the outside world (*lahir*) and the inner self (*batin*), a concept which is particularly prevalent in Java. We also focus on the special meaning of the heart as a metaphorical center of feeling and inner knowledge, and as a point of access to the transcendental and the divine. The central theme here is the way deep and persistent suffering is tied to the idea of transcendental healing.

Here, the respondent describes both a conflicted, unsettled heart and a frightening mixture (*campur aduk*) of feelings which disrupts her inner order:

> When I felt *trauma*, I felt fear (*takut*), it was a feeling of horror (*ngeri*), everything was confused (*campur aduk*). It is hard to imagine; I cannot describe it in words, neither in a single word nor in a combination of words. (Mas Restu, Sendang)

13.4.1.1 Lack of Recovery as Extreme Suffering Discourse

During the earthquake, Mbah Suloyo was also buried in her house and severely injured. At the time of the interview, she was physically impaired and reliant upon the help of other people. She reported that she considerd her persistent, severe suffering, deep disappointment, and pain to show her lack of recovery (*sakit tidak sembuh sembuh*). She did not use the term *trauma*.

> I am sick and just won't recover (*sakit tidak sembuh-sembuh*). I am jinxed—not for a few days, not just for a few months; it seems like it will take years for me to recover. So my thoughts start to stray (*pikiran saya kemana-mana*), as if my thoughts were uncomfortable (*tidak enak di pikiran*). (Mbah Suloyo, Mulya Sari)

It was clear from meeting with Mbah Suloyo that she was not capable of fulfilling her role as defined by her sociocultural context. In addition, she felt alienated from the communal feeling associated with taking on family responsibilities. She was unable to earn any money toward the treatment of her injuries or permanent disabilities; she received no financial support from the community and far too little from her family. Not only did she suffer as a result of her limited physical mobility, her lack of financial resources, and her negative experiences with treatment, but she also experienced suffering and worry in connection with hidden tensions within her family. She complained that the care provided for her—particularly by her children, and also by her extended family—was insufficient. This suffering, combined with the unfulfilled expectations regarding her cultural role, led to doubt and feelings that she no longer wished to live. These feelings represented a sociocultural and religious taboo that drew accusations from her family members.

13.4.1.2 Complete Suffering and Lack of Motivation as Extreme Suffering Discourse

Another respondent, Bu Suprapti, did not describe herself as traumatized even though she touched upon a number of suffering narratives in her interview. Her husband and children were buried in the house and injured. One of her children died and the surviving children began to display challenging behaviors after the shocking event. Bu Suprapti was forced to learn how to handle these changes. She was not able to forget these experiences; the events evoked intense fear *(ngeri)* and deep pain. She described her pain as "complete suffering" (*menderita sempurna*), because she lost everything. Because of the severe mental strain she suffered, she lost all sense of motivation for several months.

> I felt really down (*nglokro*), and I really didn't have any motivation for anything (*ngga' punya semangat apa-apa*). (Bu Suprapti, Sido Kabul)

In spite of everything, she fought to care for her surviving children. Ultimately, she described being successful in accepting her suffering, reconciling with the higher being, and calling upon divine wisdom (*hikmah*) to gain deeper insight into these past events.

13.4.1.3 Weeping Sickness (*sakit cengeng*) as Extreme Suffering Discourse

One type of suffering or instability, described idiosyncratically by the participant as weeping sickness (*sakit cengeng*), but not *trauma*, seems to be less intrusive. Pak Wagimin was not injured during the earthquake. He claimed that his experience of the earthquake left him psychologically overwhelmed and confused (*bingung*).[2]

---

[2] In a figurative sense, *bingung* means something like *light confusion* in the sense of inner unrest and chaotic or disordered feelings and thoughts.

> For about ten days I was so confused (*bingung*), because the parents of the child had not yet visited him at all. I also thought about clothes, food, and different things. I was very confused (*bingung*) (laughing). I rarely took a bath or even changed my clothes. (Pak Wagimin, Sendang)

He described his mental state since then as weak and compromised; his problems included difficulty controlling his feelings, because a range of different events triggered sudden "weeping spells" (*cengeng*).

As a result of her injuries from the earthquake, Bu Sutini suffered from persistent pain and limited mobility when she was interviewed; she described her condition as an unsettling or trembling of the heart (*hati belum tentram, hati gemetar*), and reported that she still remembered this catastrophic event. She felt an inner instability, reacted strongly to different stimuli, and cried at the slightest provocation. She described her uncontrollable feelings as an illness or "weeping sickness" (*sakit cengen*).[3] Her weeping spells indicate a lack of inner strength, internal crisis, and an emotional reaction to her social environment. In order to preserve social harmony, she avoided open tension with others. As in the case of Pak Wagimin, this shocking experience resulted in suffering associated with strong emotional agitation and strain that could persist over a long period of time.

> Now, I have weeping sickness (*lara gembeng; sakit cengeng*). If, for example, one of my children is grumpy towards me, saying this and that, then I cry and feel hurt. (Bu Sutini, Sendang)

13.4.2 Mourning as a Trauma Discourse

> Trauma refers to the feeling of your heart (*rasa hatinya*), when it is still disappointed (*gelo, kecewa*) and sad (*susah*) about losing a family member. If my house were destroyed, turning to dust [I wouldn't care], as long as my family were still complete. [...] Property can be bought again, but how about lives? (Pak Kartono, Sido Kabul)

For Pak Kartono, *trauma* refers to the disappointment and sorrow caused by the irreversible loss of a loved one. Here, he describes how he handled the death of his granddaughter:

> When I lost my granddaughter, I felt stress (*stres*). Until recently, I was still traumatized (*trauma*), I still saw her playing, although she had died, so how?... What was it with me? If my mind was not strong, I would have gone go crazy (*gila*). [...] Because I still saw her. (Pak Kartono, Sido Kabul)

[3] In this context, *sakit cengeng* means prone to sudden crying. The term stems from the slang spoken in Jakarta (Javanese: *lara gembeng*).

13.4.3 Shock from Perceptions that are Reminiscent of a Traumatic Experience

The term *trauma* was also used to describe the situation in which, for a period of time following the earthquake, sounds or other perceptions which were reminiscent of the earthquake shocked (*kaget*) the person in question.

> For example, until about 6 months after the earthquake: Whenever there was a sound of a car causing vibrations, or for any small reason, I was shocked (*kaget*). It reminded me of the earthquake. Because the sound was... greng.. [...] I also asked some of my neighbors about it, and I found out that two other neighbors were also traumatized. They were shocked (*kaget*) when hearing the particular sound. (Pak Jiyo, Sido Kabul)

So a phenomenon described as a symptom of trauma from the medical discourse was likely to be a widely shared post-earthquake reaction.

13.4.4 Reasonable Fear and Worry as Trauma Discourse

Our interview participants used the word *trauma* in the sense of a deep distress as well as in the sense of a reasonable fear or worry (*khawatir*) and risk or caution. In the following example, the respondent used the word *trauma* to refer to the caution that one shows when entering houses that are in danger of collapse:

> In my opinion, *trauma* was when we were clearing the rubble and were afraid it could suddenly collapse again, like before. Sometimes I ran. And even when I was encouraged to enter, I still wanted to run. (Mas Naryanto, Sido Kabul)

This statement refers to the worry (*khawatir*) that there could be another earthquake. In the following statement, the respondent's own *trauma* was described as a feeling (*rasa*) of diffuse worry based on the risk of future threats:

> Trauma is when you have the feeling (*rasanya*) [and wonder], how it would be if another earthquake or a tsunami occurred. (Pak Siswanto, Sido Kabul)

In a further example, Bu Romlah used the term *rasa* (feeling) to refer to the fear of an existing threat:

> If we have, for instance, already experienced an earthquake—as we have—that earthquake experience is really frightening (*bener-bener menakutkan*). So the feeling of trauma (*rasa trauma*) is that we are afraid (*takut*) that such an incident will happen again. (Bu Romlah, Sido Kabul)

Rasa trauma means the fear of something concrete and defined. This feeling materializes as a reasonable fear which draws a justifiable connection between emotion and a real threat. In the second statement, the feeling (*rasa*) behind the problem is referred to as *trauma* and is connected specifically to the idea that the house could be destroyed again in the future. Here, *trauma* functions is a kind of risk evaluation mechanism and the associated *rasa* is a (reasonable) perception (see Chap. 15 regarding future threats).

13.4.5 Suffering of Children

The idea that being shocked (*kaget*) and enduring emotional disturbances can lead to illness is a common conception in Indonesia (see Hay 2004). It is presumed that shock has a general effect which can trigger many types of illness. Children are viewed as particularly vulnerable to this phenomenon. In 1961, Geertz wrote that practically all types of care for children (and particularly young children) in East Java focus on ensuring that children are not exposed to shocking or frightening experiences.

Pak Basuki from Sendang reported that after the earthquake, his child was silent, disinterested, and fearful. The child reacted quickly to sounds that were reminiscent of the earthquake, often clung to her parents and wanted to be carried constantly. Pak Suwondo from Sido Kabul described how his children were afraid of another earthquake; they did not feel comfortable in their own home and became fearful when they saw the house. They were afraid that in the event of another earthquake, they would be unable to flee and would be buried inside the house. This fear was so strong that the children avoided entering the house and sometimes even refused to do so when asked to. Bu Suprapti spoke about her daughter, who was alone in a room as tiles began to fall from the roof. She reported that her daughter was stressed (*stres*) and in her estimation, traumatized (*trauma*). Her child developed challenging behaviors, e.g., collecting trash. She was unable to do anything but be patient and attentive. However, after a year, she noticed a dramatic improvement.

Special trauma healing groups and other types of support for children were offered by students and other nonprofessionals. Groups also offered opportunities for recreation and activities as well as psychosocial and pedagogical support. The mothers and fathers in the villages tried to help improve the children's mental state by offering them special attention, explanations, and opportunities to calm down and build motivation (*semangat*). They attempted to help them to occupy themselves or distract them by playing or engaging them in discussion. They encouraged them to play with other children in the hopes that they would not think about the event, and eventually forget it.

13.5 "Cultural Specifics in Suffering"

We attempted to describe and categorize the different types of earthquake-related sufferings. In doing so, we used the vague concept of *trauma* as a register for this connection to the disaster and identified additional meanings in the local concepts of suffering that were not defined as *trauma*. The spectrum of disaster-related suffering was very broad. It extended from a common, shared suffering experience shortly after the event ("we were all traumatized"), cautionary measures, and reasonable fear of a real threat, to a fear of earthquake-related signals, sorrow, and severe, long-term unsettling, or distress of the heart. The local criteria for determining severity included duration, intensity of reactions, use of the local concept of being ill (*sakit*), e.g., weeping sickness, and a severe impairment of the inner self (*batin*) and the heart (*hati*). Another sign of severity is a guarded attitude around others.

A common characteristic of deep distress is an all-encompassing, nonspecific impairment that includes a moral (demoralization in the sense of Priya (2010)) or religious dimension which is also expected to supply the solution to the problem (see below). The confusion, or the state that is perceived as a distressing mix between inner orders—with their relationships to the transcendental and the social—leads to a loss of inner calm and peace and is connected with a lack of inner or mental strength (*kekuatan mental*). Browne (2001) noted: "Regarding emotional expression, it is often stated that the Javanese seek to maintain a smoothness (*ikhlas*, *tenteram*) in both emotional demeanor and behavior (Geertz 1960, 1983; Keeler 1983, 1987)" (p. 152). He emphasized that the Javanese tend to avoid being surprised or expressing troubling emotions and fear a loss of control. For individuals suffering from deep distress, the core issue is not a specific, treatable problem, but rather a general condition that developed when the individual endured a terrible, frightening disaster-related experience that he or she was unable to handle.

The term *rasa* (sensation or feeling) appears in all forms of suffering. The complex meaning of "rasa" plays a prominent role in literature about Java (see Ferzacca 2001; Beatty 1999; Stange 1984; Geertz 1960, 1974). Ferzacca (2001) sees a Javanese philosophy of embodiment in the "logic of *rasa*." He cites Geertz (1973), who classified the meaning as "sense-taste-feeling-meaning" (p. 124). Geertz (1960) stated that the link to the heart is of central importance for the connection between feeling and meaning in the "*rasa*" concept. *Rasa* is not only seen as a feeling or sensation but also viewed as a path to intuitive knowledge, a concept that plays a major role in Java (Stange 1984; Beatty 1999). The word *rasa* is also used to mean the essence of a substance, or its true identity. It serves as a personal instrument that leads to true insight (Mulder 1990). Through *rasa*, the individual experiences his or her true inner reality. It represents the connection to transcendental reality.

Feeling and reason are not separate elements. The Western dualism of reason on the one side, and a physical, emotional level on the other stands in contrast to the local understanding of *trauma* as a combination of reasonable worry and a deeply felt (physical and emotional) sense of fear. In Western thought, one tends to separate the emotional/physical aspect or pathologize it (as in posttraumatic stress disorder; PTSD). The excerpts from our interviews with our Javanese respondents give an entirely different impression: the horror is related to a spiritual, moral order (in the sense of a warning from God) and directly linked to reasonable worry, which, in the Western model, tends to be understood in the terms of the technical rationality of risk management.

The local understanding of *rasa* is linked to another Javanese concept, which, for our interview participants, was related to the new concept of *trauma*. This concept is the specialized construction of the self through the juxtaposition of the outer (*lahir*) and the inner (*batin*) components.

In Javanese culture, strong emotions (such as shock, deep sorrow, crying, and rage) and passions are considered to be rude (*kasar*). They must be controlled; otherwise they could lead to illness, unseemly behavior, and strain in social relationships. In extreme cases, these emotions could lead to the feared condition of a loss of control or running amok (*ngamuk*) (see Browne 2001). In Java, this term is used to refer to even moderately aggressive actions (see Zaumseil 2006). The expression of strong feelings belongs to the realm of the outer self (*lahir*), or the individual's external actions (behavior), motions, gestures, and verbal communication. The delicate inner self (*batin*) corresponds to the subjective consciousness. The individual must constantly strive to refine (*halus*) this side of his or her personality; its destruction would carry grave consequences for both the inner and outer sides of the individual.

In the following list, we attempt to clarify connections between the signs of suffering mentioned by our interview respondents and the local categories *lahir* and *batin*. *Batin* and *lahir* are fluid concepts that have no clear-cut and mutually exclusive definitions. For our respondents they are relevant orientations which structure their suffering experience in the sense of belonging more or less to *batin* or *lahir*.

Signs of suffering belonging more to the inner (*batin*) realm:

- erratic mind (*batin tidak karuan*)
- chaotic feelings, emotional chaos (*perasaan campur aduk*)
- unsettled feeling (*rasa tidak tenang*)
- worried, concerned (*cemas*)
- deep shock (*kaget di hati*)
- intense fear/horror (*ngeri*)
- persistent fear (*ketakutan terus*)
- disappointment (*kecewa; Javanese: gelo*)
- worry (*rasa kawatir, rasa tom-toman*)
- sadness (*sedih*)
- heavy-hearted (*susah*)
- (re)appearances (*terbayang–bayang*)
- confusion (*bingung*)
- daydream (*bengong*)
- ruminate (*merenung*)
- anxious (*was-was*)
- mental exhaustion (*pikiran capek*).

Signs of suffering belonging more to the outer (*lahir*) realm:

- anger (*marah*)
- sensation of pounding heart (*deg-degan*)
- startled, shocked (*terkejut*)
- showing signs of nervousness and panic
- tremors, trembling (*gemetaran*)
- bodily exhaustion (*badan letih*)
- crying (*menangis*)
- anorexia; lack of appetite (*tidak ada rasa nafsu makan*)
- sleepwalking (*Javanese: turunelari*)
- wandering (*mondar mandir*)

The list is given here to characterize the specific and vague experience-near local concept of suffering as represented in the descriptions of our respondents. It should be understood as giving the elements of a picture and not as a list of rational and technical definitions.

13.6 Healing: Coping with Suffering

The basic conception of subjective suffering and impairment after the earthquake centers on a potentially deep change in an individual's internal state which persists on a more or less long-term basis. This is an unstable, confusing general state or internal configuration, not a specific problem with a solution. Distress of the heart is not treated using specific measures, such as those employed for certain types of trauma therapy or coping strategies; the methods are less specific. These methods follow the same principles as coping with any type of disaster and can be formulated in the same dimensions: coping takes place in the transcendental, material, social, and life conduct dimension.

People who experienced suffering were talked about and expressed their own experiences in an indirect way as a return to a state of peace (*tenang*) and heartfelt calm (*tentram hati*). They viewed their mental state as an impairment and aimed to return to a prior, balanced inner state.

> If there is an error (*error*) in our mental condition (*mental*) or our soul (*jiwa*) or our thoughts (*pikiran*), that is, if we cannot see the reality, then we will become like that. (Pak Nurdin, Sido Kabul)

Most of the villagers we spoke to felt as if they had been changed by the suffering they experienced; they had passed the test of the higher being and attained an enlightened state. In the following statements, respondents share their hope that the injured heart can be healed from the inside.

> A sick (*sakit*) heart or a wounded (*luka*) heart can recover, or the conscience (*hati nurani*) can recover on its own. If one possesses the old knowledge—the Javanese way is the old knowledge isn't it—you can make use of it. It means: whatever it is, we accept it—how do you say, because, everything is God's will, and we are not allowed to reject it. (Pak Kartono, Sido Kabul)

In the next statement, suffering and healing also revolve around the heart:

> I want to strive, so I can have a peaceful (*tentram*) heart. That way, whatever happens, my heart will not palpitate (*deg-degan*). So far, I still cannot [stay calm]. I hope that I can heal my heart, because as long as I am ill, I cannot be peaceful (*tentram*). (Bu Sutini, Sendang)

The basic thought is that one must *indirectly* create the conditions necessary to allow healing to occur from the inside. This can take place, for example, through an appeal to the higher being, patience, letting go of the things that have happened, accepting these events as inalterable, performing everyday tasks, and promoting harmony in social relationships, etc. In this indirect way, the general dimensions of coping (religious, material, social dimension, and principles of life conduct) are reflected in the ways in which individuals handle extreme suffering. In the following, we show how affected individuals apply the dimensions of coping we discussed in order to handle the distress of the sick or wounded heart.

13.6.1 Local Concepts for Handling Fear and Extreme Suffering

There is a wide range of local concepts, ideas, and recommendations for handling fear and extreme suffering. The few villagers who are unable to overcome the psychological wounds they suffered during the earthquake were viewed as ill and provided with special care and protection. However, affected individuals are rarely referred to psychosocial or psychiatric specialists. There is no conception of professional treatment. This is understandable, as the necessary resources are often unavailable or villagers are not aware of these resources in the first place. This type of coping, which takes places with a very limited amount of professional support, is imbedded in a specific moral order and heavily influenced by the social and religious context of the local cultural setting. There is no culture of therapy and therefore no resources for this type of treatment; spiritual experts are responsible for these tasks. Because of this, descriptions of suffering are often directly linked to recommendations for handling suffering. The limited resources, the precarious economic situation, and the lack of an insurance system to treat physical injuries became increasingly apparent after the earthquake, particularly in the case of enduring suffering. The cost of treatment must often be weighed against the basic resources required for survival.

The respondents were aware and proud of the fact that their cultural background, with its strong spiritual/religious framework, helped to prepare them to handle suffering and twists of fate. The characteristics of the local forms of coping with extreme suffering include:

- differentiation and diversity,
- general availability of knowledge (as opposed to exclusivity of professional expertise),
- lack of specificity, applicable to any type of misfortune, and
- descriptions of suffering and coping which are often directly connected and viewed as related.

The psycho-religious ideals and orientations that we discussed as part of the religious dimension (see Chap. 12) are central to coping with extreme suffering and distress of the heart. These ideals, such as surrender (*pasrah)*, acceptance (*nrimo*), and gratitude (*syukur*) serve as general orientations in everyday life, as principles of life conduct and are viewed to be effective, indirect ways of healing distress of the heart. Many of these orientations are regarded as virtues which extend to practical, everyday coping activities, and therefore into the material dimension of coping. These principles of life conduct are strongly linked to social activities and relationships within the village.

13.6.2 Case Study: Bu Geno

Bu Geno is 50 years old. She had been alone during the earthquake and spent hours buried under rubble, where she had been hardly able to breathe. She had screamed for help, but nobody had come. Her husband had freed her from the rubble, but her leg had been severely injured during the rescue attempt. In our interview, she described her suffering as “wall *trauma*” (*trauma sama tembok*). She reported that she still experienced pain and suffered from limited mobility. Her husband had left his job as a carpenter out of a sense of duty to care for and support her.

Throughout the process of handling extreme suffering, her main goal has been to establish a sense of inner security and peace of the heart (*aman, tentram di hati dan pikiran*). At the time of the interview she still sought out safe places to sleep that were far away from the wall; she preferred to sleep in a bamboo house rather than a stone house. Even after two and a half years, her experiences during the earthquake were still fresh in her mind and she feared that her injury would make it impossible for her to flee in the event of another earthquake. According to her, a person can make only vague predictions; God will make any final decisions. She accepted (*nrimo*) her suffering and pain as her fate in life (*nasib*). She believed that denying her fate could cause spiritual imbalance and illness. For her, faith (*iman*) and trust are resources that have helped her to handle extreme suffering. Both have given her the strength she needs to recover from her unsettled heart. She described making an effort (*usaha*) not to be faint-hearted (*tidak kecil hati*). Over time, she has learned to confront her fear and involuntary memories more calmly and patiently. The related beliefs stopped her from brooding (*banyak pikiran*) and helped her to feel a sense of inner satisfaction and peace (*tentram*).

Other attitudes, such as patience (*saba*r) and gratitude, are also important to Bu Geno. Patience has been an important instrument in the creation of a stable mental state. The *untungya* stance described in Chap. 11, or the life philosophy “fortune in misfortune,” has been an important aspect of her coping process. In spite of her severe injury, she retrospectively evaluated, “I was still lucky when the earthquake happened.” Instead of dying, Bu Geno continued to live with her injury. To remain thankful—even in the midst of extreme suffering—means to trust in God and strive for inner satisfaction through all types of life situations. She thanked God for the chance to live and heal, for her optimistic outlook toward the future (see Chap. 11), and for her job and her family.

However, in addition to her personal attitude toward life, which is based on the cultural-specific principles of life conduct, Bu Geno reported that social support also played an important role in the process of healing her distressed heart. She sensed continued support from her family, her neighbors, and her circle of friends. At the time of the interview, although she was still in pain and it was difficult for her to stand or sit, with the help of her husband, Bu Geno had been able to continue her work producing and selling krupuk. She reported that her family was very understanding of her continued fear and did not pressure her. They always provided her with words of advice, encouragement, emotional support, and a sense of hope. Without the burden of pressure, they tried to remain calm and relaxed (*santai*) and face these challenges together.

For Bu Geno, the earthquake not only caused severe physical injury and mental suffering, but also resulted in material loss. For this reason, it is important to mention that she received free professional medical treatment including medicine, a small personal loan to allow her to resume her home production business, and, like many others, financial support to help rebuild her house.

13.7 Concluding Remarks

In Chap. 2, we discussed the understanding of the diagnostic category of PTSD as stipulated in the American Diagnostic and Statistical Manual of Mental Disorders. This international text lays out a universal definition for a specific individual illness which is linked to dysfunction. Different national health and social systems take different approaches to providing professional therapeutic and care services[4] for individuals with this condition. Mental trauma is a concept that has only recently been recognized as an illness by the Western medical and psychological experts. In countries in which there is still no strong trend toward medical professionalization and where medical resources are limited, local ideas and practices as well as family and community aid are of central importance. This is evident from Zaumseil's (2006, 2010) previous study in the same region. His investigation focused on acceptance, family, and community care (*mengemong*), in addition to drastic measures used to control individuals who have been diagnosed as mentally ill (see Zaumseil 2010).

Our aim was not to develop or measure universally defined diagnostic categories for a PTSD. Rather we wanted to illustrate the ways in which those affected by a disaster describe their form of suffering and the ways they utilize ideas from global disaster help discourses and the concept of *trauma.* In the interviews and stories about disaster-related suffering in Java, local and global elements are connected in the sense of glocalization (Robertson 1995). In all countries, there is a rift between lay (or folk) concepts (also known as public beliefs) of health and illness and professional standards (see Angermeyer and Matschinger 1999). Ferzacca (2001) investigated the highly pluralistic urban medicine in the nearby city of Yogyakarta. He found a complicated and creative mixture of health-related ideas. The categorization of different aspects as modern or traditional is value-driven. In this regard, there is a tendency to associate modern influences with new illnesses (*sakit modern*) and view traditional practices as beneficial to health. Our description of the ways in which the people of Bantul employ the imported trauma concept shows a similar, creative mixture, which is closely related to everyday experience.

As we discovered, extreme, disaster-related suffering was described as fear (*takut*), intense fear (*ngeri*), shock, worry, and deep disappointment about loss and death. Individuals affected by a disaster have a strong tendency to normalize (rather than pathologize) these feelings. This tendency toward the *normalization* of extreme suffering is connected with an additional tendency to view the condition as a temporary situation, which can improve through consideration and social support. Suffering is combated using *nonspecific* methods and psycho-religious orientations which help to relieve all forms of misfortune. An overview of the elements involved in such nonspecific forms of coping with extreme suffering is offered in Fig. 13.1.

[4] In Indonesia, only state employees have a right to claim financial support for medical treatment. In the villages we visited, no one received trauma therapy.

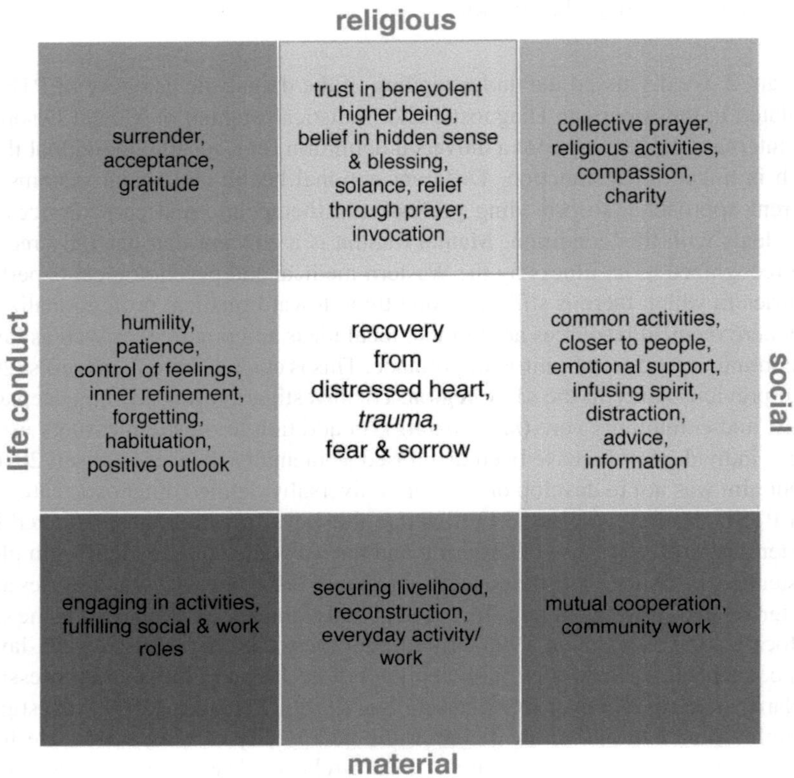

Fig. 13.1 Multiple Dimensions of Dealing with Extreme Suffering in Java

The figure illustrates the general dimensions of coping (see Part III). The areas of intersection between the religious, social, and material dimensions and the dimension of life conduct are shown in the corners of the diagram.

The subjective meanings of suffering are linked to the sociocultural context and can only be understood as a function of this context (see Chap. 3).[5] Experiences of suffering are culturally constructed and connected to the local moral order, which must be viewed within the historical framework of local economic relationships and political structures. For example, some families rely on the services of traditional healers to treat persistent physical suffering because they are unable to afford the cost of medical treatment. In this context, normalizing approaches are the only option for handing extreme psychosocial suffering, which accompanies, and indeed is inseparable from, somatic pain.

Extreme suffering plunges the inner self (*batin*) into a chaotic mixture (*campur*) or confusion (*bingung*), endangering the inner connection to and faith in a higher

[5] According to Cassell's (2004) definition of suffering, "a person may suffer if he or she is not able to meet the socio-moral demands in the local moral worlds" (p. 38).

being as well as trust in the self and the environment. These phases of confusion of the heart are considered to be normal. Respondents reflected on these phases, emphasizing the importance of healing the heart. In the ideal type view, this can be achieved by accepting fate (*nrimo)*, surrendering (*pasrah*) power over one's heart to the higher power instead of struggling against destiny, showing patience (*sabar)*, and experiencing gratitude (*syukur*). This allows the individual to reestablish his or her inner connection to the divine, or cosmic, and gain insight and wisdom (*hikmah*). Inner healing has a reciprocal relationship with the outer self, leading the individual to engage in recovery and survival-oriented behaviors. This behavior dispels inner chaos and painful thoughts. The reestablishment of the individual's inner (*batin)* balance positively affects all social relationships and motivates (*semangat)* the individual to fulfill his or her obligations.

We conclude with Priya's (2012) view that it is useful to "co-construct participants' experiences from their own perspective" (p. 212). As stated in the beginning, we showed that the process of suffering and healing is inherently subjective, local, and pluralistic in nature. Priya went so far as to accuse a purely symptom-based understanding of suffering of delegitimizing the experience of afflicted persons, and thereby enhancing their suffering. We think that the normalizing view of suffering shows great potential in terms of local wisdom, which is also highly prized on the local level (see Chap. 3). The understanding of suffering, as shown by respondents' use of the concept of *trauma* is glocal: the local does not stand in opposition to the global, or modern. On the contrary, although local wisdom is viewed as a traditional phenomenon, it is currently in the process of being reimagined. We agree with Priya that the decontextualization and individualization of suffering are extremely detrimental to the sufferer. This view does not argue against professional treatment of severe, persistent psychosocial suffering. However, this treatment must display a strong sensibility for the context and its relationship to the sufferer.

Acknowledgments The editors would like to thank Devin Martini for translating this chapter from German into English.

References

Angermeyer, M. C., & Matschinger, H. (1999). Social representations of mental illness among the public. In J. Guimon, W. Fischer, & N. Sartorius (Eds.), *The image of madness* (pp. 20–28). Basel: Karger.

Beatty, A. (1999). *Varieties of Javanese religion: An anthropological account. Cambridge studies in social and cultural anthropology*. Cambridge: Cambridge University Press.

Browne, K. (2001). (Ng)amuk revisited: Emotional expression and mental illness in Central Java, Indonesia. *Transcultural Psychiatry*, *38*(2), 147–165.

Cassell, E. J. (2004). The *nature of suffering and the goals of medicine* (2nd ed.). New York: Oxford.

Charmaz, K. (1999). Stories of suffering: Subjective tales and research narratives. *Qualitative Health Research, 9*(3), 362–382.

Ferzacca, S. (2001). *Healing the modern in a Central Javanese city*. Durham: Carolina Academic Press.

Geertz, C. (1960). *The religion of Java*. Glencoe: The Free Press.

Geertz, C. (1973). *The interpretation of cultures: Selected essays*. New York: Basic Books.

Geertz, C. (1983). *Local knowledge: Further essays in interpretive anthropology*. New York: Basic Books.

Geertz, H. (1961). *The Javanese family. A study of kinship and socialization*. New York: Free Press of Glencoe.

Hay, M. C. (2004). *Remembering to live. Illness at the intersection of anxiety and knowledge in rural Indonesia*. Ann Arbor: University of Michigan Press.

Keeler, W. (1983). Shame and stage fright in Java. *Ethos, 11*(3), 152–165.

Keeler, W. (1987). *Javanese shadow plays, Javanese selves*. Princeton: Princeton University Press.

Kleinman, A. (1988). *The illness narratives: Suffering, healing and human condition*. New York: Basic Books.

Mulder, N. (1990) *Individuum und Gesellschaft in Java*. Saarbrücken: Breitenbach.

Priya, K. R. (2010). Research relationship as a facilitator of remoralization and self-growth: Postearthquake suffering and healing. *Qualitative Health Research, 20*(4), 479–495.

Priya, K. R. (2012). Social constructionist approach to suffering and healing: Juxtaposing Cassell, Gergen and Kleinman. *Psychological Studies, 57*(2), 211–223.

Radley, A. (2004). Suffering. In M. Murray (Ed.), *Critical health psychology* (pp. 31–43). Hampshire: Palgrave Macmillan.

Robertson, R. (1995). Glocalization, time-space and homogeneity-heterogenity. In M. Featherstone, S. Lash, & R. Robertson (Eds.), *Global modernities* (pp. 25–44). London: Sage.

Stange, P. (1984). The logic of *rasa* in Java. *Indonesia, 38,* 113–134.

Star, S. L., & Griesemer, J. R. (1998). Institutional ecology, 'translations' and boundary objects: Amateurs and professionals in Berkeley's Museum of Vertebrate Zoology. *Social Studies of Science, 19*(3), 1907–1939.

Zaumseil, M. (2006). Der alltägliche Umgang mit Schizophrenie in Zentral-Java. In E. Wohlfart & M. Zaumseil (Eds.), *Transkulturelle Psychiatrie. Interkulturelle Psychotherapie. Interdisziplinäre Theorie und Praxis* (pp. 331–360). Heidelberg: Springer Medizin Verlag.

Zaumseil, M. (2010). Diversity politics and management: Der Umgang mit alten und neuen Verschiedenheiten. Zwei Beispiele aus Berlin und Yogyakarta (Indonesien). In H. Keupp, R. Rudeck, H. Schröer, M. Seckinger, & F. Straus (Eds.), *Armut und Exklusion – Gemeindepsychologische Analysen und Gegenstrategien* (pp. 63–79). Tübingen: dgvt-Verlag.

Chapter 14
Disaster Aid Distribution and Social Conflicts

Silke Schwarz

14.1 Introduction

Increased questioning of the business of humanitarian help (Arnold 2012) has led to the development of minimum quality standards for the delivery of humanitarian aid. Demands for conflict-sensitive program management have led to the development of guidelines for interventions and programs that avoid creating or reduce social conflicts and rebuild the psychosocial welfare of disaster-affected communities (Sphere Project;[1] Active Learning Network for Accountability and Performance in Humanitarian Action (ALNAP);[2] Do No Harm approach by Anderson 1999, 2000, 2004). This is a major challenge considering the range and amount of material resources that need to be distributed in the course of reconstruction after any disaster.

Mainstream psychological coping theories that are predominantly individualistic and apolitical tend to neglect diverging interests and social conflicts. An exception is the universalistic social-psychological *social support deterioration model* developed by Kaniasty and Norris (1993). According to this model, a post-disaster social bitterness may emerge due to dissatisfaction with aid, social support, interpersonal constraints, and conflicts, which leads to increased levels of distress and pathology (Kaniasty 2012). What continues to be problematic with this model is its emphasis on subjective impressions of adequate support (*perceived support*). The actual *received support*, while also contributing, does not completely determine the perception of adequacy (Kaniasty and Norris 1993; Kaniasty 2012). Therefore, a favorable social construction of post-disaster mutual assistance and support may have a positive impact on health and well-being (that is, it is not always dependent on actual, communal, and material circumstances).

[1] http://www.sphereproject.org/. Accessed 11 May 2013.

[2] http://www.alnap.org/. Accessed 11 May 2013.

S. Schwarz (✉)
International Academy for Innovative Pedagogy, Psychology and Economics gGmbH
at Freie Universität Berlin, Malteserstr. 74-100, 12249 Berlin, Germany
e-mail: silke.schwarz@fu-berlin.de; silgnschwarz@yahoo.de

M. Zaumseil et al. (eds.), *Cultural Psychology of Coping with Disasters*,
DOI 10.1007/978-1-4614-9354-9_14,

Hobfoll (1998, 2011), in particular, points to the material and power-influenced dimensions of coping processes, as well as the difficulties people have when counteracting the widespread, rapid, and often long-term impact of resource loss, especially when objective circumstances signal this loss. Those with power, status, and privilege meet conditions that allow a further accumulation of resources, which Hobfoll (2011) calls *caravan passageways*, and which effectively exclude those who lack power, status, and privilege. These passageways are responsible for access to cultural capital, material goods, and social support. In Hobfoll's approach, it is acknowledged that social structures of discrimination and privilege have a significant influence on a person's resource dynamic, and that power differentials are potentially reproduced in coping processes: people who lack status and power experience continuous social discrimination almost independently of their own behavior. This can be particularly evident in the way disaster aid goods are distributed and to whom they are denied. Besides Hobfoll's approach, sociological theories of social conflicts and their resolution (Deutsch 2000; Maiese 2003; Kurtz and Ritter 2011; Wagner-Pacifici and Hall 2012) as well as social capital approaches (Grootaert and Basterlaer 2002; Dudwick et al. 2006) capture these dimensions of power and conflict.

This chapter examines the socioculturally distinctive features, specific imbalances of power, and diverging individual and collective ways of dealing with disasters and related aid that contribute to a locally specific way of coping with disaster aid goods and associated social conflicts (and which cannot be grasped by the above depicted universalistic approaches). For instance, does the social standard for maintaining harmony (*rukun*) counter the development of social bitterness? In what way may it hinder resolutions of social conflicts? This chapter highlights how good intentions can have negative effects on the culturally specific social fabric of recipient communities by hindering recovery and coping processes. Prior social conflicts within a community may be reinforced and new conflicts can emerge, while other problems may be resolved through the aid distribution processes. The provision of external material resources therefore needs to be seen as being in a complex, long-term interplay with culture-specific personal as well as communal dynamics and political negotiation processes. This chapter explores the contributing elements of conflict dynamics and subsequently demonstrates the variety of ways of coping with conflicts.

14.2 Aid-Related Social Conflicts

In the disaster context we investigated, a multitude of aid goods were distributed: (1) food and nonfood materials (such as cooking utensils, sanitary products, tents, blankets, and clothing), (2) medical aid, (3) material resources to rebuild communal infrastructure such as wells and roads, (4) material resources to rebuild temporary and permanent shelters, (5) resources for economical recovery such as livelihood programs, (6) specialized and medical aid goods for people injured by the earthquake (such as medicines, crutches, and wheelchairs), (7) psychosocial programs for trauma and healing, (8) disaster management training, and (9) awareness-raising and capacity-building programs (for example on gender justice).

14.2.1 Challenges to the Social Fabric

The material characteristic of aid goods enormously affects conflict dynamics. There is a difference between being betrayed by someone about food aid and housing reconstruction, for example, because the amount of material resources differs considerably.[3] The intensity of a sense of injustice does not, however, depend solely on tangible and quantifiable material features. The socioculturally specific meaning attributed to these resources further moderates the emergence of possible conflicts about distribution processes. For example, aid goods were partly considered as "God's gift" (*berkah*) by many villagers, that is, as being given and taken by God, which implies no sense of entitlement to receive these goods. Whether this position was only expressed in the interview context in order to present oneself in line with a socioculturally specific moral of modesty or was genuinely perceived in this manner remains unanswered. Nevertheless, expectations and a sense of entitlement about receiving aid from the government and other institutions are important features of possible conflicts because they influence the evaluation of distribution practices as just or not. Moreover, there is a need for critical awareness about the criteria to receive aid and possible appeal proceedings.[4] These beliefs and expectations evolve in the context of institutionalized power structures which, in our case study, means an ill-equipped Indonesian social security system in normal and in times of crises. This has an effect on whether being a disaster survivor automatically instills a sense of entitlement to ask for help from public entities or whether the delivery of aid goods is considered an act of charity.

Our interview data show that skepticism and suspicion toward hidden agendas sometimes emerged when villagers were offered aid provided by organizations with specific mainstreaming agendas. For example, the founding of a women's cooperative associated with a large amount of monetary funds was harshly criticized by the male-only hamlet development committee in Sido Kabul who feared losing control in communal affairs (see Chap. 16). Such perceptions were not helped by the fact that disaster aid goods were distributed in very different ways and according to a wide range of eligibility criteria. The heterogeneity of aid sources contributed to nontransparent procedures that allowed some to increase their own wealth, an outcome which led to further suspicion and discontent. Moreover, issues of private versus public aid sources as well as the use of that aid fuelled suspicion and resentment. For example, some villagers complained about families that received aid from private sources and kept it for their own use rather than sharing it. This practice contradicted the solidary feeling of everyone having the same fate as earthquake survivors, which underpinned the call for a collectivization of privately acquired goods (see Chap. 10).

A general lack of coordination was often pointed out as a common source for social discord, disappointment, and resentment. For example, the distribution mode

[3] The earthquake in 2006 Bantul, Java, Indonesia, has been characterized as a "shelter-led emergency" (Wilson and Reilly 2007, p. 5). In this respect, funds distributed to provide for shelter reconstruction were also a major source for social discord.

[4] The three examined hamlets vary dramatically with regard to critical awareness about aid distribution and appeal processes, as a nongovernmental organization (NGO) empowerment program had only been carried out in Sido Kabul after the earthquake.

of *first-come-first-served* for building temporary shelters in Sido Kabul contributed to a dynamic of competition between survivors. Those who came late only received lower quality building materials or sometimes nothing at all. The norm of conflict avoidance led to a tendency that feelings and reasons associated with social discord and disappointments were only expressed indirectly; for example, by calling the aid distributer "too lazy to coordinate" rather than directly talking about corrupt practices. Usually, villagers who voiced complaints and expressed feelings of injustice and discontent were those who did not receive relief goods at all (or only received smaller amounts), as they saw others enrich themselves by taking a disproportionate share of the available aid.[5] This lack of coordination was fostered by the absence of monitoring systems that opened the door for arbitrary practices, that is, for rule bending and breaking, corruption, and nepotism,[6] all of which led to perceived injustices and social aggravations.

These problems point to the importance of the quality of the performance of communal leaders. Several neighborhood leaders (Pak RT) were not able to fulfill their function of managing the disaster aid distribution; because some were too old, and others had to take care of their injured and emotionally disturbed family members, they neglected their communal obligations. Moreover, in Sido Kabul, for example, the leader of the hamlet (Pak Dukuh) died shortly before the earthquake. Thus, a temporary hamlet leader was accountable for the distribution of aid. He was appointed by his superior instead of being elected by his fellows and, as a result, was less trusted and accepted compared to his predecessor. Many interviewees discussed irregularities and accused him of increasing his own wealth during his term. For the most part, government reconstruction funds were reduced by those who were in charge of distributing aid, that is, the hamlet and neighborhood leaders and on the upper administrative levels. The difference between the funds received and those distributed to the community was used to increase the private wealth of leaders and administrators or rededicated for community projects. Most villagers regarded only the latter option as a legitimate redistribution of aid.

Reconstruction money was distributed in three phases. For some, these were moments of hope that they could finally meet the criteria for receiving aid, while for others these phases were moments of further disappointment. A prominent example for aid-related injustices refers to the hamlet development committee[7] in Sido Kabul that was in charge of deciding who would meet the criteria to receive funds from the Java Reconstruction Fund (JRF; see Sect. 4.2). Some villagers voiced their discontent and anger over some house tenants receiving reconstruction funds twice

---

[5] For instance, an NGO donated reconstruction tools which were placed in the house of the temporary hamlet leader in Sido Kabul. Everybody who needed the tools was allowed to borrow them. However, the tools soon disappeared eliciting disappointment and anger among the villagers who still needed to use them.

[6] This was usually referred to as KKN (= *korupsi*, *kolusi*, *nepotism*), that is corruption, collusion, and nepotism.

[7] All of the committee members were men and the committee included formal or informal neighborhood leaders and the hamlet leader. All of them had powerful positions within their community before the disaster struck which indicates the persistence of the ever-present village hierarchies and gender disparities.

(both from the government and the JRF) and about people who received government reconstruction money even though their houses were neither destroyed nor inhabited. Again, it was usually villagers who felt unjustly treated who voiced complaints during the interviews. Conversely, corruption, fraud, and the social conflicts that resulted from these practices were hardly mentioned and even rejected during interviews with the people in charge. Rather, those in power depicted the earthquake as bringing "blessings" (*berkah*) and enriching everyone, especially due to the sufficient and sometimes plentiful disaster aid. Those villagers whose houses actually had been destroyed reported that the amount of reconstruction money was insufficient to rebuild and that they had to take on debts. In contrast, those in power tended to accuse them of not being prudential with regard to their management of aid funds. In general, villagers had to deal with different distributed amounts of housing money, which provided another potential source of conflict and envy between neighbors and even family members. Officially, government reconstruction aid amounted to 15 million Indonesian rupiah (around US$ 1,600), whereas reconstruction aid from the JRF amounted to 20 million Indonesian rupiah (around US$ 2,133). In practice, there were wide variations in the final amounts received or left over after redistribution.

In conclusion, villagers categorized injustices as either "unintentional" (due to limited help, people not being able to be met at home during distribution rounds, etc.) or "intentional." The latter were mainly associated with intense and enduring feelings of being betrayed, excluded, cheated, and left behind.

14.2.2 Diverging Senses of Justice

The Global Network of Civil Society Organisation for Disaster Reduction[8] developed a checklist for good local governance. According to their document, aid policies should aim to ensure inclusion and participation, capability, accountability, transparency as well as coherence (O'Brien et al. 2012; Carnalt and Dale 2012). In general, diverging understandings or senses of justice may refer to modes of aid distribution processes (that is to forms of *procedural justice*) as well as to subjective feelings of what justice means in regard to disaster aid (that is to *concepts of justice*).

One commonly voiced standpoint with regard to concepts of justice is that all villagers should receive the same amount of aid, regardless of the pre-disaster economic status (rich or poor). This position is based on the understanding that all villagers share the same fate of being an earthquake survivor and it is probably supported by the collectively shared ideal of harmony and togetherness. The competing, though also commonly voiced, position is to argue for differentiated modes of distribution, that is, for a needs-oriented distribution of goods in which similar conditions should be treated similarly. Conflicts in this regard arose due to inconsistent evaluations of these conditions or weaknesses, vulnerabilities, and levels of need (see Chap. 10).

---

[8] Homepage of the Network available at: http://www.globalnetwork-dr.org/home.html. Accessed 9 August 2013.

Another disagreement referred to the reference unit for allocating disaster aid. Some villagers argued for the number of family members, and still others for households to be the relevant unit of reference. The practice of distributing the same amount of relief goods per household was justified with the habit of communal practices of mutual assistance (*gotong royong*). In normal times, it is usually one member per household who is obliged to participate. However, others wanted individual entitlements for receiving aid goods. In this case, individuals become the main reference units so that people could be treated equally or in accordance with their needs again (for example, a large family would gain more disaster aid than a small family).

With regard to procedural justice, the following two features were highlighted: adhering to top-down predefined standards or following commonly agreed upon rules. The former required a certain level of trust in the authorities, while the latter approach connected with the communal practice of deliberation (*musyawarah*). With communal deliberation, the related discussion rounds should have ensured transparency and supported common agreements on priorities and procedures. However, these forums were also criticized for the pervasive influence of village hierarchies and thus for being undemocratic.

The above described aid-related disagreements produced feelings in many interviewees of having been taken advantage of.[9] Villagers reported being disappointed (*kecewa*), feeling discontent (*nggak puas*), not accepting something sincerely or wholeheartedly (*nggak menerima dengan ikhlas*), feeling envy (*iri*), feeling jealous (*cemburu*), feeling hostile (*memusuhi*), not liking someone (*ngak suka*), feeling truly hurt (*merasa sakit benar*), being angry (*marah*), and hating (*benci*). These emotions were considered to run counter to feelings of being in harmony (*rukun*) with others.

14.3 Coping with Social Conflicts Along Aid Distribution Processes

The handling of aid-related social conflicts can be regarded as a coping challenge, while the following situational elements (Clarke 2005) seemed to hinder or enable the enforcement of violated entitlements in the sociocultural context of our research site.

We found that the enduring value and practice of harmony and togetherness (*rukun, kebersamaan*) severely limited the possibilities to react upon perceived injustices in a direct manner. The ideal usually translates into a tendency toward conflict avoidance, leaving problems rather unresolved. We did, however, identify various aspects that counteract this ideal. For instance, a communal critical awareness about citizens' rights can result in an environment that is conducive to confronting injustices, as was the case in Sido Kabul. In addition, social standing within the community

[9] The object of these emotions was other family members, neighbors, more distant persons such as the hamlet leader, or even entire communities. For instance, hamlets or neighborhoods inhabited by comparatively many civil servants had better connections to flows of government aid than other hamlets or neighborhoods. Families with migrant workers also had better access to money in order to rebuild emergency and permanent shelter. These differences in accessible aid—due to differences in bridging or linking social capital—contributed to feelings of injustice.

is important. For example, the wealthy and former civil servant, 71-year-old Pak Zamroni from Sido Kabul, had been the head of a communal group for 17 years. In social terms, his social standing was quite high, even though he and his wife were the only Christians in the Islamic hamlet. He knew about his rights and was therefore not easily intimidated by the authoritative manner of some aid distributors. He explained that this made him dare to speak up much more easily compared to "ordinary villagers" (*orang kecil*).

Additionally, demonstrating the virtue of downplaying the importance of the material world—even if this was only evident as a form of discursive positioning during the interviews—by referring to spiritual and social morals, appeared to inhibit villagers from engaging in activities to demand aid that they had previously been denied. In contrast, corruption is also regarded as a sin (*dosa*) and is, therefore, forbidden (*haram*) according to Islam. This ideology encouraged activities to openly criticize corruptive practices and to support practices that aim to achieve social justice within one's community.

The source of injustice plays another important role. Is it a powerful village figure (*tokoh*) who is responsible for the unjust treatment of oneself or is the source of injustice a neighbor or an external institution? In the latter cases, villagers described being more comfortable when complaining about injustices. Moreover, asking for help for oneself or one's family was sometimes associated with revealing one's neediness or inability to be self-reliant. This could lead to feelings of shame[10] and result in other people gossiping, as striving to acquire material things is considered greedy and egoistic, not modest. Bu Suprapti from Sido Kabul put it this way, "Do not strive for satisfying all your desires (*nongso*), but accept whatever you are given." Asking for aid or financial compensation for one's neighborhood or hamlet, instead of asking for help for oneself (or one's family), had greater legitimacy and was therefore easier to carry out. For example, in Sido Kabul, the temporary hamlet leader sold teak wood from the communal graveyard and kept the money for himself, an action that resulted in joint action being taken by villagers. Accordingly, if fraud occurs on a communal level, collective actions can be carried out and actions such as protesting were presented as a more accepted way of reacting to injustice (see Sect. 14.3.2 for more details).

Eventually, the timing of protests and complaints also affects coping behavior because at some point people can realize that justice may no longer be achieved and thus focus on the hope that practices will be better in the future or simply give up hope. In our research context, once relief goods had been distributed, people tended to keep silent about any experienced injustices (until opportunities to talk to external parties, such as our research team, occurred). Last but not least, the dynamics of dealing with social conflicts along aid distribution processes is influenced by communal events prior to and following the disaster, such as communal elections for the hamlet leader.

[10] Expressed with *riku*, that is, feeling awkward and *malu*, that is, feeling ashamed.

14.3.1 Person-Centered Reactions

The strategies applied by villagers to handle the injustices they experienced can be arranged on a continuum, with confrontational, clarifying, and direct (assimilative) strategies on one pole, subversive strategies in the middle, and indirect, accommodative, and accepting strategies on the other pole. The verbalized end goals were to regain an inner balance and to achieve material compensation. Most strategies tended to be reactive. The groups of subversive and clarifying strategies are closest to prevention because they include efforts to mitigate or avoid the emergence of future possible social injustices. In our case study, subversive and accepting strategies dominated.

Clarifying Strategies A clarifying strategy was rarely described by interviewees. According to villagers, this is due to its confrontational aspect. The anticipation of shame and discomfort, the fear of being discriminated against and socially excluded in the future, feelings of not being entitled to aid or being confused about the criteria for entitlement all reduced the use of this type of coping strategy. On the contrary, having a good social standing and having proof of one's accusations fostered the probability of confronting the person in charge. Having proof was considered the best means to exert pressure on the alleged perpetrator. Nevertheless, social sanctions (such as being excluded from future communal meetings or government poverty programs) sometimes had to be endured by those who confronted the alleged perpetrator. Obviously, it is easier for people with more material resources to take this route compared to those who depend entirely on public aid. The few villagers who applied this clarifying strategy had a good social and economic standing before the earthquake. They claimed that their intentions had an ideological basis, such as hoping to restore justice or change the behavior and attitude of the alleged perpetrator in the long run. If they kept silent, this could have been misinterpreted as making corrupt actions appear "legal," that is, as accepting the wrongdoings of the elite as a normal practice. For accusers, the confession of the perpetrator, combined with the will to do better, was presented as consoling *and* reconciling.

In general, the act of confrontation should be in line with local ethical standards, that is, one should confront in a polite and gentle (*halus*) manner so that a good relationship is still possible in the future. Control over the inner self rather than an uncontrollable outburst is, therefore, a necessary competence for a strategy of clarification:

> Even if forgetting the feeling of being hurt (*sakit hati*) is the hardest thing for me, I admit it, but I have to take care of my feeling and have to be able to follow our etiquette (*unggah ungguh*). (Mas Naryanto, Sido Kanul)

"Ordinary villagers" (*orang kecil*) usually approached the aid distributor in order to find out information regarding entitlements and to clarify nontransparent procedures. This was usually done in the hope that they would receive material compensation. In many cases, they based their claims on comparisons with others. During our interviews, they emphasized the difficulties of prevailing against authorities when there was a lack of transparency with regard to procedures and the right to receive what they thought they were entitled to.

Subversive Strategies In order to ensure social harmony, subversive strategies appeared, for the most part, to be the preferred strategy.

Some villagers rejected help that was associated with unjust practices, thus signaling disagreement. Rejecting help went hand in hand with a self-reliant and modest stance, that is, even though a person may feel entitled to receive aid, they usually did not hope for it. Conversely, striving for self-reliance or rejecting aid could be regarded as an act of arrogance (*sombong*) by the surrounding community. Its enactment might be considered confrontational and was only done if the person and the family had alternative reconstruction resources. Moreover, the rejection of aid sometimes led to intrafamilial conflicts. For example, the former youth leader, Mas Naryanto from Sido Kabul, refused to accept reconstruction money from the Java Reconstruction Fund, as he would have had to bribe the temporary hamlet leader. Bribing the leader would contradict his ideological principles and make him feel ashamed, he explained. For his wife, however, it was rather difficult to accept his decision, as they had to share the house with their parents-in-law instead of having their own home.

Some villagers also shared their aid goods with people who did not get any. This generous strategy was also usually only applied if sufficient and alternative resources were available. For instance, those who received aid from their friends and relatives shared it with others (collectivization of private aid). The belief in a just world fostered their generosity. For example, the earthquake was often referred to as a test (*ujian*) by God that would reveal the good and bad characters of humankind; in this context, generosity indicated a good character and generous actions were said to be rewarded by God in the afterworld.

Another common strategy was communicative exchange and emotional sharing with like-minded people. In contrast to direct confrontations and clarifications, social harmony could be ensured on the surface, that is, people behaved normally—greeted one another and engaged in "chitchats"—and only in the background was it possible to express disappointments and anger.

However, some interviewees felt so affected that it was not possible to maintain harmony in their interactions with others. In order to contain their uncomfortable feelings, they withdrew socially and avoided meeting the person they had a conflict with. Opting for social withdrawal was often associated with a person's self-perception of their socioeconomic standing as that of an "ordinary villager" (*orang kecil*), that is, one whose social standing is not sufficient for direct confrontations. As a result of this strategy, even four years after the earthquake, some villagers still did not participate in the communal *gotong royong* practices, as they felt to have been treated unjustly during the distribution of aid. This nonparticipation signaled their discontent and animosity. Sometimes the alleged perpetrator realized this indirect criticism, but sometimes he was not aware of it. Villagers could also refuse to support the alleged perpetrator in the future. During the election for the hamlet leader in 2008 in Sido Kabul, for example, two of the three candidates were accused of corruption and fraud and thus denied support during the election by many who felt treated unjustly. However, villagers who did not support the current hamlet leader complained about not having received invitations to communal events in the aftermath of the elections. In sum, one can withdraw oneself and one can also be excluded by others. In Sido

Kabul, the temporary hamlet leader who was accused of fraudulent misappropriation of public aid was said to have lost respect and social standing. He was ridiculed, gossiped about by his fellow community members, and excluded. He also withdrew from the community and no longer participated in the community's mutual assistance practices.

Accepting Strategies The majority of villagers reported accepting and accommodative strategies, in order to regain an inner balance and to maintain social harmony.[11] Some villagers applied an instantaneous accepting stance that is silently accepting without prior attempts to influence the practice that was perceived as unjust. Acceptance was also practiced after unsuccessful attempts to receive just treatment, for example, after confronting the distributor.

In the context of the distribution of relief goods and possible neighborly conflicts, the majority of villagers, irrespective of their social standing, described having immediately accepted whatever was given to them and not complaining about what had been denied. Overall, it was usually those who perceived themselves as "common villagers" (*orang kecil*), that is, those with a relatively low educational background and socioeconomic status, who enacted an accepting stance. They described not seeing any chances for acting on the basis of their concerns or they felt that their efforts would not have been successful. Confrontations with the elite initiated by "ordinary villagers" (*orang kecil*) would also be regarded as rude (*kasar*). In our research context, *kasar* is a very negative and devalued ascription. Similarly, being confrontational toward someone who has a higher social rank is labeled *ngeyel*, or being stubborn—a stance and practice that attract highly moral scorn from the majority of villagers. Furthermore, some interviewees balanced the costs and benefits of fighting for social justice. Most villagers concluded that securing future access to resources had more weight. Furthermore, there was a strong feeling among many of not being entitled to aid goods. This was reinforced by the fact that many irregularities occurred behind closed doors. This lack of transparency impeded any action being taken against corruption and nepotism in the aid distribution process.

All the villagers interviewed shared a socioculturally specific condemnation of direct expressions of intense and, in particular, negative emotions. Indirect manners were instead considered more appropriate for people to use to convey what they thought and felt. In this moral framework, criticism is equated with an emotional outburst and loss of control, which are both socioculturally condemned affective practices.

> The words from a person can be painful. In the end, one can become sick; one can be put to rest in the hospital. [. . .] If a person wants to express the content of one's heart, this cannot be done. . . this is not possible, and then it is repressed. (Mas Ngabdul, Sido Kabul)

The repression of direct emotional expression may contribute to prolonged feelings of being hurt. Some interviewees said the stronger feelings of discomfort and a sense of injustice persisted for around two years, although shorter and longer variations

---

[11] This may partly be due to a methodological bias created by relying mainly on interview transcripts instead of behavioral observations for example. The interviews conducted by Javanese interviewers may also have further contributed to a moral pressure to, at least verbally, maintain highly valued positions of harmony and modesty.

were also reported. Three to five years after the event, however, only a few individuals reported enduring intense feelings of discomfort and injustice.[12]

Attempting to achieve inner peace and repose were presented as more important goals than attempts to seek clarification from elites and attempts to receive a just resolution. Inner peace is associated with psychosocial and religious well-being and longevity, whereas inner unrest is believed to lead to illness and further distress. Strategies such as the *thought-stop* technique or an *inner shifting of priorities* were described by participants as ways to restore this inner balance (see Chap. 11). The most common *beneficial comparison* strategy in the context of aid-related conflicts was the "better-than-nothing"attitude, which probably had a basis in a lack of critical awareness about citizens' rights and entitlements. *Coming to terms with one's past* was also emphasized: without the ability to forgive and forget, the feeling of carrying an emotional burden might increase and even shorten one's lifetime. Even though the effects of not having received aid were still felt in daily life, interviewees indicated that if one could forget this would alleviate one's aching heart. The "art of forgiving" as a sort of self-reconciliation strategy was said to prevent the deepening and prolongation of conflicts. Forgiveness was usually combined with the *hope for a better future*, in both the worldly life and the afterlife. All in all, the majority distanced themselves from intense and enduring unpleasant feelings and accepted what had happened by using the strategies described above.

14.3.2 Communal Endeavors and Recommendations

A wide range of understandings regarding justice led to numerous suggested recommendations regarding the improvement of aid distribution practices and the handling of social conflicts. In this section, the focus will be on procedural justice in relation to communal processes of decision-making and modes of aid distribution.

Internal Affairs During the disaster aid distribution process, the village elite (*tokoh*) was in a powerful position with hardly any monitoring or control systems in place. The roles of common villagers were mainly to receive aid or implement decisions made by the elite. In contrast to a democratic-participative community-based disaster management approach, a stark power imbalance existed.

Some people in charge described applying strategies that attempted to enact redistributive justice in response to perceived or actual cases of injustice. Reconstruction funds were distributed in several phases (partly due to different aid sources). Accordingly, villagers who did not receive anything in the first round could expect something in the following distribution phases. Calming promises by the elite which

[12] Persistent feelings of conflict related to the level of the personal relationship between alleged perpetrator and the person who felt betrayed. This interpersonal stance was not negotiated on a communal level which helped to limit disturbing and unsettling open social conflicts. Emotions were rarely expressed toward alleged perpetrators, but were rather shared with like-minded persons or family members.

aimed to achieve redistributive justice may therefore be considered a strategy that some alleged perpetrators of distributional irregularities used to compensate some people when they had previously been denied aid.

The following example of fraud carried out by the elite in Sido Kabul illustrates possibilities for a collective action against those in power. The temporary hamlet leader asked each villager with a newly built house to pay 50,000 Indonesian rupiah (around US$ 5.35) in order to apply for a building license. Over the next three years, however, not one of the villagers received a license. They complained to Pak Lurah at the next administrative village level. Due to this public accusation at the office of his superior, the temporary hamlet leader conceded and confessed. Pak Lurah threatened to sentence him to prison if he did not repay the stolen money. The accused leader promised to repay what he illegally took. We assume it was easier for the community to publicize this misbehavior of the temporary leader for two reasons: first, it concerned the whole community, not just individuals[13] and second, villagers could complain to a third party outside their community. As a communal, long-term consequence of this turmoil, the temporary leader withdrew socially, as described earlier.

Looking toward the future, "ordinary villagers" (*orang kecil*) voiced their wish to assume a different role in the context of disaster aid. They mainly asked the village elite for improved distribution of information to the community and an assurance of transparency by inviting all family heads to *musyawarah*—a communal discussion forum, not only the elite.[14] Sometimes creating transparency can simply mean providing explanations about people's rights and entitlements and informing villagers of the modes of distribution that have been agreed upon elsewhere. Several villagers who were not members of the elite demanded that the discussion forum should not only be used for information provision (as was the case in 2006) but argued that the forum should also provide a chance to participate in the decision-making process itself. They asked for an explication of the role and function of the elite in disaster aid distribution processes and argued that it would be optimal for the whole community to decide together who is most in need of aid. Many "ordinary villagers" (*orang kecil*) wanted somebody to be in charge of coordinating the distribution of aid goods so that the guidelines could be followed and eligibility criteria met by recipients. The role of the elite would then be more administrative with officials being accountable for a smooth and regular process of distributing aid goods, while the power of the elite would be restricted by the practice of the *musyawarah*. In the long run, the elite was considered responsible for initiating social activities in order to reinstate and ensure social harmony, for example, by communal mutual assistance (*gotong royong)* or other village rituals such as the Javanese shadow puppet play called *wayang kulit*.

External Affairs The coping efforts and suggested recommendations described by villagers differ depending on whether they relate to conflicts within a hamlet or to conflicts with third parties (such as aid agencies or the government). In the latter case,

---

[13] As noted previously, the prospect of appearing greedy and materialistic often stopped people from using confrontational personal strategies against the perpetrator(s) of perceived injustices.

[14] In Sido Kabul, many villagers also demanded the participation of female representatives as the head of the family is usually male (see Chap. 16).

an entire community or a coalition of several communities can become the agent for protest against the experienced injustices of third or outside parties. For instance, earthquake survivors successfully organized in order to protest against the National Electricity Company. They refused to pay any fees as long as they had no houses and were granted free electricity for one year. Another example involved a communal protest against a donor organization. In Sido Kabul, people refused to accept aid in form of toilets, as the aid provided was not sufficient for all inhabitants. Thus, none of the villagers received any in order to prevent social disagreement and envy.

Several communities also took action against the local government and its related reconstruction program. Of the 30 million Indonesian rupiah (around US$ 3,210) of funds originally promised by the government to homeowners, only 15 million Indonesian rupiah (around US$ 1,600) were disbursed. This disappointed and even enraged many disaster-affected people and a demonstration was organized to protest and pressure the government to disburse the funds more quickly. Each household was socially *obligated* to send one representative to the demonstration, as the villager Pak Gunanto from Sido Kabul explained:

> It was due to solidarity (*solidaritas*). [...] I was afraid of being expelled by the society, by the neighbors, so I joined them.

Only civil servants did not dare to participate in the demonstration as they would have felt "uncomfortable" (*tidak enak*), even though they supported the idea of the demonstration itself. As a reaction to these confrontations, the Sultan and Governor of the Province of Yogyakarta expressed an understanding attitude toward the protest and discontent, that is, a reaction which is in line with socioculturally appropriate morals. However, this probably did not make a major contribution to the resolution of social conflicts and disappointments. Nevertheless, the Governor Hamengku Buwono X. admitted possible faults during the government's management of the disaster, a confession that was absent at the communal level, and which might have consoled at least some villagers:

> I could understand when there were demonstrations which were used as channels of expression of unbearable emotion. If the government might have shown a lack of appropriate public services, the commencement of the reconstruction phase will become a new stepping stone to build a closer relation and better understanding full of empathy so that the process runs well and reaches the targeted goal. (Hamengku Buwono X 2008, p. xv)

14.3.3 Institutionalized Efforts

Several institutions were involved in managing perceptions and feelings of injustice, ranging from the local government to NGOs.

Government Reconciliation Program A reconciliation program was initiated in 2008 in order to reunite villagers who had experienced social divisions (*rasa perpecahan*) as a result of aid distribution processes and to rebuild trust in the government reconstruction program. The local government provided funds per hamlet (two million

Indonesian rupiahs which is approximately US$ 214), as well as per neighborhood (one million Indonesian rupiahs or US$ 107). Each hamlet and neighborhood leader could decide which kind of joint activity would be put into practice to achieve reconciliation (for example, eating together, praying together, etc.).[15]

The evaluation of the program varied although most of the formal leaders described the reconciliation program as a success. According to Kaniasty (2012), sufficient advertising for high-quality social cohesion is necessary in order to mitigate the social bitterness resulting from secondary stressors and auxiliary losses. Formal leaders promoted social cohesion by referring to "local wisdoms," such as the highly valued harmony ideal, which was (re)constructed during these meetings.

Conflicts were neither discussed nor were they resolved openly. Rather, leaders asked for any discord to be forgotten, which led the majority of "ordinary villagers" (*orang kecil*) in our research context to assess the program as "not so helpful" in overcoming the aid-related social conflicts. Conflicts and related feelings of hurt were reportedly too intense to be overcome by only holding a meeting which did not address or clarify the underlying problems. Some went as far as to suggest that the program might have contributed to the legalization of corruption, as fraud was covered up by the discourse of harmony and the imposition of a new norm of silence about previous aid-based disagreements.

Nongovernment Initiatives Only two days after the disaster, 26 NGOs located in the Province of Yogyakarta joined together and formed a network. The main goal was to empower civil society to take an active part in the recovery and reconstruction process through coordinating the aid that was streaming into the area.

In selected hamlets, NGOs disseminated information on citizens' rights. Villagers were able to practice verbally presenting and defending their rights and claims. Meetings with governmental representatives and common villagers were also organized.

The position of an ombudsman was also established. Villagers felt more at ease to confide in someone from outside their village, as it diminished worries about future social sanctions and negative effects from their own village elite. The ombudsman could then exert pressure by making his surveys public while informants remained anonymous.

Another strategy was to raise public critical awareness in general. The internationally financed NGO called *Institute for Development and Economic Analysis* (IDEA)[16] established an office in Yogyakarta town and conducted a survey, tracking the disaster budget from the national to the local government. IDEA' s Indonesian staff members published a report in 2007 (IDEA 2007) which caused public turmoil as corrupt practices and mismanagement were revealed. Subsequently, many newspapers reported these issues which further intensified public awareness.

---

[15] However, not all villagers seemed to know about this program and not all neighborhood leaders implemented it. Some decided to buy communal goods such as plates and glasses that could be used for any future communal feast, instead of organizing a specific reconciliation festival.

[16] http://ideajogja.or.id/. Accessed 12 May 2013.

Recent Developments In 2002, the *Corruption Eradication Commission* was established at a national level. Since the fall of Suharto in 1998, an NGO called *Indonesia Corruption Watch*[17] has also been active. In September 2006, Indonesia became the 107th country to ratify the *United Nation Convention Against Corruption* (UNCAC; National Coalition of Indonesia for Anticorruption 2009). These efforts have already demonstrated some small effects in the wider context of our research site. For example, the regent (Pak Bupati) Ibnu Subiyanto of the regency Sleman nearby the volcano Merapi was imprisoned due to corruption in 2009 (Rosser et al. 2011).

14.4 Concluding Remarks

Models of community resilience are based on good governance, participation, and transparency. In our case study, it is crucial to consider these concepts in the context of Indonesia as an emerging postcolonial country with a specific history. We have shown that the available structures of local governance led to several post-disaster distribution conflicts, inducing secondary stress cycles that had to be coped with. At least temporarily, this decreased communal resilience for future disasters. Conversely, according to Norris et al. (2009), a community's ability to handle or even prevent conflicts would demonstrate community resilience.

The accumulation of further wealth, opportunities, and resources by people who have power and material resources appears to be a universal phenomenon in post-disaster situations that invokes a dramatic moral offense in the eyes of those who suffer from losses and lack resources. Against the background of initial empathetic waves of mutual willingness to help after a disaster, this offense is experienced even more intensely and creates despondency and disillusionment, especially with regard to values of social togetherness and solidarity. The *deterioration deterrence model* (Kaniasty and Norris 1993; Kaniasty 2012) depicts this universal phenomenon. In this chapter, we have shown the specific sociocultural forms of corrupt practices and other offenses. In addition, culturally specific dimensions of coping with social conflicts generated by aid distribution processes were highlighted.

Overall, everyone could tell a story about experiencing or observing the misuse of disaster aid and associated unpleasant feelings. The feeling of being treated unjustly during the aid distribution process, that is, receiving nothing or less than others, can reduce the sensed level of social harmony and the social capital of affected communities (and thus negatively affect its resilience). Strikingly, however, the majority of interviewees claimed no connection between aid-related conflicts and the communal *rukun* level or reported temporary reductions of *rukun* only; they usually located these at an individual and not a communal level. The continuous fostering of this collectively shared harmony discourse may have prevented the development of a profound social bitterness along with the corrosion of communal ties. Indeed, it seems to have actually contributed to personal and communal well-being because it provided a way of avoiding the escalation of conflict and open, emotional confrontations with members of the village elites.

---

[17] http://www.antikorupsi.org/eng/. Accessed 12 May 2013.

However, the common social standard of maintaining harmony (*rukun*) should not be misunderstood as a fatalistic acceptance of any injustice. As demonstrated earlier, many villagers employed socioculturally appropriate strategies to counteract injustice, albeit in a rather indirect manner. The cultural legitimacy of certain resistance and negotiation strategies can change and develop in new directions. The colonial-feudalistic history of Java needs to be taken into account, as well as the democratization and decentralization in Indonesia that has taken place after the 1998 fall of the authoritative-centralistic rule of Suharto. Empowerment, individual and collective agency, freedom of expression, and nonhierarchical forms of negotiating diverging interests are now enforced and are becoming more accepted due to increasing globalization, connections to world economies, democratization processes, and the use of newer forms of communication (Berninghausen et al. 2009). The moralizing discourse about the demerit of asocial stances and materialistic orientations served to counteract the arbitrary decisions of powerful members of village elites. Nevertheless, the heritage of a paternalistic social order is one that encourages and conceals fraud, corruption, and nepotism due to a lack of socially and politically grounded control mechanisms. In this regard, the official, top-down-implemented reconciliation program needs to be evaluated critically as it seems to have enhanced co-option and silenced complaints instead of introducing sustainable resolution of conflicts at the village level.

Overall, our analysis demonstrated how social structures of discrimination and privilege had a significant influence on individual resource dynamics, and how power differentials were reproduced in coping processes: people who lacked status and power experienced further social discrimination almost independently of their own behavior (see Hobfoll 2011). Only smaller readjustments of social morals and related manners to counteract social injustices could be achieved—associated with the risk of losing valuable resources such as a decline in the social standing, appearing stubborn and greedy, and above all risking future denial of access to resources such as not being invited to communal meetings anymore. These transformations were driven by those with a powerful social standing within their communities. An NGO-led program raising critical awareness of the community fostered this development and contributed to the emergence of a public discourse against corrupt practices of the village elite.

Acknowledgment The editors would like to thank Elise Serbaroli for her assistance in editing this chapter.

References

Anderson, M. B. (1999). *Do no harm: How aid can support peace or war*. Colorado: Lyenne Rienner Publishers.

Anderson, M. B. (Ed.). (2000). *Options for aid in conflict. Lessons from field experience*. Cambridge: The Collaborative for Development Action. http://www.cdainc.com/publications/dnh/options/OptionsManual.pdf. Accessed 29 June 2012.

Anderson, M. B. (2004). Experiences with impact assessment: Can we know what good we do? Berghoff Forschungszentrum für konstruktive Konfliktbearbeitung. http://www.berghof-handbook.net/uploads/download/anderson_handbook.pdf. Accessed 29 June 2012.

Arnold, M. (2012). International planning systems for disaster. In B. Wisner, J. C. Gaillard, & I. Kelman (Eds.), *The Routledge handbook of hazards and disaster risk reduction* (pp. 603–616). London: Routledge.

Berninghausen, J., Kerstan, B., & Soeprapto-Jansen, N. (2009). *Schleier, Sarong, Minirock. Frauen im kulturellen Wandel Indonesiens*. Bremen: Kellner-Verlag.

Carmalt, J. C., & Dale, C. H. (2012). Human rights and disaster. In B. Wisner, J. C. Gaillard, & I. Kelman (Eds.), *The Routledge handbook of hazards and disaster risk reduction* (pp. 61–70). London: Routledge.

Clarke, A. (2005). *Situational analysis. Grounded theory after the postmodern turn*. Thousand Oaks: Sage Publications.

Deutsch, M. (2000). Justice and conflict. In M. Deutsch & P. T. Coleman (Eds.), *The handbook of conflict resolution: Theory and practice* (pp. 43–68). San Francisco: Jossey-Bass Inc. Publishers.

Dudwick, N., Kuehnast, K., Jones, V. N., & Woolcock, M. (2006). *Analyzing social capital in context*. Washington, D.C.: World Bank.

Grootaert, C., & van Basterlaer, T. (Eds.). (2002). *Understanding and measuring social capital: A multidisciplinary tool for practitioners*. Washington, D.C.: World Bank.

Hamengku Buwono X. (2008). Learning from the 27 May 2006 earthquake. In D. Karnawati (Ed.), *The Yogyakarta earthquake of May 27, 2006* (pp. xi–xviii). Belmont: Star Publishing Company.

Hobfoll, S. E. (1998). *Stress, culture and community*. New York: Plenum Press.

Hobfoll, S. E. (2011). Conservation of resources theory: Its implication for stress, health and resilience. In S. Folkman, & P. E. Nathan (Eds.), *The Oxford handbook of stress, health, and coping* (pp. 127–147). New York: Oxford University Press.

Institute for Development and Economic Analysis (IDEA). (2007). *Disaster budget tracking: kemana dana bencana mengalir? temuan satu bulan pasca gempa*. Yogyakarta: IDEA.

Kaniasty, K. (2012). Predicting social psychological well-being following trauma: The role of postdisaster social support. *Psychological Trauma: Theory, Research, Practice, and Policy, 4*(1), 22–23.

Kaniasty, K., & Norris, F. H. (1993). A test of the support deterioration model in the context of natural disaster. *Journal of Personality and Social Psychology, 64*(3), 395–408.

Kurtz, L. R., & Ritter, D. (2011). Conflict resolution, provocation or transformation? Ask Gandhi. American Sociological Association. http://works.bepress.com/lester_kurtz/36. Accessed 14 Feb 2013.

Maiese, M. (2003). Distributive justice. http://www.beyondintractability.org/essay/distributive_justice/. Accessed 31 Mar 2013.

National Coalition of Indonesia for Anticorruption (NCIA). (2009). Weakening of Corruption Eradication Commission (KPK) in Indonesia. Independent Report to the 3rd Conference of State Parties to the United Nation Convention Against Corruption. http://www.antikorupsi.org/sites/antikorupsi.org/files/doc/Umum/independentreportofUNCACimplementationinindonesiaqatar09.pdf. Accessed 7 June 2013.

Norris, F. H., Tracy, M., & Galea, S. (2009). Looking for resilience: Understanding the longitudinal trajectories of responses to stress. *Social Science & Medicine, 68*(12), 2190–2198.

O'Brien, G., Bhatt, M., Saunders, W., Gaillard, J. C., Wisner, B. (2012). Local government and disaster. In B. Wisner, J. C. Gaillard, & I. Kelman (Eds.), *The Routledge handbook of hazards and disaster risk reduction* (pp. 629–640). London: Routledge.

Rosser, A., Wilson, I., & Sulistyatno, P. (2011). Leaders, elites and coalitions: The politics of free public services in decentralised Indonesia. http://www.dlprog.org/ftp/download/Public%20Folder/1%20Research%20Papers/The%20Politics%20of%20Free%20Public%20Services%20in%20Decentralised%20Indonesia.pdf. Accessed 22 Feb 2013.

Wagner-Pacifici, R., & Hall, M. (2012). Resolution of social conflict. *Annual Review of Sociology, 38*, 181–199.

Wilson, P., & Reilly, D. (2007). Joint evaluation of their responses to the Yogyakarta earthquake. www.alnap.org/pool/files/erd-3611-full.pdf. Accessed 24 Apr 2010.

Chapter 15
Facing the Future: Villagers' Visions of Resilience

Silke Schwarz

15.1 Introduction

Disaster management, among other things, refers to the process of mitigating or avoiding the future impact of disasters, ideally in a sustainable manner. Risk is the probability of harmful consequences caused by vulnerability with respect to a hazard. In Chaps. 1–3, we showed that risk can be understood as something objectively measurable (that is, for example, the grinding of two continental plates indicating an earthquake risk zone or a community's proximity to the sea associated with tsunami risks), as a risk that is subjectively experienced (that is, the personal perception and idiosyncratic handling of risks), and in terms of sociocultural considerations (that is, as collectively shared meanings attributed to the risk and socioculturally valued codes of conduct for dealing with the risk). The relationship between these three poles is handled and understood differently in such research disciplines as geography, sociology, and psychology.

The question of how a risk is currently being handled and how this risk management may be optimized in the future is of primary importance. Moreover, risks can be modeled at a range of levels. Within macro-level approaches it is possible to theorize risk as embedded in a sociocultural context, adopt a historical and global perspective, and emphasize collective dimensions of coping (Bankoff 2007, 2010, 2012; see Chap. 1). In contrast, there are approaches that focus on the individual and (over-)emphasize cognitive and rational dimensions of risk perception and management. The latter is the case in mainstream psychology, which distinguishes various future-oriented coping forms from a reactive coping style in which the harmful event has already taken place (see Chap. 2).

In this chapter, we locate risk within the triangle of objective, subjective, and collectively shared dimensions and highlight the way in which it is embedded in the everyday practices and symbolic worlds of those who live in disaster-prone regions.

S. Schwarz (✉)
International Academy for Innovative Pedagogy, Psychology and Economics gGmbH
at Freie Universität Berlin, Malteserstr. 74-100, 12249 Berlin, Germany
e-mail: silke.schwarz@fu-berlin.de; silgnschwarz@yahoo.de

M. Zaumseil et al. (eds.), *Cultural Psychology of Coping with Disasters*,
DOI 10.1007/978-1-4614-9354-9_15, © Springer Science+Business Media, LLC 2014

Our specific areas of interest are the socioculturally specific future-oriented heuristics (Gigerenzer 2008) that are used in particular settings and the question of which emotions, intuitions (Slovic and Västfjäll 2010), and principles of life conduct (see Chap. 11) emerge in communities located in disaster risk zones.[1] So far, little is known about the specifics of future orientations in disaster-prone areas (Holman and Silver 2006) and about the sociocultural specifics of these orientations. Based on these ideas, this chapter begins with an exploration of the general understandings of future within the three villages under investigation.[2] We analyze how villagers incorporate the danger caused by environmental hazards into their lives. The relationship of these future orientations to preventive action is discussed in the following sections. This chapter closes with understandings of a socioculturally specific sense of safety and the resources devoted to achieving it.

15.2 Understandings of Future and Related Risks

15.2.1 Orientations Toward the Future

In research, the relationship between future orientations and processes of coping after traumatic events is still unclear: some of the research claimed that positive orientations have emerged, while other studies identified the emergence of negative orientations during the process of coping and development (Holman and Silver 2006). Optimistic outlooks, in particular, tend to foster preventive action (Seginer 2010).

Due, among other things, to Indonesian grammar, villagers described the future as a vague concept of "tomorrow" (*hari besok*) and "time that will come" (*masa yang akan datang*). This "tomorrow" was predominantly associated with personal, familial, and communal goals, aspirations, wishes, and desires; it was mostly seen as a bright future, a better life than before, and was connected with happiness, fun, and the realization of dreams. Moreover, the future was sometimes also understood as a time full of possible surprises, something one has not intended to achieve or has not longed for and perhaps even as something to be feared of. These images of a gloomy future were very rare.[3]

---

[1] Gigerenzer (2008) and Slovic and Västfjäll (2010) formulate universalistic assumptions about human functioning; however in our research, the focus is on socioculturally specific collective and individual coping processes within the process of learning to live with ongoing hazards.

[2] Results reported in section 15.2.1 are derived from a participatory research program conducted in 2011, five years after the earthquake. Several communal groups were invited to research meanings of and views about the future, stimulating a common discovery process. Due to the very open character of this research question and approach and our dependence on preexisting communal groups with their own interests and agendas, the research illuminated the diverse and rich understandings of future-oriented stances within three disaster-stricken village communities.

[3] Adolescents, in particular, verbalized fears and related them to their possible futures with respect to the educational, vocational, and familial aspects of their lives.

In general, when talking about the future, villagers reflected upon earlier hopes and desired goals that they held in the past and which they had learned to adjust in the trajectory of their lives. This demonstrates the interweaving of past, present, and future outlooks. The relatively high level of hope and optimism in comparison with prospective fears and worries (a finding that misleadingly has been called overoptimistic bias, see Chap. 1), as noted in previous chapters, may be a product of the unique character of our research site. "Javanese culture" restricts the expression of troublesome emotions through normative devaluation processes (see also Beatty 2005):

> Regarding emotional expression, it is often stated that the Javanese seek to maintain a smoothness (*ikhlas, tenteram*) in both emotional demeanor and behavior (C. Geertz 1960, 1983; Keeler 1983, 1987). Heider (1991) notes the strong desire of many Javanese to avoid surprise and other troubling feelings, focusing on the maintenance of order. (Browne 2001, p. 152)

According to Seginer (2008), hope may also emerge to counter adverse conditions. This refers to both precarious socioeconomic conditions as well as disaster-prone geographical surroundings, both of which apply to our research site. Future orientations relate to specific domains of life. Seginer (2008, 2010) referred to these as *core prospective domains* and asserted that these domains are characterized by universal themes such as a higher education, work and career, and marriage and family. In our case study, however, collective and religious dimensions of life play a further crucial role. For example, the distinction between this mortal world and an afterlife is critical. A person's expectations regarding the afterlife (that is, whether or not the afterlife is feared or longed for) depends on the worldly deeds and accumulated merits in the mortal world. Anticipating the quality of an eternal afterlife was said by several villagers to have an impact on daily routines in the present, because in order to amass merit, one's life needs to be acted out in accordance with religious and sociocultural guidelines.

When talking about prospective hopes and fears, villagers referred to different social reference units and considered personal, familial, and communal interests. As individuals, they expressed different types of future orientations: staying physically healthy, improving one's level of education, finding a good job,[4] increasing happiness by leading a more peaceful life instead of overemphasizing the material aspects of life, and enhancing one's religious life.[5] Familial goals expressed by (usually married) adults were: improving the health of one's children or the entire family, improving the

[4] This goal was usually voiced by children and adolescents and a gender difference was reflected in the type of answers given. In general, women reported feeling less obligated to take on a productive role. Some of the prospective jobs mentioned by girls were: teacher, doctor, beauty specialist, and nurse. Examples mentioned by boys included: soldier, police officer, doctor, teacher, entrepreneur, soccer or badminton player, and artist.

[5] On the subject of work and career, economic issues were mainly presented as a challenge and possible future burden as participants were highly aware of the precarious economic situation of their families. This needs to be considered against the backdrop of a discourse on increased economic

educational prospects for one's children, attaining a better future for one's children in general, improving family finances (for sheer survival—that is, to meet daily needs—or to build a better future for one's children or fulfill communal financial obligations), making one's partner happy, and eradicating domestic violence. Children voiced the wish to provide for their parents, a desire which was usually expressed as a conflict between the obligation to stay within the village in order to care personally for their parents and the drive to move away from the village to get a well-paid job. In addition, several villagers mentioned group-specific goals, such as the wish to improve the external perception of the group involved in the eradication of domestic violence. Some of the communal interests expressed by the villagers included: improving the village environment (for example, by raising ecological awareness), improving the level of communal knowledge and skills (for example, with regard to civil rights), improving village morals (by aiming at a socially understood sense of collective well-being, as well as social harmony as an end in itself, and a communal sense of security), improving the village economy and infrastructure, and strengthening the religious community.

These socioculturally informed meanings of expressed future orientations contain highly valued codes of conduct (see Chap. 11) and need to be viewed in the context of power structures. Influential villagers (*tokoh*) publicly promoted these desired future outlooks, raising them to the level of a powerful public discourse, from which individuals were hard-pressed to distance themselves—at least during the interview situation. Moreover, gender-specific, power-related disparities can be assumed, as it is usually men who serve as communal or religious leaders and therefore they contribute disproportionately to these publicly propagated discourses. In addition, it is usually men's networks that are formally institutionalized and therefore men rather than women have access to and control over valuable resources, such as information.

A hopeful, optimistic future orientation is critical for successful coping processes in disaster areas, that is, to initiate preventive action and afford psychological adaption processes after a burdensome event (Kotter-Kühn and Smith 2011). Astonishingly, the topic of disaster was not raised at all while talking about future outlooks. Instead, villagers emphasized desired developmental trajectories and expressed an optimistic outlook. For example, for the fifth anniversary of the earthquake, a communal feast named *The healthy walk*[6]*—reflection of the earthquake* was held near Sido Kabul. Above all, speakers highlighted general developmental progress as well as the excellence of participating hamlets, for example, by referring to the academic

hardship in general (which is also due to global economic dynamics). In this regard, religion served as a source of hope in times of extreme poverty, while also acting as a reminder to exercise modesty and to adjust one's hopes to the reality of one's situation.

[6] The concept of a "healthy walk" can be found in other contexts as well, usually combined with commemorations of certain events in the past. It consists of a joint walk in the surrounding area through several hamlets and the participants are usually automatically entered in a tombola as well. For the fifth annual commemoration of the earthquake, the tombola prizes included a motorbike and a goat.

and athletic achievements at regional schools. We do not interpret this tendency to focus on development as progress as a form of repression that may prevent villagers from engaging in appropriate disaster-related precautions (see below).

15.2.2 Perceptions of Disaster-Specific Risks

The personal and collective perceptions of hazards and other threats held by inhabitants of risk zones are related to a geographical place of residence. Smaller quakes are common in the research site. Sido Kabul and Sendang lie on earthquake fault lines; Mulya Sari does not directly. Instead it is close to the sea, placing it within the tsunami risk zone.

The vast majority of interviewees displayed a high awareness of disaster risk. The area was generally described as a "red zone" (*zona merah*) and "crisis area" (*daerah rawan*). These technical terms and related forms of technological knowledge were transferred via information campaigns and simulation exercises that have taken place since the earthquake in 2006.[7] Many claimed that this new knowledge intensified feelings and thoughts of uncertainty, unrest, and insecurity. This draws attention to the distinction between perception and concern, with the former being the subjectively and socioculturally informed awareness of existing risks and the latter being the personal and collective relevance attributed to perceived risks. In general, the impact of disaster-specific knowledge and explanations can be considered a double-edged sword. A hazard-specific, technologically informed awareness can have troubling effects on individuals and communities:

> Since the quake, until now, [the area] has been continuously monitored. There were some people taking pictures, and distributing copies. I am not sure if they wanted to frighten us or if they told the truth; I don't know. But they said the [tectonic] plates would go wild, like that. (Bu Suprapti, Sido Kabul)

The majority of people, however, claimed to feel both safe and unsafe at the same time after having learned that their hamlet is located within an area that is at risk of earthquakes or tsunamis. This is in part because science-based knowledge can also play a role in refuting rumors that evoke fears. Related worries and uncertainties were reported to have eased or even eliminated by information sessions. Furthermore, knowing about the sheer impossibility of escaping from certain risks can help to relativize concerns (see also below). Villagers were well aware of the fact that environmental hazards (such as landslides, floods, earthquakes, tsunamis, or volcanic eruptions) are not confined to Java or even to Indonesia:

> I saw on TV that every place in the world has its own disaster. Even if I moved there, it doesn't mean that I would be safer there compared to staying here. (Pak Samino, Sido Kabul)

---

[7] Though not all villagers participated in these programs, the information still spread informally in forums not related to the disaster and through everyday encounters in village life. Furthermore, mass media spread information about the risks of living in a zone full of disaster-specific hazards.

People's concerns were based on their knowledge that they lived in a disaster-prone area and that it was not possible to make concrete predictions about the next earthquake.[8] Those who believed in predicted time frames reported feeling safer:

> About safety, it's clear that we're safe. Since according to the prediction, a similar earthquake will happen in 50 years again. That's what old people say. (Pak Munarman, Sido Kabul)

Others reported that they did not spend a lot of time thinking about the time frame of a next possible earthquake. They believed that it is Allah's decision if and when another disaster will strike. In general, villagers referred to a number of different sources for their predictions: dreams as premonitions, predictions by religious or scientific authorities, or stories passed on from previous generations.

In psychological cognitive-oriented models, risk awareness or perception and risk concern are two steps on the path to preventive action (for an investigation of problematic presumptions, see Chaps. 1 and 2). In the following section, we will elaborate on the relationship between the future scenarios described above and preventative action.

15.3 Components of Disaster Preparedness and Mitigation

The villagers we interviewed talked about engaging in a historically developed, science-based, and socioculturally specific mixture of the following preparation and mitigation strategies.

15.3.1 Geographical Location

Coping processes, among other things, are modified based on the geographical location of a person's place of residence. Different geographical conditions are associated with different types of hazards, and therefore there are a wide range of best practices for preventive action. For instance, Mulya Sari is located in a red zone for tsunamis. Therefore, villagers had considered the closest hills, trees, and higher plateaus which would allow them to escape tsunami waves. In addition, a dam was built between the hamlet and the river. In contrast, Sido Kabul and Sendang are located in a red zone for earthquakes. In the case of these villages, mitigation measures focused primarily on building earthquake-resistant houses.

Furthermore, Bantul is close to the northern volcano, Merapi; the capital of Bantul is located at a distance of approximately 35 km from the volcano. Merapi is one of the most active volcanoes in Indonesia. It is best known for its nearly continuous volcanic activity, a phenomenon characterized by the extrusion of viscous lava domes. Lava

[8] The villagers had different opinions as to when the next earthquake will occur (in a few years, in 30, 50, or 100 years).

dome growth increased during March 2006 and was rapidly followed by periods of multiple rockfalls and dome collapse events which continued until June 2006.[9] In October and November 2010, the volcano erupted again. The lava traveled 15 km to the south and caused more than 360 deaths (see Chap. 4).[10] Though the Bantulnese were not directly affected by evacuations or material damage in 2010, we heard vicarious concerns about people, friends, and relatives living close to the volcano.

Even though humans can only partially influence geographical conditions in order to mitigate potential risks, one always has—at least in theory—the possibility of moving to a safer place. In the immediate aftermath of the earthquake, aftershocks were still frequent and rumors about the area being swallowed by the sea were common. Many villagers reported thinking about moving away in order to protect themselves and future generations from harm. When the aftershocks ceased and feelings of uncertainty subsided, however, for the majority of people, moving away was no longer a genuine option. This is explained by their lack of financial resources to migrate coupled with the desire to stay within the village community. Another reason relates to the argument mentioned above: that all regions in Indonesia, and even worldwide, are perceived to be more or less hazardous. A sense of belonging to that particular place[11]—that is, to one's home—and a sense of social embeddedness seemed to compensate for disaster-related worries by giving people a feeling of well-being:

> It seemed that my heart is attached to this place, Mbak. In some other place, I'd have to adjust myself. In my own place, it's just comfortable (*enak*), even if it is dangerous. Every place has its own danger. (Bu Jiyo, Sido Kabul)

A few villagers however, deliberately chose a slightly different location for their newly built homes in the hope of achieving a better or, as Pak Ratman from Sido Kabul said, a "healthier future":

> Now we moved here to the empty area. I wouldn't have felt happy if I'd built a new house there. [. . .] It would always remind me of the event. The land was already unhealthy.

In the long run, villagers reported that it is more important to learn how to live with risk and threat instead of avoiding them. In this regard, moving away was not considered to be an option anymore.

15.3.2 Disaster-Specific Measures

In general, mitigating and preventive strategies can be more (see Sect. 15.3.2.) or less (see Sect. 15.3.3.) focused on disasters. The latter case also centers on economic,

---

[9] This drew attention to the volcano and it was a huge surprise to both officials and villagers when the earthquake struck Bantul at the end of May instead of an expected volcanic eruption.

[10] http://miavita.brgm.fr/pressroom/Pages/ayearafterthe2010Merapieruption.aspx. Accessed 12 May 2013.

[11] See also Prewitt Diaz's (2008) concept of sense of place.

sociocultural, and religiously understood risks and captures socioculturally specific features of dealing with risks. The former denotes general measures which apply to any disaster.

15.3.2.1 The Role of Government and Nongovernment Institutions

According to most interviewees, a number of different groups are expected to cooperate in order to improve Indonesia's disaster management and to balance top-down and bottom-up approaches. These groups included community members, communal health cadres, the village elite, teachers, entrepreneurs, local and central government officials, the military, and nongovernmental organization (NGO) activists.

Government entities, however, were described by people as carrying the main responsibility for disaster management. This may be due in part to newer attitudes or beliefs that have developed after the earthquake in 2006. Communal leaders are considered to be representatives of the local and national government and are mainly responsible for coordinating and communicating tasks between their community and higher governmental bodies. According to several villagers, in cases in which the government cannot meet the population's needs, NGOs, political, or private entities are expected to step in and provide resources needed by the population. They also argued that the government should assess disaster risk and assume responsibility for decisions, for example, in case an evacuation was necessary or if long-term migration was inevitable. Many villagers also noted that it is the government's responsibility to provide aid during the emergency and reconstruction phases in such a way that self-reliance is sustained.[12] In Sido Kabul, communal leaders were expected to determine which disaster aid is needed and should write proposals to the local government to obtain funds. They were seen as responsible for general community program planning as well as for communicating these plans to higher bodies, protecting vulnerable groups, protecting natural resources, forming disaster management groups, and making disaster management plans.

Since the earthquake in 2006, government and nongovernment institutions provided a number of services and resources for risk-mitigation purposes: technical devices (for example, early warning system for tsunamis), installation of marked escape routes, compilation and provision of demographic maps showing vulnerable and resilient households within villages, formation of communal disaster management groups, information (for example, regarding earthquake-resistant building standards), psychoeducational training, and real-life simulations of best practices and escape routes in emergency situations (such as training people to restrict post-disaster calls to avoid crashing the telecommunications network).

[12] The relationship between disaster risk reduction, community empowerment, and community development was emphasized by communal leaders and villagers alike, and justified by underlining the value of self-sufficiency (*mandiri*).

15.3.2.2 Communal Disaster Management Groups

In Sido Kabul, a communal disaster response group was formed in 2009 through an initiative of an internationally funded NGO. It consisted of 25 members and seven board members. The hamlet leader was automatically named as the leader of the group.[13] The group's main goals were to prepare for and mitigate disaster risks, reduce possible deaths, restrict material damage, and address the sociocultural erosion of collective values (such as the spread of increasingly individualistic and materialistic orientations). The group was expected to disseminate best practices within the community, take charge during the emergency phase, coordinate rescue attempts and distribute aid goods.

Similar groups were formed elsewhere through both government and nongovernment local initiatives. While local and international features of disaster management become intermingled, the local specificity is still extremely important: during disaster management group meetings, the specific social fabric (*rukun, kebersamaan*), the history of communal self-help practices (*gotong royong*), and the revolving funds (*arisan*) were highlighted through comparisons with other disaster contexts. A code of conduct described as understanding, caring, and compassionate (*peduli, kasihan*) and solidarity between villagers was reported to contribute to the development of risk-reducing ways of relating to the environment. For example, avoiding throwing waste products into the river in order to minimize the risk of floods was legitimized by the discourse of caring for one's surroundings. Moreover, international technical-oriented concepts and discursive arguments were emphasized. Participant-observation revealed that during psychoeducational sessions, concepts such as social vulnerability, capacities, threats, and risks were introduced alongside the phases of disaster management cycles.

15.3.2.3 Training and Simulations

Villagers have been provided with training and simulations in the form of workshops which offer top-down instructions rather than negotiated solutions. For example, in Sido Kabul, an international NGO provided an earthquake-specific training program.[14] Participants reported having more appropriate preventive or crisis strategies (for example, hiding under door frames) compared with nonparticipants, who did not report specific courses of action that they would follow or who claimed they would

---

[13] This power-reproducing organizational structure of communal disaster management is typical of village structures. All board members took on either official roles or informal, but respected, functions, such as neighborhood leaders or health cadres.

[14] Originally, 30 sessions in three groups (separated for women, men, and youth) were planned, and then reduced by half due to protests from villagers. The community had been the target of an overwhelming amount of NGO-led programs (see Chap. 16), and reported boredom and increased time pressure as, in addition to completing the training sessions, they also had to handle the responsibilities of daily life as well as reconstruction after the disaster and resume their income-generating activities.

just run away in the case of a disaster. Conscious knowledge of what can and needs to be done (such as having escape routes in mind) was said to have a calming effect. Villagers often referred to the importance of staying calm *and* cautious (*waspada, hati-hati, prihatin*) instead of either panicking or cognitively avoiding the risk.

However, these educational measures are not always implemented and they do not always reach all members of a village community, as not everyone was invited to these training programs.[15] As the date of the next earthquake is unknown, some villagers reported that they were hesitant to engage in mitigating efforts, such as keeping an emergency tent or a medical kit. Besides, villager Bu Kusminah from Sido Kabul explained that it is not necessary to collect and keep important documents in an emergency bag because as she was not attending school and does not have any money, her only important document would be her identity card. Furthermore, securing furniture to the wall was not feasible:

> We heard about those wardrobes during the training. We have a narrow space for living, right, Mbak? [. . .] If these wardrobes were moved to the side, I would be seen in my sleep by, for instance, guests. [. . .] I won't do it like that then. (Bu Kusminah, Sido Kabul)

Overall, the identified tendency to neglect precautionary measures may be due to inappropriate modes of delivering the information to the villagers, for example, by overlooking local habits and contexts. This can result in a less commitment to apply newly acquired knowledge and skills. One of the most important factors seemed to be to connect to villagers' experiences, ways of thinking, and worldviews. One positive example is the hamlet of Mulya Sari and its preparation for tsunamis. In this case, government staff provided concrete examples, illustrated the distance between the beach and the village of Mulya Sari, and addressed the condition of the land and its relation to the expansion of tsunami waves by describing the well-known characteristics of the southern beach's waves. This information was repeated continuously over the course of the training sessions.

15.3.2.4 Disaster Knowledge and Communication Flows

During a workshop organized by our Indonesian research partner in 2010, representatives of the education ministry and of the regional body for planning and development, lecturers in communication science, scientists from the center for disaster research, and donors during the 2006 earthquake agreed on the necessity of providing comprehensive information and appropriate ways of communicating this information to communities through training programs and simulation exercises.

Long-term mitigation requires, among other things, intergenerational communication. To make risk mitigation practices sustainable, parents need to communicate to future generations about possible hazards and risks as well as educate children about how to handle these risks and what to do in case of an emergency. However, communicating about possible prospective threats can also induce anxiety, feelings

[15] Some villagers assumed that invitations were granted based on favoritism from the communal elite. Nonparticipants had to rely on others who were willing to spread their knowledge.

of insecurity, and worry. This is why some parents avoided discussing these matters thoroughly with their children.

Before the earthquake in 2006, village communities already relied on a drum made from bamboo or wood, called *kentongan*, which is struck to sound an alarm. Hearing the drums, villagers know they should take refuge and search for a safe place outside of their homes. These long-running practices are combined with technological–rational measures, such as knowledge of escape roads to be taken when *kentongan* are beaten. Newly installed escape route signs now indicate the way.

Elderly villagers in particular tended to refer to prior experiences with disasters. They remembered and compared death tolls and levels of destruction and this led them to question what might be done better in the future. They usually felt that building materials and construction standards were particularly important, because wooden houses were responsible for far fewer deaths compared to stone houses stone houses used nowadays.

15.3.2.5 Housing and Infrastructure

Villagers received information and training about how to build earthquake-resistant houses (for example, by using 6–12 mm iron struts, employing an increased number of escape doors, building foundations reaching into the ground, etc.). However, the vast majority of newly built houses do not comply with safety standards (see Subagyo and Irawan 2008). Relevant information arrived too late—that is, after governmental reconstruction money had been distributed and reconstruction had already started. Moreover, considering the villagers' habits, it would have been more effective to deliver this information verbally or in the form of exercises rather than, for example, by distributing booklets as the case was after 2006. In addition, after distributing the reconstruction money, the government did not employ any monitoring and control measures, a condition that was identified as a cause of low building standards. Furthermore, different safety standards were propagated by different agencies. The lowest standards were stipulated by government agencies and higher standards were required by international and national organizations, such as the Java Reconstruction Fund or the International Organization for Migration (IOM). Another hurdle in the implementation of safety quality standards involved the cost of materials. In Sendang, the IOM built one disaster-resistant sample house. However, the building materials used for this sample house were far too expensive so that none of the villagers could afford to rebuild similar houses. Knowing that their own house met only the lower standard intensified many villagers' reported feelings of insecurity and worry.[16]

Nevertheless, many new houses were reinforced with iron bars of some form. And the new, iron-reinforced houses were reported to feel safer to those living in them than their previous houses. In practice, feeling safe translated into the expectation that the house will not immediately collapse, but will nevertheless provide enough

[16] These concerns were probably only raised at the time they were inquired about. After this, they may have been forgotten during daily routines.

time to run outside. Feeling safe also meant that the building materials used are not as heavy as to cause potentially deadly injuries. However, it was acknowledged by many villagers that even if all the standards were met, a residual risk always remains.

15.3.3 General Safety Precautions

Besides disaster-specific measures, great emphasis was placed on general safety precautions. This was explained by villagers' uncertainty with regard to the timing of next earthquake. Additionally, villagers reported that continuously dealing with the risk of a disaster is unhealthy and burdensome:

> There was a man who asked about the house, the size, and the rooms and so on. And then I asked him, "Why does this need to be written?" "Oh it's okay, Mbak. It needs to be considered in case there are any earthquakes in the future, so that we can figure out what is wrong with the house." And then I directly said, "Oh, I don't want another earthquake, Pak!" So the man was laughing, "I don't want it either, but in case there's another one. Who knows?" So he answered like that (laughing). So I always had the word "earthquake" in my mind. "Oh, there'll be another earthquake later." (Bu Sumiarti, Sido Kabul)

Villagers also described engaging in activities that would increase their resilience, although these activities were not necessarily disaster-specific. The coping processes presented below may have developed because of the broader context of living in a disaster-prone area and because of other factors, such as the preexisting level of poverty and low education levels combined with a postcolonial history.

15.3.3.1 Economic Survival and Precaution Strategies

With regard to financial security in an ongoing economically precarious situation, several strategies seem to have been developed by villagers. Mention here can be made of the *arisan* tradition (that is, rotating savings and credit associations), diversified income-generating activities, and a group approach to farming and business in general.

Resuming daily income-generating activities was reported to be an important factor in coping with past losses and, even more importantly, as a way to face an insecure future. Being able to look after oneself economically is a highly valuable sociocultural asset in the context of our research site, and villagers indicated that it helped to restore a feeling of normality in insecure times. The *pasrah-nrimo-usaha*-concept plays an important role here: one does not need to think about when there will be another disaster; this would be disruptive for performing one's duties and fulfilling one's roles. Surrendering to God and focusing on acceptance instead helps individuals not to ponder too much on uncertainties and helps them to distract themselves through work and daily routines. For example, a duck breeder claimed that when he was being entertained by his animals while caring for them, his concerns about the future dissolved. In these cases, being prepared means working as effectively and patiently as possible while praying for safety.

15.3.3.2 Environmental Precautions

NGO activists, along with several local politicians, began to push a discourse of environmental sustainability. For example, in order to promote the idea of sustainable development and environment protection, activists highlighted the possible economic benefits. A group of entrepreneurs was approached and invited to process the skin of cassavas into cookies, crackers, or *nada de cassava* instead of throwing it into the nearby river—which contributed to water pollution. In addition, during their talks for the fifth anniversary of the earthquake disaster, local politicians pointed out that humans have a responsibility to treat the environment carefully, promoting a caring or *peduli* attitude.

15.3.3.3 Social Precautions

On a communal—that is, a hamlet-wide (*dusun*) or neighborhood-wide (RT) level—certain collective practices and shared values were highlighted when facing the future. The interviewees emphasized issues of communal self-reliance and solidarity: villagers themselves decide on communal problems and challenges during discussion forums (*musyawarah*)[17] and collectively share the burden of helping to promote village development using *gotong royong*. Villagers reported an increased number of communal feasts and rituals in the aftermath of the earthquake. In addition, religious ceremonies became more frequent. The issue of social embeddedness, expressed by references to *rukun* (now Chap. 10), was assigned a crucial role by villagers; they associated it with a feeling of belonging, probably comparable to the *sense of community* described by McMillan and Chavis (1986).

In addition, the issue of familial embeddedness and strong family ties was raised. Family roles were associated with certain responsibilities, such as caring for injured family members and providing financial support for poorer family members. The family was mainly presented as promoting feelings of safety.

15.3.3.4 Enhancing Codes of Conduct

Several codes of conduct described in Chap. 11 and elaborated on in the context of extreme suffering in Chap. 13 add to the individuals' capacity for coping with insecure futures and related worries. In general, an individual's ability to consider different possibilities for agency while staying calm, patient, and optimistic and

[17] Nondemocratic aspects of these discussion forums have been criticized by some, as it is only men who are invited and as it is usually those with a good standing in their community or with formal functions who make decisions.

striving to improve one's personal, familial, or communal situation was reported to be an asset in helping that individual to face the future. Awareness helps to inform the individual about what can be controlled and what needs to be accepted going forward. It describes a state of inner preparedness that involves knowing how to face a disaster and what to do when a, b, or c happens. It was also evident in an attitude to life that the individual is prepared to die at any time:

> One of the meanings of the earthquake in our life is that we have to be careful (*hati-hati*). Human life is not eternal. Sometimes a disaster can threaten our life. We have to be ready. We have to prioritize our preparedness. There are two important issues. Firstly, we have to get ourselves close to God because a disaster may strike anytime. Secondly, we have to prepare how to face it. (Pak Jiyo, Sido Kabul)

This type of inner awareness and behavioral preparedness is considered to be a typical Javanese virtue (for example, see the Government of Yogyakarta Special Province 2008).

15.3.3.5 Transcendental Measures

Preparedness measures are also influenced by folktales and beliefs inherited from ancestors, religious practices, and the local culture. For example, common prayer sessions, called *pengajian,* were reported to be held in order to help villagers face the future with a new sense of strength. The goal is to ask for safety and welfare. Knowing about the hazards of one's place of residence, while being simultaneously unwilling or unable to move away, makes individuals feel unsafe. Individuals cope with these feelings by believing in and surrendering themselves to God:

> Personally, I can only submit myself to God (*pasrah*). What else can I do? It's impossible for me to move away from here (laughing). Besides, I don't know where to go. Personally, I submit myself to God (*pasrah*); what goes around comes around (*ya sudah*). (Pak Jiyo, Sido Kabul)

Humans cannot know when God will send the next disaster or when they will die; in the wake of God's almightiness, people become weak and even powerless, and as a result, they may feel fear. By turning to God, one is empowered to control this fear by acceptance (that is by accepting the weakness or even powerlessness of humankind). This inspires feelings of calm, especially when facing an insecure future. *Pasrah* and *nrimo* mean accepting everything that comes from God and being grateful for all of those things, even when one is struck by disaster and poverty. Earthquakes are interpreted as a test from God, which one should try to pass successfully. Without accepting God's will and the tests that it involves, hardship may develop into health problems, which, ultimately, will also require acceptance, as this 65-year-old woman explained:

> If I accept (*pasrah*) what God Allah gives me, it means that I am thankful (*bersyukur*) and accept (*nrimo*) everything [. . .]. Whether I am given a fortune or not, I am still thankful to God. If I am not thankful, like if I am protesting "why I am not given this and that", I will become sick (*sakit*). And when we're sick and we do not accept it (*tidak nrimo*), it means that we don't accept (*nrimo*) God's will. (Bu Ngatini, Sido Kabul)

In order to be safe (*aman*), it is not sufficient for the *lahir* (the outer) to be accepting; the *batin* (the inner) needs to be accepting as well, indicating a sort of authenticity.[18] *Pasrah* and *nrimo* bring about a sincere or *ikhlas*-attitude, leading to calmness, and translating into the following stance: one does not know what, where, and when things will happen, so one should accept this fact instead of dwelling on it and entering a state of *pusing*. This term literally translates to headache, but here it also refers to an inner imbalance and panicked mind. *Pasrah* and *nrimo* express a kind of basic confidence that one will be protected by God as long as one believes in God and brings his or her heart, soul, and conduct closer to God. *Pasrah* and *nrimo* support an optimistic and serene future orientation, encourage a self-reliant attitude and translate into the following stance when in relation to the future: whatever happens, one must take the high road, avoid dwelling on things and enjoy life.

This accepting stance is sometimes associated with more or less disaster-specific preparedness strategies. Our data distinguish between the following two discursive coping positions: Firstly, *pasrah* and *nrimo* help individuals not to abandon their routine activities and habits, that is, to maintain their capacity to act. Acceptance, a general stance of precaution (*waspada*), and patience (*sabar*) enable individuals to endure adverse conditions such as an insecure future. Many villagers considered earthquakes to be a test or a challenge (*ujian*), or as an orientation point which leads them to reconsider or change the direction of their conduct in life. An active effort (*usaha*) can and should be made (for example, running away in case of tremors instead of ignoring them, but without panic) but, on the contrary, and as a last consequence, humanity's fate (*nasib*, *takdir*) is determined by God and therefore cannot be influenced. Second, some villagers (especially elderly and very religious people) expressed the opinion that any kind of disaster-specific preparation is pointless as it is not within the power of humankind to influence earthquakes and their consequences. On this view, the only preparation strategy is to follow the rules of the Qur'an and Allah in daily life. By orienting oneself closer toward God by engaging in increased religious behavior, *ibadah*, and belief, *iman*, one is prepared to die at any time without having to fear punishment for one's sins in the afterlife. In both positions, it was important to maintain good relationships with neighbors and family members so that no problems were left unresolved.

15.4 Resources for a Sense of Safety

According to the villagers we interviewed, a sense of safety or resilience not only refers to prospective hazard-induced disasters but also has a much more comprehensive meaning. A sense of safety relates to different areas of life; it is a complex phenomenon encompassing diverse features, such as social and cosmological embeddedness as well as economic security. From this point of view, it is possible to

[18] For an explanation of the concepts of *batin* and *lahir* see Chaps. 11 and 13.

explore diverse sources and resources for feeling safe or unsafe; that is, for feeling resilient or feeling vulnerable.

Feelings of uncertainty, fear, and unease were triggered by repeated smaller earthquakes that have taken place since the large earthquake in May 2006.[19] Many villagers reported that memories of the 2006 earthquake were automatically activated; they described being scared (*kaget*) and experiencing a variety of automatic reactions. For example, some villagers described a feeling of unease or disquiet when they are in a stone house. They would feel safe only outdoors or in bamboo houses where the risk of being injured is much lower. Feelings of uncertainty also developed because villagers received information regarding safe building standards after their houses had already been rebuilt (see above). In the end, however, villagers usually concluded that it is up to God to determine whether the houses stand firm, and who will survive or be physically harmed.

In general, feelings of safety or resilience are strongly associated with feeling comfortable (*nyaman, enak*). Villagers referred to a number of sources of and resources for achieving this kind of sense of safety: (1) disaster-specific training would help individuals to feel calm and safe again, because they would know what needs to be done in case of an emergency and thus feel prepared (*siap*) and able to attain a state of caution (*waspada*), instead of merely being afraid of an unavoidable but unpredictable earthquake. (2) The absence of larger earthquakes in the recent past and the expectation that the next large earthquake will not happen in the near future was another helpful resource. There were no stronger earthquakes in the region in the months prior to the interviews and focus group discussions and roughly half of the interviewees described feeling safe and calm. (3) Houses reinforced with (at least some) iron were believed to contribute to a sense of safety. (4) According to the villagers, the "feeling of recovery" from rebuilding one's own house and communal infrastructure instilled a source of safety as part of the understanding of self-reliance and trust in one's own agency. (5) Family embeddedness was also emphasized:

> As long as our family's heart works peacefully (*tenteram*), we'll feel safe (*aman*). I just let the other things happen. I don't care about them (*biarin*). (Pak Wiryo, Sido Kabul)

(6) Stable family economics were highlighted as a source of security as well. For example, it was important to be able to pay for a good school education for one's children and meet communal financial obligations. (7) In addition, communal embeddedness was crucial. Villagers reported an increase in activities aimed at maintaining social harmony (*rukun*) (such as night watch, communal meetings and rituals, as well as Qur'an recitations called *pengajian*). Neighbors who provide material assistance, advice, and supportive social interactions in general also helped to foster social embeddedness, and engendered a sense of well-being and feelings of safety (see also Chap. 10):

[19] Other hazards, such as mudslides or volcanic eruptions, were perceived as irrelevant by villagers. The impact of these types of disasters would not extend as far as the villagers' place of residence. Floods were the only other risk mentioned.

> Although I live next to the river, I still feel comfortable (*nyaman*) here. Because I know all my neighbors here, everyone is good to me. [...] [I feel] comfortable and safe. So the most important thing is that we have to be good with our neighbors. [...] If there's something happening, we have to help each other, not necessarily with money. Maybe we help to think through something. (Bu Nurdin, Sido Kabul)

(8) Finally, a cosmological embeddedness is evident from the analysis of the interviews and group discussions. Many villagers reported feeling more secure because trust in God has increased since the 2006 disaster. Religious services have increased dramatically; people say more prayers and their strengthened faith was reported to have added to the feeling of harmony with cosmic forces and thus contributed generally to a feeling of safety.

Overall, in practice, a colorful mixture of these elements when coping with future disaster-related hazards was usually revealed: do not have any problems with society, do not have any problems with your family, do have the courage to correct your faults, do build your relationship with God, and do employ disaster-specific strategies if possible.

15.5 Concluding Remarks

Even though the process of handling risks relates to future events, general psychological models of future orientations (Seginer 2008) assume that these orientations are bound up with positive expectations rather than with concerns (see Chap. 2). As we have shown, risk and the future seem to be very different issues. Personal, familial, and communal futures often were not viewed from the perspective of risks in general or the specific risk of another earthquake for which special preparation is required. When villagers were asked directly, however, they showed a keen awareness of the fact that they live in a highly disaster-prone area. Nonspecific, general goals of earning a living and maintaining a certain level of social embeddedness dominated our discussions about the future. Therefore, concerns about being threatened by disasters need to be seen in relation to other future-related hopes, such as social harmony and familial or communal economic development. Consistent with Hobfoll's (2011) terminology, we highlighted a sort of resource investment principle in the sense of a future-oriented coping strategy which helps to prepare individuals and communities for possible resource losses in general and results in resource caravans, or a pooling of resources.

If we adopt the perspective of the normality of threat proposed by Bankoff (2007, 2010, 2012) about the Philippines, then uncertainty and risk must be considered normal factors in life. In our study, hazardous events were presented as recurring cycles rather than as singular events, a factor which highlights dynamic processes of long-term coping, as well as lifespan and related individual and communal developmental processes. Furthermore, living with permanent threats (that are not necessarily disaster specific but economic, social, and transcendental as well) needs to be seen against the backdrop of sociocultural-specific principles of life conduct, such as the stance of "happiness in sorrow and worry in the face of happiness" (*prihatin*-stance, see Chap. 11). It helps individuals to accept risks as an integral part of life, to be aware of risks, and to prepare for them in the best way possible. This stance is combined with the practice of distracting oneself by focusing on other areas of life and on desired outcomes in order to prevent stress processes from exceeding communal and individual capacities.

From a Western perspective, it appears that villagers only make partial arrangements for disaster precaution. Technological risk measures appear to be integrated into daily practices only in a pragmatic manner. Their application is not always done in an "effective" way as these imported concepts and strategies sometimes do not fit with conditions in the hamlets, and can compete against local configurations of relevance and confront resource limitations in village life (that is, limitations in economic and social capital). Therefore, disaster-specific precautions can be limited by the local sociopolitical and sociocultural order and harsh economic conditions. Moreover, collectively shared and personally held meanings assigned to the previous earthquake experience are reactive coping processes with implications for general future-oriented precautions. This includes interpretations of the earthquake (and tremors) as a reminder, or as a test. These reframings are associated with the willingness to improve oneself and to do better in the future. Preparedness is something that villagers above all try to achieve from within themselves (as a sort of inner preparedness). In contrast to Western concepts, the focus is placed less on controlling the situation and developing technical and physical preparedness, but more on religious, personal, and social measures, probably also as a result of limited material resources. However, a combination of both that strikes a balance between physical–technocratic and inner preparedness was usually presented as the best practice. Thus, disaster-specific precautions with physical–technical features need to be seen as complementary to inner measures rather than as excluding each other: it is possible for individuals to anticipate and exercise control while also letting go and surrendering. The contrasting view is the Western-inspired, international framework of risk management, which highlights control as the only way of dealing with adversity and disaster.

In Chap. 1 we showed that Western approaches to risk reduction focus on the external, technocratic preparedness strategies following this control paradigm. This is linked to Western understandings of science, knowledge, enlightenment, and a specific assumed relation between humankind and nature. The preparedness found in our case study is process-orientated and thus open-ended ("Whatever will happen, I will be ready to deal with it."). Probably, this is due to the specific characteristics of the disaster context itself. If earthquakes are perceived as unpredictable, that is, if even science is not yet able to predict them, one must rely on other techniques and sources for a sense of safety. In this regard, the type of preparedness that we found in our research site is nonspecific and includes the risk of earthquakes, along with other uncertainties and hardships of life such as the fragility of human relationships. On the contrary, feeling comfortable and secure fits with a general feeling of being in good hands in a cherished, harmonious community that has a strong religious life. This general feeling of safety and embeddedness seems to assuage feelings of being threatened and has a stabilizing and calming effect on daily routines while promoting feelings of solidarity through religious and communal rituals.

In sum, when Western-inspired risk management is applied to or imported into countries with different sociocultural frameworks, it is important to understand the complex notions of preparedness that result. On the island of Java, human agency and concepts of the inner and outside realm are constructed in a very different way when compared to Western thinking in which surrendering is closely linked to powerlessness and considered to be rather devaluing or disempowering. What can at first appear to be an overemphasis on powerlessness combined with the idea of surrendering to a benevolent higher power, however, ultimately resulted in increased hope and reliance on a positive outlook, and supported active engagement in pragmatic action.

Acknowledgment The editors would like to thank Devin Martini for her assistance in editing this chapter.

References

Bankoff, G. (2007). The historical geography of disaster: 'Vulnerability' and 'local knowledge'. In G. Bankoff, G. Frerks, & D. Hilhorst (Eds.), *Mapping vulnerability* (pp. 25–36). London: Earthscan.

Bankoff, G. (2010). No such thing as natural disasters. http://hir.harvard.edu/no-such-thing-as-natural-disasters? Accessed 16 June 2013.

Bankoff, G. (2012). Storm over San Isidro: "Civic community" and disaster risk reduction in the nineteenth century Philippines. *Journal of Historical Sociology, 25*(3), 331–351.

Beatty, A. (2005). Feeling your way in Java: An essay on society and emotion. *Ethos, 70*(1), 53–78.

Browne, K. (2001). (Ng)amuk revisted: Emotional expression and mental illness in Central Java, Indonesia. *Transcultural Psychiatry,* 38(2), 147–165.

Gigerenzer, G. (2008). *Rationality for mortals. How people cope with uncertainty*. New York: Oxford University Press.

Hobfoll, S. E. (2011). Conservation of resources theory: Its implication for stress, health and resilience. In S. Folkman & P. E. Nathan (Eds.), *The Oxford handbook of stress, health, and coping* (pp. 127–147). New York: Oxford University Press.

Holman, E. A., & Silver, R. C. (2006). Future-oriented thinking and adjustment in a nationwide longitudinal study following the September 11th terrorist attacks. *Motivation and Emotion,* 29(4), 389–410.

Kotter-Kühn, D., & Smith, J. (2011). When time is running out: Changes in positive future perception and their relationships to changes in well-being in old age. *Psychology and Aging, 26*(2), 381–387.

McMillan, D. W., & Chavis, D. M. (1986). Sense of community: A definition and theory. *Journal of Community Psychology, 14*(1), 6–23.

Prewitt Diaz, J. O. (2008). Integrating psychosocial programs in multisector responses to international disasters. *American Psychologist, 63*(8), 802–827.

Seginer, R. (2008). Future orientation in times of threat and challenge: How resilient adolescents construct their future. *International Journal of Behavioral Development, 32*(4), 272–282.

Seginer, R. (2010). *Future orientation: Developmental and ecological perspectives*. New York: Springer.

Slovic, P., & Västfjäll, D. (2010). Affect, moral intuition, and risk. *Psychological Inquiry, 21*(4), 387–398.

Subagyo, B., & Irawan, V. (2008). Building local governments and communities that are more resilient to hazards. In D. Karnawati (Ed.), *The Yogyakarta earthquake of May 27, 2006* (pp. 23.1–23.8). Belmont: Star Publishing Company.

The Government of Yogyakarta Special Province (2008). Reconstruction based on local wisdom (*Saiyeg Saeko Kapti*). In D. Karnawati (Ed.), *The Yogyakarta earthquake of May 27, 2006* (pp. 25.1–25.8). Belmont: Star Publishing Company.

Chapter 16
Critical Perspectives on Gender Mainstreaming in Disaster Contexts

Silke Schwarz

16.1 Introduction

Since the 1990s, the field of international disaster management has made increasing efforts to overcome the dichotomies between disaster management and development, between crisis and everyday life. Emergency assistance supplied at short notice should nevertheless have a sustainable impact by contributing toward achieving the so-called Millennium Development Goals.[1] Gender justice is understood to be one of the ultimate goals of aid-related development as well as contributing to development and disaster risk reduction. It is regarded as a condition in which the different interests and needs of the genders are recognized and equitable power relations and fields of responsibility exist between men and women (Wichterich 2010; Ariyabandu and Wickramasinghe 2005; DAWN; Duryog Nivaran;[2] Schwarz 2012; United Nations [UN] 2000; United Nations/International Strategy for Disaster Reduction [UN/ISDR] 2007).

[1] In the year 2000, 189 states committed to reaching development targets by 2015, ranging from increasing gender equality and women's empowerment to halving extreme poverty rates (http://www.un.org/millenniumgoals/; accessed 10 August 2013).
[2] DAWN stands for *Development Alternatives with Women for a New Era*. DAWN was founded in the Philippines in 1984 and nowadays consists of a broad network from Africa, Asia, Latin America, the Pacific, and the Caribbean (http://www.dawnnet.org/index.php; accessed 29 July 2012). The Duryog Nivaran network is active primarily in South Asia (http://www.duryognivaran.org/; accessed 29 July 2012).

S. Schwarz (✉)
International Academy for Innovative Pedagogy, Psychology and Economics gGmbH
at Freie Universität Berlin, Malteserstr. 74-100, 12249 Berlin, Germany
e-mail: silke.schwarz@fu-berlin.de; silgnschwarz@yahoo.de

M. Zaumseil et al. (eds.), *Cultural Psychology of Coping with Disasters*,
DOI 10.1007/978-1-4614-9354-9_16,

Although this goal appears unequivocal in terms of its broad conceptual design and values, the question remains as to which exact direction change should take. In the specific context of a Javanese village after a disaster, what is it that is felt normatively desirable or just in terms of gender relations?[3] There can be strong differences and, in some cases, even contradictions about what is subjectively perceived as fair or desirable. Should men and women increasingly occupy the same positions within village politics? Should women be encouraged to act mainly in accordance with certain Islamic perspectives of a primarily reproductive role? Should men be supported above all in their position as breadwinners? Which routes toward increased gender justice seem possible? Which potential obstacles lie in the way? When attempting to be socioculturally sensitive and critical of power relations, it is essential to raise these questions (Anderson 1999, 2000, 2004).

> Disasters are not neutral. [...] Recovery interventions are also not neutral: they can increase, reinforce or reduce existing inequalities. (ALNAP 2008, p. 8)

In order to answer them, the mainstreaming of gender[4] is examined in the Javanese village community Sido Kabul struck by an earthquake. The community helps to clarify what is possible when a group of several nongovernmental organizations (NGOs) works together on issues of social justice and gender.[5] In this context, most institutions were organized in a network with funding provided by the Ford Foundation and an Indonesian institution acting as the on-site intermediary organization. The program began twelve months after the earthquake and was scheduled to run for one year.

Among others, the NGO Rifka Annisa[6] provided information about gender equity (*keseteraan gender*), educated female villagers about violence against women (including the legal situation pertaining to this), and promoted women's reproductive health and children's health. A communal domestic violence group was formed and weekly exercise classes for women were offered. However, even with the addition of a small, informal micro-credit group (*arisan*), the number of members of this contested group had only slightly increased at the time of my study.

---

[3] More information about possible tensions within, amendments to, and legitimization of externally funded, internationally propagated gender policies with Western connotations in disaster relief and socioculturally specific movements can be found in Schwarz (2012).

[4] Depending on changing paradigms, this sort of gender politics has been labeled by various terms: women in development, women and development, empowerment, gender and development, human rights-based approach, gender mainstreaming, work with men, diversity approach, or the LGBT approach (lesbian, gay, bisexual, transgender) (Wichterich 2010).

[5] This distinctiveness also restricts possible generalizations of the results to other contexts or villages.

[6] The organization's homepage (also in English): http://rifka-annisa.or.id/; accessed 4 May 2012.

In contrast, becoming a member of the communal groups that were affiliated to the NGOs ASPPUK,[7] ICBC,[8] or IHAP[9] had a far more widespread appeal. These organizations offered small loans to village women, at first exclusively for female entrepreneurs, but extended later to a wider circle of women. Besides the financial support, business-related training and gender-specific educational events (similar to those by Rifka Annisa) were also organized. The target group of all these programs was exclusively women, most of whom were married.

As part of the extensive relief efforts, a hamlet development committee was founded—consisting exclusively of men—as well as a cattle breeding group, which was used to carry out educational work on the subject of civic rights. This group was also directed primarily at men. Members of the Rifka and ASPPUK groups participated only temporarily in this training. The views of both villagers and activists (that is, the staff of the above-described NGOs) will be reconstructed in this chapter.

The theoretical chaps. 1–3 illustrated the ways in which a traditionally narrow psychological understanding of coping has gradually been broadened. Instead of reducing coping to individual, subjective, and intrapsychic (primarily cognitive) aspects, it is understood as a process of societally assimilative and accommodative development in this chapter. This approach corresponds with Norris et al.'s (2008) focus on the community as a unit of analysis. They ask which courses of development are possible for a community after a drastic experience such as a disaster (and subsequent relief interventions). A resistant developmental path is seldom found in empirical research: it refers to a process of social conservation or a "post-event functioning, adapted to pre-event environment" (p. 130). A resilient dynamic describes development in the direction of social change, to a level of "post-event functioning, adapted to [the] altered environment" (Norris et al. 2008), whereas a vulnerable dynamic describes a continuing state of community dysfunction. In psychology, coping and adaptive functioning is more a question of wellness and function than of social justice. Only resource-oriented approaches to social capital illuminate structures of domination that are close to the ideas of Hobfoll's (2011) *caravan passageways* and the *access model* of Wisner et al. (2004). These approaches are helpful to integrate a critical and political perspective into a psychological understanding of coping. The same is the case with the framework proposed by the scientific community under

---

[7] ASPPUK stands for *Asosiasi Pendamping Perempuan Usaha Kecil* and means a union supporting small entrepreneurs. The organization's website: http://www.asppuk.or.id/; accessed 7 Oct 2012. As part of the ASPPUK program, a women's cooperative with nine business-specific subgroups (food, agriculture, and ceramics, as well as trade) was formed.

[8] ICBC stands for *Institute for Community Behavioral Change*. The organization's website: http://www.icbc-indonesia.org/; accessed 12 May 2012. ICBC was active under the Ford Foundation network with its rehabilitation program to deal with the destroyed houses in Sido Kabul and was directed primarily at men. The NGO was then active again in the hamlet from April 2008 to May 2009, funded this time by the Malaysian *Force of Nature Aid Foundation* and had a specifically female target group.

[9] IHAP stands for *Institute of Hak Asasi Perempuan*, the Institute for Women's Rights. The organization's website: http://ihap.or.id; accessed on 10 May 2012. The NGO had already been in the hamlet in August 2006 and was not integrated into the Ford Foundation network.

the umbrella of the International Strategy for Disaster Risk Reduction (UN/ISDR 2004). There, resilience is seen as the *capacity for change*. This definition is suitable for the previously described research purposes to investigate possibilities for more profound social change, where it is important to increase resilience not only for impending disasters but also in relation to future risks to allow for robust and sustainable development.

The term *gender* is understood differently depending on gender-theoretical assumptions, and as such is now regarded as the central "multi-dimensional and contested concept of feminist theories" (Frey 2003, p. 27).[10] I use postcolonial and deconstructivist feminist theories in order to gain a perspective on gender that is historical *and* critical of power relations. In this chapter, gender is seen as a sociocultural construct. It describes a social practice, characterizes social roles, and is anchored in social structures. It is thereby apparent in social interactions and is reflected in political and economic dimensions of life. Ultimately, it is also written into the mental state of people as a multitude of internalized discursive positions. Gender relations are produced both through discourse and through social interactions, as well as being structured by these in turn (Lorber and Farrell 1991; Errington 1990; Narayan and Harding 2000; Bourdieu 2005; Mae and Saal 2007; Hermans and Hermans-Konopka 2010).

16.2 Gender-Specific Developmental Ideals

What kind of gender relations does a village community endorse after a disaster and the implementation of various gender mainstreaming programs? The greater the diversity and contradiction among the desired gender ideals of each individual in a community, the more potential there is for social conflict, which could in turn inhibit social change. Of course, a diversity of opinions also promises a variety of possible models that could offer directions for change.

At a basic level, almost all interviewees agreed that desirable and equitable gender relations were characterized by *treating one another respectfully*: "it's about respecting and appreciating one another as husband and wife" said Bu Mariana from Sido Kabul.

However, there are various, sometimes contradictory, ideas and feelings about what treating one another respectfully exactly means. Some men and women expressed a preference for clearly separated areas of responsibility, which I refer to as complementary orientation. Their tasks were judged to be equitable and, on this view, men and women should complete one another, compensating for each other's "shortcomings" and reinforcing one another when solving problems. Mas Bambang described this ideal as follows:

> We're already predestined (*takdir*) as counterparts, right? [...] Humankind is created in relation to one another, so that one is stronger when confronted by life's problems.

[10] Translated from German by Sarah Howard.

Other participants described an equal distribution of tasks as being desirable. They tended not to assign men and women roles, abilities, rights, or obligations on biological grounds. Social gender roles were experienced as being in flux.[11] Within family life, this means that both men and women should complete household chores and be responsible for childcare, as well as both playing a productive role through paid work. Villagers with an egalitarian attitude sanctioned political leadership and participation by women and men alike. The gender activists who were interviewed consistently subscribed to this egalitarian line of thought.

The shared norm of respectful cooperation perhaps represents a common and basic value when faced with the almost contradictory positions of egalitarianism and complementarity. In both cases, a recognition and acceptance of the other person, with his or her "shortcomings," was aspired to, and the equal worth of the genders was emphasized despite certain differences. Gender justice (*keadilan gender*) is equated with harmony and togetherness (*kerukunan, kebersamaan*) as well as differentiated from the extremes of feminine or masculine dominance, as described by Bu Mariana:

> A woman shouldn't challenge her husband too much, either. We [women] should always respect and value [our husbands], as long as the woman is not oppressed.

However, compared to these abstract, ideological ideals that lie between the two poles of egalitarianism and complementarity, the range of personal, familial, and communal everyday practices is extremely diverse (see Schwarz 2012 for more details).

16.3 Recovery Interventions Aiming at Gender Justice

The ideals presented earlier were formulated in light of the experience of numerous gender mainstreaming programs. In the following sections, tensions in the use of social change instruments are discussed and the genderized use and uptake of micro-credit schemes is examined. My analysis illustrates the implications and limitations of interventions and programs designed to promote profound and sustainable social change in the context of disasters and gender mainstreaming.

16.3.1 Overview of Instruments for Social Change

The possibilities for social change moving toward more just ways of living after disasters have been studied in various sociocultural contexts (Ariyabandu 2003; Chowdhury 2001; Yonder et al. 2006; Bari 1998). Some studies, however, describe contrary dynamics with a tendency toward retraditionalization (Bradshaw 2001, 2002; Hoffman 1999).

[11] Those with a complementary attitude described more rigid gender concepts, often based on religious and biological arguments.

The importance of NGOs in development work—as well as in the quest for gender justice—has increased steadily. They are characterized by less pronounced hierarchies than state institutions, as they claim to work in a way that is largely participatory and based on an empowerment approach. However, NGOs are increasingly criticized for creating new dependencies, which contradicts their stated aim that interventions should help local communities to accumulate social capital. Their focus on short-term duration programs is also regarded with skepticism (see Buckland 1998). In general, the frequently short-term financing policies of development projects mean that programs usually increase only forms of physical and human capital in a top-down process, rather than establishing the political and social capital necessary for securing a certain level of sustainability for a project. In contexts such as these, Kabeer's (1994) distinction between gender-neutral, gender-specific, and redistributive political action is often used in order to assess the distribution of resources between men and women. Only a redistributive policy will allow sustainable and far-reaching transformation of existing gender relations, enabling more just forms of living.

To achieve their aims, NGOs use a multitude of programs, which Buckland (1998) classifies as follows:

- Income-generating activities (usually in the form of peer-monitored loans),
- Provision of social services (for example, elementary education), and
- Organizational work in the community (for example, through the formation of micro-credit groups).

16.3.2 The Micro-Credit System

Worldwide, the number of informal credit systems has increased over the last 30 years (Ghazali 2003), not least because of various development and gender mainstreaming programs (Buckland 1998). Credit schemes are widespread in the Indonesian context, such as in the field of family welfare (Momo et al. 2002). In disaster management and poverty-related development work, it is common practice to focus on livelihoods (see, for example, Carney et al. 1999). As part of a disaster-related loss of human capital, assets, employment, markets, and the costs of relief measures, restoring livelihoods is regarded as central to the process of recovery. According to official guidelines, complex and sustainable livelihoods should be supported during reconstruction processes following disasters (ALNAP 2008).

How are small loans connected with the concern for gender justice? One fundamental assumption is that having one's own income and control over it automatically promotes detachment from familial and patriarchal control systems. Micro-credit schemes are thought to support this process. An improved financial position (such as through a micro-credit scheme) is thought to improve a woman's negotiating or bargaining position within the family and the community. There is broad public acknowledgement of this impact of micro-credit schemes; they are widely used, despite conflicting empirical findings about their effectiveness (Bloemen 2010; Agarwal 1997).

In Java, micro-credit groups are part of a longer history and tradition of the so-called *arisan* associations that are either for men *or* women. Besides Geertz's (1962) view that the micro-credit group produces solidarity, above all they are also often the only way of saving money or receiving financial support in times of need (Wolf 1992). Family economies in the Javanese context have already been examined frequently by researchers. Depending on when the research was carried out, different theoretical and thematic priorities have been set, resulting in contradictory assessments.

Studies carried out after the independence of Indonesia, for example, portray Javanese women as independent, economically autonomous, and equal or superior to their male counterparts (Geertz 1961; Jay 1969).[12] From another anthropological viewpoint, women are seen as neither subordinate nor superior to men, but rather as having a kind of indirect influence and *other* forms of power (Koentjaraningrat 1967; Keeler 1990). From a third and final perspective, inspired by a feminist branch of research, it is assumed that economic autonomy and patriarchal control coexist and that belonging to certain classes and the level of poverty both act in a generally restrictive way upon autonomy and freedom. Therefore, though Javanese women gain a relatively high level of agency in terms of their real economic power, this is inextricable from the formal authority of the men (Berninghausen and Kerstan 1984; Kerstan and Berninghausen 1991; Berninghausen et al. 2009; see Wolf 1992).

Viewed in this light, which limitations and potential benefits ensue from the popular instrument of micro-credits in the specific context of a central Javanese village, when these are provided as assistance for reconstruction following a disaster? Which roles, responsibilities, and duties, *and* which kinds of influence and decision-making powers, are attributed to women and men?

The productive role is associated with power structures, as it is accompanied by access to and control over certain resources, whether social networks, information, or financial resources (see also concept of the bargaining position, Agarwal 1997). In Sido Kabul, four main familial professional constellations could be distinguished based on occupational practices: the first cluster of *Only Male Earner* describes families in which the husband worked as a ceramicist, civil servant, craftsman, farmer, or factory worker, thereby acting as the sole breadwinner for the family. The second cluster of *Primary Female Earner* summarizes families in which the woman pursued regular work and generated the majority of the family income, for example, as a civil servant or by producing or trading food. The husband often earned an inconsistent wage through work in the agriculture or handicraft sectors. The third cluster of *Paid Employment of Both* can be divided again into those who worked outside the hamlet as employees in factories or as civil servants and those working within the hamlet, for example, in the ceramic or food industries; this latter

[12] Wolf (1992) attributes decades of influence on subsequent gender research projects by the works by Geertz (1961) and Jay (1969), who both argued that women's control over the family income was an indicator of their level of autonomy, therefore suggesting the high status of Javanese women.

subcategory often meant earning a relatively irregular and similarly low wage and being more available at home. The fourth and final cluster of *Joint Entrepreneurship* describes families who ran a company together, either in ceramics, terrazzo, or in food production such as noodle manufacture.

How is the family income divided up and who decides on its use?

When the man is the sole breadwinner, the chance seems to be higher (though only slightly) that he also takes a leading role in managing the family's finances. In cases where both the women and man are in paid employment, it was usually the woman who managed the family finances and seldom both partners together. Even in family businesses, large or small, it was the woman who assumed responsibility for both domestic financial management and keeping the business accounts. This is justified by the argument that man would have a natural tendency to be wasteful and hedonistic, while a woman on the other hand could be economical and thrifty and would be better able to keep an eye on the family's various financial obligations. Interviewees of both genders produced these stereotypical genderized accounts, regardless of whether they otherwise presented themselves as adopting an egalitarian or complementary stance of the division of labor in households. The male shortcoming was seen by both men and women as a matter of common knowledge and was not generally regarded as being objectionable or shameful in any way. In her role as financial manager, participants noted that the woman is obliged to ration the money in such a way that it is sufficient for all familial needs. Furthermore, she always assumes a social responsibility by ensuring that the family can meet the diverse financial obligations to the neighborhood network. The obligation to budget well with the existing and often scant finances, while considering the needs of *all* family members *as well as* communal obligations, was seen by some women as a burden, as they felt left alone to deal with financial problems. A woman is supposed to be responsible for borrowing money from relatives or other acquaintances in times of financial need, or for seeking additional sources of income. In this respect, the female financial management and its implications for the gendered power relations on Java is contradictory:

> Actually, the woman has a strong position. That is the strength of the Javanese woman. They are in the position to manage the family. [...] [But] if the husband has no money, and no job, then the wife has to work, whether she wants to or not. (Activist Mbak Surti)

The role of the financial manager does not necessarily equate with that of the decision-maker. For participants, either a shared decision (*rembug, musyawarah*) was made about internal family affairs, which was presented as the ideal practice, or the man was seen as being the ultimate decision-maker.

For example, Bu Nurmini, who ran a ceramics business with her husband (*Joint Entrepreneurship* cluster), pointed out that when she wanted to buy clothes or shoes, she asked her husband first. She would make her own decision only about items for daily use such as buying soap. If her husband forbade her to buy something, then she would defer her needs or desires. She said that she followed her husband's estimation as to how important each family member's needs are; and yet, she kept no record of their financial situation, so her husband would have to trust her in terms of expenditure with regard to items such as buying spices for the kitchen. The lack of accounting means that the woman has a relative freedom, which can be considered as rather low, as everyday kitchen purchases entail only small expenditures. The final decision-making power was attributed to the man by Bu Nurmini, even if the woman is responsible for managing the finances.

Others emphasized the illusory character of this presentation: the woman only formally respects her husband in his social role as head of the family (*kepala keluarga*) and in order to uphold this pretense, she would ask him for permission (*minta ijin*) if she wants to order cassava, for example.

Regardless of the question of the actual decision-maker, the financial management of the family per se was not perceived as being sufficiently important to constitute an increase in the bargaining position of women (Agarwal 1997); instead, having her own work and income were presented as more important:

> Silke Schwarz: "Can looking after the money strengthen the position of the woman within the family? [. . .]"
> Mas Zaki: "Not necessarily, either. In my opinion, it's more about [. . .] earning money herself. [. . .] That can increase the woman's bargaining position. [. . .] The most important thing is that she has her own income."

In all of the four familial occupational clusters described earlier, regardless of whether they hold egalitarian or complementary views, people emphasized that the man remains in the role of head of the family. He was consistently declared as having the main responsibility for the family's economic situation, and the woman was identified as a supplementary earner and financial manager. The masculine role assignment as the one in paid employment and main earner appears to need no further legitimation. Indeed, a man had to justify being unemployed, while female employment necessitated an explanation such as that it was based on economic necessity, a new consciousness or awareness of gender justice, or that employment was simply facilitated by access to capital through the NGOs and their small loans.

Overall, women were still positioned in everyday discourse in the role of supplementary earner 2–4 years after the NGO programs. Even though this justifies female employment to some extent, it maintains the discourse of men as main breadwinners, irrespective of the real income levels of women and men. Among other things, this tenaciously persistent gender bias contributes toward genderized trainings in certain professions and a wage gap in which the amounts earned by men remain mostly inaccessible to women. Male salaries were consistently higher in the hamlet studied, justified by men's main breadwinner role. The material advantages for men on the employment market are named by Demetriou (2001) in reference to Connell (1995) as the *patriarchal dividends of the external hegemony*.[13] Conversely, female villagers enter into a so-called *liberal trade* (Sa′ar 2005) through their discursive strategies: they verbally confirm dominant discourses and power relations and subordinate themselves to them. The self-designation of supplementary earner does, however, ensure a certain amount of agency when female employment is declared supportive of the male's primary responsibilities and is thus considered to be justified. It counters the

[13] An external hegemony denotes the power relations between men and women, whereas an internal hegemony describes the relations of men among themselves.

discourse of women being the *konco wingking*-literally meaning "the friend in the background"; that is behind her husband-who is primarily responsible for household chores and children's education.

In sum, to what extent can the employment of a woman, supported by a micro-credit loan, help to promote gender justice? According to the interviewees, female employment can lead women to gain more courage and confidence as they make a meaningful contribution to the family and village economy, thereby earning recognition, respect, and support from their husbands and other men in the hamlet. The employment of women was also seen as increasing the likelihood that men would become involved in the household chores and childcare, although the male level of critical awareness about the flexibility of gender roles was crucial in practice. Critical gender awareness on the part of men and their willingness to play a supportive role could be strengthened through awareness-raising events, according to the villagers.

However, in Sido Kabul, it appears that while the employment of women and the women's cooperative (which came about due to the micro-credit system) has increased the public presence of women's economic role in the community, this has not led them to gain any political decision-making power in the hamlet. In addition, adverse effects of female employment and the micro-credits were stated, such as multiple burdens, a lack of time for other activities, or financial burdens (such as marketing problems or the potential to fall into debt traps).

16.4 Implications for Social Change: Between Transformation and Conservation

> Disaster response is no magic bullet. [. . .] Clearly, there are limited opportunities for promoting social changes after disaster. (ALNAP 2008, p. 8)

Various strategies for social change have been applied to increase gender justice in the hamlet of Sido Kabul (see previous text). In development work, gender analysis is commonly employed to ascertain the success of gender mainstreaming programs.[14] In this research, an *area of life approach* was used to examine the extent to which the gender relations have changed in the eyes of the interviewees (see Fig. 16.1). There are both similarities and differences between this approach and conventional evaluative methods of research which Rossi et al. (1988) defined as "the systematic application of social science research methods in order to assess the concept, details, implementation and uses" (p. 3)[15] of social intervention programs.

In contrast to conventional summative or formative evaluation research, the focus of this research is not the exact mapping of program contents to program effects, but rather in-depth research at the site of a village community in which many different programs had been conducted over an extended period of time with different

[14] For an assessment of each gender analysis procedure with respect to the objectives of this research, see Schwarz (2012).

[15] Translated from German by Sarah Howard.

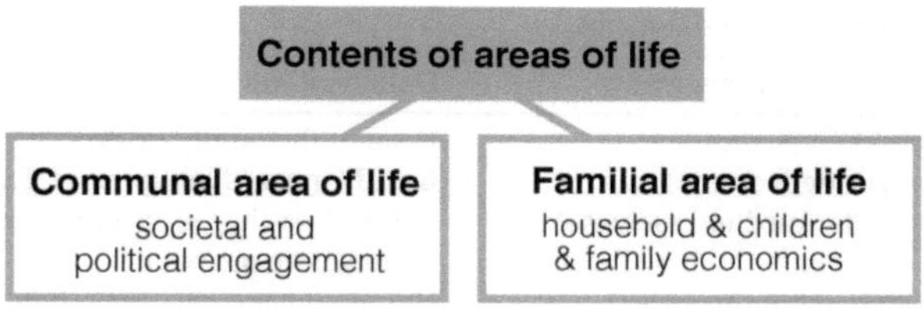

Fig. 16.1 Overview of Areas of Life

objectives. Most existent evaluations are project-based (from the perspective of an auxiliary actor or at most, a network of actors) and neglect the question of what other actors at the scene (including those affected themselves) are able to effect or prevent through their activities (see, for example, Wilson and Reilly 2007; Rifka Annisa 2008). What typifies work on the ground, however, is exactly that interplay between a variety of organizations and other actors with heterogeneous objectives working with or against one another. This research's focus on village sites instead of single programs allows for the long-term effects of *all* of these changes on the ground to be considered from multiple perspectives.

The aim of this research was a comprehensive analysis of the various areas of life that programs attempted to change. These can be descriptively defined as a familial area that includes both reproductive aspects (*household and children*) as well as productive dimensions (*family economics*) and a village communal area, containing both *engagement in society* and *political participation* (see Fig. 16.1).[16]

In retrospect, the villagers presented the real and ideal responsibilities and tasks of men and women not as something static, but rather as undergoing change. Notably, women are increasingly being assigned with economic, social, and political responsibilities, a trend that was framed positively especially by egalitarian oriented interviewees as progress, "a leap forward." Overall, villagers and activists assigned the current gender-specific roles in the following order of decreasing priority as shown in Table 16.1. The direction of change is indicated in brackets.[17]

In their assessments, villagers noted numerous contrasts. Two tendencies were crucial, that is, to contrast the past with present times as well as to contrast one's own family with others:

[16] I carried out the division into the different areas of life deductively, with the aim of enabling both a differentiated and a comprehensive analysis. It may not, however, correspond to the views of the interviewees. It is especially in the West that areas of life are often dichotomized into a public and private sector and then endowed with certain values. This seemingly "natural" dichotomy in the social sciences and humanities between public and private has been questioned by gender researchers (for example, by Pateman 1989). The main problem with this division is that it expresses a hierarchical arrangement of these areas, running along the lines of a gender-specific binary that is often not explicitly addressed nor challenged. Andro- and Eurocentric assumptions have been identified by various critics as the basis of this hierarchy-creating dichotomy (Bargetz 2009; Benn and Gaus 1983; Collins 1991; Dahlerup 1987; Elsthein 1981; Hauser 1987).

[17] The directions of change indicate general trends, but the contradictory and complex issues are likely to be obscured. As the results are presented in greater detail, the issue of multidimensionality becomes apparent (see later).

Table 16.1 Dominant Role Assignments

Dominant Feminine Role Assignments	Dominant Masculine Role Assignments
Household and children (same)	Head of the family (same)
Family economy (strong increase)	Breadwinner (slightly more flexible)
Engagement in society (medium increase)	Political participation and engagement in society[a] (same)
Political participation (slight increase)	Household and children (slight increase)

[a] Both roles were seen as equally important by some of the interviewees, while for the majority, the social role was of greater importance

> Through the different layers of time inherent in the act of telling, the opportunity to choose a position is multiplied. [...] At the same time, the various, newly-updated levels of time allow the teller to behave towards the former self. (Lucius-Hoene 2010, p. 595)[18]

The former situation tends to be associated with a lack of gender justice and with an existence for village women exclusively in the role of a housewife (see the *konco-wingking* discourse mentioned earlier). Female productivity was construed as something new. These contrasting demarcations fulfill a particular function, depending on the person and the context. The tendency to contrast the past with present times or one's own family with others can be read as an expression of a *new* gender awareness ("Nowadays, we have equal rights compared to our parents"), or as a positive self-projection ("We have always been egalitarian in contrast to others").

In the field of communal participation in particular, powerful implications for the gender relations arise.[19] It is important to begin by differentiating more precisely between the various understandings of participation held by villagers: Is it political or communal participation (*area of life specificity*)? Moreover, the extent of participation should be distinguished (*participation level*) because only then can there be an adequate interpretation of perceived gender-related changes as well as the corresponding stabilities in village life. I use the distinction made by interviewees, the majority of whom distinguished between activities concerned with communal development or communal politics where decisions are made and activities of mutual aid or local self-help, known as *gotong royong* (see also Chap. 10).

16.4.1 Societal Engagement

In terms of gender-specific understandings of *gotong royong*, the emphasis is more on the social unit of the family and the (neighborhood or hamlet) community rather than on the individual and her or his gender. The highly esteemed sociocultural

[18] Translated from German by Sarah Howard.

[19] For detailed elaborations with regard to individual-, household- and communal-related dynamics of transformation and conservation, see Schwarz (2012).

ideals of maintaining harmony (*rukun*) and protecting communal interests were reported to be more important than gender differences. Verbally, both men and women were described as being treated with equivalence and respect—no one would be glorified.

According to the strict Muslim Pak Nurdin, *gotong royong* does not automatically mean men's work, for example, when cleaning the graveyard. The important thing, he concluded, is harmony (*rukun*) and that a member of the family takes part; it is not important whether this person is a man or a woman, young or old. A respected village figure (*tokoh*) criticized the lack of cohesion between the genders with regard to communal work. He appealed to people to lay aside qualms and to commit to the village and community interests:

> So sometimes we lack of togetherness (*kebersamaan*). Like women feel that this is not our place, and also men think that this is not our own place to *gotong royong*, so basically we have a lack of togetherness. Like for example there's *gotong royong* in the graveyard, so only men come (laughing) since women feel uneasy to come. They should not feel like that since it's for public interest. But also, if sometimes women are assigned to go *gotong royong* in the graveyard, men also feel uneasy to come. So sometimes we have a lack of cooperation. (Pak Suwondo)

Nevertheless, a highly genderized view of work was linked to different skills which are ascribed to the genders on both biological and religious grounds: it is women who are expected to prepare food and to be active in the health and educational sector, whereas men are involved in issues relating to infrastructure and conducting rituals. In visits of condolence, both genders participate. However, it was felt that only the combination of both genders can lead to successful development for the hamlet.

The bulk of the workload is seen to rest on the shoulders of men, for whom participation is mandatory as the head of the family (*kepala keluarga*). The metaphor of a motorcycle that is passing by compared to one that is stopping was used to illustrate the different degrees of freedom associated with the roles taken by men and women:

> I already told you that women take a part but just a little, or even not at all... If we put it in an analogy; women are like a passing by motorcycle. But men are like a stopping motorbike. [...] [Women] are not obliged [...]. Men take more roles. Women have already had their own business. (Mas Naryanto)

Within the group of male villagers, further *gotong royong* roles were noted depending on age. For example, young men take care of the road construction, while elderly men are responsible for the less physically strenuous work of cleaning the roads. Within the group of unmarried people, there is no division between the genders in their contributions to communal work. Both girls and boys are responsible, for example, for the cutting of trees along the road. It is only once a man is married that he has a duty to participate. And only in cases where no male representative of the household (*kepala keluarga*) can attend would a woman take the male role in *gotong royong*. Overall, no gender-specific changes were reported in the area of *gotong royong* before and after both the earthquake and related NGO programs.

16.4.2 Political Engagement

Decision-making dynamics in the context of local self-help (as to what needs to be done, how, and by whom) refers to the topic of *participation in village politics*. In this area of life, a general trend toward an increase in female participation was postulated, while male involvement in village politics was presented as staying the same. Women were seen to be participating increasingly in social decisions, to be taking a more active role in public life, and to be more involved in village meetings since the earthquake, and especially since the NGO programs. Only when they were questioned further did most of the villagers and activists elaborate on what they mean by political participation,[20] so that on closer inspection, female participation in village politics (in terms of having a right to speak out and any power in decision-making) actually was nonexistent at the time of the interviews. Members of both of the decision-making forums, the hamlet development committee and communal meetings, were exclusively male.

The women's cooperative, which was initiated by the NGO ASPPUK, was regarded as a public space and understood by many as a form of active participation in village affairs. It is in this respect that feminine political participation has increased, according to many villagers. Women increasingly had a presence in public life because of the cooperative and its meetings. The money that the women managed in the cooperative, the training they received, and their economic success also have attracted public attention. Moreover, with the emergence of ASPPUK groups, a power structure had formed in parallel to the so far male-dominated structures of the hamlet development committee and communal political meetings.

It is likely that this form of economic participation influences the political culture of the hamlet and vice versa. Increased freedom of movement as a result of participation in the micro-credit groups can help, for example, to deconstruct limiting taboos about feminine participation in politics as meetings for village politics are usually conducted in the evenings. The evening meetings of micro-credit groups have led to other evening meetings between women becoming more acceptable.

Nonetheless, numerous persistent barriers to women's participation in local politics were reported, which was vehemently objected to particularly by those villagers (and activists) with an egalitarian mind-set. They were critical that mixed-gender activity was declared to be unethical on religious grounds, a discourse that regulates the continued exclusion of women from village politics. According to many villagers, women must take responsibility for the children and household in the absence of their husband, for example, if he takes part in the evening meetings of village politics. Motherhood therefore stands in the way of political participation, in contrast with fatherhood in this representation.

[20] Participation in a disaster management group, in community health care, or the electoral committee was mentioned. Communal groups, however, remained largely gender-separated. Women were involved in the health, consumer, and economic areas, men in village development.

Just as the household and children are seen as the domains of women, village development was viewed by some as something masculine or aggressive. This perception can support the lack of willingness to participate in village politics that was voiced by several women. The characterization of women as shy and politically disinterested has a similarly restraining effect on change:

> My experience until now has been as follows: when there is a meeting, and men and women are there, well women usually say less. [...] For sure, women must take the initiative to express their opinion. [...] If not, then it means that they will always continue to be dominated by men. [...] Yes, that's really the key to empowering women: the women have got to show initiative. (Activist Mas Helmi)

In contrast, others suspected that the male-occupied village apparatus seeks to maintain its power. According to Mbak Ineng, it is not a lack of female confidence that prevents women from speaking in mixed-gender groups, thereby limiting their political participation. She herself would like to, and could do so, but the meetings are led entirely by men and women are excluded because it is men who issue the invitations.

In what ways could women's participation in village politics be increased? Above all, egalitarian oriented men and women spoke out in favor of structural support offered in the form of invitations by those holding local power. The practice of distributing invitations was considered to express structural power relations, by which a singularly male body of power regulates access to village politics. Lobbying constituted another focus. The Sultan living in Yogyakarta City, for example, was seen as being in a powerful position to influence gender awareness and promote structural support for women's participation in village (and regional) politics:

> According to Javanese custom, a woman's position is really that of a friend in the background (*konco wingking*). [...] That is a concept that needs changing. And in actual fact, that is very difficult, because it is from, perhaps... well in my opinion it comes from the sultanate itself. [...] [The Sultan] has not yet spread awareness among his people about what gender is. And here in Yogya, well, the old people here, [...] they very much admire the Sultan. (Mas Zaki)

The activists furthermore regarded motivational and public speaking training for women as being necessary, as well as introducing quotas for committees.

16.5 Concluding Remarks

What insights do the results of this research provide in terms of the purpose and success of gender mainstreaming programs in the process of coping with an earthquake and related reconstruction efforts? Disasters and external assistance have considerable potential to effect change within social structures and power relations. The exceptional event of a disaster and subsequent flows of assistance are likely to be accompanied by crisis-ridden economic, political, and cultural processes as well as shifts in the gender relations and identities.

The earthquake investigated here served as a "door-opener" for NGOs to do gender work and receive funding provided to assist with reconstruction. However, the earthquake alone was represented as insufficient by itself to encourage reflection on or changes in gender relations. The awareness-rising work initiated by several NGOs focused particularly on promoting an understanding of egalitarian goals. This led to some changes because concepts of gender (*gender*), gender justice (*keadilan gender*), gender equity (*keseteraan gender*), and gender equality (*kesamaan gender*) were introduced into public discourses and given further legitimacy and strength. These terms have become increasingly popular and common. Other issues such as illegal trafficking (*trafficking*) and domestic violence have also become part of the discourses of the village community.

The more diverse and contradictory the objectives expressed by individuals in a community are, the greater the potential might be for social conflict. Egalitarian ideas, for example, seem at first glance to be diametrically opposed to views of complementarity. Especially when power structures are affected, (temporary) resistance on the part of those in power—which is men in most villages—can arise and lead to conflicts. The projects focusing exclusively on women, particularly in the economic sphere, initially produced envy among men and led to conflicts as men felt excluded. Those in power were apparently used to regulating money and aid and they demanded some of the money for themselves in order to "protect" the women against mismanagement. The male-run hamlet development committee called for detailed reports on all activities and financial statements of the women's cooperative, despite not having the authority to do so. Cooperative members presented this "taking-care" as being paternalistic and as continuously limiting women's power.[21]

On the contrary, ideas about what *should* be in gender relations are rarely one-dimensional, but rather characterized by complexity, fluidity, and contradictions. Furthermore, the types of relation between ideals and everyday life practices can be enormously different. It is just this variety and contradictory nature of gender relations that can hold potential for transformation. Regardless of this variety, activists and villagers alike referred to a collectively shared benchmark, the basic ideal of treating one another respectfully, which helped to avoid open conflict.

At the outset, resilience was defined as the capacity to bring about social change (UN/ISDR 2004). In this respect, the possibility for expanding the meaning of Central Javanese ideas (such as that of treating one another respectfully) seems to represent a particular Javanese resilience:

> We are seeing that in Indonesia, old and new values do not need to be seen as being in contrast to one another, nor need the old values be uncritically replaced by the new. The conflicting values and role requirements do not supersede each other, but rather continue to exist side by side. Instead of the confrontational "either... or..." attitude typical of Germany, the conciliatory Asian "both... and..." can be found in Indonesia. (Berninghausen et al. 2009, p. 81)[22]

---

[21] When compared with the Rifka group with its focus on domestic violence, the example of the women's cooperative clearly demonstrates that the gender dimension cannot be disentangled from socioeconomic aspects of power. The cooperative's money which had to be managed seems to have decidedly rekindled the conflict, whereas the domestic violence group—even though it was contested—did not lead to the same level of public criticism and conflict.

[22] Translated from German by Sarah Howard.

Instead of insisting on Western ideas such as the rights of women, locally specific symbolism was gradually being expanded to create greater acceptance rather than resistance about women's roles being equal to those of men in Java. The first signs of a readjusted gender order have become visible in the community of Sido Kabul, whereas rather than radical change, a more gradual process of change is taking place. The reference to existing, locally specific values about which there is a consensus, such as the ideal of respectful coexistence of men and women (as an expression of the Javanese "both... and... " principle) can simultaneously act both in an empowering *and* a restrictive way. Time will tell where the interplay between holding onto existing structures and simultaneously introducing innovation will lead. For example, it appears to be increasingly acceptable in public that women play a productive role comparable to that of men, while at the same time the discourse of the main breadwinner being a masculine role is vehemently maintained. These (ambiguous) achievements were driven by Javanese activists who are familiar with Javanese symbolism and how to use it. All in all, this upholds the necessity for a transcultural feminist psychology *and* caution against trying to impose Western ideas upon stakeholders worldwide:

> It is important to remember that white middle-class women from the economic North have dominated the feminist movements. Moreover, many aid workers and the people creating treatment plans and policies for humanitarian operations also represent the goals and ideals of privileged Western societies, so that most of the tactics and strategies employed by humanitarian psychosocial staff are informed from this world view. (Hudnall and Lindner 2006, p. 13)

Acknowledgements The editors would like to thank Sarah Howard for translating this chapter from German into English.

References

Agarwal, B. (1997). Bargaining and gender relations. Within and beyond the household. *Feminist Economics, 3*(1), 1–51.

ALNAP (Active Learning Network for Humanitarian Practice) (2008). Responding to earthquakes 2008; Learning from earthquake relief and recovery operations. London: ALNAP. http://www.alnap.org/pool/files/ALNAPLessonsEarthquakes.pdf. Accessed 10 May 2013.

Anderson, M. B. (1999). *Do no harm: How aid can support peace or war.* Colorado: Lyenne Rienner.

Anderson, M. B. (Ed.). (2000). Options for aid in conflict. Lessons from field experience. Cambridge: The Collaborative for Development Action. http://www.cdainc.com/publications/dnh/options/OptionsManual.pdf. Accessed 29 June 2012.

Anderson, M. B. (2004). Experiences with impact assessment: Can we know what good we do? Berghoff Forschungszentrum für konstruktive Konfliktbearbeitung. http://www.berghof-handbook.net/uploads/download/anderson_handbook.pdf. Accessed 29 June 2012.

Ariyabandu, M. (2003). Women: The risk managers in natural disasters. http://www.ssri.hawaii.edu/research/GDWwebsite/pdf/Ariyabandu.pdf. Accessed 10 May 2013.

Ariyabandu, M., & Wickramasinghe, M. (2005). *Gender dimensions in disaster management. A guide for South Asia. Kirulapone.* Sri Lanka: ITDG South Asia.

Bargetz, B. (2009). The politics of the everyday: A feminist revision of the public/private frame. In I. Papkova (Ed.), *Reconciling the irreconcilable*. Wien: IWM Junior Visiting Fellows' Conferences. http://www.iwm.at/index.php?option=com_content&task=view&id=130&Itemid=125. Accessed 29 June 2012.

Bari, F. (1998). Gender, disaster, and empowerment: A case study from Pakistan. In E. Enarson & B. H. Morrow (Eds.), *The gendered terrain of disaster—through women's eyes* (pp. 125–131). London: Praeger.

Benn, S. I., & Gaus, G. F. (1983). The public and the private: Concepts and action. In S. I. Benn, & G. F. Gaus (Eds.), *Public and private in social life* (pp. 3–27). London: Croom Helm.

Berninghausen, J., & Kerstan, B. (1984). *Die Töchter Kartinis. Berichte und Reportagen aus dem Leben indonesischer Frauen*. Berlin: Express Edition.

Berninghausen, J., Kerstan, B., & Soeprapto-Jansen, N. (2009). *Schleier, Sarong, Minirock. Frauen im kulturellen Wandel Indonesiens*. Bremen: Kellner-Verlag.

Bloemen, H. (2010). An empirical model of collective household labour supply with non-participation. *The Economic Journal, 120*(543), 183–214.

Bourdieu, P. (2005). *Die männliche Herrschaft*. Frankfurt am Main: Suhrkamp.

Bradshaw, S. (2001). Reconstructing roles and relations: Women's participation in reconstruction in post-Mitch Nicaragua. *Gender and Development, 9*(3), 79–87.

Bradshaw, S. (2002). Exploring the gender dimensions of reconstruction processes in post-hurricane Mitch. *Journal of International Development, 14*(6), 871–879.

Buckland, J. (1998). Social capital and sustainability of NGO intermediated development projects in Bangladesh. *Community Development Journal, 33*(3), 236–248.

Carney, D., Drinkwater, M., Rusinow, T., Neejes, K., Wanmali, S., & Singh, N. (1999). Livelihoods approaches compared. London: Department for International Development (DFID). http://www.odi.org.uk/rapid/projects/R0093/Abstracts/doc056abs.html. Accessed 29 June 2012.

Chowdhury, M. (2001). Women's technological innovations and adaptions for disaster mitigation: A case study of charlands in Bangladesh. Paper presented at expert group meeting on 'Environmental management and the mitigation of natural disasters: A gender perspective'. Ankara: United Nations Division for the Advancement of Women (DAW) & International Strategy for Disaster Risk Reduction (ISDR).

Collins, P. H. (1991). Work, family, and black women's oppression. In P. H. Collins (Ed.), *Black feminist thought: Knowledge, consciousness, and the politics of empowerment* (pp. 45–68). New York: Routledge.

Connell, R. W. (1995). *Masculinities*. Sydney: Allen & Unwin.

Dahlerup, D. (1987). Confusing concepts—confusing reality: A theoretical discussion of the patriarchal state. In A. S. Sassoon (Ed.), *Women and the state. The shifting boundaries of public and private* (pp. 93–127). London: Hutchinson.

Demetriou, D. (2001). Connell's concept of Hegemonic Masculinity: A critique. *Theory and Society, 30*(3), 337–361.

Elshtain, B. J. (1981). *Public man—private women. Women in social and political thought*. Princeton: Princeton University Press.

Errington, S. (1990). Recasting sex, gender, and power. In J. M. Atkinson & S. Errington (Eds.), *Power and difference. Gender in island Southeast Asia* (pp. 1–58). Stanford: Stanford University Press.

Frey, R. (2003). *Gender im Mainstreaming. Geschlechtertheorie und -praxis im internationalen Diskurs*. Königstein: Ulrike Helmer.

Geertz, C. (1962). The rotating credit association: A "middle rung" in development. *Economic Development and Cultural Change, 10*(3), 241–263.

Geertz, H. (1961). *The Javanese family: A study of kinship and socialization*. New York: Free Press of Glencoe.

Ghazali, S. (2003). Kut (informal rotating credit) in the livelihood strategies of urban households in Penang, Malaysia. *Area, 35*(2), 183–194.

Hauser, K. (1987). *Strukturwandel des Privaten? Das "Geheimnis des Weibes" als Vergesellschaftungsrätsel*. Berlin: Argument.

Hermans, H., & Hermans-Konopka, A. (2010). *Dialogical self theory. Positioning and counter-positioning in a globalizing society*. Cambridge: Cambrigde University Press

Hobfoll, S. E. (2011). Conservation of resources theory: Its implication for stress, health and resilience. In S. Folkman & P. E. Nathan (Eds.), *The Oxford Handbook of stress, health, and coping* (pp. 127–147). New York: Oxford University Press.

Hoffman, S. (1999). The regenesis of traditional gender patterns in the wake of disaster. In A. Oliver-Smith & S. Hoffman (Eds.), *The angry earth: Disaster in anthropological perspective* (pp. 173–191). New York: Routledge.

Hudnall, A. C., & Lindner, E. G. (2006). Crisis and gender: Addressing the psychosocial needs of women in international disasters. In G. Reyes & G. A. Jacobs (Eds.), *Handbook of international disaster psychology* (pp. 1–18). Westport: Greenwood.

Jay, R. R. (1969). *Javanese villagers. Social relations in rural Modjokuto*. Cambridge: MIT Press.

Kabeer, N. (1994). *Reversed realities. Gender hierarchies in development thought*. London: Zed Books.

Keeler, W. (1990). Speaking of gender in Java. In J. M. Atkinson & S. Errington (Eds.), *Power and difference. Gender in island Southeast Asia* (pp. 127–152). Stanford: Stanford University Press.

Kerstan, B., & Berninghausen, J. (1991). *Emanzipation wohin? Frauen und Selbsthilfe in Java, Indonesien. Kritische und selbstkritische Forschungsberichte zur Dritten Welt*. Frankfurt am Main: Verlag für Interkulturelle Kommunikation.

Koentjaraningrat (1967). Tjelapar: A village in south central Java. In Koentjaraningrat (Ed.), *Villages in Indonesia* (pp. 244–280). Ithaca: Cornell University Press.

Lorber, J., & Farrell, S. A. (Eds.). (1991). *The social construction of gender. Newburry Park*. USA: Sage.

Lucius-Hoene, G. (2010). Narrative Analysen. In G. Mey & K. Mruck (Eds.), *Handbuch Qualitative Forschung in der Psychologie* (pp. 584–600). Wiesbaden: Verlag für Sozialwissenschaften.

Mae, M., & Saal, B. (2007). Einleitung. In M. Mae & B. Saal (Eds.), *Transkulturelle Genderforschung—Ein Studienbuch zum Verhältnis von Kultur und Geschlecht* (pp. 9–17). Wiesbaden: Verlag für Sozialwissenschaften.

Momo, F., Prihantinah, T., Marinova, D., Stocker, L., & Muchira, L. (2002). Empowerment: Finding voices and strategies to combat globalization. *Community Development Journal, 37*(4), 361–374.

Narayan, U., & Harding, S. (2000). *Decentering the center: Philosophy for a multicultural, postcolonial, and feminist world*. Bloomington: Indiana University Press.

Norris, F. H., Stevens, S. P., Pfefferbaum, B., Wyche, K. F., & Pfefferbaum, R. L. (2008). Community resilience as a metaphor, theory, set of capacities, and strategy for disaster readiness. *American Journal of Community Psychology, 41*(1–2), 127–150.

Pateman, C. (1989). *Feminist critiques of the public/private dichotomy. In C. Patema. The disorder of women. Democracy, feminism and political theory* (pp. 118–140). Cambridge: Polity Press.

Rifka Annisa (2008). *Bojoku wis gender lho...! Kisah penyadaran nilai-nilai kesetaraan laki-laki & perempuan di desa*. Yogyakarta: Rifka Creative Communication.

Rossi, P. H., Freeman, H. E., & Hofmann, G. (1988). *Programm-Evaluation: Einführung in die Methoden angewandter Sozialforschung*. Stuttgart: Enke.

Sa′ar, A. (2005). Postcolonial feminism, the politics of identification, and the liberal bargain. *Gender and Society, 19*(5), 680–700.

Schwarz, S. (2012). *Eine kritische und kultursensible Sicht auf das Mainstreaming von Gender in einem Katastrophenkontext: Umstrittene Gendergerechtigkeitsvorstellungen, ein heuristisches Modell sozialen Wandels und Strategieprozessvorstellungen. Betroffenen- und AktivistInnensichtweisen*. Doctoral dissertation, Fachbereich Erziehungswissenschaften und Psychologie, Freie Universität Berlin.

United Nations (UN). (2000). Report of the ad hoc committee of the whole of the twenty-third special session of the General Assembly. General Assembly. Official Records. Twenty-third special session. Supplement Nr. 3. A/S-23/10/Rev.1. New York. http://www.un.org/womenwatch/daw/followup/as2310rev1.pdf. Accessed 24 June 2011.

United Nations/ International Strategy for Disaster Reduction (UN/ISDR) (2004). Living with risk. New York: United Nations. http://www.unisdr.org/files/657_lwr1.pdf. Accessed 12 Dec 2010.

United Nations/ International Strategy for Disaster Reduction (UN/ISDR). (2007). Gender perspective: Working together for disaster risk reduction. Good practices and lessons learned. Geneva. http://www.unisdr.org/files/547_gendergoodpractices.pdf. Accessed 24 July 2012.

Wichterich, C. (2010). Gender als politisches Projekt: Wie bitte geht's zur Geschlechtergerechtigkeit? Berlin: Friedrich-Ebert-Stiftung. http://library.fes.de/pdf-files/iez/07025.pdf. Accessed 24 July 2012.

Wilson, P., & Reilly, D. (2007). Joint evaluation of their responses to the Yogyakarta earthquake. http://www.alnap.org/pool/files/erd-3611-full.pdf. Accessed 30 Jan 2009.

Wisner, B., Blaikie, P., Cannon, T., & Davis, I. (2004). *At risk: natural hazards, people's vulnerability and disasters* (2nd ed.). London: Routledge.

Wolf, D. (1992). *Factory daughters. Gender, household dynamics, and rural industrialization in Java*. Berkeley: University of California Press.

Yonder, A., Akcar, S., & Gopalan, P. (2006). *Women's participation in disaster relief and recovery*. New York: The Population Council.

Part V
Conclusion

Chapter 17
Concluding Remarks

Manfred Zaumseil, Mechthild von Vacano, Silke Schwarz, Gavin B. Sullivan and Johana E. Prawitasari-Hadiyono

This book focused on the productive tension between the universalist views of coping and disaster, and the particular ways in which disaster and coping processes unfold in local contexts. Critically reviewing the literature on disasters and coping, we developed a theoretical argument for a cultural psychology of disaster coping which is grounded in an understanding of people being inseparably enmeshed with their contexts.

Our *cultural* approach is not an argument for examining location-bound cultural differences (people *having a culture* and acting according to it), but rather for examining the *multiple, hybrid, dynamic, and contested cultural ways* that people relate to their contexts, while simultaneously (re)producing and being shaped by them. Based on an in-depth case study of the 2006 Java earthquake, we developed our

M. Zaumseil (✉) · S. Schwarz
International Academy for Innovative Pedagogy, Psychology and Economics gGmbH at Freie Universität Berlin, Malteserstr 74-100, 12249 Berlin, Germany
e-mail: zaumseil@zedat.fu-berlin.de

M. von Vacano
Institute for Social and Cultural Anthropology, Freie Universität Berlin, Landoltweg 9-11, 14195 Berlin, Germany
e-mail: m.vacano@fu-berlin.de

S. Schwarz
e-mail: silke.schwarz@fu-berlin.de; silgnschwarz@yahoo.de

G. B. Sullivan
School of Social, Psychological and Communication Sciences, Leeds Metropolitan University, City Campus, LS1 3HE Leeds, UK
e-mail: g.sullivan@leedsmet.ac.uk; gsullivan34@yahoo.com

J. E. Prawitasari-Hadiyono
Center for Research and Community Service, Christian University of Krida Wacana, Jl. Tanjung Duren Raya No. 4, 11470 Jakarta, Indonesia
e-mail: jeprawitasari@ukrida.ac.id

Universitas Gadjah Mada, 55281 Yogyakarta, Indonesia

M. Zaumseil et al. (eds.), *Cultural Psychology of Coping with Disasters*,
DOI 10.1007/978-1-4614-9354-9_17,

theoretical argument and exemplified how coping research can be contextualized and used to account for the psychological, social, geographic-material, historical, and political particularities. Our approach is committed to the project of cultural psychology which aims to transcend "the many familiar and foundational psychological binaries; that is, person–situation, individual–environment, culture–social structure, and self–society binaries in which people are conceptualized as separate from their 'surrounding' contexts" (Markus and Hamedani 2007, p. 6). We agree with the view that such an endeavor requires the transdisciplinary integration of sociological, anthropological, and historical perspectives with psychological studies of coping and disasters. Social scientist disaster research, for example, offers a perspective on disaster as a constellation of specific material and socioeconomic conditions, or constructionist sociological research illuminates the social nature of disasters as a discursive field, where different forms of deprivation and suffering are negotiated. While anthropological–historical approaches highlight the cultural normalization of risks in geographic regions where societies have been living in hazardous environments for centuries, Bankoff (2003) described these societies as having developed "cultures of disaster" (also see Anderson 1968).

The cultural *psychological* characteristic of our approach focuses on *subjective* coping processes in a disaster context. Since we understand subjectivity as inherently contextual, we challenge the common psychological terminology and conceptual tools by questioning its individualist assumptions regarding the psychological subject and its functioning. Revising the appraisal-based coping model, we argued for a social-constructionist broadening of the idiosyncratic conceptualization of individual appraisal. In other words, our argument was that the way a person assesses a stressful situation depends on the larger context that shapes how she or he sees, experiences, and acts in their communities and the world. In our view, disaster survivors are individuals who, on the one hand, draw their orientations from a world of shared meanings, social relations, and experiences with the physical world and, on the other hand, actively (re)produce this world. The traditional cognitivist bias was counterbalanced by a practice-oriented theoretical approach, which allowed us to present coping processes as embodied practices and to integrate the physical experience and the "doing" of coping into our research.

Our approach replaces the causal relations of common coping models with referential relations of meaning. Within this interpretative approach, the causal models of traditional coping research serve as a heuristic device, as a frame, rather than a modeling of cause and effect relations between quantifiable variables. For example, instead of correlating variables of spirituality or religiousness to coping processes and outcomes, we seek to understand the contextual relevance of (religious) cosmologies and practices, and their interrelation with other aspects of life. For such an endeavor, the sharply defined and categorized variables of quantitative universalist coping research can serve as sensitizing concepts for qualitative interpretative research; however, this requires a critical approach to the cultural assumptions and values inherent in these variable categories.

In order to overcome the foundational binaries and biases of Western psychology, we represented *coping* as *a complex material-symbolic, cognitive-embodied, and individual-social process*. The notion of complexity is borrowed from other research on disasters as we consider it a helpful reference point for coping research. This borrowed notion helped us to broaden our research perspectives and sensitize our awareness for the local settings we analyzed. In order to handle this complexity approach, we developed a simple analytical framework that touches upon the key theoretical characteristics of coping (mentioned earlier) and closely relates to the core issues with coping that are particular to our research site. The resulting multidimensional framework for coping with disaster incorporates material, social, religious, and principles of life-conduct dimensions (see Part III).

The multidimensional framework is intended to be a tool for untangling the complexity in various coping contexts; however, any application of the framework in another research context might require the dimensions to be adapted. For example, in less (explicitly) religious contexts, a cosmological dimension might be more productive or in another context, a personal dimension might be more suitable than the principle of life-conduct dimension we outlined. Accordingly, the framework is a rather flexible research strategy, instead of being simply another universal model of psychological functioning. The dimensions constitute anchors in a web of complex referential relations of meaning and suggest that each element of coping can be seen and analyzed from any dimensional angle. Thus, the separation into dimensions is an analytical strategy to grasp the multiple connections and interrelations between key aspects of coping. Prayer, for example, is not just a matter of religion. It can be a social activity, a form of communicating one's own piety to an outside community, and a physical bodily practice. The "Javanese" work ethic that our respondents evoked through the high value of effort and economic independence can be considered an empowering principle of life conduct and a resource for economic recovery, all framed within a religious cosmology of divine omnipotence.

Our analysis challenged the tendency of functionalist reduction in psychological coping theory and presented a broader sociopolitical perspective on coping: *Coping processes are contingent on micro- and macro-dynamics of individual life-courses, community processes, and global histories*. Coping processes involve multiple potentially contradicting constellations of interest, which do not necessarily relate to "coping" itself, but to other dynamics that are not necessarily disaster related. Thus, any researchers in the area of coping need to think beyond coping and ask the critical question of what is subjectively at stake for the different actors involved when they cope in the ways that they do. A post-colonial, power-critical perspective points to the larger patterns of motivation and to structural limitations of personal and collective agency. For instance, if our respondents interpreted the disaster as a divine admonishment, they were able to address their criticism regarding any social condition that required improvement. In talking about the disaster, village residents negotiated what role Islam should play within their everyday village life, working within a much broader discourse on interpretations of Islam in Indonesia and its role in national identity. Any meaning-making is to some extent political, since even answers to the metaphysical question of "why" the disaster occurred easily move toward attributions of blame involving individuals and communities. While explicit blaming discourses were rare in our interview data, respondents were still concerned about potential blaming dynamics.

Another example is the discourse of Javanese local wisdom. The regional government presented the earthquake recovery process as a success story, identifying Javanese cultural values as its key ingredient. Comparisons of the region's recovery to the recovery process in the Aceh province after the 2004 tsunami were common. Within the cultural plurality of the Indonesian nation, this discourse draws on a representation of Javanese culture as a superior way of (Indonesian) life: humble, hardworking with a strong sense of collectivity, and as a proto-cultural ideal for the postcolonial Indonesian nation. The "Javanese" values of communal work (*gotong-royong*) and community harmony (*rukun*) have a long history of ideological exploitation by political elites (and problematic reification through Western anthropological research), though they are still meaningful codes of conduct for the village residents of our research sites (see Bråten 2005). The cultural values of economic independence and self-reliance were important subjective features of recovery. Communal work practices were an important resource for the post-disaster cleanup and the physical reconstruction of village infrastructure; however, it was a political idealization to expect most of the community-based housing reconstruction to be accomplished by such a system of reciprocal unpaid labor. From the perspectives of villagers, such a large demand on the available workforce exceeded the capacities of communal work, and they complained about the material consequences of this idealization. The government reconstruction fund only calculated material costs and took for granted that the communal workforce would achieve reconstruction goals.

The function of any harmony discourse by the relevant political elites at village, regional, and national Government levels seems obvious. Nevertheless, the cultural value of *rukun* is much more than an ideology, it is a crucial subjective experiential modus of relating to social context. To most of our respondents, being involved in a harmonious (*rukun*) community was an important aspect of life and a positive resource for agency and support. This ideal served as an important counterbalance to social bitterness over corruption and social offenses. *Rukun* is embedded in a broader cosmology and experienced as a key resource for maintaining a general sense of safety (or a general sense of preparedness) because community harmony is closely associated with personal feelings of inner peace. With this notion of individual well-being blending into community well-being and vice versa, the concept of coping can be expanded to a communal level and coping framed as *societal assimilative and accommodative development* rather than as an individual, subjective, or intrapsychic (above all cognitive) process. Such a perspective enables to critically inquire into different ways people understand and obtain social justice in general (see Chap. 14) or in regard to gender relations within a village community (see Chap. 16).

Extracted from the context of disaster coping after an earthquake, our data also offer general insights which may expand the common universalist psychological conception of the human subject as a goal-striving individual (see Taylor 1989) who attributes her or his merits and efficacy to herself or himself. The triad of acceptance, surrender, and effort, which was a central theme of coping with adversity/disaster in our research context, transcends the reductionist fatalism–control dichotomy that is common in the psychology and disaster literature (see Chap. 12). Humans can only accept and surrender against the cosmological backdrop of divine omnipotence and human relative powerlessness. But not striving for control does not equal passivity. The value of effort requires humans to give everything within the limits of their capacities, while the results of these attempts remain unpredictable. Imbued with deep religious meaning, acceptance, surrender, and effort are also fundamental pragmatics of life or codes of conduct (see Chap. 11). As such, they are rooted in shared socio-cultural values but interpreted and practiced heterogeneously by individuals. Within the local understanding, these codes of conduct are not static qualities of a person. Rather, they represent desired developmental trajectories toward personal and religious refinement (*kehalusan*). In daily lives as well as in times of crises, these codes of conduct serve as context-specific resources or as "local wisdom" for adequate functioning, in order to foster a positive image of the self, family, and community as well as to fulfill one's role in a positive manner or maintain inner balance. To enact these codes of conduct when confronted with a crisis situation is a different coping strategy than directly attacking a problem in a goal-directed manner. Such virtue orientation is an indirect way of approaching challenging situations, and, thus, requires that the anthropological assumptions of common coping theories are reworked. The triad of understanding, positive reframing, and benefit finding points to a positive accepting stance toward any given situation, as exemplified in the religiously framed concept of gratitude (*syukur*). From this triad, a culturally specific balance between accommodative and assimilative coping processes emerges. By ignoring or denying one's loss of resources, their subjective relevance to the person can decrease and allow her or him to focus all attention on those aspects that she or he still deems within the scope of her or his influence.

The question of when, why, and with what consequences a specific coping style is employed depends on the experience of individually, collectively, or transcendentally located agency. Instead of locating resources for agency (and agency itself) only in the individual, which happens with constructs like self-efficacy or self-perceptions of locus of control, collectively shared and transcendental realms proved to be at least as relevant for participants at our research sites. While Western approaches to risk reduction focus on external, technocratic preparedness strategies within a control-paradigm, the preparedness we found in our case study was process orientated and, thus, open-ended ("Whatever will happen, I will be ready to deal with it."), unspecific and embedded in the general fragility of living conditions. People have come to live with multiple sources of uncertainty of which disaster hazards are one challenge to feelings of security. Against this backdrop, principles of life conduct, such as the stance of "happiness in sorrow and worry in the face of happiness" (*prihatin*-stance) need to be interpreted. "Risk" is thus a rather broad category, and equally broad risk measures are integrated in a pragmatic manner into daily practices. On the other hand, sometimes "proper" disaster risk reduction strategies either compete against local configurations of relevance, do not fit the conditions in a village, or are constrained by resource limitations in village life (that is, finite amounts of economic and social capital). In the ways that village residents in our study related to future uncertainties, they emphasized feeling comforted and secure through a rather general feeling of being in good hands in a cherished and harmonic community. Further consolation and support was found in the omnipotence of the divine. People therefore put their future in divine hands and trust in the benevolence of a higher power. Their faith provides believers with hope and a positive outlook on the future and thus supports active engagement in pragmatic action.

Disaster touches on fundamental issues of human existence, such as life and death, human–nature relations, social support networks, and micro- as well as macro-power structures. As our case study illustrated, studying societies in disaster can therefore teach us a lot about the ways people see, experience, and act in their worlds (cf. Oliver-Smith and Hoffman 2002). Conversely, in order to understand coping processes in their real-life complexity, we need to integrate these subjective sociocultural experiences, desires, and fears into disaster research. We hope that our cultural psychological approach to coping with disasters contributes to the broader field of disaster studies.

Acknowledgements The editors like to thank Elise Serbaroli for her assistance in editing this chapter.

References

Anderson, J. W. (1968). Cultural adaption to threatened disaster. *Human Organization, 27*(4), 298–307.

Bankoff, G. (2003). *Cultures of disaster. Society and natural hazard in the Philippines*. London: Routledge.

Bråten, E. (2005). Resurrecting "Java": A call for a "Java"nese anthropology. In H. Antlöv & J. Hellman (Eds.), *The Java that never was. Academic theories and political practices* (pp. 21–42). Münster: LIT.

Markus, H. R., & Hamedani, M. G. (2007). Sociocultural psychology: The dynamic interdependence among self systems and social systems. In S. Kitayama & D. Cohen (Eds.), *Handbook of cultural psychology* (pp. 3–39). New York: Guilford.

Oliver-Smith, A., & Hoffman, S. M. (2002). Introduction: Why anthropologists should study disaster. In S. M. Hoffman & A. Oliver-Smith (Eds.), *Catastrophe & culture* (pp. 3–22). Santa Fe: School of American Research Press.

Taylor, C. (1989). *Sources of the self: The making of modern identity*. Cambridge: Harvard University Press.

Glossary

arisan	Informal lottery; rotating savings and credit associations; micro-credit groups
batin	Inner realm of a person; essential aspects of personhood
Bu	Form of address for an older, respected female; literarily: mother (*ibu*)
desa	administrative village unit above hamlet (*dusun*)
dusun	Hamlet; administrative unit below village (*desa*) and above the neighborhood unit RT
gotong royong	Mutual assistance; cooperative action; communal practices; community work
hikmah	Deeper or hidden meaning; wisdom
hormat	Respect
kebersamaan	Togetherness
kearifan lokal	Local wisdom
kejawen	Javanism
lahir	Outer realm of a person; material and physical aspects personhood
Mas	Form of address for a (young) man; literarily address for an older brother
Mbak	Form of address for a young women
musyawarah	Joint decision making; mutual deliberation
nrimo	Accept
orang kecil	Ordinary or common people; literarily: little people
orang awam	Ordinary or common people; literarily: lay person
Pak	Form of address for an older, respected male; literarily: father (*bapak*)
Pak RT	Head of the neighborhood unit
Pak Dukuh	Head of the hamlet
pasrah	Surrender
pengajian	Religious gathering for recitation of the Quran
posko	(= *pos koordinasi*) Coordination post
pokmas	(= *kelompok masyarakat*) Community-based reconstruction group

M. Zaumseil et al. (eds.), *Cultural Psychology of Coping with Disasters*,
DOI 10.1007/978-1-4614-9354-9,

ronda	Night watch
RT	(= *rukun tetangga*) Administrative neighborhood unit; unit below hamlet (*dusun*)
rukun	Harmony
tokoh	Village elite; formal or informal community leader

Index

M. Zaumseil et al. (eds.), *Cultural Psychology of Coping with Disasters*,
DOI 10.1007/978-1-4614-9354-9, © Springer Science+Business Media, LLC 2014

MIX
Papier aus verantwortungsvollen Quellen
Paper from responsible sources
FSC® C105338

If you have any concerns about our products,
you can contact us on
ProductSafety@springernature.com

In case Publisher is established outside the EU,
the EU authorized representative is:
Springer Nature Customer Service Center GmbH
Europaplatz 3, 69115 Heidelberg, Germany

Printed by Libri Plureos GmbH
in Hamburg, Germany